The Journey of the First Black Bishop
Bishop Samuel Ajayi Crowther 1806 - 1891

Jacob Oluwatayo Adeuyan

AuthorHouse™
1663 Liberty Drive
Bloomington, IN 47403
www.authorhouse.com
Phone: 1-800-839-8640

© 2011 Jacob Oluwatayo Adeuyan. All rights reserved.

No part of this book may be reproduced, stored in a retrieval system, or transmitted by any means without the written permission of the author.

First published by AuthorHouse   8/24/2011

ISBN: 978-1-4634-0734-6 (sc)
ISBN: 978-1-4634-0733-9 (hc)
ISBN: 978-1-4634-0732-2 (e)

Library of Congress Control Number: 2011908330

Printed in the United States of America

Any people depicted in stock imagery provided by Thinkstock are models, and such images are being used for illustrative purposes only.
Certain stock imagery © Thinkstock.

Because of the dynamic nature of the Internet, any web addresses or links contained in this book may have changed since publication and may no longer be valid. The views expressed in this work are solely those of the author and do not necessarily reflect the views of the publisher, and the publisher hereby disclaims any responsibility for them.

Contents

Introduction:		vii
Chapter 1	Bishop Ajayi's Birth Place.	1
Chapter 2	The Culture of His People	7
Chapter 3	A Continent in Ruins	19
Chapter 4	Era of Slave Trade in Africa	31
Chapter 5	The Exeter Hall Meeting: June 1, 1840	42
Chapter 6	The Early Missionary Journey To The Continent of Africa.	53
Chapter 7	Bishop Crowther as a Slave Boy	68
Chapter 8	Bishop Crowther as a Foundation Student of Fourah Bay College in Sierra Leone.	85
Chapter 9	First Niger Expedition of 1841	97
Chapter 10	Second Niger Expedition of 1854	110
Chapter 11	The Third Expedition & Planting of the Seeds of Christianity along the Banks of Niger in 1858 by Samuel Crowther.	124
Chapter 12	Bishop Crowther's Missionary Works at Abeokuta:	141
Chapter 13	Bishop Crowther's Meeting with Queen Victoria & Prince Albert at Windsor Palace.	156
Chapter 14	Consecration of Samuel Ajayi Crowther as the First Black African Bishop of the Church of England.	165
Chapter 15	Crowther as the First Bishop of His People:	176
Chapter 16	Bishop Crowther – The Atlas of Modern Nigeria Economy and Government:	190
Chapter 17	Early Missionary Activities on the Banks of River Niger:	207
Chapter 18	Bishop Crowther and Episcopal Crisis	227
Chapter 19	The Brave and Fearless Nationalist Missionaries after Bishop Crowther	242
Chapter 20	Early Political Trumpeting in West Africa	260
Chapter 21	The Scramble for Africa's Enormous Wealth.	275

Chapter 22	The Hassles of the Colonial Administration in Nigeria	285
Chapter 23	Nigeria's Preparation for and at the gate of Independence:	301
Chapter 24	Independent Nigeria and the Civil War	317
Chapter 25	If African Continent is to be totally Free and Independent, What is to be done?	329

Introduction:

On the morning of 6th of September, 2005 after listening to the early morning news regarding the aftermath of the Katerina category five hurricane that recently devastated substantial part of the gulf region in the Missisipi and New Orleans city in the US, I sat down on my desk to map out my writing strategies on this book concerning the journey of an individual that walked through thick and thin to make his mark on the sands of history. Much had been written and said about this illustrious son of Africa but writings and sayings about him would continue to flow in the minds of his people from generation to generation for as long as the spiritual anointing endowed him by Almighty God Himself continue to flow without an end.

For couple of days now, we have been watching, listening, and reading about the present conditions and situations of the people that once lived very happily in their homes in the city of New Orleans and its environ on the television screens, radio sets and some other media means and who are now facing the worst and the most horrible situations of their lives from the hands of the mother nature. The current situation is very acute and devastating because the city of New Orleans and other places in this region are sitting right now on waters and New Orleans is seriously under siege. According to the news reaching the whole world about this calamity, many lives have been lost in thousands; people have been evacuated from their homes and taken to save areas in the region and farther in millions; some sick people have been packed together in an airport lobby and reception halls that now serves as make-shift hospitals where they are being treated for one ailment or the other. But one thing to note here is that the present day problems of the people of this region are not without the knowledge of God and it is only Him alone that can reveal the knowledge of how to fix these problems to His people. He would surely deliver the affected cities and their inhabitants; He would Himself console the families of the dead people in this disaster; make ways for the orphans and re-settle the lives of the widows and widowers affected in the present complicating problems. The proud and courageous people of the affected places would once again come back to their beloved cities from far and near where they are now taken to as their save heaven to congregate at the centers of these cities to worship and serve their true God.

The journey of Bishop Samuel Ajayi Crowther was similar to what is now happening to the people of the present day gulf coast region of the US with only little variation. In his own situation, he was separated from his family through the evil hands of the slave traders and what now befalls the people of the gulf coast region is entirely from the hands of the mother-nature. But all the same, the results from both events are that people are devastated, displaced and exposed to all sorts of human hardships and degradations. His journey was not without bad and good tastes. It was full of hills, mountains, low and high levels of land, very dry deserts, marshy flood plain areas and a lot of green field areas. I first heard and learnt about the story of Samuel Ajayi Crowther when I was in elementary two in 1947. We were only told about him as a young slave boy that was taken captive from his town of Osogun and sold to the white slave traders in Lagos. And, that the slave traders took him to their country from where he later learnt their language and eventually became a Bishop. It was the little information made available to our teachers of this time from the colonial school superintendents who were mainly whites that were passed on to the brains of the little ones about this illustrious son of the land. But thanks to God that all of us that are still living today would always remember this name and where he came from in the Yoruba Nation of the entity called Nigeria.

This book is not intended to be the full story or a complete biography of the Bishop but only an important reference to the great job he was able to do to uplift and improve upon the lives and status of the black race from the devastating impressions that the foreign people of his time had about his people. All sorts of names were coined out to describe the black race of the world during the past centuries. Some people and nations labeled them with such stigma such as people of the Dark Continent, heathen people; people living on top of the trees in the jungle, people born with tails under their pants like monkeys, and people with very low intelligence. But thanks to people like Bishop Samuel Ajayi Crowther who during his lifetime proved the stigmatic labels wrong and very untrue about his people. He substantiated his facts through the knowledge, skill and administrative excellence he demonstrated to the whole world and to the amazement of the then rumormongers and destroyers of people. I would therefore agree with a fine African historian that wrote: "all worthwhile historical writing is primarily an artistic exercise, consisting in an attempt to master a large body of facts and to present a small selection of them in the proportion and form that seems most meaningful at a particular moment of time".

Before the popular nineteenth century exploration by the people of Europe that opened the doors of African continent to the outsiders for religious, economic and colonial ambition, the people of the continent had been living in affluence and maintained established governments. At the outset of European colonial career, Portugal for example propagated a genuine policy of assimilation they called "assimilado", a system that was designed to give Africans the right of citizenship of Portugal. But this system with its friendly opposite "apartheid" became features of colonialist mythology. When her explorers reached Congo River in 1483, they found a kingdom of complete administration, whose inhabitants worked iron, copper, and metals, wove mats and clothing from raffia of palm-cloth, raised pigs, goat and sheep, chickens, cattle and grow their own foods. The king of Mani-Congo, Nzinga-a-Cuum, and his successor, Mbemba-a-Nzingz, who reigned from 1506 – 1543 as Dom Afonzo I, not only adopted Christianity himself, but, did his utmost to spread the new faith amongst his subject.

The industrial activities of the Africans, which preceded the arrival of the Europeans to the coast of Africa, actually demonstrated the highly connected intellectual skills of the people. But when the initial good gesture of these people metamorphosed into hyena type of gesture in form of slave trading, the steady progress of industrialization of the people had a big set back. This deadly disease disorganized nearly all the fabrics of their system and threw them overboard. They became confused, disillusioned and disoriented. Their scientist and strong men in the community had now been taken captive and thrown into plantations in a foreign land without any hope of return to their native lands. Their noble men, princes and princesses were now being killed in the mid sea and thrown into the ocean to feed the fishes and reptiles. Their culture was changed forever.

The impression created by the outsiders to the continent during the eighteenth and nineteenth centuries regarding the continent and its people was so devastating and misleading to such a level that those impressions still bleed fresh blood from the streams of people from Africa about how their people and their land were being badly painted. Some people of today still carry this old placard in their minds and thoughts that Africa is a land bleeding with poverty, hunger, disease, malnutrition, wars, disasters, and all kinds of political, social and economic instabilities. Anywhere in the world that famine, conflicts and coup d'etat are mentioned, African continent would immediately come to mind as the factory where these calamities are being manufactured.

The original intention of the early missionaries was strictly connected to the Bible principles and philosophy that says: "Go ye into the world and preach the gospel". But by gradual process, slave trading sneaked itself into the big show, followed by colonialism and watered both down by neo-colonialism. The continent of Africa that is the second largest continent of the world is known to have offered the world the largest arable agricultural land that produces products such as cocoa, coffee, palm, cotton, rubber, sisal, timber, tea and others. It has the largest desert in the world – the Sahara with promising potential mineral resources buried therein millions of years back and yet undiscovered. The continent has many useful rivers that can be used for people and products transportation from one country to another. African continent is considered by the scientists as the richest continent in the world because of its largest shares of the world's mineral resources that includes gold, petroleum, diamond, cobalt, phosphate, tin, iron, platinum, chromium, coal, natural gas, lime stone, gypsum and others.

Undoubtedly, the journey of Bishop Ajayi Crowther began as a slave boy that was sold to the white slave traders by his own people for material exchange and little amount of money. He was captured during the civil wars of 1821 when the Moslem (Foulahs), the "Yoruba Mohammedans" attacked his hometown of Osogun in the Yoruba nation. The story had it that Osogun town was surrounded by these foulahs when the majority of the men and women of the town had already gone out to the farmland for the day's various businesses. Some went to the fields to graze their animals while those with domestic skills remained behind to attend to their businesses.

This fateful day was the day that the town of Osogun was to have its turn of the sorrowful fate of ruin, desolation and deprivation caused by the inhuman acts of the slave traders and their agents. Houses were ruthlessly set on fire and the inhabitants fled the town for the safety of their lives.

When Ajayi's father who was a weaver and who was carrying out his business in the open place in his courtyard saw the rampage, he ordered his family members to flee. He decided to enter into his house and never reappeared again. There could be the possibility that he decided to commit suicide or decided to stay in the building while the house was set on fire by the raiders. In the African tradition and culture of this time, whenever there was an imminent disaster approaching someone's family compound, the head of the family or the owner of that compound would send away the wives, the children and other members in the family to a protective place and wait behind to face the consequences such disaster might brought to the compound. Another way out is that if the demands of the raiders are outrageous to be met by the owner of the compound, he may decide to take away his own live so as to bring honor to the rest of the family members that are left behind. Any of these suggestions could be the reason why Ajayi's father never re-appeared again. Ajayi in the company of his mother and two sisters were asked to flee by his father and they did flee.

This day marked the beginning of Bishop Ajayi Crowther's ordeal in this wicked world, as he was then a young boy who had no idea of what life contained. Ajayi, the mother and the sisters could not reach the save heaven the father had in mind for them but instead, they all ran into the welcoming hands of two out of the numerous raiders that attacked their town. The raiders were happy as they had a good catch and immediately put nooses around their necks and kept them with others under the same affliction. According to the story, they were all marched to Iseyin another nearby major town where Ajayi was exchanged for a horse. This was how this young boy was separated from his mother and two sisters for another quarter of a century before they miraculously reunited again. His new owner now took him to Ijaye, which was another slave trade market center in Abeokuta where he was sold to a Mohammedan woman trader. This new owner was planning to take him to Popo market for resale at a higher profit the next market day, which was to be near. When Ajayi heard of this plan, he became sick and dejected and now began to realize that it was now obvious that the possibility of reuniting him with the rest of the family members was now remote and he became more sickening physically and emotionally.

This new development pierced his mind to shreds and as a result, he unsuccessfully attempted to commit suicide by trying to strangle himself to death in the night. He was lucky to be rescued. The suicide action by Ajayi prompted the woman trader to hurriedly want to get rid of him for an exchange of tobacco leaves and a bottle of an English wine offered her by an Ijebu trader. Ajayi was successfully transferred to this Ijebu trader for the prize of tobacco leave and a bottle of wine and the new Ijebu-master now took Ajayi to Lagos slave market where he was finally sold to the Portuguese traders. The Portuguese traders put Ajayi on a ship with other slaves and set out at sea on a journey to the newly discovered world – North America. This young boy became more disillusioned and now finally concluded that every hope of life for him had been lost and the end had cruelly come to him in reality.

But God was kind enough to re-open Ajayi's case file and sent it to the Sea master - the British anti-slavery warship called **Myrmidon** to attack the Portuguese schooner carrying Ajayi to an unknown destination, and destroyed it at sea. Ajayi himself confirmed that 102 out of the 189 slaves on board the Portuguese schooner perished in the attack. He was now freed and in the save hands of the British crew in the **Myrmidon** in company of other rescued slaves. They were taken to Sierra Leone this time not as a slave but as a freed boy. In Sierra Leone, he now found to himself a new home, a new country with new people and new environment entirely. But interestingly, Ajayi never forgot his original place of birth and the people he left behind including his beloved father, mother, his two sisters and other half brothers.

The devastating results that slave trading left on the people of Africa in their home bases or where they ultimately found themselves at the end of the journey would forever remain in the memories of every generation in the continent of Africa. The generation yet un-born would always feel very badly when they learn that a continent that is the most polyglot continent in the world, with about 800 – 1000 different, separate and distinct languages was reduced to three main foreign languages – English, French and Portuguese through the domination of its colonialists and their agents. They would feel sad when they read the stories of how African countries usually have little or no say in the prices of the products and minerals extracted from the soil of their continent. Their foot will be lifted off the ground when they will be told that at one time or the other in the past their people are "price takers" instead of "price makers". As part of the commercial injustices meted to African continent, the two countries - Nigeria and Ghana for example that produces large cocoa beans for the world's consumption are never allowed for a very long period of time to put their own prices on this product. Instead, some people would sit down some where in a tiny corner of the world to package the prices they feel alright for them and send it and even vetoed it on the producers without allowing for any protest or price redress.

The spread of Christianity throughout the continent in the nineteenth century saw a mark of success for the future of the continent. During the twentieth century, the world began to see the germination of the seeds of freedom and liberty sewn by our past missionaries such as Bishop Ajayi Crowther, John Venn- the first secretary of CMS, Thomas Birch Freeman, Lott Carey, Robert Moffat, David Livingstone, Bishop Mackensie and the great orators that delivered superfluous speeches at the meeting in Exeter Hall on June 1, 1840, which bordered on how to arrest the destruction of mankind that was prevalent in Africa and some other places of the world as at then. Threat to human dignity was one of the main issues that preoccupied the minds of the men and women of God that volunteered to walk across the dangerous paths in Africa in the face of hardship, hostility, hunger and other indifferences to plant the tree of unity, hope, knowledge and power we see growing in action today in the continent. We all appreciate their concerted efforts and sacrifices.

Chapter 1

Bishop Ajayi's Birth Place.

Bishop Samuel Ajayi Crowther came from a rich and complex society. The religion of his people "Yoruba Mythology" is regarded to be one of the world's oldest and widely practiced religions that its origin dated back to several thousands of years. In Africa it is a major religion that is widely practiced in different forms and by different groups of people throughout the land. The religion has given credence and origin to several New World religions like Santeria in Cuba, Candomble Umbanda and Batuque in Brazil. It is interesting to note that when many ethnic Yorubas were taking as slaves in the nineteenth century to Cuba, the Dominican Republic, Puerto Rico and the rest of the New World, they carried along with them their religious beliefs and as soon as they began to settle down in their new locations, they never forgot to pass-on this beliefs to their new generations. This is why we see this religions still being practiced and recognized in those countries today.

There was never a time in the history of the Yoruba mythology that the Supreme God they call Olorun or Olodumare has ever been relegated to the back door or not respected and recognized as the Supreme being contrary to the erroneous propaganda of the slave traders and their agents that first came into the land. Before the arrival of the colonialists with Bible in their left hands and swords in their right hands, the Yoruba people like other communities in the continent had been communicating effectively with this Supreme being in their own divine ways and the Supreme being they call Olorun is ever ready to listen to their supplications and help them to solve their problems.

In the case of when the Yoruba wants to talk to Olorun/Olodumare (God), they believe that no human being can go straight to the Supreme Being because of the transferred belief that no one sees His face. In this regard, they thought it as a mark of respect and their being humble unto God to go to Him through the spirits of their dead heroes whom they knew very well about their courageousness during the time they were alive to present their suplecations before the holy throne. What they needed doing at any time they have problem is to call on the spirit of the dead hero of their choice or the one being worshiped in their family set-up, which they believed he now resides in heaven to directly make their supplications to God on their behalf. It was the general believe of the people of this generation that it is only the dead that were capable of seeing God face-to-face. They also had the belief that this messenger hero would bring back answers to their requests as fast as possible. These dead heroes were later recognized as deities (the Orishas) in Yorubaland and elsewhere in the continent.

If we study the relationship of this belief that was in place in the land of Yoruba before they even heard anything about Jesus Christ, to what Jesus Christ himself said in the Bible that: "I am the way and anyone that needs to go to the Father will have to go through Him", it is then possible to see similarity in the words of Jesus Christ to the belief of the ancient Yoruba mythologists. Another fact to bear in mind here is the words of Jesus Christ in John 14:12-13 where he said: "Verily, verily, I say unto you, he that believeth on me, the works that I do shall he do also; and greater works than these shall he do; because I go unto my Father. And whatsoever ye shall ask in my name, that will I do, that the Father may be glorified in the son". What Jesus Christ was saying here was a matter concerning the time He would be residing with the Father in heaven. Because it is when one dies that he is qualified to see God in heaven.

Bishop Ajayi Crowther came from the society and the community that practiced this type of religion and believed in the superiority of various Orishas that to them served as the mouthpiece of God (Olorun). Some if not all the deities that existed in the Yoruba land, which predated Christianity and Islam are still recognized in every community of the land and people still talk to Olorun through them. Though the beliefs in Christianity and Islam have turned these Orishas unto satanic instruments but we should all remember that before the advent of these religious bodies, people of the land had been effectively communicating with God through the divine knowledge of these Orishas. The Bible and Koran have come to stay in the land and there is no doubt about this but the question that comes to mind is that are there no satanic instruments in existence in the minds of the believers of these two religions? Of course YES, then what do we say about them? Are we going to call them Saints or anything else?

The slave boy was born in a town called Osogun in Ife South Local Government area in the jurisdiction of Kere town of Osun state in Nigeria around 1807. Long before the 15th century, much of today's Nigeria was divided along the line of small states, which can be identified with the modern ethnic groups that trace their history to the origins of these states. These early states included the Yoruba kingdoms, the Edo kingdom of Benin, the cities of Nupe, and Hausa cities. In the course of the expansion of Kanem, other numerous small states sprang up around the west and south of Lake Chad, Borno, which was initially the western province of Kanem, became independent in the late fourteenth century. There was no doubt about it that, the existence of other states were not in place but oral traditions and the absence of archeological findings and data do not permit an accurate dating of their antiquity.

The Yoruba kingdoms have been no doubt the dominant group on the west bank of the Niger. Historically, they are of mixed origin and the product of the assimilation of periodic waves of migrants who evolved a common language and culture. These two areas of their life style still bounds them together as monolithic group of people till today. Understandably, the Yorubas were organized in patriotic descent groups that occupied village and city communities that subsisted mainly on agriculture. In their villages, they ascribe every authority to the head of the village, which in most cases is the head of the family unit or clan head. They always rally round this head to see that the lives of the community are save and that everything goes on well with everybody in the community. Through communal efforts, they help each other in their farm works especially at the beginning of the field clearing and planting season on rotational basis, which they call *aaro*. Because of their interest in this industry, they are able to contribute immensely to the production of such produce such as cocoa beans, palm, coffee, yam tuber and other cash and non-cash crops.

From about the eleventh century A.D., adjacent village compounds, which Yoruba people called *ile,* began to come together into a number of territorial cities like in which their loyalties to the clan became subordinate to a dynastic chieftain in allegiance. This transition produced an urbanized political and social environment that the foreign missionaries met in place by the time they came in. Apart from their keen interest in agriculture, the brass and bronze used by Yoruba artisans was a significant item of trade, made from copper, tin, and zinc either imported from the North Africa or from mines in the present Northern Nigeria and across the Sahara.

The Yoruba people so much cherished their religion and culture and from their day one on this planet earth, they have been giving recognition to the Supreme Being called Olorun or Olodumare. The word Olodumare is interpreted to mean the only Being that has everything in abundance and this is why they usually look unto him for the supplies of their needs. The lesser deities, some of them formerly mortal, and who performed a variety of cosmic and practical tasks are as well recognized and respected in their order of seniority. One of them was **Oduduwa** who the people regarded as the creator of the earth and the ancestor of the Yoruba kings.

According to Yoruba history, **Oduduwa** was believed to have founded the city of Ile-Ife, which is the cradle of the Yoruba land and dispatched his grandsons to establish other cities, where they reigned as priest-kings and presided over all things that belong to their domain. The city of Ile-Ife was the center of as many as over 400 native religious sects whose its traditional rights and authority was vested and lays in the hands of the chief custodian of the people's rights and obligations - His Royal Highness, the Oni of Ife, concerning the welfare of the city and its inhabitants.

During the fifteenth century, Oyo and Benin became both political and economic powers of the South West region of what is now the present Nigeria. These two cities surpassed Ile-Ife because of their economic domination but Ile-Ife preserved its status as a religious center of the people by all means. The respect given to the priestly functions of the **Oni** of Ile-Ife and the recognition of the common tradition of origin that bounds the people together were crucial factors in the evolution of Yoruba ethnicity. This was why the **Oni** of Ife was recognized as the senior political official of the people not only among the Yorubas but also at Benin in Edo land where he formally invested Benin rulers (Obas) with the symbols of temporal power.

The Yoruba wars of the nineteenth century tore the community into shreds. Oyo, which was the great exporter of slaves in the eighteenth century, had collapsed in a civil war after 1817 and by the middle of the 1830s the whole Yoruba land was swept up in these civil wars. New centers of power began to emerge as a result of the wars. Places like Ibadan,

Abeokuta, Akure, Owo and Warri were now appearing to have contested control of the trade routes and sought access to fresh supplies of slaves, which were necessary to repopulate the turbulent countryside. During this period, the British that were one time in the business of slave trading now began to withdraw from the business and show an intense course to block the coast of slave trading. This blockade required some sort of adjustment in the slave trade along the Lagoons that stretched from Lagos, while the domestic market for slaves were now being converted to be used as farm laborers and as porters to carry commodities to market places and this new arrangement easily absorbed the many captives that were a product of the Yoruba wars.

Few of the Yoruba cities of today especially those that lie along the war routes of those days started their existence as war camps during the period of chaos in which Oyo broke up and when the Muslim revolutionaries who were allied to the caliphate conquered Northern Yoruba land of Ilorin and its environ. Ibadan, which now became the largest city in black Africa during the Nineteenth Century, owed its growth to this fact and the role it played in the Oyo civil wars. The Oyo wars and slave raid were complementary exercises among the Yoruba of the early 19th century, reason being that they needed money to buy the firearms with which they fought in a vicious cycle war and enslavement. Around this period, their military leaders were well aware of the connection between guns and enslavement.

The nineteenth century era recorded two unrelated developments that were to have major influence on almost all areas that now constitutes the Nigeria of today. These two developments ushered in a period of radical changes in the live of the people. First, between 1804 and 1808, Usman dan Fodio who established the Sokoto caliphate was fighting his Islamic holy war, which not only expanded to be the largest empire in Africa since the fall of Songhai but which also had a tremendous impact and influence on large population of Muslim Africa to both west and east of the continent. Secondly, in 1807 Britain declared the transatlantic slave trade to be illegal. This was an action that occurred surprisingly at a time when Britain itself was in the business of shipping more slaves to America than others in the business group.

The transatlantic slave trading did not end until 1860s, but was gradually replaced by other means of trade in form of such commodity such as palm oil. The shift in trade now had serious economic and political consequences in the interior of the country because it was to take some years for the people to adapt themselves to the new trend. The current situation opened the doors for the British to intervene in the affairs of Yoruba land and the Niger Delta. There was the need for the people to buy essential commodities imported from the foreign countries for survival and the only way open to them in this regard was to allow the missionaries and their trading partners to have a place among them for the continuation of this purpose.

By gradual trading process, and huge interest of the government of Britain, what we now see today as Nigeria was moulded out of fragments of independent states and tribes. After initial contact with Great Britain in 1849, Lagos became a colony of the British Crown in 1861. In 1924, the Northern and Southern Protectorate established by the British in 1900 were united to form one country – Nigeria. In 1954, Nigeria acquired a status of confederation and in 1960, it acquired independence from Britain and in 1963, it was constituted as a republic.

In principle, Nigeria is a secular state. The Nigeria Constitution of 1963, 1979 and 1989 guaranteed religious freedom. But what we are seeing happening in the country's history of today has been characterized by tensions between the two giant religious bodies – the Christian and the Islam that often lead to violent outbreaks. In these new waves of violence, many lives have been lost and many people have been rendered homeless and displaced. The stability of the country now depends on the constructive relationship between the two warring religious bodies.

If foreign agents that brought the two religions to Africa can manage our affairs from their home bases for upwards of 60 – 70 years without any serious traces of religion conflicts, why then can't we as Africans find a way of compromise where we can resolve once and for all the petty conflicts and rancours that always lift up their ugly heads in our society. I believe we have so many problems at hand to face rather than wanting to help God to do His business. I know from here till eternity that we are in no way qualified to advise God in any form. He does not need any help or advice from any of us on how to govern his people, instead it is the people that will have to continually going to Him for knowledge and wisdom in all the things we do.

Chapter 2

The Culture of His People

What is now known as Osun state in Nigeria today was in the old larger Western Region of Nigeria created immediately after the exit of the British Administrators in Nigeria. The area featured very prominently during the first and subsequent indigenous administrations of late Chief Obafemi Awolowo and Chief Samuel Ladoke Akintola who was an indigene of the state and host of others. Bishop Samuel Ajayi Crowther came from a small town of Osogun in Osun state, which is populated mainly by Yoruba people and unified by a general language spoken throughout Yoruba land. This is the area of Yoruba land where there are groups associated with particular dialects version of Yoruba language slightly different from the one being spoken in other geographical areas of the land. Among the major dialects from this area are the ones associated with the Oyos, Ifes, Ijeshas and Igbominas. But no matter how dialectic the Yoruba language is being spoken in one area, the people from other areas would still catch up with it and would not have problems of assimilating the contents and the dialog contained.

Osun state, according to 1991 National Population Census has a population of 2.2 million people made up of 1.079 million males, and 1.123 million females. It occupied a landmass of approximately 8,602 square kilometers and was carved out of the old Oyo state of Nigeria. The state is bounded in the west by Oyo state, Ondo and Ekiti states in the east,

Kwara state in the north and Ogun state in the south. This is the reason why people say that Osun state lies in the heart of Yoruba land and a state of living spring because of the Olumirin water falls at Erin-Ijesha and the internationally recognized Osun festival that deeply rooted its history and originality at the banks of the popular river Osun in Oshogbo township, which is also the state administrative headquarters.

Ancient Yoruba religion, their culture and traditions have been a thing of many centuries and generations before the arrival of the foreigners into their land. History had it recorded that Yoruba nation was the making of their great ancestors and deities through the divine instructions of Olodumare (God). Some of such ancestors were Oduduwa or Odua, Obatala, Olokun, Sango and others. In Yoruba mythology, the ancestors and the deities of Yoruba land are giving much respect, honor and recognition the way other religious bodies of the world honor and respect their ancestors and Saints. There are many sides to the story of how Odua, the progenitor of Yoruba people came into being and how he founded his people and their kingdoms. During the living periods of these ancestors and deities, we all know that the art of writing was never invented then and as such it was impossible for the historians to have first hand information about their existence and the quality of the life they lived. Yoruba mythology like all other histories before the art of writing was invented had to go through the same process of information dissemination, which was from generation to generation by persons in the communities or in the family set-up.

The history of Odua, the progenitor of Yoruba people went thus. One school of thought propounded the number one theory in this form: It was generally agreed that hence the language was unwritten for a very longtime, then information about his existence was handed down through oral means i.e from generation to generation. The first oral story had it that the Yoruba people sprang from Lamurudu who was one of the great dynasties of Mecca. This king had a son called Odua and Odua was known to be highly influential in the kingdom of his father just like what we see today regarding the position of the Royal families of places like Saudi Arabia and other kingdoms around this region. He was highly involved in the practice of idolatory as against the nomenclature and religious practice of the people of the Middle East, which is predominantly of Islamic tendencies.

His intention was to establish idolatory as state religion with the help of a chief priest called Asara. Asara had a son called Braima who was brought up as a Muslim and a stronger believer in his Islamic religion. Braima in all ramifications detested and abhorred idol worshipping and he was targeting an opportunity whereby he would deal ruthlessly with this new group of idol worshippers.

One day, a royal edict came out to all men of the kingdom that they should go on three days hunting expedition for the on-coming festival to be held in honor of the gods. Braima used the absence of all the city's able bodied men as an opportunity for him to carry out his long planned attack on the houses of the gods scattered around the city of Mecca. He single handedly used an axe to destroy all the gods and finally hung his axe on the neck of the image of the major idol in the city. When the men came back from their hunting expedition, they found the relics of the havoc he had done to their gods. Braima was immediately summoned, tried and found guilty. He was burnt alive.

From the result of this action, civil was erupted and Lamurudu was slain and all his children were driven out of Mecca. Odua went eastward while the other children went westward. Ile-Ife was no doubt already in existence by the time Odua came in mysteriously. The town was under the leadership of Obatala, Agbonniregun and others but was incessantly under the attack of the near-by community called Igbo (not the present people from Ibo land). These Igbo people would come in the nighttime dressed in raffia clothes to raid Ile-Ife of their belongings and set their houses on fire – the houses of this time were roofed with leaves and grasses. Ifa oracle was consulted on what to do to conquer these Igbo raiders through Agbonniregun. The people were told that Olodumare – the Supreme Deity would descend down to them a savior in a short while. No sooner that they heard this message from Olodumare that Odua actually came down through a chain from the sky. It was a miracle to the people at first time that this mysterious person came the way Agbonniregun described his sudden appearance in the land. From thence forth, they began to have double assurance that their freedom had actually come.

Some time later, the Igbo raiders came in to attack Ile-Ife as usual but this time, Odua's presence with his magical powers helped the Ife people to soundly defeat them outright. When everyone in the town saw the demonstration of Odua's powers in the battlefield, the chiefs and the elders of the town decided to bestow on him the kingship of the town. Odua was qualified for this position because he was able to provide the needed security that no one could provide to the people of the town before he arrived. There was a conflict of power between the acting monarch of Ile-Ife, which was Obatala before Odua came and the now new ruler who was Odua. Before his selection according to Yoruba culture and tradition,

Ifa oracle had to be consulted and when consulted, its chief priest – Agbonniregun announced the consent of Olodumare of Odua's choice as the king..

Although, Obatala who was leading the city as the acting monarch before Odua came in was not supportive of this new development. On the account of this, he began to organize a revolt against the new ruler. He rallied the support of Esu and some other high chiefs in the town. While he was on this course, Odua had a dream one night when it was revealed to him that the kingdom of his father in Mecca was in chaos and under a very heavy attack by some groups in the city. He had to leave for Mecca to arrest the situation and promised his people at Ife that he would come back in due course. While he was away, the mantle of leadership moved back to Obatala again. Obatala this time did every possible means to see that Odua did not come back to the throne again but his plan was futile because in the end, Odua came back with some of his native people from Mecca. He regained back his leadership authority and by this time his only son Okanbi had grown into manhood, got married and producing children. In fact his seven grand children that began to establish kingdoms in Yoruba land had been born to his son Okanbi before he came back to Ile-Ife the second time. These grand children and there children established many prominent cities in Yoruba nation.

Another version of the story of how Yoruba came into being was that Olodumare, descended down a chain from heaven to the center of Ile-Ife town and it was through this chain that Odua and the first group of Yoruba people descended unto the earth. On their way coming from heaven, they had with them a life cock-chicken, some dusts of earth in a container and a palm kernel. When Odua dropped onto the earth, he poured a little bit of the dust powder he brought with him unto the primordial water and asked the cock to spread it all over, hence the earth was formed. He then put the kernel into the ground that had been formed and it began to grow with sixteen branches, which represented the first sixteen original kingdoms of Yoruba nation.

Another version of the origin of Yoruba was cosmogonical in theory with two variations. The first variation of the cosmogonic myth was that Orishanla called Obatala was the arch-divinity who was given the power by the Supreme Being (Olodumare) to create the solid land out of primordial water and the power to mould human beings to populate the land that had been formed. It was said that Obatala descended from heaven on a chain, carrying with him a small snail shell full of earth powder, palm kernel and a five-toed chicken. Obatala was to empty the content in the snail shell on the primordial water and allow the chicken to spread it all over. This Obatala did to the satisfaction of Olodumare. The next task was the making of the human beings in robot form without life. When he completed this assignment, Olodumare Himself gave breath of life and the making of human beings was complete according to the first version of the cosmogonic myth theory.

The second variant was that Obatala was given the task but on his way onto the earth, he got drunk half way and was unable to complete the assignment. When Olodumare was worried about the second journey of Obatala unto the earth, he had to send Odua to go and find out what went wrong with Obatala. On his way to the earth, he found Obatala where he was deadly drunk half way. What Odua did was that he took over the task and completed it. Thus the ancient people had the belief that it was Odua who completed the task by creating the land according to the instruction of God - Olodumare. The particular spot where he dropped down from heaven and where he redeemed the water to become land is up till today called Ile-Ife. This is why the city is considered the sacred and spiritual home of the Yoruba nation. Interestingly, when Obatala woke up and remembered what had happened to him half way from heaven, he became embarrassed and he made it a taboo for any of his worshipers or devotees not to cultivate palm wine drinking habit. Obatala was forgiven of his wrong action by Olodumare, and after the land had been created by Odua, Obatala was then given the responsibility of moulding the physical bodies of human beings.

Others in the schools of thought regarding this issue believed in the existence of the city of Ile-Ife before the arrival of Odua with his super natural powers that he used in defeating the Igbo raiders. In whatever facts or believe that we can bring out of these mythical theories about the origin of the Yoruba people, it was established that the Yoruba nation started its journey from its ancestral city of Ile-Ife, which was the center from which all Yoruba people dispersed to their present locations in the land. Whichever way we see the origin of the Yoruba nation, an idea that the Yoruba people originated from the Middle East is somehow remote to be considered. If actually the city of Ile-Ife had been in existence before the arrival of Odua, it was illogical to believe that he founded the city. On the other hand, the theory that supports the idea that he was sent by Olodumare from heaven to go and find out about the mission of Obatala to the earth could be an acceptable mythical theory. The story of how God formed the earth in the Old Testament in the Bible had close similarity with what we find in the cosmogonical myth theory of the completion of Obatala's assignment by Odua.

As Odua was able to stop the Igbo raiders, the city was now at peace. He then got married to one of the beautiful ladies of the community named Olokun. This woman after staying with her husband for many years had no child by him. It is always a taboo for the king of any kingdom in Yoruba land not to have heir to the throne and because of this, Olokun went out on her own to arrange another marriage for the king so that he would have a heir to succeed him after his death. All these arrangements were made without the knowledge of the king. The second wife named *Osara* was welcomed into the palace court and in a lesser time, she was pregnant and bore a male child named Okanbi. The story had it further that this second wife of Odua was be-witched, powerful and arrogant particularly to the senior wife – Olokun. When Olokun could no longer swallow the incessant insults from the junior wife, she decided to pack out of the palace and made her way onto the Sea side where she finally became the goddess of the ocean and the patron of the deities.

When Odua died, his grand children dispersed out of Ife to found their kingdoms throughout the Yoruba land. These were the children born unto the only child Odua had – Okanbi and who later found different kingdoms in Yoruba land:

(1) Olowu of Owu (Son of a daughter) – Ogun state of Nigeria
(2) Alaketu of Ketu (Another son of a princess) Ketu is now located in the present Republic of Benin
(3) Oba of Benin in Edo state of Nigeria
(4) Orangun of Ila – Osun state of Nigeria – the eldest grandson of oduduwa
(5) Onisabe of Sabe
(6) Olupopo of Popo
(7) Oranmiyan of Ile-Ife and Oyo – Osun & Oyo states of Nigeria. He was the youngest of all the princes and who was charged with the responsibility to administer Ife dynasty after the exit of Odua by Odua himself.
Odua was considered not to be dead physically but was taken away by the spirit of the whirl-wind called Aaja just the way prophet Elijah was taken away to heaven in the Old Testament.

Oranmiyan was noted to be a great warior, a diplomat, a medicine man of Ile-Ife and the founder of Oyo kingdom. The reason why he left his kingdom at Ife was his intention to travel to the Middle East to avenge his grand father's expulsion from the city of Mecca. But when his expedition failed due to the disagreements between him and his war generals and the people traveling with him, he had to abandon the expedition half way. He was ashamed to return to Ile-Ife because of the unsuccessful expedition. He therefore appealed to Etsu of Nupe who had authority over the territory of the northern part of Yoruba land as at then for a place to stay. His Royal request was granted and he founded Oyo kingdom there and became the first Alafin of Oyo. Because of the cordial relationship between Oranmiyan and the Etsu of Nupe, the later gave his daughter in marriage to the former and this woman later became the mother of Sango who was crowned the fourth Alafin of Oyo. He reigned after Alafin Ajaka who was taken captive by his cousin the Olowu of Owu for being a weakening monarch that would allow the Fulanis to penetrate into the Yoruba nation through its fast expanding kingdom by then. When Alafin Ajaka was released through the mythical efforts of his brother Sango from his captivity place in Owu, the Oyomesi (the traditional kingmakers and Government in Council in Oyo) banished him to Ipodo and later installed Sango in his place as the fourth Alafin of Oyo.

We cannot but refer to the importance of some of the deities that played important roles in the structural building of the Yoruba people in the ancient times. Among the numerous Orishas (deities) that the Yoruba people recognized and cherish till today are the followings:

(1) Sango ………..The god of sky & Thunder
(2) Osun ………... Goddess of fertility and water
(3) Ifa ………….. God of divination
(4) Egungun……. Symbolizes all dead ancestors
(5) Orunmila…… The oracle god
(6) Ogun ….. God of Iron and war equipment
(7) Yemoja…….. The divinity of Ogun River in Nigeria
(8) Olokun……… The mother of all bodies of Water and owner of the ocean and many others.

Sango for example is worshipped in nearly all the cities and communities in Yoruba land and some other places of the world. Apart from the fact that he was the fourth king of the Yoruba city of Oyo and who was deified after his death, he is always remembered for his hot temper, gallant courage and quick action. He was a no-nonsense personality when he ruled Ile - Ife and Oyo kingdoms. Sango was one of the important deities that many ethnic Yorubas that were taken as slaves to Cuba, the Dominican Republic, Puerto Rico, Brazil and the rest of the New World in the 19th century carried with them to their new destinations. The Yoruba people in these countries up till today continued to worship this powerful deity of their ancestors.

During the lifetime of Sango, he had three wives from which his favorite because of her excellent cooking was Osun, a river goddess in Oshogbo. His first wife was Oba, who was another goddess of river. The third wife was Oya, who commands rainstorm at will and the goddess of River Niger. The story behind the courtship between Sango and Oya was a mysterious love affair. One day at the market place in Nupe, Sango met Oya and sized her as a beautiful and mysterious person. He asked her for an acquaintance but Oya shunned him off. Sango being a great magician from his birth immediately noticed that the lady was not an ordinary human being but a spirit in the human cover. He decided to secretly follow her until she entered into the jungle where she usually keep her animal skin on every market day and changed in to human body as a person. The following market day after the day's business and Oya was ready to go home, Sango moved faster than her to the particular place where she used to keep her animal skin and Sango stole the skin and hid himself around the corner. When Oya came to the spot where she usually kept her skin, she couldn't find it and she began to search everywhere for her animal skin, yet she was unable to find it. It was now becoming too worrisome to Oya as it was getting too late for her to go back home. She now stood motionlessly thinking about what had happened to her skin and when she had no solution, she bursted into flight range. As she was about to begin deadly incantations on whomever stole her skin dress, Sango appeared to her from his hideout and stopped her furious actions. Sango confessed to her that he was the one that took her skin dress and he was not ready to release it to her. He then commanded her that she should follow her home to be his new bride. Oya pleaded passionalately with Sango that she was ready to send as many animals to him to kill in his lifetime but Sango too refused her offer and remained adamant because he new the type of enormous magical powers that he would gain from Oya being his wife. At last both of them struck a deal of secrecy that none of them would ever reveal the guided secret to anyone. She finally agreed to follow Sango home to become Shango's third wife.

Oya knew and understood Sango inside out and she knew that the greatest of all the powers that Sango had was in the thunder bolt that used to bring fire out of Sango's mouth each time he was angry and this thunder bolt always lived in Sango's stomach. She was a great diplomat. She knew to which level Sango could go to whenever he is angry with anyone either in the family circle or around his subjects. With the power in this thunderbolt, Sango had won so many wars and Oya was clever enough to think of the safety of her husband's kingdom first. She realized that should Sango one day fly into high range with his subjects, he could destroy them with fire. She actually knew that Sango was capable of destroying the whole kingdom in less than a minute if he wanted to. Because of this, Oya began to plead with her husband to give to her for save keeping the thunderbolt. After so many persuations and lobby, he finally agreed to give it to her for save keeping but warned her not to loose it or keep it closer to her private part because if she does, the power in the thunderbolt will drastically reduced or be made impotent forever. She agreed to all the conditions.

But Oya broke her own part of the promise as she kept the thunderbolt close to herself and thereby rendered the power in the thunderbolt reduced. She actually guessed correctly about the attitude of her husband. One day when Sango's authority was undermined by one of his subject and he wanted to deal with him, he asked Oya for the bolt but by the time the bolt was given to him, he realized that more than half of its power had gone. He was highly enraged and used the remaining power in the bolt to destroy his palace killing everyone therein including his own children. Realizing the deadly action he had inflicted upon himself, he decided to move out of his kingdom in anger and was on his way back to his mother's land in Nupe. Shango was never hanged as against the impression the people had but mysteriously disappeared like his grandfather (Oduduwa) half way between Oyo and Nupe. He was later defied by his people.

Osun is another powerful and loving deity recognized and worshipped by the ancestors and the present generation of Bishop Ajayi's people in Osun State where he came from. In Yoruba mythology Osun is a spirit-goddess who reigns over love, intimacy, beauty, wealth and diplomacy. Osun is beneficent and generous, and very kind. She is believed to give children to barren women but had a horrific temper similar to that of her husband Shango, though it is difficult to anger her. She was the second wife of Sango and as such, Oba the first wife was her rival. This rivalry between them when they were both living as human beings is still demonstrated when they both became goddess of two different rivers. This can be seen where the two meet in a turbulent place with difficult rapids that symbolized their rivalry at the intersection of Osun and Oba rivers.

A few of what has been said about the culture of the Yoruba people serves as a pointer to the beginning of the journey of every Yoruba sons and daughters irrespective of where they are located. It is also an indication that people like Bishop Ajayi Crowther and others in his category whose names have been forgotten but did excellent works for the progress of Yoruba land did not come to this planet without a source. The story of his life was not expected to begin at the time when he was captured as a slave boy but from his formative years preceding that time. We should assume that because of the ugly situation he found himself and the type of ordeal he went through before his life was re-shaped embittered him so much that he himself never wanted to discuss anything about his past with anybody. Other reasons could as well be assumed that the early missionaries of African descents were ashamed to discuss about their origin and where they came from for some reasons best known to them.

Before we all grew to our present levels in life, our biography never started at the beginning of the present level but from our birth walking itself through thick and thin before we get to our present levels. The Supreme Deity that we call by different names in different areas of the world that created all human beings is never stupid. He has his reasons for creating us to where He created us and for what purpose He created us.

Bishop Samuel Ajayi Crowther was one of the African heroes to be respected, honor and even to be conferred with the Sainthood title assuming he had come from the cultural background of the colonialists. It is saddening to note that even the Africans whom he fought for with every drop of the blood in his veins have not even fully accorded him the rightful position he is suppose to occupy among his peers. The great work he did with others in his generation in the continent to free their people from the hands of their oppressors and slave traders of the past centuries and the new ones that are now raising their ugly heads again is a thing to be recognized in all nations of Africa.

The world should know that Samuel Ajayi Crowther came from the continent that has a long period of cultural arrangements that is set by the Supreme Being for His own needs and for the development of mankind. The cultural background of his people that helped to broaden his mind and interacted with his philosophical storage when he was working on the interpretation of English version of the Bible and songs of hymn into his mother tongue with the help of his other Yoruba slave brothers and sisters did not come from the blues but from the interest they had for their future generations. This same cultural training he had in the first fifteen years of his life helped him in his first and second Niger expedition to the amazement of his masters. It helped him to build the difficult relationships he had with his own people of Abeokuta, Niger Delta, Lagos, Freetown, Lokoja and other areas where he worked and visited during his missionary journey.

Traditional African religion played a vital role in the establishment of the Christian faith in Africa. We should all accept the fact that overseas missionaries did not bring God to Africa and God has never been seen as a strange object to the people of Africa from day one of their existence as human beings. Spiritual activities like prayer, thanksgiving and the offering of sacrifices to God were well established facts of life for the existence and continuation of the African community. One would notice that when Africans are worshiping and praising God, some of the words they use in doing this in their mother tongues could not even have any equivalent in any of the foreign languages that the overseas missionaries brought to the land.

The God described in the Bible is none other than the God who is already known in the framework of the traditional African religiosity. The missionaries who introduced the gospel to Africa in the past two hundred and fifty or more years did not bring God to the continent. But instead the only God, known at everywhere in the world brought the missionaries at His own convenience and time. The missionaries only came to the continent to proclaim the name of Jesus Christ but the name of God they met on the ground in different areas they visited never changed. For example, it was the same names of God that were already in existence in Africa before the Europeans arrived - such as Mungu, Mulungu, Katonda, Ngai, Olodumare, Asis, Ruhanda, Jok, Modimo, Unkulunkulu, Chineke and thousands more that the missionaries equally used without changing any of these names. Why? Because they perfectly knew that these were not empty names; and that, they were names of the one and the same God, who created the heaven and the earth including every thing therein. It has been obvious that in the immediate past time, some people attempted to take credit for the making of Bishop Samuel Ajayi Crowther thereby trying to neglect some important versions of his lifetime, which helped to mould him and deposited him into the hall of fame. Could this be a deliberate oversight or being regarded as injurious to their faith, belief or intentions?

Jacob Oluwatayo Adeuyan

It is only the God of the universe that can answer these questions correctly because my answers which may be on the same level with your answers may be misinterpreted into various versions that may not in the end do good to anyone of us.

Chapter 3

A Continent in Ruins

African continent has always been seen by people from other continents as a dark continent that cannot produce enough light to illuminate itself except help comes from outside. To the contrary, the early explorers that began their expedition to Africa around 15th century met progressive developments in the area they first landed. Diogo Cao of Portugal came to the mouth of the Congo River in the middle months of the year 1483. On the bank of the majestic brown River, Cao and his men anchored their ship and began to establish friendly relations with the leaders of an African community. He left four Portuguese companions to be conducted with gifts and messages to the paramount chief dwelling in the interior and he pursued his coastal voyage to the south of the River.

When he came back from the arid shores to the south, Cao discovered that the four Portuguese he left behind had been retained at the Manicongo court. In retaliation, Cao seized four Africans. The Africans he seized were only taken as hostages for the safety of the Portuguese ambassadors – if they were still alive. Cao took these African men with him back to Portugal promising the local prince who was a relative of the supreme chief that he would return them in fifteen months time. Cao's action was to be turned into a masterstroke of diplomacy by the Portuguese king and his advisers. The king and his advisers mapped out an alliance with the Manicongo. Accordingly every effort was made to impress the hostages with the wealth and spiritual values of Portugal and from victims of a kidnapping, the unsophisticated visitors were transformed into messengers of goodwill, who were able to explain to their chief better than any Portuguese the benefits to be gained from friendship with Europeans.

The return trip of Diago Cao to the Congo in 1484 or 1485 was more of a triumphal embassy than another voyage of expedition. On his way back, he carried with him rich presents for king Nzinga-a-Cuum and the traditional messages of hope that the Manicongo would embrace the Christian faith. The king welcomed their gesture and was receptive to the persuasion. He prepared a small group of his people to be sent to Portugal so that they may be trained in European ways of life, and asked that Joao II send his missionaries, builders and traders to train his people. The king was overwhelmed by the story told him by the four hostages taken to Portugal by Cao.

Joao's response to the request of Manicongo chief was a fleet of three ships dispatched to Congo in 1490 carrying priests, skilled workers, tools and religious objects. The purpose of the expedition was initially peaceful and missionary in content. They were to seek alliance and not to conquer. The Manicongo, his eldest son Afonso, and various notables of his court were baptized while the technicians and priests who remained in Mbanza were busy carrying out their respective task of instruction.

Dom Afonso-King of Congo(1492-1540)

When Manicongo died, he was succeeded by his young Christian son, Afonso, who reigned between 1492 until 1540 or thereafter. During the period of 1492 until 1506 little was known of events in Congo because it was apparent that Portugal did not send men and supplies to Mbanza on regular basis as it was in the past. The residents of the newly populated Sao Tome began to trade for slaves in the area and the Old king Manicongo used this opportunity of the absence of Europeans to lapse into his traditional habits and turned against the few remaining priests. When Afonso became the new king, he was confronted with factious nobility and cancerous slave trading. The problem of the continent now began from where the supposed modern civilization entered the land.

The long reign of Afonso I or Mbemba-a-Nzinga, the Christian king of a pagan land represented a period of turmoil. Afonso was versed in the Portuguese language and as well familiar with Portuguese history and customs. But his opportunity to change the customs and destiny of his people was destroyed by one of the side effects – the slave trade – of the civilization that he had accepted. From the beginning of his reign, Afonso was bedeviled by the intrigues of the Lords proprietor of Sao Tome who made the Congo a commercial and often political dependency of the island.

The slave trade became the dominant interest of his kingdom. The missionaries that were sent to the Congo in 1508 succumbed to the moral climate of the capital tendency, they began to participate in the commerce until some of them died of fever or succeeded in returning to Portugal in between life and death. His reign was also marked by a steadfast though frustrated dedication to bring the benefits of European culture to the Congo. His greatest flaw was a naïve refusal to believe that some Portuguese were able to betray the virtuous principles he had been taught to hold. In the early 1540s Afonso died, and with him went the last hope for the success of the Congo experiment.

Between the 5th & 15th century AD, a succession of powerful kingdoms in West Africa began to emerge; spanning a millennium and their great wealth was based on trade rather than conquest. Admittedly a lot of warfare goes on between these kingdoms only to enable the ruler of the most powerful state to demand the submission of the lesser states. It was nothing of dangerous game or intent but only the background to the main business of controlling the caravans of merchants and camels. The routes run north and south through the Sahara. And the most precious of the commodities moving north is African gold. The first kingdom to be recognized in this region for its supply and that established full control over the southern end of the Sahara trade was Ghana. Ghana is well placed to control the traffic in gold from Bambuk, in the valley of the Senegal. Gold was known to be the most valuable African commodity that attracted the interest of the foreigners around this time. Other products that were in demand around the Mediterranean were ivory, ostrich feathers and the colanuts while important commodity coming to the south from the north of Africa with the caravans was salt, which is essential in the diet of African agricultural commodities.

Ghana remained the dominant kingdom of West Africa for a very long time, from before the 8th century to 13th. The evidence of the prosperity resulting from its gold produce was evident in the town of Jenne – by AD 800, which was clearly known to be a thriving town on the Niger. In the 13th century the gold field of Bure, on the upper area of Niger, became more important than Bambuk. The shift in economic power that was followed by a political change was as a result of when a warrior named Sundiata conquered Ghana and established the even more extensive kingdom of Mali that stretched from the Atlantic coast to beyond the Niger. In the 15th century, the Mali kingdom too declined and was replaced for a while by another power – that of Songhay people that built their capital in the city of Gao. At the end of 16th century Gao too lost its dominant position when the new foreign power established its presence on African coast, with a new religion, Christianity and new intention of domination.

The great trade routes to the north, through the kingdoms first of Ghana, then Mali and Gao actually provided a market for the produce of other regions of the West Africa. During the period, it was difficult for small communities in other areas to coalesce into more powerful states because of the condition of life in the tropical rain forest. The early kingdoms around Sahara area seized the opportunity of savanna terrain to move trade, people and camels to foster their trading activities beyond their geographical territories.

Despite all the difficulties experienced by the people of this period a state emerged among the Yoruba people in 11th century called Ife. This state is famous for its sculpture technology. Ife lies west of the Niger and just within the border of the rain forest with the economic advantage of being close to a gold field at Ilesha. In the 15th century Ife was eclipsed by a neighboring kingdom of Benin, which is lying within the region of southeast of Ife in what is now the present Nigeria. It was in this city of Benin, when the Portuguese merchants arrived in 1470s that they were greatly impressed by many elements of Benin including the type of government that was in place. They were also struck by the sophistication of life in the Royal palace of the Oba of Benin and how the people of the city conducted themselves in orderly and responsible manner. Benin kingdom was noted for their brass sculpture technology which they brought with them from Ife - their ancestral base.

Benin's fame was based on factors other than the fact that it became a name internationally known for its cast-metal sculpture and power. It is a coastal kingdom, which the Portuguese met when they reach the mouth of River Niger in the 1470s, bringing back to Europe the first news of superb African artifacts and of the ceremonial splendor of the Oba of Benin. In terms of extent Benin was no match for Oyo kingdom, which was then its contemporary to the north. Though over the centuries, Benin stretched its dominance from the Niger delta in the east to Lagos in the west.

One would be amazed to think of what went wrong with the sophisticated technology that was already in place in every where in the continent of Africa as far back as in the 5th century through to 15th century AD when the foreigners began to infiltrate into the people's system. We should not forget that the African scientists of this era did not know or even heard anything about Sir Isaac Newton's law of motion or of any other world known scientific works that guided them through class room training to the factories. The sudden change was a terrible turn around in the course of African journey to the world technological base. If kingdoms such as Ghana, Ife, Benin, Oyo, Congo kingdoms, Sokoto caliphate, Kanem kingdom and others in the continent could link up in trade and transfer of technology among one and another without the influence of Britain, France, Portugal, Germany, Italy and others in Europe around this ancient times, why should people now be saying that such continent is a dark or underdeveloped continent?

In 1947, one of the senior officials within the Portuguese Colonial administration attempted to show Portugal the reality of its rule. Henrique Galvao, who was then a member of Salazar's Uniao Nacional, reported to the Portuguese National Assembly on conditions in the African empire as thus: Entire frontier regions are being depopulated, and only old people, sick people, women and children are now found there……. The most accurate description of this impoverishment is given us by the catastrophic fall in the birthrate, the incredible level of infant mortality, the growing number of sick and infirm, a well as the mortality figures due to various courses, the most important being the conditions of work and the recruitment of laborers.

On 9 September 1952, Henrique Galvo was charged with plotting a coup d'etat and sentenced to a preliminary three years in prison. He was kept in goal on a series of different charges until 1959 when he finally escaped from prison hospital to the Argentinian Embassy where he was granted political asylum (information from Portugal in Africa by James Duffy).

The problem of African continent that emanated from the 16th century when the outsiders began to pry round its quiet coast in search of plunder or trade is worth mentioning. The north of the continent received the attention of the two most powerful Mediterranean nations. The Barbary Coast that stretched from Algeria to modern Libya was disputed between the Spanish and the Turks with the Turks prevailing. The remaining other parts of Africa, from Morocco down to the Cape and from the east to the west coasts, European interest was only pioneered by the Portuguese.

The Portuguese in their exploration along the coasts of Africa had an underlying intention. Initially their purpose was to sail round the continent to the spice markets of the east. But when they discovered good trading potentials along the coasts of Africa, they began to develop trading interest and lasting presence in Africa at all cost. On the west of the continent their interest was in the slave trade to feed the newly found plantations in the New World. For this purpose they settled in both Guinea and Angola. On the east, they were attracted to Mozambique and the Zambezi River by the news of the fabulous wealth in gold of a local ruler, the Munhumutaba.

Because of their treacherous interest in this ruler's wealth, the Portuguese established in 1531 two settlements far up the Zambezi – one of them at Tete, which is about 260 miles inland from the Sea. Luckily enough, the Munhumutapa and his gold mines remained beyond the grasp of the intruders. But Portuguese involvement in this region was seen to become sufficiently strong to survive into 20th century. The Portuguese enjoyed a very strong monopoly on the long sea route round Africa throughout the 16th century without rivals from any continent or any nation of the world.

But in the early 17th century, the situation began to change when both Dutch and the British came together to form the East India Companies. In 1659, the British ships sailed to the Island of St Helena far out in the Atlantic and made the place their possession. In 1652, the Dutch selected a harbor at the southern tip of Africa, nesting beneath Table Mountain at the Cape and this settlement had momentous impact in history. The expansion of the Dutch colony at the Cape represented one of the significant developments in Africa during the 17th and 18th centuries.

The second was the vast increase in the long-established African slave trade. This was where the European ships especially from Britain picked up their human cargo at collection centers along the west coast of Africa and transport the slaves in appalling and degrading conditions, across the Atlantic Ocean to plantations in the West Indies and continental America.

Because of the greedy attitude and self propelled wealth grabbing characteristics of some of the ancient native administrators of Africa especially their rulers and kings, who prosper greatly from the slave trading, had no interest in allowing the foreign partners to move to the inland but caged them in the coastal settlements where the real trading was taking place. This was what happened in the places such as in Guinea and Nigeria where the activities of the foreigners were limited to the ports of Bissau and Lagos respectively. In the case of Guinea, the slave trading became the business of the local people and economy with raids of the inland to procure captives. It was suggested that more than a million men, women and children were supplied from here across the Atlantic.

The land that is endowed to African people by their Supreme Deity (God), had now been stolen away from them by their greed ancestors and their accomplices. The African children both male and female were now being lumped up together like dead fishes in a container ready to be shipped to a foreign land whose climate, terrain and topography they do not know or understand. They were totally severed from their loved peers and the foundations of their lives were up-rooted from its base. The Mother Nature had now sent a terrible calamity, which is worse than the winds and storms of the highest category of hurricane ever to be witnessed in the history of mankind to the continent of Africa. This heavy wind blew off almost all the human structures in the continent.

The trading commodity – slave trade that sneaked itself quietly into the people's system like an armed robber in the midnight dealt a deadly blow on their future hopes and aspirations as people. It was actually a devastating blow that will ever remain with them till eternity. Because of the funny trading activities that spread over the land, African technological bases were actually destroyed to their foundational roots. Their scientists that were taken captive and thrown into the wilderness could no longer gather their brains together any more. Some of them died en-route their journey to the plantations of their captors in a foreign land. Those that were able to make the journey to its destinations were made to forget everything they left behind in their laboratories and factories. They now had to begin a new life at their different ages with the supply of cutlasses, shovels, diggers and hoes in their hands to work in the plantations of their masters. For them not to eat out of the fruits of their labor their mouths were now padlocked and their clothes became tattered and ragged. They had no shoes to wear neither do they have descent places to keep their heads at night. They were now too far away from their ancestors, homes, ever flowing rivers, beautiful land with green pastures and vegetations and that splendid oxygen that their jungle nature always provided them at their seasons.

Things now began to fall apart for those left behind because the center could no longer hold itself together as their cities now became desolate. It was only heaven that could account for how many African bodies that were thrown over-board the ship to feed creatures in the Atlantic Ocean after if they were certified dead or not because of lack of attention, poor meals and conditions. These and other reasons were the painful sorrows of a continent that was once quiet and walking on the path of development like other continents of the world of the time. The windfall of slave trading that hit the continent below the belt left devastating results for every growing kingdom from Morocco down to the cape. These kingdoms were yet to sweep off the ground clean of the barbaric mess that slave trade brought for them when another wave of hurricane storm began to gather itself together and on its way back again into the continent.

This time, it was no longer slave trading but something more serious than the former blow. The scrambling to divide and partition the continent into units that would easily become accessible to the foreign raiders began around 1857 when the idea to discover the source of the Nile became an obsession of the 19th century. Everyone in the ancient world agreed on the fact that this great river was at the heart of one of the world's first civilized continent but yet no one knows where it's enriching waters came from.

The first serious attempts to explore far up the river of the White Nile were made from 1839 on the order of Mohammed Ali, the then ruler of Egypt after it had been established from the 17th century that the Blue Nile waters flow from Lake Tana in Ethiopia and merged with White Nile at Khartoum. But the White Nile comes from further south, in impenetrable equatorial region. The explorers of Mohammed Ali reached a point slightly upstream of Juba, where rising land and tumbling rapids make it impossible for them to continue any further on the river. To continue this exploration, there was the need to use land approach towards the elusive headwaters. In 1856, the Royal Geographical Society of London planned another expedition to carry out this assignment and Richard was chosen to lead the expedition because of his past astonishing pilgrimage he made in 1835 to

Mecca when he disguised as a Muslim with a relatively inexperienced John Hanning Speke. In December 1856, both of them arrived Zanzibar where they spent six months to plan their journey into the interior of Africa. In June 1857, they set off from the coast of Bagamoyo and later reached Tabora in November of that year after following the well-trodden routes of Arab merchants that was the long-established hub of east African trading routes.

Richard Burton

It was at Bagamoyo that they were told of the three great Lakes in the region. To the south is Lake Nyasa, to the west is Lake Tanganyika and to the north Lake Victoria. It should be a strange concept to Africans that Europeans should be described or to have taken credit of discovering geographical features in Africa on which the local people are able to provide them with information and routes to those features. In the course of exploring the source of the White Nile, such names as Grant, Samuel Baker and his intrepid Hungarian wife Florence Von Sass, Livingstone, Stanley and scores of African natives that worked with them on this noble course may never be forgotten for the role they played. Among these explorers, Stanley's achievement turns out to be a pivotal event in the 19th century European involvement in the continent. The last installment of the mid-century saga of exploration was actually the first chapter of the subsequent scramble for Africa.

In September, 1876 and in recognition of the work done by European explorers particularly Stanley in the African continent, a ruler of one and relatively insignificant nation in Europe – Belgium – Leopold II invited the world's leading African explorers and experts to a lavish conference in Brussels. He invited them to join him in setting up an International African Association for the purpose of opening it to civilization. The king emphasized in his opening remarks that in this he has no selfish designs. "No, gentlemen, if Belgium is small, she is happy and satisfied with her lot". But in a subsequent letter to the Belgium ambassador in London, he was more frank when he wrote that, " I do not want to miss a good chance of getting us a slice of this magnificent African cake". Leopold's interest can be taken as the beginning of the scramble for Africa.

Leopold II had no one to help him achieved his hidden plans except Stanley who had navigated the Lakes in central Africa and knew of the rich commercial products mainly ivory and rubber that he had observed in the Congo basing. In September 1877, news reached Europe about the success of Stanley's exploration. On his journey back to England, Leopold sent agents to intercept him. The agents approached him in January 1878, in the railway station at Marseilles, and invited him to accompany them immediately to Brussels. Stanley declined the invitation on the ground that he wanted Britain to benefit from the riches, which he had discovered in his expedition journey to the Congo Basing. When he reached England, he preached to the politicians, businessmen and philanthropists a renewed version of David Livingstone original message. Both of them saw it as a glorious venture for Britain as a duty and opportunity if they could take commerce and Christianity into the heart of Africa. But their clarion call fell on deaf ears.

Within six months, in June 1878, Stanley sent a message to Leopold II that he was coming to Brussels. Stanley now agreed to work for Leopold for five years. His task was to create a viable link between Boma and Stanley Pool – the lake that was the all important strategic site on the Congo. While Stanley was faced with a lot of difficulties in his task especially on the construction of road in the area where there was a rising land cutting off the flow of the river, he was unaware that a French rival, Pierr Savorgnan de Brazza had stolen a march on him. Brazza had spent the years between 1875 – 8 exploring the Ogoone River, north of the Congo in Gabon. When he heard of the Stanley's discoveries, he was eager to claim the Congo for France. In his short-cut plan, Brazza won French support for a bold plan to forestall Stanley at his own strategically placed Stanley Pool. Brazza started his journey up the Ogooue River late in 1879. By September 1880 with Stanley still miles downstream, Brazza was already in Stanley Pool introducing himself to the local ruler king Makoko. Within days, the Monarch had put his Royal seal on a solemn treaty, placing his kingdom under the protection of France and also agreed not to have any dealings with any Europeans other than the French.

On Brazza's way back after he had secured Stanley's Pool, he met Stanley where he was still busy constructing road to the pool through the forest. He did not tell him of the deal he had struck with king Makoko.

In the summer of 1881, when Stanley reached his Pool, he discovered the unpleasant truth when he saw a tricolor flying over a guard post (on the site of what later became Brazzaville). Stanley was refused all assistance from the local people, and even the local markets were closed on him. When he saw that he had no option, he crossed to the south where he met a friendly ruler, Ngaliema who later became his blood brother when they met in 1877. In 1882, Stanley established a foothold in Ngaliema's kingdom on a site, which he named Leopoldville after the king of Belgium who contracted the task to him. The race between the two explorers now resulted in the first unmistakable partitioning of an African territory into French Congo on the north of the River and Belgian Congo to the south of the River.

The high level of Leopold's ambition now alarmed the larger European powers. Initially, they did not show any interest in any race for African territory. But if there was to be much race, they could not afford not to be part of it. The 19th century brought increasing European involvement in the continent. In the north of Africa, it was the economic interest that caused France to annexe Algeria and Tunisia. This situation brought reluctant Britain into close involvement in Egyptian affairs. In West Africa, where there was no any European involvement other than coastal trade where they originally had depots for the purchase and embarkation of slaves, now began to see different purpose for the foreign traders.

Past and present patterns of trade lie behind the French involvement in the Ivory Coast, which originally was a source of ivory and slaves; in Senegal for valuable gums and slaves. The same trading situation explained the British presence in Ghana for their gold and slaves and in Nigeria mainly for slave trade. Originally the Germans were entirely objected to the idea of colony. In 1883 the history recorded it that Bismarck was so uninterested in a colonial presence in Southwest Africa. But he later changed his mind because of the failure of the British government to send any reply to his query about Angra Pequena. He had earlier asked the British to confirm that this German outpost at Angra Pequena may rely on the protection of the Cape colony. The failure of the British to send a reply to his query prompted him in 1884 to send a secret cable ordering the annexation of the region.

In November 1884, Bismarck invited the powers to a West African conference in Berlin. In his opening address, Bismarck emphasized the philanthropic concept of colonialism, evoking the original ideal of the three Cs, Commerce, Christianity and Civilization. Other decisions of the conference included the guarantee of free trade in the Congo, and free navigation on the Niger and Congo Rivers. The significant underlying assumption of the conference was that Africa was about to be consumed in its entirety by Europe. In 1886, a British colonial administrator, Harry Johnston, submitted a roughly sketched map to the Foreign Office suggesting how the continent should be divided. Every single corner of the map is allocated to Britain, France, Portugal, Germany, Italy, Spain and Belgium. The continent was divided among the Europeans. The land and all its mineral resources including its rich forests and people are now passed on to the foreigners, who, eats close to 95% of the pie. Administration of the continent is now being put together by the conferences of colonial kings, queens, noblemen, businessmen, bishops, lords and even peasants of European continent that by all standards there should not be a counterpart of their equals in African continent. The foreigners now own large holdings in the land while the sons of the soil were made to work for their artificial masters for meager monthly allowances, which could hardly take care of their responsibilities for couple of days. In each kingdom, they carved out to themselves some large acreage of land where they built their secluded residential houses faraway from the natives and called this area GRA (Government Reservation Areas). Everything was made comfortable and available for them at the expense of the people's labor and wealth. All these put together accounted for the first ruins of the continent.

Chapter 4

Era of Slave Trade in Africa

The 1926 Slavery Convention described slavery as "the status or condition of a person over whom any or all of the powers attaching to the right of ownership are exercised". Therefore, a slave is a person who cannot leave his/her employer without explicit permission of that owner, and who will be returned if escaped. Control over a slave may be accomplished through official or tacit arrangements with local authorities by the masters who, belongs to a class in the society because of their social or economic status. The slaves work for their masters without any pay and they have no right to reject any of their master's instructions either good or bad. The International Labor Organization (ILO) defines this cruel labor services (slavery) as a form of forced labor. Forced labor represents all form of work or services that is extracted from any person under the menace of any penalty and for which the said person has not voluntarily offered himself or herself.

The business of slave trading was one of the oldest business commodities of the ancient time. In the 17th century, slavery was used as a way of punishment against the native Catholics in Ireland by the conquering English Parliament armies. Between 1649 and 1653, the New Model Army under the command of Oliver Cromwell conquered the Ireland and thousands of Irish Catholics were forced into slavery while their land was confiscated and the people were transported to the West Indies as slaves.

The Arab world too traded in slaves like many other cultures of the time. During the beginning of the 8th century, the Moors were known to have constantly raiding the Mediterranean coastal areas and would sometime carry away the whole villages to the Moorish slave markets on the Barbary Coast. The slave trade from East Africa to Arabia was dominated by Arab and African traders in the coastal cities of Zanzibar, Mombasa and Dar Es Salaam.

The transatlantic slave trade that increased the tempo of the business in the late 18th century was when the largest numbers of slaves were captured by their own people in West Africa and shipped them to the colonies of the New World. Prior to this time and precisely in the 16th century, the bulk of slaves exported from Africa were shipped from East Africa to the Arabian Peninsula and Zanzibar was the leading port for the trade. These Arab traders differed from European traders in the sense that the Arab traders would often capture slaves themselves thereby making them to penetrate deep into the continent for their catch. Their market also preferred the purchase of female slaves to male slaves for promiscuity purposes.

During the ancient times, external slave trading was carried out through the routes across the Sahara. But when the introduction of camel transportation arrived from Arabia in the 10th century large number of slaves, were transported annually to the north through this means. It was estimated that from the 10th to 19th century, some 6000 to 7000 slaves were transported north annually and over the time, this added up to several million people passing through this route to the north. The black slaves taken to the north of the continent were better mixed and interrelated with each other than their counterparts taken to America. Frequent inter-marriages suggested that the black slaves were quickly assimilated in North Africa because of their easy proximity. But unlike in the Americas where the slaves were mainly servants rather than laborers, and greater number of females were taken to work as chambermaids to women of the masters. Where women were not found to fill this gap, it was not uncommon to turn male slaves into eunuchs.

During this period, mighty kings in the Bight of Biafra near modern day Senegal and Benin formed the habit of selling their captives to European slave traders in return for such commodities such as metal cookware, rum and gin. In fact, Europeans often acted as junior partners to the African rulers, merchants and middlemen in the slave trade along the West African coast. Two factors contributed immensely to this dependency:

    (1)   The coastal geography and

(2) The diseases of West Africa

The seasonal wind patterns along the Atlantic coast of Africa always generate heavy surf and dangerous crosscurrents, which in turn buffeted a land almost entirely lacking in natural harbors. Hazardous offshore reefs and sandbars also complicated the matter further for seafarers along the West African coast. Because of these factors, European commerce in West Africa took place in most cases on the ships anchored well away from the shore. Before this could be efficiently done, they had to rely on the efforts of skilled African canoe-man whose ability to negotiate across the hazardous stretch of water between the mainland and the waiting ships. In places where the Europeans were able to conduct trade on the mainland, their presence and activities were limited by epidemiological problems that impeded their livelihood and threatened their lives. Malaria, dysentery, yellow fever, and other diseases reduced the few Europeans living and trading along the West African coast to chronic state of ill health and earned Africa the name of "white man's grave".

Based on the hazardous health factor, the European traders had to rely heavily on the African rulers and mercantile classes at whose mercy they gained access to the commodities they desired. At this period, European military technology was not effective enough to allow them the access by means of force on a consistent basis until the 19th century. Therefore they had to listen to the dictates of the Africans especially those elite coastal rulers and merchants who controlled the means of coastal and river navigation, under whose authority and to whose advantage the Atlantic trade was conducted. It was a big mistake when people of yesterday asserted that the Europeans brought civilization to the continent of Africa. In fact, when the Europeans first initiated trading relationship with West Africa in the mid-15th century they met established, well positioned and highly developed political organizations plus healthy competitive regional commercial networks. This was why it was easy for them to relate comfortably with the ruling class of the land when they came in. How could they have succeeded easily in their trading missions if virtually they met on the ground the zero level of intelligence of the people they were to successfully trade with? Long before the existence of some of the nations in Europe, caravan routes had long linked the people of Sub-Sahara territories with the North Africa and the wider Mediterranean and Middle Eastern worlds.

In the business of slave trading, African had long been involved in it before the arrival of the Europeans in 15th century. The business was not new to them at all because they were well involved in trans-Saharan trade in slave's long time ago. When the Europeans came in with broader knowledge of this business, the African rulers and merchants only tapped into their pre-existing method of ideas, skills, and networks of enslavement to supply European demand for slaves. Enslavement was often a byproduct of much local warfare between the powerful kingdoms and less powerful ones; kidnapping of people, or the manipulation of religious and judicial institutions. In the past in West Africa, military, political and religious authority determined who controlled access to the Atlantic slave trade. It was this type of opportunity that some African elites, such as those in the empires of Dahomey and Ashanti used to their benefits and profit by enslaving and selling their brothers and sisters to European traders. In actual fact the damage that these elites did cannot be forgotten easily but can only be temporarily set-aside in the minds of the offshoots of their victims. It should not be forgotten that the children of these African elites and those of their commercial partners were not captured or sold into slavery at any time during this deadly era in the history of the continent.

It is obvious that the slaves came into the market in various forms and from different sources. About half of these slaves came from the societies that sold them. They could be criminals, heretics, the sick mentally, the indebted and those who had fallen out of favor with the rulers and noblemen in the society. During this era, capital punishment and human sacrifices almost disappeared because slaves or prisoners that were being used for rituals before the advent of slave trade now become far too valuable to dispose of in such manners. The rulers and the merchants now preferred to sell their peers to European traders rather than wasting them without any profit to be accrued on them.

Other sources came from military conquests of other states or tribes. This source alone contributed almost half of the total slaves exported out of African continent during the peak of the trade in the 18th and 19th centuries. Because of the great economic interest attached to this trade by the slave merchants, it has been contended that slave trading greatly increased violence and warfare among the kingdoms all in the pursuit of slaves to keep the business going. During the period of late 18th century, which was classified as the peak period of the slave trade, the traders and the rulers of the African states received a great deal in exchange for selling some of their population into slavery. Hundreds of thousands of muskets, large quantities of cloth, gunpowder, alcoholic products, and metals were being shipped to Guinea and other ports along the coast of West Africa.

At this period also for example, Guinea trade with Europe, which included significant exports of gold and ivory was close to 3.5million pounds sterling per year. By contrast, the trade of the United Kingdom, which was seen as the economic super power of this century, was about 14million pounds per year over this same period of the late 18th century.

Though one could assume that the standard of living for those left behind increased substantially but the region gradually became divided into highly centralized and powerful nation states, which was in preparation for the next wind of colonialism and permanent annexation of some states. Such nations as Dahomey and the Ashanti confederacy benefited immensely from this program because it created a class of very wealthy and highly europeanized traders who began to send their children to European schools and universities. If we look at it very closely, we can see that the first group of African children that made their ways to institutes of higher learning generally belongs to these rulers and the partners of European traders. It took several years and decades before the children of the ordinary peasants from the main land began to breathe - in the oxygen of the new wave of civilization.

No one disputes the horrific and devastating harm that the trade of slavery did to the regions where the slaves were taken from and to the personality of the slaves themselves. Over the years, the effect of the trade on African societies is much debated. In the 19th century, some people especially the abolitionists saw slavery as an unmitigated evil. This view continued with scholars such as Basil Davidson into the 1960s and 70s, who conceded that it might have had some benefits but still acknowledged its largely negative impact on Africa. In the premises of argument, one may agree that some people benefited immensely from the outcome of the trade. The traders and the members of their families were well protected and well fed from the profits of the trade. But what can we say about the families of the victims, and the slaves themselves? What did they stand to gain in a situation where the breadwinner of a family was taken away from his home and permanently being severed from that home and his family forever? What can we say about those that did not make the trip to its destination and died on the voyage? What type of compensation that was due to this group of people?

The Atlantic slave trade, which was described as the most horrible type of business in the history of mankind estimated that some 12 – 20 million slaves were shipped out of Africa for the Americas and some other places, out of which some 15% died on the terrible voyage. Those that died on the Sea were just offered as a great feast for the fishes in the ocean. Of what benefit then was the perished numbers of African slaves on their voyage to the continent of America and other places as a whole? Although these numbers are hotly disputed by some scholars, and precision is quite difficult, but yet, the general consensus of opinion today is that these numbers are fairly accurate and reliable. In the absence of an epidemic disease, it is hard to believe that over 90,000 people will be dead naturally from a population of around 25million people of Guinea that was taken as slaves in a year during the peak of the slave trade in Africa.

The irony of the whole episode is that the African slaves that were taken to various places of the world to work in the settlers estates in America, Cape Verde, Portugal, Spain and those that were sold in Madeira and other slave markets did not forget about the harm done to their persons and the beginning chapter of the appalling commercial interests and activities that took them away from their base to become sojourners in foreign lands. The labor of the slaves in the plantations growing cotton and indigo; employed in weaving and dying factories where the commodities were transformed into cloth did not leave a chance for common sense. For example, the cloth produced out of the labor of the slaves without given them adequate remuneration for their services were used in exchange in Guinea for the acquisition of new sets of slaves.

Because of this rapid and great turnover of slave commodities, the Portuguese merchants were enjoying the monopoly of the transportation of African slaves to their colony in Brazil and in the Caribbean and America where there was the need for the development of labor-intensive plantations growing sugar, cotton, and tobacco. It is a fact that the slave merchants and their African accomplices had no reputation of deep compassion for human dignity. This trade triggered so many things that were favorable and unfavorable to the continent of Africa in particular. In the first place, it opened up the importance of the continent and its abundance of mineral resources to the outside world. Between 1500 and 1800 centuries, the kingdoms in the continent particularly those that occupied the coastline of West Africa, such as Benin and Oyo empires in Yoruba land and the Manicongo kingdom in the Congo eagerly welcomed the Portuguese traders with open arms and both people were benefited greatly from the first chapters of their association book. These kingdoms were gradually incorporated into European mercantile and capitalist activities.

The period of initial contact of these early Europeans with African continent in the late 15th and early 16th centuries began with an amazing process, which if it had been followed, African and European history would be entirely different from what we later saw. During the initial contact, the Europeans regarded the Africans as an exotic but nonetheless dignified and equal partner in civilization and the same line of thinking came from the Africans to the Europeans. Both the Portuguese and the Africans of this time were speculating about what they could learn from each other. The kingdoms of Benin, Oyo, and the Manicongo sent ambassadors, intellectuals, and students to Lisbon and to Rome to study the European ways and to represent their civilizations to the Europeans. This beginning of African and European contact, which was then seen as very promising and, which would have produced a far different and wonderful world, was cut short by the discovery of American continent where intensive-labor activities would be needed to cultivate the fertile newly found land.

It then became evident that the agricultural exploitation of the new land would require immense amount of cheap labor. At first instance, the Spanish and the Portuguese tried to enslave the Native Americans, but they bolted away and easily disappeared among other Native Americans while some died under the burden of strenuous working conditions. They tried to use other Europeans but when these Europeans escaped, they also blended easily with the European populations and they would become difficult to differentiate. These difficulties posed a great threat to the ambitions of the Spanish and the Portuguese and what do they do next? They turned to their African ruler friends of the past and by 17th century, the traffic in human slaves from Africa became competitive and a flood.

When the estate and farm land owners in the new founder lands discovered the strength and energy deposited by nature in the body structure of a black man, the strength of the trade increased tremendously. The results from the slave labor now began to yield much fruits to the plantation owners. The middle passage called the crossing of the Atlantic Ocean to the Americas that was endured by slaves after being laid out in rows in the holds of ships, and which was only one of the bad elements of the well-known triangular trade engaged in by Portuguese, Dutch, French and English was one of the worst degradations ever meant for any humans in the history of mankind. Ships bringing slaves to the Caribbean ports would now take back with them sugar, indigo, raw cotton and coffee to Liverpool, Nantes, Lisbon or Armsterdam. The ships leaving European ports for West Africa would also carry with them printed cotton textiles and other junky materials to their African business partners in exchange for human slaves. Some of the materials such as copper utensils and bangles, pewters, plates and pots, iron bars, which was more valuable than gold by then, hats, trinkets, gunpowder and firearms and assorted alcoholic beverages some of which were originally from India were brought to the shores of Africa as instruments to depopulate the continent.

The continuation and expansion of this deadly trade began to shrink the population of the continent. Some historians concluded that the total loss in persons removed from the continent and those who died on the ardous march to coastal slave marts and those killed in slave raids, far exceeded the 65 – 75 million people left behind in the Sub-Saharan Africa at the end of the trade. There has also been speculation that during this slave raid in Africa, females were most often captured as brides, with their male protectors being a "bycatch" who would have been killed if there had not been an export market for them. There are always two sides to a story as we have it to a sword. Matters didn't go down well for either the Spanish colonies or others in the game in the New World. Experimental slavery in the Spanish colonies began with the indigenes in the Caribbean but when their population was shrinking due to imported European diseases, they resorted to the use of African slaves instead. Between 1502 and 1518, Spain transported hundreds of Spanish-born Africans, called *ladinos* to the Caribbean Islands, to work as laborers, especially in the mines. It was later discovered that this arrangement didn't work out properly because the free Spaniards were reluctant to do manual labor that was required in the mines. Therefore, the proponents of this idea declared that the rapid diminution of the indigenous population required a consistent supply of reliable workmen and women.

The mainstay of the Brazilian economy during the colonial epoch was the use of slavery, especially in mining and sugar cane production. It was recorded that 37% of all traded African slaves and more than 3million of them were sent to this country alone. The plantation owners actually saw the immense usage of African slaves in the sugar plantation in many ways. First, African slaves had strong immunities to European diseases. The white workers had very low immunities to fend off deadly diseases of the Caribbean region such as malaria. Secondly, the benefits of the slaves far exceeded the amount invested to purchase them. After the first 2 – 3years, it was established that slaves would work off their worth, and plantation owners would begin to make profits on them. This was why the plantation owners in the new found lands made a lot of lucrative profits out of the labors of the slaves despite the fact that about 10% death rate per year from the total number of slaves were recorded due to harsh and inhuman working conditions.

The technological position in the labor industry during this period was relatively too low and because of this harsh intensive manual labor to work in the sugar cane fields was the only option. The slaves working in those fields were made to use hoes to dig trenches where sugar cane sticks were planted. They were also made to use their bare hands to spread manure during the time of mulching. This hazardous technique alone accounted for almost 25% of the death rate recorded for the slaves and, which reduced their life span to an average of eight years. Due to overwork of the slaves, day in day out without any resting period, the death rates for Caribbean slaves were much higher than the birth rates. This ugly situation and harsh conditions led to increasing number of slave revolts, campaigns against slavery in Europe, and in the end, the abolition of slavery in the European Empires began to find its roots.

In the colonial America, the first sets of slaves were brought in as indentured servants, and not as slaves. They were made to serve as servants for seven years and were brought only to the British North American colonies, especially to Jamestown, Virginia in 1619. Under the European rule, slavery began with the importation of indentured laborers, and then followed by the enslavement of indigenous people in the Caribbean. When the demand was becoming higher than expected, they eventually turned to the importation of African slaves through a large slave trade. The shift from indentured servants to African slaves was prompted by a growing lower class of former servants who had worked through the terms of their indentures and now thus become competitors to their former masters. The newly freed servants did not have enough means to support themselves comfortably because of the monopoly of the only moving commodities of this time, which was in the Tobacco business and, which was mainly dominated by large planters. For this reason, the economy of the freed servants plummeted and the only way out for them was to cause domestic unrest that culminated into Bacon's Rebellion.

Through the Northwest Ordinance of 1787 (also known as the freedom ordinance) under the Continental Congress, slavery was prohibited in the Midwest. In the East, slavery was not abolished until years later. The importation of slaves into the United States was banned on January 1, 1808; but not the internal slave trade, or involvement in the international slave trade externally. The issue of slavery in the country agitated a lot of controversy among the free states of the North and enslaved Southern states, which later culminated in the lunching of a massive political, cultural and economic struggle. Refugees from slavery fled the South across the Ohio River to the North via the Underground Railroad, and their presence in the Northern region agitated the Northerners.

The Dred Scott decision of 1857 asserted that slavery's presence in the Midwest was nominally lawful and this turned Northern public opinion further against slavery. After the passage of the Kansas – Nebraska Act, armed conflict broke out in Kansas Territory over its admission into the Union, which had to be clarified as either a slave state or a free state. But this question was left to the prerogative of the inhabitants. When the issue was not resolved on time, it prompted the spontaneous action of the radical abolitionist – John Brown in the mayhem and killing in "Bleeding Kansas". In the end, the Anti-Slavery legislators took office under the banner of the Republican Party.

In the election of 1860, the Republicans brought Abraham Lincoln into Presidency. Although Lincoln did not appear on the ballots in most Southern states and his election divided the nation along sectional lines. After decades of controlling the Federal Government, the Southern states seceded from the US to form the Confederate States of America. The Northern leaders like Lincoln and others viewed the prospect of a new slave nation, with control over the Mississippi River and the West, as unacceptable. This eventually led to the outbreak of the Civil War. The Civil War marked the end to chattel slavery in America. Lincoln's Emancipation Proclamation of 1863 was a symbolic gesture that proclaimed freedom for slaves with the confederacy. This proclamation made the abolition of slavery an official war goal and it was implemented as the Union soldiers captured territories from the Confederacy. Slaves in southern part of the country were now librated and freed by Union armies. And many of them joined the Union Army as workers or troops. Legally, slaves within the United States did not become free not until the final ratification of the Thirteenth Amendment to the Constitution in December 6, 1865 (with final recognition of the amendment on December 18), eight months after the cessation of hostilities.

In 1807, the House of Parliament in London enacted legislation prohibiting British subjects from participating in the slave trade. Indirectly, this legislation brought down the collapse of Oyo Empire that was at the peak of its international recognition. Britain that was the major transporter of slaves to the Americas now withdrew from the trade. Furthermore the French had been knocked out during the French Revolution that began in 1789 and by the Napoleonic wars of the first fifteen years of the 19th century. The French and the British that had been the major purchasers of the slaves from the ports of Oyo resulted in the unsettled economy of Oyo kingdom. Ironically, the political troubles in Oyo came to a stand still after 1817, when the transatlantic market for slaves once again boomed. Instead of Oyo kingdom to continue enjoying the boom of the business it had already known and which had put the kingdom on the map of the then world and which had also established it as a powerful nation of the time in West African Coast, Oyo now became the source of supplying slaves to the slave market with its own population.

British legislation forbade ships registered under the British registry to engage in the slave trade and the legislation also applied generally to all flags as it intended to shut down all traffics in slaves coming from the ports of West Africa. With the aggressive and meaningful actions of the British ships patrolling the Mid-Atlantic Ocean for the capture of illegal slave trade ships on the Ocean, other countries previously engaged in the business more or less hesitantly followed the British lead. The Dutch government was actually the first country to declare the trade illegal in 1792. It was certain that not all the nations that was formerly strong in this business that approved the illegality of the trade at the on-set, but gradually the campaign for the eradication of the trade and the substitution for it with other commodities increasingly resulted in British intervention in the internal affairs and the structures of Nigerian region during the 19th century and ultimately led to the decision to assume jurisdiction over the Coastal areas of the country.

Britain was determined to put halt to the traffic in slaves fed by the Yoruba wars, and responded to this frustration by annexing the port of Lagos in 1861. Thereafter, Britain gradually extended its control along the coast and into the mainland. Its intervention became more visible in the 1870s and 1880s as a result of more pressures from the missionaries especially the Church Missionary Society (CMS) in London and the native liberated slaves returning home from Sierra Leone. The issue of protecting the British new method of trade in this region prompted the dictates of various treaties that inevitably led to the amalgamation of the North of the country with the South and further annexations of some other Coastal areas. This created another form of slavery of the whole country into the hands of their colonial master for the next sixty years of perpetual bondage – 1900 to 1960.

Chapter 5

The Exeter Hall Meeting: June 1, 1840

The menace and blunders created by slavery in the universe of the time called for meetings and conventions that invited people and delegates from all walks of life and Anti-Slavery organizations throughout the world.

The venue of the first world meeting was at Exeter Hall, The Strand, London and the date was June 1, 1840. The history of Exeter Hall went thus: The ground on which Exeter Hall stands was formerly occupied by a menagerie (place where wild animals are kept), but, owing to the roaring of the lions, the horses in the strand were becoming frightened and the place was cleared away

Exeter Hall

in 1829. The need for a religious work, which should also provide a home for the various organizations, had long been felt, and the site was acquired by a number of influential men for that purpose. On March 29, 1831, in the presence of an immense audience, the first Exeter Hall was opened, Sir Thomas Barin being in the chair. The first building was considerably smaller than what it is today, but the cost was considered large for the sum of 30000 pounds sterling. In 1850, various improvements were made, and the Hall was lengthened and given modern face-lift.

It was in this Hall, on June 1, 1840, that the Prince Consort made his first public appearance in England, when he presided at a meeting for the abolition of the slave trade. His speech was most successful, and he wrote to his father that it was received with great applause, and seemed to have produced a good effect in the country. A few days later on the 12th of June, 1840, another famous meeting of the Anti Slavery Convention was held there where Venerable Thomas Clarkson, then in his 81st year presided and in his feeble voice, appealed to the vast assembly for a few minutes meditation before opening this famous Convention. Because of the popularity of Exeter Hall, many famous meetings have been held within its walls. Stanley's first lecture on his return from the Congo Expedition was given here, and in March, 1895, members of the Royal family were here to listen to F. C. Selous lecture on his "Travel and Adventure in South Africa".

It should be remembered also that it was "Exeter Hall" that saved Uganda for the British Empire, because it was here that the Church Missionary Society organized a meeting that raised 11,000 pound sterling before the Parliament voted 20,000 pound sterling to support the 40,000 that the British East Africa Company needed for the Railway survey that eventually secured Uganda for the British Empire. Many great names have been associated with the old platform chair, which is still preserved in this great Hall. Such big names as Brougham, Guizot, David Livingstone, Lord Shaftesbury, Clarkson, and Wilberforce have all taken this chair at Exeter Hall.

The historians of the 19th century recorded that the city of London had never known public meeting like one of 1st June 1840, in its life history. From as early as 6 o'clock in the morning, the streets around Strand had been fully flooded by people wanting to have a good view of the important personalities that were to attend this august occasion, as they made their way by carriage to Exeter Hall. The doors of the Hall were to be opened by ten o'clock and the first speech was not due until after 11am.

Jacob Oluwatayo Adeuyan

The Box Offices where tickets were to be bought for this day had been witnessing long queue of people, two or three days before and large some of money had been offered by those hoping to gain admission. London city itself was fairly busting with zeal and an excitement because the citizens wanted to catch glimpse of Queen Victoria's new German Consort en route to his first public engagement in Great Britain. The city was radiating warm air of appreciation for the organizers of this meeting because the time had in the end come when the dignity of man should be put in the right place and when a permanent stop had to be put to the traffic in human beings in the regions of West Africa and other places in the world.

One of the reasons that prompted this meeting was the question of how to stop the trade of slavery in West Africa, which still lingered almost half a century after its official abolition and where cannibalism and other horrific incidents were said to flourish. For almost a year, since the birth of Society for the Extinction of the Slave Trade and the Civilization of Africa, the British Government had been laying the plans to dispatch an expedition of three steamships to West Africa to subdue slave trade activities in the region. The Exeter Hall meeting was an intensely moral occasion that touched the minds of every attendee and ordinary spectators on the streets of London.

The meeting's real significance was that it marked the beginning of unparalleled growth and development in the missionary journey in Africa. What had been taught as impossible things in the missionary circles for years, suddenly unfolded themselves from the understanding of a Christian minded people. The success of the meeting increased the energy needed to persuade their deep obligation to go forth and proclaim the message of the Gospel to the degraded people in Africa and elsewhere in the world. They were as well now ready to rally to this course with obsessive enthusiasm and ready to send their agents out to the world in an increasing flow, supporting them with money, goodwill and with esteem on a large scale. It had never been said in the history of any nation of this time, that there was anything ever to match the great interest of the British subjects in their Christian missionary, which now began to form itself into shape. It was actually a selfless preoccupation.

The subject of discussion at this public meeting of June 1840, which was the drive against slavery and the planting of the seed of missionary instinct were not quite different from the motives of the founding fathers of the group that organized this meeting. William Wilberforce had been one of the founding fathers of the Church Missionary Society (CMS). In the formative years of the CMS, it had been faced with struggle even for recognition by its supposed parent – The Church of England, which it represented. Unfortunately, Wilberforce was no longer around to witness the beginning of the harvest season of the fruits of the spiritual and economic tree he helped to plant and grow.

In his place in the CMS since 1822, was Thomas Fowell Buxton, who was known to be the crusade leader against slavery. It was under the leadership of Buxton at the CMS head office that the Society for the Civilization of Africa had been formed. It was he that planted the seed of the idea for Niger Expedition upon which the British Government was now about to support.

Thomas Fowell Buxton

Buxton wanted a more extensive force to be used against the slave traders in West Africa than what the Royal Navy had yet managed to provide; because despite the numerous Anti-Slavery Legislations that had been passed in the past, none of them was effective. The traffic still went on unchecked.

Beyond the immediate and specific steps as the operation of gunboats in African waters, Buxton had a vision of something greater than that. The real remedy, he argued, "the true ransom for Africa will be found in her fertile soil". And in a phrase that was to become a battle-cry of the missionaries for some years to come, he declared that: "it is the Bible and the plough that must generate Africa". His thinking was that with the introduction of a commerce based upon Christian standards and western commodity, the profiteers in human flesh and misery would have their trade undercut and disappeared.

He then proposed that treaties must be made with local chieftains and exploration must be made into the agricultural and commercial potential of the continent and the initial security of Africa to be placed under the Union Jack. Buxton opposed to the idea of the British to erect a new empire in Africa as hitherto in India. This was the plan to which the British Government at once gave its ready consent. Based on the Government's assent, the Comptroller of Steam Machinery was making preparations to get his vessels ready for the mission and the Anti-Slaving lobby and the missionary people too were grooming themselves for a new move to implement hence the need for Exeter Hall meeting on June 1, 1840 was timely.

The pavement of the Strand was now becoming over crowded and people were eager to get in so early. The influx of people trooping in prompted the officials to open the doors one hour before it was intended and long before ten o'clock every space in the hall had been filled with people except the reserved seats for the invited dignitaries and committee members. The hall was densely filled with highly respectable audience from all walks of life. Observers that recorded account of this day said that by half past ten the assembly had started to get a little restive, and because of this, the Exeter Hall organist amused them by playing voluntary tunes, which was warmly applauded.

As the organist was lowering the tunes from his organ, the Prince, accompanied by Buxton and the committee members appeared on the platform. This moment was attested to that not only did the entire audience stood to honor the Prince but they clapped, waved their handkerchiefs and hats as well and there was more cheering when the organist played the national anthem. Prince Albert himself was astonished and was scarcely able to utter a sentence without punctuating cheer during his opening speech. This was the moment when the Prince seemed to feel the truly English enthusiastic reception that greeted his remark in his slightly foreign accent. The Prince in his remark said that, "he was deeply regretted that the benevolent and preserving exertions of England had not yet succeeded in ending the African slave trade; but he trusted that there would be no relaxing of these efforts, let us therefore, trust that Providence will prosper our exertions in so holy a cause, and that under the auspices of our Queen and her Government, we may at no distant period be rewarded by the accomplishment of the great and human object for the promotion of which we have this day met. There was a loud and long-continued cheer that followed his great remark.

This gathering was to be graced by either the Bishop of London or the Archbishop of Canterbury but both were engaged in different church activities on this day, but they both sent their goodwill messages and reasons for their inability not to be physically present. They as well sent their graceful prayers for the deliberations of the day. Notwithstanding of their absence, seven other Bishops turned up and took their sitting among the secular notabilities. Sir Robert Peel, the darling of the Tory party, Mr. Gladstone, the French Ambassador, M. Guizot, were all there to take their sits in the place of honor. There were a dozen or so peers of the realm in the gathering and one of them was the leader of the Roman Catholic lay community in Britain, the Duke of Norfolk; for this was a cause in which all men of goodwill and human love could forget their sectarian differences and act together for the total freedom for their fellow human beings under bondage.

The Society did a wonderful job because from the beginning, they included in their ranks every shade of Christian opinion in Britain. The primary agenda of the Society was to right the wrongs anywhere they may be found and this was why this very week had seen those making representations on behalf of the Jews of Damascus, who were being persecuted and slaughtered by the Moslem Mehemet Ali. The Bishop of Ripon and Lord Ashley both of whom were in this meeting came to present a memorandum to Lord Palmerston expressing deep sympathy for all the cruelty inflicted upon those inoffensive people and to ask Her Majesty's Government if not to obtain redress, at least to prevent a recurrence.

Sitting in this great Hall unnoticed by anyone and who made no contribution to the debate; who was not recognized by the reporters that covered the occasion and who was sitting down quietly in the audience; who was destined much more than anyone else in the meeting of the day at Exeter Hall, in London and in the whole world, to exemplify the spirit, which was now being proclaimed and released as benison upon devalued Africa, who was a twenty seven years old medical student from Charing Cross Hospital, who had come from Scotland armed with a great deal of native tenacity and complex missionary instinct that was all of his design. This was David Livingstone who by his inner Godly spirit now walking very closely to his ordination ceremony that would transform and elevate him into priesthood and at the same time a doctor of medicine.

Before that year came to an end, Livingstone would have sailed out for Africa to achieve his lifetime's obsession of such heroic fame with such epic proportions, that would kill the slave trade and exalt the Christian missionary profession than all the fascinating meetings of nobility, of Bishops, of politicians and of enthusiastic members of the public that might have taken their places in Exeter Hall or anywhere else in the universe. If actually this day's heroic work marked the concrete platform of the missionary success story, people later saw that it was Livingstone that translated it into fable.

One of the great speeches and longest of them all was the one made by Fowell Buxton. His was a highly impassioned piece of oratory that struck the nail by the head and, which actually goes to the roots of the problems facing African continent of the time. Buxton exclaimed about the present state of Africa as it was proved upon facts and evidence that could not be disputed by anyone as one of the universal slaughterhouse in the universe. He asked what was its trade and religion. A trade in the bodies of its inhabitants and its religion was human sacrifice. He remarked that its trade swept off and moved down multitudes every day in the year and every hour in the day. It is a trade where thousands were destroyed in the nightly combustions, which took place – thousands feel by day traveling the burning sands; and as to slave ship, it was impossible to describe, except in the words of Scripture that said: "A pestilence walketh upon the waters"; nay, the very shark knew the slave ship to be a barque of blood, and expected from it his daily sustenance.

Buxton re-iterated the program of his companion and that of his in this crusade against slavery that they wanted peace for Africa; they wanted to establish industry which should till the land and out of the land extract a ransom for that unhappy continent, that industry which would transform the face of the continent. Furthermore he said that they wanted commerce for that continent, by which they should carry away the superfluities of Africa, and take to her the produce, which the skill and machinery of this country (Great Britain) could offer. And above all, they wanted to establish religion in Africa-loud ovation from the audience.

Another vibrant speaker of the day as the long meeting lumbered into the June afternoon was Sir Robert Peel. When he rose to speak, the warmly standing ovation he received, from the audience was very much close to the one received by the Prince at the start of the meeting, because almost every hat and handkerchiefs went into the air one more time. He created a sensation when he read the contents of a document issued by the shipping companies, which logged commercial transactions earlier in 1840 on the East African coast. Sir Robert's extracts reported how a Spanish brig containing nine hundred slaves had been hit by a storm off Mozambique, how six hundred of these wretches had been suffocated when the hatches were battened down, and how another one hundred had perished before the vessel could return to harbour. And when asked Sir Robert icily? Had the brig put about to the safety of Mozambique? No! It merely pulls there to obtain fresh supply of human cargo.

All speakers at this meeting made eloquent speeches and remarks that touched on the nerves of the subject matter. But one speaker whose speech concisely expressed a thought that was believed to be uppermost in the minds of the people was the one made by Mr. Gurney, a member of the Society's committee. He enlarged upon the commercial opportunities that could follow after cleaning Africa of all its pagan practices. He elaborated on the commercial opportunities that might follow from the Niger Expedition the British Government now had at its hand. Gurney anticipated the day when the British might be in a position to obtain wool and indigo in large quantities from Africa to feed their home industries. He reminded the audience about the unsophisticated great population that Africa had and he then asked – might not artificial wants be created for them? Such wants would produce civilization and increase commerce. He was greatly applauded and finally he remarked that the olive branch would do more to produce civilization than the musket and the sword and those exertions would be the means of hastening that day when Christianity would cover the earth as the waters covered the sea.

The concluding speech of the day was, summarized by Buxton when he said that he had not forgotten the military triumphs of the British nation, but there was now open to Britain a road of glory more illustrious, noble and purer than the battles of Waterloo or Trafalgar had opened. Therefore, to arrest the destruction of mankind, to throw a blessing upon a continent now in ruins, to give civilization and to spread the mild truths of the Gospel over a region in comparison with which the British empire was but a speck upon the ocean was a higher and nobler road, and his desire and prayer was that Her Majesty might tread it. This was a text that was to inspire the missionary enterprise for a hundred years to come.

Minutes before Buxton rounded off the meeting, he announced the names of those that donated money to the course of the Society as thus: Prince Albert subscribed one hundred and five pounds sterling and also directed that his name be put down as an annual subscriber of ten pounds; the Duke of Northumberland had offered fifty pounds, the Bishop of London twenty five pounds, the Bishop of Lincoln – twenty pounds, the Primate of Ireland – twenty five pounds, Lord Ripon who had been sitting as chairman since the departure of the Prince offered fifty pounds. Other donators were asked to put down their donations at the committee room or at the foot of the stairs.

No sooner that the successful and, well attended meeting of the Exeter Hall ended that the World's Anti Slavery Convention took place in London in the same month of June 1840. The call for this Convention invited delegates from all Anti Slavery Organizations throughout the world. In America, women had been playing a great role in the plight of slaves and for this reason, several American Societies saw it fit to send women as delegates, to represent them in that such an important assembly. Unfortunately, after traveling three thousand miles to attend a World Convention, it was disappointedly discovered that women were not allowed to form a part of the constituent elements of this august assembly. The propagandist of the Convention John Bull when inviting the friends of the slaves never thought that women, too, would answer to his call. One could imagine the crash down of the spirit of those women who had in the past spoken to promiscuous assemblies, voted on men and measures, prayed and petitioned against slavery, women who had been mobbed, ridiculed by the press, and denounced by the pulpit, who had been the cause of setting all American Abolitionists by the ears, and split their ranks asunder.

The men in the committee that organized this Convention had heard about the activities of these American heavy weight women who had played great roles in the course of freedom for the slaves in North and South America and else where in the world. Their fears of these formidable and belligerent women must have been somewhat appeased when Lucretia Mott, Sarah Pugh, Abby Kimber, Elizabeth Neal, Mary Grew of Philadelphia who was in her modest Quaker costume, Ann Green Phillips, Emily Winslow, and Abby Southwick of Boston, all of them of refinement and education, and several, still in their twenties, landed at last on the soil of Great Britain to contribute their own quota to the course of exterminating the slave trade in all its ramifications.

The venue of the Convention was Freeman's Hall and the date was June 12, 1840. The delegates began to troop in as early as the hours of the morning. On entering the vestibule, one would notice small groups gathering here and there, earnestly discussing the best disposition to make of those women delegates from America. Lucretia Mott in her usual characteristics of cool, calm and firm manner person insisted that the delegates had no discretionary power in the proposed action, and the responsibility of accepting or rejecting them must rest on the Convention. The argument on the debate of this issue went high in the air and lasted for couple of hours before it was resolved in favor of the men delegates.

Many spoke eloquently in favor of the acceptance of American women delegates into the business of the Convention and many spoke against it as a violation of the English tradition, which does not allow women to be on the same equal level with men in the generational set up of the time. One particular speaker whose speech touched most on the rights of women and the cultural prejudices of men was George Thomas whose some extracts from his speech are herewith reproduced: He said at the middle of his speech that it seems that the grand objection to their appearance among us is this, that, it would be placing them on a footing of equality, and that would be contrary to principles and custom. For years, the women of America have carried their banner in the van, while the men have humbly followed them in the rear. It is well known that the National Society solicited Angelina Grimke to undertake a mission through New England, to rouse the attention of women to the wrongs of slavery, and that distinguished woman displayed her talents not only in the drawing room, but before the Senate of Massachusett.........

Regarding the customs of England, which some speakers used to buttress their argument in favor of disallowing women to participate in the business of the Convention, George Thomas responded by saying that in America we listen to no such arguments. If we had done so, we had never been here as Abolitionists. We cannot yield this question if we would; for it is a matter of conscience. But we would not yield it in the ground of expediency. In doing so we should feel that we were striking off the right arm of our enterprise. We could not go back to America to ask for any aid or support from the women of Massachusetts if we had deserted them, when they chose to send out their own sisters as their representatives here. In conclusion he pleaded with the Convention to admit them. But if they choose not to do so, the responsibility rests on their shoulders. He made it clear to everyone in the Convention that Massachusetts cannot turn aside, or succomb to any prejudices or customs even in the land she looks upon with so much reference as the land of Wilberforce, of Clerkson, and of O'Connell. It is a matter of conscience, and British virtue ought not to ask us to yield.

As the hour was becoming late, Mr Phillip's reply was brief, consisting of the corrections of few mistakes made by different speakers. The vote was taken and the American women were excluded as delegates to participate in the Convention by over whelming majority. However, the debates in the

Convention had the effect of rousing English minds on how to put more oil to burn down the tyranny of sex, and re-awaken the American minds to the importance of some definite actions toward woman's emancipation. As Lucretia Mott and Elizabeth Cady Stanton were walking arm in arm down the Great Queens street that night, reviewing the exciting scenes of the day, they both agreed to hold a woman's right Convention on their return to America, as the men to whom they had just listened had manifested their great need of some education on that question. Thus was how a missionary work for the emancipation of women in "the land of the free and the home of the brave started". As the ladies were denied their right in the Convention, they kept up a brisk fire morning, noon, and night at their hotel on the unfortunate gentlemen who were domicile at the same house with them. The ladies of the Convention were fenced off behind a bar and curtain, similar to those used in the old time churches to screen the choir from the public gaze.

Chapter 6

The Early Missionary Journey To The Continent of Africa.

Many African writers have written extensively concerning the issue of early missionary's journey into the continent of Africa. Some have credibly concluded and proved right that it was not the Europeans that brought God to the soil of Africa instead they brought with them confusions and discord among the people. It was glaringly seen that before the coming of the white missionaries to the continent of Africa, African people had already been solidly grounded in the knowledge of God, and the concept of Trinity was evidently present in the people's day-to-day worship. An ethnic group in Western Kenya for example, where early white missionaries worked, the Supreme Being was addressed in three dimensions: *Wele Baba, Wele Mukhobe, and Wele Murumwa* meaning God the Father, God the Herald, and God the messenger respectively. God the Father, *Wele Baba*, was also dignified with a variety of attributes such as, Mumba, meaning the Creator: *Wele Murumwa* has the attributes of the Holy Ghost, who was sent as messenger to reveal the mysteries of secrets to the people.

From the tribe where Bishop Ajayi Crowther came from, God the Father was known to be addressed as **Olodumare, Olorun Orun, Olorun gbogbo Agbaiye or Eleda ohun gbogbo.** All these attributes refers to the only God of heaven because the people believed that He is the only one that controls everything and who has everything in abundance and that He lives in heaven and no one else like Him. The Holy Spirit is regarded as pure spirit that travels between the earth and heaven to deliver messages either from the people to the Supreme Being or from Him back to the people. The translators of the Bible and Koran into different languages of Africa used the existing attributes of God, which they met in use at different locations in Africa to interpret either the English or Arabic versions of the Holy Books to carry the required effective meanings to the people. They did not invent their own new languages during the script writings of those Holy Books. The name God the Herald, carries with it the concept of spokesmanship. The people believed that in the Holy of Holies in the Heaven, there are lesser beings that have the capabilities of talking to God face-to-face and request for the needs of the people down the earth from Him, which the white missionaries called angels.

Each of the personalities mentioned above functions with equal power and they source that power from the Supreme Being called **Olodumare.** This is deep theology that the early missionaries failed to comprehend or which they misconstrued and misinterpreted. To them this was a mythology associated with fetish or ancestral worship. Important factor to the gap between the early missionaries and the people they supposed to evangelize was the issue of language. Hardly were any of the early white missionaries understood or were fluent in any of the African languages of the area they worked for many years. This pointed to the fact that they brought religion in one hand and a big rod to cane the people on the other hand, which actually surfaced during the colonial era in Africa. For the reasons best known to them, they did not for one time lived with the people or interact with the people at the grass root. They spoke to them through interpreters, which some were half baked in the European languages.

When the missionaries came into the soil of Africa, the entire African way of life completely changed. In the first place the Africans were made to throw off their names for Western names. The African worshipers were made to move from their sanctuaries, the African shrines, to a church decorated in Western styles. They were taught to face the Alter instead of the rising sun while praying. In truth, the various activities of Christian missionary societies had a profound impact on African societies. The standard of living of the converts changed and they began wearing European style clothes, walking the European walk style on the streets and segregated themselves from their peers and people. In short, the converts were made to feel contemptuous of their own traditional institutions that for many centuries had held communities together.

It was of recent time that some Catholic churches in some African countries, began to conduct their services in the language of the people. In the past all Sunday services were conducted in Latin language. The worshipers would only attend Sunday services to watch the Reverend Father talking to himself only, while the servers would carry the candle sticks up and down the Alter because at least majority of the natives may not understood what he was saying in Latin language. In the post missionary era, God has become remote and very much limited to the confines of Western theology. The African worshipers were now taught to preach, address and worship God in the manner in which He was introduced to them at the onset.

The Western missionaries of the early years failed to identify themselves with the ethnic ambitions and the idiosyncrasy of the people. The improvised superior intelligence they claimed to acquire over the low or none available of any sort to the Africans prevented full development of the African Christians. Their presence actually destroyed the superior qualities of African Christianity. For over half of a century or more, most of the churches in Africa received instructions and guidelines from either London or Rome as to how to run those churches that are physically erected on the soil of Africa and attended mainly by African people. This singular act removed independence, courage, bravery and daring self-reliance, and readiness to face challenges and difficulties from the regimes of the puppets they put to manage those churches.

Many missionaries went to Africa with the notion that the continent could only be civilized by introducing Christianity, formal education, capitalism, and industrialization. Adu Boahen was right to see colonial conquest as just another way of accomplishing this mission. He argues that the missionaries collaborated with the colonists to produce the African in their European image. If there is a desire to destroy a community, all that is needed is to first of all destroy its base, which is its culture. Every other thing would fall into place and this was what the missionaries and the colonists were able to achieve in the African continent.

African names including that of Bishop Samuel Ajayi Crowther, their music, dance, art, marriage, system of inheritance, laws and others were excluded from school and college curricular and church programs. The recent canker worm now eating deep into the fabrics of the modern African people, especially those from English speaking nations in Africa is the rejection of their mother tongue for foreign language. If you go to the homes of those intermediate class people in Lagos and other principal cities for example, hardly could their children speak to you in their mother tongue languages. The only means of discussion in those homes are now English language and nothing else. This reminded me of my primary school days when a notice was conspicuously displayed in each of our class rooms reading thus: "No vernacular language is allowed to be spoken in this class". The new move is now the effect of neo-colonialism that is spreading very fast throughout the land and which needs serious attention of the leaders in the continent.

Christianity came into the North of Africa as early as the 1st century AD., but it was only in the 19th century, when the colonial scramble in Africa by Europeans was advancing, that Christianity seriously increased its presence. In what later became Southern Rhodesia and now New Zimbabwe, the first mission station was opened in Inyati, very close to Bulawayo in 1859 by the London Missionary Society through Reverend Robert Moffat (David Livingstone's confidant and father-in-law). In 1737 George Schmidt of the Moravian church of the Brethren was dispatched by the Dutch Reformed church in Armsterdam, to the Cape of Good Hope shortly after his release from a German prison, where he had spent six years as a penalty for his Protestantism. Record showed it that Christianity had been introduced to South Africa with the arrival of Jan Van Riebeck and his 126 followers in 1652. In 1751, the Society for the Propagation of the Gospel (SPG) dispatched Thomas Thompson to the Gold Coast at a salary of seventy pounds sterling a year and at Cape Coast (modern Accra) he settled down to turn Africans into Christianity.

In this part of the west coast of Africa, Thompson discovered that the Africans would not listen to his teaching more than once a week while some of them would demand for a tot of liquor for the price of their attendance. After four years of labourous work, he returned to England a sick man but while he was at the coast, he had sent three African natives to England for education. A few years later, only one of them made it to the top and that was Philip Quaque who later became SPG's Missionary School Master and Catechist in Gold Coast. Thompson concluded in his work in the missionary field where he wrote in a tract entitled: *The African Trade for Negro slaves shown to be consistent with the Principles of Humanity and with the Laws of Revealed Religion.*

The reckless statement was a shocking hypocrisy to his followers in the missionary works and to twentieth-century men and women of sensitive piety in that age. It was an established fact that, slave trading was but the way of the world of this time. In spite of a succession of Popes who castigated slavery and slave ownership, the story had it that the Catholics who sailed with Henry the Navigator's captains around Africa in the 15th century, who established various Portuguese colonies there maintained the right of the white man to possess and use Negro slaves. To cap it all, there was a confirmed rumor that a Jesuit monastery in Loanda in the 16th century was endowed with 12,000 slaves; and when the slave trade was developed between Angola and Brazil, the Bishop would sit on his throne by the quayside, blessing each cargo as it went aboard, and promising each member of it happier times in the eternal life to come. Another interesting story was that of the British famous John William Hawkins when in 1562, he went for slave trading in Sierra Leone, the Christian Queen Elizabeth of England saw nothing dangerous in lending him one of the Royal ships named Jesus for the shipment of slaves.

Early examples of Christian journey in the continent of Africa also dated back to when Christianity entered the continent through Egypt, about the time when Christian religion were legalized by Constantine the Great in 313 AD. Predating this time, it was shown that Christians fled into the desert throughout the years of persecution that preceded Constantine's edict of toleration. For many years Egypt was the center of the monastic movement, housing the most rigorous monks and some of the most creative minds of the time. The monks of the time did not decide to withdraw themselves from the cities and towns of Egypt to live in caves in the desert; they did so because they wanted to physically and symbolically separate themselves from the world and according to their religious belief.

One of the earliest Hermits or solitaries (the monks) was St Anthony who went out into the wilderness to practice solitary ascetic Christianity in 285 AD and organized a form of monastic life for his followers. He died in 356 AD, at the age of 105 years. Other reasons they advanced to support their decision were in part that Christianity had become a cheap commodity for everyone to buy since the emperor Constantine had converted to Christianity; their veneration of the Christian martyrs, who had given their blood and their lives for their faith and the third reason was that they wanted to act as champions and intercessors for the Christian community because they saw prayers as their main task in the body of Christ, and saw themselves as the first line of defense in the struggle against Satan.

The Egyptian monks were known to be living in the desert as hermits or communities but as well remained a powerful force in the Egyptian church that did not hesitate to use their power and influence to impose a greater rigor on the church when the need was necessary. Example of this was when they came out to support Bishop Athanasius very strongly in return for his identified sympathy with the monks when he was forced to live among them in the desert during the time he was driven into exile over the Arian controversies and the resultant political infighting. At the turn of the fifth century, the monks also came out in full force as part of campaign against paganism, storming into the cities and towns, smashing and burning pagan images and temples, including the Temple of Serapis in Alexandria, home of the Museion, or great library of Alexadria.

By the second century, Alexandria had become the intellectual and philosophical capitol of the spreading Christian faith. Between 150 and 215 AD lived one of the highly educated and well-trained classical philosophers of the time, Titus Flavius Clement who was later known as Clement of Alexandria. His conversion to Christianity took him to the East to study under Assyrian, Palestinian and Hebrew teachers. He ended up in Alexandria where he came to study at the Cathecal School of Alexandria under Pantaenus, the dean of the school. He later succeeded Pantaenus as the dean of the school.

Clement's work was recognized in all Christian circles of the time as he tried to combine the best of pagan Greek and Roman learning science with the Christian faith. He saw it as his task to demonstrate to the pagans that Christianity was intellectually respectable and philosophically rigorous, and to Christians that Christianity was not only for the uneducated, but that Christians must no longer "fear philosophy as children fear a scarecrow". His affection for the Greek philosophers made him to say that: "the law is for the Jew what philosophy is for the Greek, a school master to bring them to Christ". Clement believed that the Greek philosophers understood the truth revealed in God's creation and that God had in fact planted seeds of the Truth in all rational creatures. He agreed that there was very much about Christianity that was philosophical and intellectual and at times he stated that ignorance was in fact worse than sin.

In AD 451, the tension in the theological scene that had been tearing apart the Christianity set-up in the region for ages was now cooling down with the emergence of new diversion from the main problematic issues. The Monophysite controversy was now a main issue at the Council of Chalcedon, and continued the theological, political, social and philosophical tensions between the Christians at Alexandria and the Christians at Antioch. The Alexandrian Monophysites were condemned by the Council and ultimately changed the direction of Christianity. The Alexandrians immediately separated to become the Egyptian Coptic Orthodox Church. The new church both in Egypt and Ethiopia now remained the dominant form of African Christianity from the Moslem invasion to the coming of the Missionaries in the 19th century.

The major issues between the two warring groups revolved around the nature of Christ, which had been the subject of heated theological debate in the Eastern Church since the time of Arian controversy and the Council of Nicea. Both sides agreed upon the divinity and humanity that are joined in Jesus Christ. The problem arose when they began to think about the fact that God, which is the divine nature of Christ, was unchangeable, immutable and eternal, while the human nature in him is changeable and temporal. The Antiochian theologians therefore contended that Christ's human nature need to be fully and truly human if he were to be the saviour of human beings, while the Alexandrians tended to stress Christ's divinity and his role as teacher of divine truth. This theological problem raged between the two factions for sometime and it came to a peak when any reigning bishop, if supporting any idea from either one of the two schools of thought, he would be prepared to defend his beliefs in the philosophy of the theory he supported when attacked or questioned.

When Nestorius, a representative of Antiochene School, became the Patriach of Constantinople in 428 AD, Alexandrians immediately began to look for a way to attack him. They finally found one when Nestorius suggested that it was inappropriate to call Mary the bearer of God but the bearer of Christ. What he was trying to bring to light then was that Mary was the mother of Christ's human nature, but Christ's divine nature was separate and eternal and did not come through his mother thereby placing a sharp distinction between his humanity and his divinity.

In the case of Cyril of Alexandria in AD 431, when he was bishop, he and the Alexandrians were convinced that God had a single, divine, nature and that he "emptied himself" to become human without losing any of his divinity. The Alexandrians succeeded in anyway in condemning the Nestorians in the Council of Ephesus.

The inability of the Council of Chalcedon, which met in AD 451 to resolve the differences between the Antiochians and the Alexandrians led to the split between the two. The Coptic Church that was labeled as Anti-Chalcedonian Church in Egypt came to be called, Cyril's formulation that

Christ was God who emptied himself to become fully human, but did not really condemn the notion that Christ had two distinct natures in one person. The Council deposed, excommunicated and exiled the Alexandrian patriach Dioscorous and immediately installed an imperial candidate by the name of Proterius in his place. The Egyptians rejected him because they saw him as an interloper and immediately elected Timothy Aelurus, an Alexandrian to the See. This development marked the beginning of the wide gap between the Imperial Church and the native Coptic Church. The Coptic Church took its independence from the empire, and survived the Arab conquests because it strongly enjoyed the support of the Desert Monks.

The religion of Islam began in Saudi Arabia early in the 7th century. It swept across the Middle East and North Africa region and neighborhood. By the middle of the century, Egypt had fallen to the Arabs because the rulers of both church and the state were the hated Imperial Chalcedonian Christians. The Coptic speaking Monophysite majority were glad to be free of Byzantine rule, and now gained a measure of religious toleration they had not known since the Council of Chalcedon, and now taxed just over a half the rate they had been taxed under the Empire.

For the first four centuries of their rule, the Arabs treated the Copts with great forebearance, which in part was because Mohammed, whose Egyptian wife was the only woman that bore him a son, had said that: "when you conquer Egypt, be kind to the Copts for they are your protégés, kith and kin". The Copts were therefore allowed to practice their religion freely, and were protected as "people of the Book" as long as they paid a special tax, called the "Geyza". Their regular payment of this taxation became an important source of revenue for the Islamic governors, and at one point the governors discouraged the idea of conversion to Islam for financial reasons. The tax advantages for those who wanted to become Muslim led to a slow decline in the Coptic population until it stabilized at just fewer than 10% of the population.

At one time, it became imperative that only those who could speak Arabic were the only scribes, magistrates, or tax collectors. From the 8th century until the late middle ages, Arabic was the official language of Egypt as Coptic ceased being a spoken language, which now turned the Coptic population into a bilingual community. The hatred between the Copts and the Muslims now began to grow wild and at an alarming rate that the Copts were now seriously hated and vilified by the Muslim population, who would occasionally rioted and burn down Coptic Churches and neighborhoods.

At the turn of the millennium, things went further into the drain pits because the administration of Caliph al Hakim who was probably insane, turned against Christians and the Jews and also did not spear the Muslims too, torturing and killing thousands of people. He forced the Christians to wear a particular type of dress, including a five-pound weight of cross around their necks, the Jews to wear a heavy bell around their necks and dismissed all non-Muslims from administrative offices. He turned loose the Egyptian mob to demolish Coptic Churches and Synagogues, walled off Jewish streets, and sealed the doors of a public bath for women, entombing alive all those who were inside. At his death, toleration returned, but the center of the Coptic Christianity now shifted from Alexandria to the new capital, Cairo and churches were rebuilt.

The religious indifferences of the time that associated itself with regional crusades brought another dark time to the history of the Coptic Church because the Coptic Christians were caught between two equally hostile forces during the 12th and 13th centuries. Muslims came to hate all Christians in the Muslim world of this time and which is still noticed today in some areas of the world, while Latin Christians despised the Copts as heretics. The Latin Christians during the crusade came to control the Holy Land preventing the Copts from fulfilling their binding religious obligations to go on pilgrimage to the Holy Land. In 1168 the Islamic capital city of al-Fusat, was burned down to the ground by it's Muslim governor, in order to prevent it from falling into the hands of the Crusaders who could use it as a fortress from, which to invade all Egypt. The predominantly Copt population of this city fled, and was made destitute overnight. The mob still hated the Copts, except when restrained by rulers who found their administrative acumen and skills useful. The restraints did not stop or prevent them from burning down their Churches and neighborhoods when embittered. But in 1320 after a particular severe season of rioting, the Christian desert monks came into the cities in retaliation and burned down Mosques and Muslim neighborhoods, then returned to the desert.

Patriach Cyril IV (1854-1861) took advantage of a period of toleration to initiate serious reforms and rebuilding including the Coptic Orthodox College, the first woman's college in Egyptian history, and establishment of a flourishing printing press. He also arranged for nation-wide clerical education in all ranks. In the last half of 20th century, the Coptic Church had engaged in extensive ecumenical dialog with other Coptic Churches, as well as Orthodox, Roman Catholic and Protestant Churches. In 1987, the Coptic Church and the Orthodox Churches finally agreed to a common statement on the nature of Christ; and lifted the mutual anathemas they had held on each other since the 5th century, and in the early 1990s, the Coptic Church and the Roman Catholic Church came to agreement on their understanding of the nature of Christ and declared one another Sister Churches.

The first groups of protestant missionaries in Africa were the former slaves that had been freed by the European and American Mission Societies. As early as in the 18th century, notable African personalities such as Philip Quaque, Jacobus Capitein, Pederson Svane and Christian Proteen were among the free slaves that returned to Africa serving as chaplains in the European forts along the coastline. Their efforts were not much seen as significant because of their Europeanized life style. They were so much identified with the European community and all of them had European wives, sometime at the instance of the mission agency that sent them.

Late in the 18th century, the situation began to change gradually as a group of "boisterously free slave Christians" who had originally settled in Nova Scotia Canada came to the West Coast of Africa to found the free colony of Sierra Leone in 1780. About 1200 of them who had fought on the British side in the Revolutionary war first emigrated to Nova Scotia for a new life but when they were unable to obtain land of their own, they arrived in Sierra Leone and settled in Freetown by an arrangement of the British Government because it paid for their voyage expenses. It was not too hard for these people to carry on their Christian duties and obligations, as they had become Christians while in North America. With the great zeal, they carried with them the boisterous Christianity tenets back to the land of their origin, refining the culture of the land with their new culture in Christian ways and spreading the message to all that would listen to them in Sierra Leone.

The population of this group began to expand because of the large influx of re-captives – those that were taken from captured slave ships and resettled in Sierra Leone. Sierra Leone now became a large and vibrant Christian community along the West coast of Africa. One of the most remarkable of these missionaries was Samuel Ajayi Crowther, who was one of the librated slave boy of only fifteen years old at the time of liberation, educated by the Anglican Missionary Society and years later ordained first as a priest and later on consecrated as the first black bishop in the continent of Africa. The Church in Sierra Leone was already established very strongly under the leadership of the wealthy and powerful settler Christians. The members and the officiating local personnel were as equally versed in the knowledge of the Bible and Christian doctrine as their counterparts from Europe and in America. Their acumen was measured through the observations, hearsays, and report writings of the foreign missionaries sent out from England and America to them; and records proved that during their interactions with the native Christians and their native officials, they did not recognized any inferiority in their knowledge of the Bible and the church doctrine.

It was not uncommon for the European missionaries to peevished in the system that was wholly under the control of the African church dignitaries, but Henry Venn, who was the Superintendent of the CMS at this time, pursued a policy that sought to establish self-sustaining, self-propagating, self-supporting native churches throughout the region. Ironically, he did not know that in Sierra Leone, the church there was already carrying the same policy of self-sustaining, self-propagating, self-supporting, and already spreading the Gospel throughout the Re-captive population of Sierra Leone with the knowledge and skills of the people on the ground. Majority of the Christians in Sierra Leone now were the Yoruba people who were rescued from the slave ships and who originally came from the coastal areas of what is now Nigeria, and who yet maintained their Yoruba identity in the new and temporary found land – Sierra Leone, while being converted to Christianity and becoming outwardly westernized.

The doors of prosperity, problems, dignity, development, backwardness and colonialism began to open when a significant number of them decided to return to Yoruba land to convert their people to the new religion, and created a flourishing church and a westernized Yoruba culture. The CMS encouraged and supported these Yoruba missionaries and ordained a large number of them as pastors, cathecists and lay readers in the churches.

The return of the Yoruba liberated slaves back home was not without problems and joy. The population of the colony – Sierra Leone was now rapidly expanding thereby creating some economic hardship on the inhabitants. Farmlands, markets and other living opportunities were becoming more and more restricted. This situation prompted many of them to look beyond the colony for every available opportunity they could grab. John Langley (an Ibo by birth) was one of the prominent traders of this time in the colony. Because of the allegation that he sold gunpowder to the Mendes, Langley was sent to prison by the Alkali of Port Lokko, on the account that he was aiding his enemies against him. In 1834 the

Governor intervened to rescue him from prison. A little while later, the traders grouped themselves together to buy the condemned slave-vessels with which they used to trade down the coast as far as Badagry and Lagos.

It was here that some of the traders were lucky enough to found people they could still recognize as members of the same family, peers and acquaintances. As Bishop Crowther described this moment two years later, he said that: **Some found their children, others their brothers and sisters, by whom they were entreated not to return to Sierra Leone. One of the traders had brought to Sierra Leone two of his grandchildren from Badagry to receive instructions. Several of them had gone into the interior altogether. Others in this colony have messages sent to them by their parents and relations whom the traders met in Badagry.**

The beginning of missionary enterprise in Nigeria was not accidental but who could first jump the gun in the race among the foreign organizations. The first to act was the Methodists through Rev. Thomas Birch Freeman, the energetic Superintendent of the Methodist Mission at Cape Coast, and who had shown outstanding abilities in the missionary works based on the account of his two visits to Ashanti. He was asked to occupy Badagry as an out-station of Cape Coast while his arrival there on 24th September 1842 marked the effective beginning of missionary works in Nigeria. He was accompanied on the trip by a Fanti man William de Graft, a native of Cape Coast and an assistant missionary.

On getting to Badagry, Rev Freeman bought a piece of land where he erected a temporary bamboo chapel and later constructed a more elaborate mission house at a cost of three hundred pound sterling and, which was described as: **a large, airy dwelling-house, fit for an European family, raised from ten to twelve feet from the ground, on twenty-two stout coconut pillars, averaging about three quarters of a ton each in weight………. It appeared a thing so novel and extraordinary, that the people were often seen standing in groups at a short distance, gazing at it in astonishment.** While working on this building, he was as well holding prayer meetings on Sundays with the Sierra Leone emigrants and the natives. Thus Badagry became the first missionary base in Nigeria where the missions hoped to penetrate into the interior of Yoruba country.

Other Christian denominations too made their tremendous impact and in-road on the continent of Africa. The Portuguese as we all know were the first Europeans to venture south of the Sahara desert with two principal motives. In the first instance, they took the sea route to explore

The Journey of the First Black Bishop

down the West Coast for exploration mission and often held missionary purposes as well. In 1490 their missionary works in Kongo had begun to yield fruits when the country became a Christian kingdom. It was on record that the Portuguese priests and missionaries joined in the protests of the Catholic Christian king of Kongo in appealing to the Pope and the king of Portugal for support against slave trade, but to no fruitful outcome. In 1840, the congregation of the Holy Ghost became an African Mission Society, while Archbishop Lavigerie, who was appointed Archbishop of Algiers in 1867, used his position to establish the Missionaries of Our Lady of Africa, known as the "White Fathers" because of their mode of dressing in flowing white Arab robes. Their Catholism was highly clerical and centralized for they readily submitted to the direction of the "office for spreading the faith" in Rome.

The description of the greatest king of Kongo Affonso I (Mvemba Nzinga) who ruled from 1506 to about 1545 was contained in a letter dated May 25th, 1516 from Rui de Anguiar to king Manuel of Portugal. Rui de Aguiar was then the missionary worker in Kongo as Vicar-General during the second decade of the 16th century. He attested to the good quality of the character of the king as a genuine and devout convert to Christianity, who sought to establish Catholism and to carry out a program of westernization in the Kongo. He also said in his letter that only a shrewd and able king could have abandoned the traditional sanctions of divine kingship and introduced new customs to challenge the old without disrupting the kingdom or loosing his throne. This king, Dom Affonso, has nothing else in mind but our Father and His manifestations. He has presently ordered that every man in his entire kingdom pay the tithe, saying that the light must be carried in front and not behind. These were some of the attributes that Rui de Anguiar showered on the king in the letter he wrote to the king of Portugal.

Many other names were recognized and remembered in the early missionary struggles in the continent of Africa and each of them played vital roles in the development of the Christian faith in the minds of the people. They as well contributed immensely in the development of commerce and government through the planting of educational seeds at every level and at different locations in the continent. Through the knowledge now being acquired by the children of Africa in various educational fields including the expansive theological area, the idea of building a virile nation began to rare up its beautiful heads in the minds of the elites and educational folks. The formation of African Christianity groups were now coming into existence and various church leaders and religious sects were beginning to emerge with different visions towards the growth and independence of the African churches.

At the beginning of the 20th century for example, great African prophets such as William Harris who was a Liberian Grebo that worked for the Protestant Episcopal Church as a teacher began to fight the Americo-Liberian rule in his country. He was imprisoned when implicated in a rebellion, which would have invited the British rule into Liberia as a liberator from Americo-Liberia oppression. Harris began his preaching journey from Liberia through the Ivory Coast and on into Gold Coast (now Ghana). He proclaimed that when he was in jail, he received a vision from the Archangel Gabriel that he had been ordained a prophet sent to prepare the way of Jesus Christ. In the vision, he said, he was commanded by the Archangel, to abandon the European clothes he took pride in, and particularly the shoes he had just ordered from America. Through his preaching many Harrian churches were established and became flourishing in Ivory Coast and its neighborhood till today.

The "Ethiopian" churches, which began in the last years of the 19th century, were the first steps into dependency. These churches, which grew up in Nigeria and in South Africa represented a conflict, not over theology, practice of polity, but rather over control of the churches from foreign lands. By the 1890s, the churches in West and South Africa were well into the second generation of Christians. These second generation Christians were fully prepared to step into leadership positions in the churches because they had now acquired enough knowledge and skills to maintain those leadership positions. On the other hand, a new generation of aggressively Westernized missionaries had begun to flood Africa in response to the call of the European colonial powers in the scramble for the continent. These new missionaries were often not impressed by the work that had been done by their predecessors in the last 50 years and they were determined to keep control of African Christianity in the same way the colonial authorities intended to control the continent.

To keep the programs of the colonialists' upright, the African church leaders were being frustrated, down-graded and reduced in ranks to the unbearable levels of authority. These disgraceful actions prompted many to leave their original mission churches to start native or Ethiopian churches patterned after the Western mission churches they had left, but now under the full control of the Africans. Many of the churches liked the style of the Christian nation of Ethiopia, which had never been colonized by any foreign nation. In Nigeria, the collapse of Bishop Ajayi Crowther and the unfavorable treatment meted out to him in the Niger Episcopate by the new crop of foreign missionaries led to unhappiness with the CMS and subsequent founding of various independent churches. In the case of South Africa, establishment of Ethiopian churches was much stronger because of the settler's racism that prevented African Christians from attaining any kind of leadership positions in mission churches. The situation of the two nations mentioned above was much of a case of hopes raised and then thwarted than it was an outright suppression of all hopes for African leadership in the African churches.

African evangelism from the perspective of the contributions of the natives helped to create awareness in the realm of the rural converts especially in those rural areas where more churches and schools were now built and made functioning. In 1920, one Joseph Sadare (Orisadamilare) a goldsmith and Sophia Odunlami a teacher started the Precious Stone Society that was an Anglican prayer group initially. Two years later they were said to have left the CMS church because of some doctrinal issues – the baptism of infants and the use of all forms of medicine, whether Western or traditional. The story further had it that another person David Odubanjo an Ijebu man founded a branch of the Precious Stone Society in Lagos, joining first Faith Tabernacle, which was an American sect that practiced faith healing, then the British Apostolic Church, a Pentecostal Church. It finally became an independent church in 1941, with the name "Christ Apostolic Church". Some of the founding fathers of the church were His Royal Highness Isaac Akinyele, the Olubadan of Ibadan and Apostle Joseph Babalola who was by profession a road-grader driver and who joined Joseph Ositelu in the revival crusade of 1930s that swept the whole of Yorubaland. The contributions of both old and new Christian denominations in Africa played a vital role during and after the struggle for independent African states of today.

Chapter 7

Bishop Crowther as a Slave Boy

Africa has been the mother of mighty sons and great daughters as it has been mentioned in the previous chapters about some of them and how her ancient cities from the North to the South and from the West to the East were the sanctuaries of learning that shown the light of Divine truth in both Christian and Muslim religions using her deep rooted African mythology science to move the wheels of these two religions forward. One of her mighty sons was the subject of this book in the person of Bishop Samuel Ajayi Crowther, who lived in the era of slave trading and introduction of Christianity into the land of Africa. There was a wide historical distance between the days of our primitive fathers and our time of the moment.

African continent has its own rich history that her children can boast of as a lineage, and find no gratification in tracing the branches of their genealogical tree. The art of writing that did not come to them not until the middle part of 19th century or thereafter does not prevent their traditional way of passing down information from generation to generation and by the mark of natural events and seasons. Some people may not be prepared to take evidences through these means very seriously but the family records which traces the descent and parentage of a person in those primitive years should be considered authentic and in fact a believable record of event.

Bishop Samuel Ajayi Crowther by birth was a Yoruba son to the fullest and he came from a great Yoruba kingdom that was ruled by Ajabo, a powerful monarch of his time at the close of the 18th century. In around 1770, this powerful monarch died and was succeeded by a famous king Abiodun Adegorolu, who by the family tree was shown to be the maternal great-great-grandfather of the Bishop. The daughter of king Abiodun named Osu became the mother of Olaminigbin, who in turn became the husband of Omo-oga-Egun and the father of Ibisomi Telerinmasa the mother of the Bishop. This woman possessed a special dignity, which was known among her people as Afala, signifying the princess or priestess of the great god Obatala (the Lord of the white cloth) whose province was to bring order and beauty out of chaos to his people. Obatala's supposed habitation is believed to be a sphere of absolute and dazzling purity.

From his father's family lineage, Bishop Ajayi belonged to the clan of "Edu" and his grandfather was the Baale of Awaiye-petu, who had relocated back into the Yoruba country from the land established by the direct grandson of Oduduwa – Alaketu in Ketu now a famous town in the Republic of Benin. He was known to be a man of great wealth, amassed from the trade of fabric weaving, specially designed for the costume of the king of Erin, and this "aso Elerin" became the recognized production of the family looms. The origin of his birth place, which his ancestors, the ancient princes of Oyo-Ile founded as a colony and was given the name Iba-Agbakin, which can be translated into "to pull through the course of life and keep on peaceful terms with the world, one needs to be very careful". No sooner that the people settled in this colony that rivalries broke out, and in due course another settlement was found and called it Oshogun now an identified town in the present Oshun state in Nigeria.

It was in this town around 1806 that the little boy Samuel was born whose destiny marked a career of conspicuous honor, dignity and usefulness, and of course the most remarkable representative of his race in modern times, the greatest ambassador of his Yoruba country, and one of the strongest pillars of modern African religion, economic and political freedom house. His Yoruba name "Ajayi" is a significant and important name in the culture of his people. The name is usually given to a child that is born with his face to the ground during the old days when natal sciences were not fully developed all over the world. The people of West Africa saw this natal peculiarity as being rare and considered it as a good forecast of remarkable future for such child.

It was the custom of the people of his time, according to Yoruba culture to consult the "Ifa oracle" (the god of divinity) as to the ways and future forecast of the little boy. Furthermore, it was a way to identify the particular tribal god that he would serve and dedicated to when he grows up into manhood among the over four hundred tribal gods in existence in his native culture. When the "Ifa" priest was consulted the way prophets of today are being consulted on matters of individual interests and concerns, the priest declared that on no account was little Ajayi be dedicated to any of the existing idols of the land. The priest told the parents that the little boy was destined to serve the Supreme Being (Olodumare), meaning that he had been chosen to carry the title of "Afa" or "Alufa" – God's priest, who would serve the maker of heaven and the earth, the great God that lives in the sky and who has all things in abundance. His parents were greatly disappointed by this flattering prophecy, because the people of this time in his locality believed that this type of God being referred to by the priest was the God honored by the Mohammedan Foulas who were then bitter enemies of the Yorubas.

The story had it that though the parents were not happy about the result of the "Ifa" oracle but they inwardly resolved to carefully watch and observe the tendencies of the mind and behaviors of their growing little boy, who, all unconscious of his importance in the world, skipped their minds. His father continued his weaving trades that earned him enormous wealth and made him prosper in the community. In those days, people that were regarded as wealthy must own to himself a home, farmland, wives and a lot of children in his courtyard. Ajayi's father was said to have these qualifications and as such he was one of the headmen or councilors in the community. This position plus his weaving industry preoccupied him much in the city and he therefore decided to handover his farmland to his eldest son – Bola. As Ajayi was growing, he would be asked by his father to go to the farmland in company of his senior brother Bola to learn how to farm and till the land. Along with the farming trade, Ajayi was a lover of poultry breeding that also earned him his own financial independence as from the age of eight. After a period of training time under his brother Bola, Ajayi had now become skilled in the tendering of various farm products such as yams, vegetables and other arable products.

In the Yoruba culture, the people believes in hard working in whatever trade that one chooses to practice and this is why it is too difficult for one to be found idle even up till today. The culture provides a proverb or saying that it is imperative for everyone to wake up early in the morning and set at his/her chosen trade or business. On account of this, the youthful Ajayi would trudge seven miles to his farm work cheering himself with one of the proverbs of his culture, inculcating habits of industry that says – "when the day dawns, every trader goes to their respective trades; the spinner would take his spindle, the warrior his shield, the weaver stoops to his shuttle, the farmer arises to his machete and hoe, the hunter takes his bow and arrow and the fishermen gets into his canoe with his fishing net or hook and set for the waters."

The farming industry of those days was so tedious because farming instruments were made locally by the blacksmiths and the levels to which their technological knowledge could carry them was then limited to the production of hoes and machete and nothing more. To cultivate a sizeable farmland, the boys and the youths of each community would organize themselves into little clubs called "Aro"- communal helping group to help each other in their farm works on rotational basis. Of such a club, Ajayi was made a captain of his club of forty youth members who doubtlessly recognized in the boy with the auspicious name that was going to make an indelible mark in the world.

Ajayi was known to be courageous and someone who had exceeding respect and honor to the religion of his parents as from his early days. This character trait in him was demonstrated at an occasion when his father's house caught fire and the man (his father) was helpless but only to call out his family out of the perilous incident crying out in pains about the danger that would afflict his gods that were in the burning house. Out of share courage, Ajayi promptly ran through the flaming doorway and brought out all the idols back to safety, amid the cheers of the neighbors, who remarked that, "This child will be a great worshipper of the gods and that one day he will restore the gods of our nation." No sooner after this inferno that the house was restored and the gods were taken back to their respective original places of honor in the family house.

The great boy was around thirteen years of age at this time and he was busy with his farm works and his poultry business. No one could imagine or forecast his future, and he himself never dreamt of any dream that one day, he would be seen as an imitation of Joseph in the Old Testament that would become a spiritual leader in a great kingdom that Egypt ever knew. Along the path of his growth, people were intelligently observing his footsteps and his scrupulous passion and observance of religious rites that enhanced his reputation as one being blessed immensely by the gods. In the light of this observation and his noble life, beneath the thatched roof building constructed with bamboo sticks and palm fronds in Oshogun town, a new era for the African race was being born.

The beautiful adolescent age of this young man, which was bubbling up amid the simple native surroundings of Oshogun, was on the eve of a new impulse, a catastrophe which, like a fallen rock from its base, should obliterate its peaceful meanderings and force it into new and tumultuous courses. People are born differently with different paths in life. Like the story of Joseph that was sold into slavery by his own blood brothers was the case of Samuel Ajayi Crowther who his beloved peers sent into captivity through slave trading and economic interest. It was given to everyone in this type of situation and at that their age to suffer in their springtide, and to drink from the cup of sorrow in the darkness, which seemed to eclipse all their radiant morning. But both lived to see the silver lining of the cloud, and to find, as we all to remember, that God's ways are always the best, and not let so because in the time of trial our eyes are holden, our body will be weak and our hearts are troubled. In the breaking of the day, as in the breaking of colanut in Yoruba culture, we cry, and it is the Lord who hears our supplications.

Years later, when the storm calmed down and the fresh winds from the ocean began blowing its beautiful sounds of trumpet and God sitting in His majestical throne smiled back from the retreating cloud, Ajayi sat down in the college room and wrote a short, but memorable story of his experience which changed his life and a precious scrap of his autobiography. The story recalled many sweet and bitter seasons of personal inter-course, when in a room at the upper level at Salisbury Square in London the venerable Bishop recounted those early days of grief to his person and the dignity of human race. Truly, he was angered, bitter and his mind was filled with emotions, his eyes were suffused with tears but the recital of the incidents that happened in his life history was broken by fervent mind of thanksgivings to God. And from his own words and writings, Bishop Ajayi Crowther now narrated the detailed second chapter of his journey in this planet Earth where things chaotically move around its axis in an unstable manner; and when everything that surrounded him appeared not to be working perfectly to his command and as if a big pit was dug around him at the center of the universe. Read the passage with little or no emotion but with pains and agony in your hearts for the type of treatment meted out to human beings of Ajayi's generation particularly in Africa because you never can tell when and where the winds will blow from towards your direction in this world.

I suppose some time about the commencement of the year 1821 I was in my native country, enjoying the comforts of father and mother and the affectionate love of brothers and sisters. From this period I must date the unhappy, but which I am now taught in other respects to call blessed day, which I shall never forget in my life. I call it unhappy day because it was the day on which I was violently turned out of my father's house and separated from my relations, and in which I was made to experience what is called "to be in slavery." With regard to its being called blessed – it being the day which Providence had marked out for me to set out on my journey from the land of heathenism, and vice to a place where his Gospel is preached.

For some years war had been carried on in my Oyo country, which was always attended with much devastation and bloodshed, the women, such men as had surrendered or were caught, with the children, were taken captive. The enemies who carried on these wars were principally the Oyo Mohammedans, with whom my country abounds, who with the Foulas and such foreign slaves as had escaped from their owners, joined together, made a formidable force of about twenty thousand; which annoyed the whole country. They had no other employment but selling slaves to the Spaniards and Portuguese on the coast.

The morning on which my town Oshogun shared the same fate, which many others had experienced was fair and delightful, and most of the inhabitants were engaged in their respective occupations. We were preparing breakfast without any apprehension, when about 9 a.m. a rumour was spread in the town that the enemies had approached with intentions of hostility. It was not long after, when they had almost surrounded the town to prevent any escape of the inhabitants. The town was rudely fortified by a wooden fence about four miles in circumference, containing about twelve thousand inhabitants and producing three thousand fighting men.

The inhabitants not being duly prepared, some not being at home, but those who were having about six gates to defend, as well as many weak places about the fence to guard against - and to say, in a few words, the men being surprised and therefore confounded – the enemies entered the town, after about three or four hours resistance. Here the most sorrowful scene imaginable was to be witnessed – women, some with three, four, and six children clinging to their arms, with the infants on their backs, running as fast as they could through prickly shrubs, which, hooking their blies (baskets) and loads, threw them down from the heads of the bearers. When they found it impossible to go with their loads they only endeavored to save themselves and their children. Even this was impracticable with those who had many children to care for, as while they were endeavoring to disentangle themselves from the ropy shrubs they were overtaken and caught by the enemies, by a rope noose thrown over the neck of every individual, to be led in the manner of goats tied together, under the drove of one man. In many cases a family was violently divided between three or four enemies, who each led his away to see each other no more.

I was thus caught with my mother, two sisters, one infant about ten weeks old, and a cousin, while endeavoring to escape in the manner described. My load consisted of nothing else than my bow and five arrows in the quiver; the bow I had lost in the shrub while I was extricating myself, before I could think of making any use of it against my enemies. The last time I saw my father was when he came from the fight to give us the signal to flee; he entered into our house, which was burnt some time back for some offence given by my father's adopted son – hence I never saw him more. Here I must take thy leave, unhappy, comfortless father! I learned sometime afterwards that he was killed in another battle.

Our conquerors were Eyo Mohammedans, who led us away through the town. On our way we met a man sadly wounded in the head, struggling between life and death. Before we got half-way through the town some Foulas among the enemies themselves hastly separated my cousin from our number. Here also I must take my leave, my fellow-captive cousin! His mother was living in another village. The houses in the town on fire were built with wood, about twelve feet from the ground, with high roofs in square forms of different dimensions and spacious areas. Several of these belonged to one man, adjoining to with passages communicating with each other. The flames were very high; we were led by my grandfather's house, already desolate, and in a few minutes afterwards we left the town to the mercy of the flames, never to enter or see it any more. Farewell, the place of my birth, the playground of my childhood, and the place, which I thought would be the repository of my mortal body in its old age!

We were now out of Oshogun, going into a town called Heh'I, the rendezvous of the enemies, about twenty miles from our town. On the way we saw our grandmother at a distance, with about three or four of my other cousins taken with her, for a few minutes; she was missed through the crowd to see her no more. Several other captives were held in the same manner as we were- grandmothers, mothers, children and cousins were all taken captives. O sorrowful prospect! The aged women were greatly to be pitied, not being able to walk so fast as their children and grandchildren; they were often threatened with being put to death upon the spot, to get rid of them, if they would not go as fast as others, and they were often as wicked in their practice as in their words. O pitiful sight! Whose heart would not bleed to have seen this? Yes, such is the state of barbarity in the heathen land!

Evening came on, and coming to a spring of water we drank a great quantity, which served us for breakfast, with a little parched corn and dried meat, previously prepared by our victors for themselves. During our march to Iseh'i (Iseyin) we passed several towns and villages, which had been reduced to ashes. It was almost midnight before we reached the town, where we passed our doleful first night in bondage. It was not, perhaps, a mile from the wall of Iseyin where an old woman of about sixty was threatened in the manner above described. What became of her I could not learn.

The next morning, our cords being taken off our necks, we were brought to the chief of our captors - for there were many other chiefs – as trophies at his feet. In a little while a separation took place, when my sister and I fell to the share of the chief, and my mother and the infant to the victors. We dared not vent our grief in loud cries, but by very heavy sobs. My mother, with the infant, was led away, comforted with the promise that she should see us again when we should leave Iseyin for Dahdah, the town of the chief. In a few hours after, it was soon agreed upon that I should be battered for a horse in Iseyin that day. Thus was I separated from my mother and sister for the first time in my life, and the later not to be seen more in this world. Thus in the space of twenty-four hours, being deprived of liberty and all other comforts, I was made the property of different persons. About the space of two months, when the chief was to leave Iseyin for his own town, the horse which was then only taken on trial, not being approved of, I was restored to the chief, who took me to Dahdah, where I had the happiness of meeting my mother and the infant sister again, with joy which could be described by nothing else but tears of love and affection, and on the part of my infant sister with leaps of joy.

Here I lived for three months, going for grass for the horses with my fellow-captives. I now and then visited my mother and sister in our captor's house without any fears or thoughts of being separated any more. My mother told me she had heard of my sister, but I never saw her any more. At last, one unhappy evening arrived when I was sent with a man to get some money at a neighboring house. I went but with some fears for which I could not account, and to my great astonishment in a few minutes I was added to the number of many other captives, fettered, to be led to the market town early next morning. My sleep went from me. I spent almost the whole night in thinking of my doleful situation with tears and sobs, especially as my mother was in the same town, whom I had not visited for about a day or two back. There was another boy in the same situation with me; his mother was in Dahdah. Being sleepless, I heard the first cockcrow, and scarcely was the signal given when the traders arose, loaded the men slaves with baggage, and with one hand chained to the neck we left the town. My little companion in affliction cried and begged much to be permitted to see his mother, but was soon silenced by punishment. Seeing this, I dared not speak, although I thought we passed by the very house my mother was in. Thus I was separated from my mother and sister, my then only comforts, to meet no more in this world of misery. A few days travel we came to the market town of Ijahi (Ijaiye). Here I saw many who had escaped from our town to this place, or who were in search of their relations, to set at liberty as many as they had the means of redeeming. Here we were under very close inspection, as there were many persons in search of their relations, and through that many had escaped from their owners. In a few days I was sold to a Mohammedan woman, with whom I traveled many towns on our way to the Poh-Poh (Popo) country on the coast, much resorted to by the Portuguese to buy slaves. When we left Ijaiye, after many halts, we came to a town called Toko. From Ijaiye to Toko all spoke Ebwe dialect, but my mistress Eyo, my own dialect. Here I was a perfect stranger, having left the Eyo country far behind.

I lived on Toko about three months, walked about and with my owner's son with some degree of freedom, it being a place where my feet had never trod; and could I possibly make my way out through many a ruinous towns and villages we had passed I should have soon become a prey to some others, who would gladly have taken advantage of me. Besides, I could not think of going a mile out of the town alone at night, as there were many enormous devil houses along the highway, and a woman having been lately publicly executed – fired at – being accused of bewitching her husband, who had died a long, tedious sickness. Five of six heads of persons who had been executed for some crime or other were never wanting to be nailed on the large trees in the market places to terrify others. Now and then my mistress would speak with me, and her son, that we should by and by go to the Poh-Poh country, where we should buy tobacco and other fine things to sell at our return. Now thought I, this was the signal of my being sold to the Portuguese, who, they often told me during our journey, were to be seen in that country. Being very thoughtful of this, my appetite forsook me, and in a few weeks I got dysentery, which preyed on me. I determined with myself that I would not go to Poh-poh country, but would make an end of myself one way or other. Several nights I attempted to strangle myself with my band, but had not courage enough to close the noose tight, so as to effect my purpose. May the Lord forgive me this sin! I next determined that I would leap out of the canoe into the river when we should cross it on our way to that country. Thus was I thinking when my owner, perceiving the great alteration, which had taken place in me, sold me to some persons. Thus the Lord, while I knew Him not, led me not into temptation and delivered me from the evil. After my price had been counted before my eyes, I was delivered up to my new owners with great grief and dejection of spirit, not knowing where I was now to be led.

About the first cockcrowing, which was the usual time to set out with slaves to prevent their being much acquainted with the way, for fear an escape should be made, we set out for Elabbo, the third dialect from mine. After having arrived at Ik-ke-ku yere, another town, we halted. In this place I renewed my attempt at strangling several times at night, but could not effect my purpose. It was very singular that no thought of making use of a knife ever entered my mind. However, it was not long before I was battered for tobacco, rum, and other articles. I remained here in fetters alone for sometime before my owner could get as many slaves as he wanted. He feigned to treat us more civilly by allowing us to sip a few drops of white man's liquor, rum, which was so estimable an article that none but chiefs could pay for a jar or glass vessel of four or five gallons. So remarkable it was that no one should take breath before he swallowed every sip for fear of having the string of his throat cut by the spirit of the liquor: this made it so much more valuable.

I had to remain alone again in another town in Jabbo, the name of which I do not now remember, for about two months. From hence I was bought, after a two days' walk, to a slave market called Ikosy (Ikosi) on the coast, on the bank of a large river, which very probably was the Lagos on which we were afterwards captured. The sight of the river terrified me exceedingly, for I had never seen anything like it in my life. The people on the opposite bank are called Eko. Before sunset, being bartered again for tobacco, I became another man's. Nothing now terrified me more than the river and the thought of going into another world. Cry now was nothing to vent my sorrow. My whole body became stiff. I was now made to enter the river to ford it in the canoe. Being fearful of my entering this extensive water, and being so cautious in every step I took, as if the next would bring me to the bottom, my motion was very awkward indeed. Night coming on, and the men having very little time to spare, soon carried me into the canoe and placed me among the cornbags, supplying me with an Abalah (a cake of Indian corn) for my dinner. Almost in the same position I was placed I remained with the Abalah in my hand, quite confused in my thoughts, waiting only every moment our arrival at the new world, which we did not reach till about four in the morning. Here I got once more into another district, the fourth from mine, if I may not call it altogether another language, on account of now and then, in some words, there being a faint shadow of my own.

Here I must remark that during the whole night's voyage in the canoe not a single thought of leaping into the river entered my mind, but, on the contrary, the face of the river occupied my thoughts. Having now entered Eko I was permitted to go any way I pleased, there being no way to escape on account of river.

In this place I met my two nephews, belonging to different masters. One part of the town was occupied by the Portuguese or Spaniards, who had come to buy slaves. Although I was in Eko more than three months I never once saw a white man until one evening when they took a walk in company with about six and came to the street of the house in which I was living. Even then I had not the boldness to appear distinctly to look at them, being always suspicious that they had come for me, and my suspicion was not a fancied one, for in a few days after I was made the eighth in number of the slaves of the Portuguese. Being a veteran in slavery – if I may be allowed the expression – and having no more hope of ever going to my country again, I patiently took whatever came, although it was not without a great fear and trembling that I received for the first time the touch of a white man, who examined me whether I was sound or not. Men and boys were at first chained together with a chain of about six fathoms in length, thrust through an iron fetter on the neck of each individual and fastened at both ends with padlocks. In this situation the boys suffered the most. The men, sometimes getting angry, would draw the chain most violently, as seldom went bruises on our poor little necks, especially the time of sleep, when they drew the chain so close to ease themselves of its weight, in order to be able to lie more conveniently, that we were almost suffocated or bruised to death, in a room with one door which was fastened as soon as we entered, with no other passage for communicating the air than the openings under the eaves drop. And very often at night, when two or three individuals quarreled or fought, the whole drove suffered punishment without distinction. At last we boys had the happiness to be separated from the men, when their number was increased and no more chain to spare, we were corded together by ourselves. Thus we were going in and out, bathing together and so on. The females fared not much better. Thus we were for nearly four months.

About this time intelligence was given that the English were cruising on the coast. This was another subject of sorrow to us – that there must be wars on the sea as well as on the land – a thing never heard of before nor imagined practicable. This delayed our embarkation. In the meantime the other troop, which was collected in Poh-poh and was intended to be conveyed into the vessel the nearest was from that place, was brought into Eko (Lagos) among us. Among the number was Joseph Bartholomew, my brother in the service of the Church Missionary Society. After a few weeks delay we were embarked at night in canoes from Eko to the beach, and on the following morning we embarked on the vessel (a Portuguese ship called the *Esperanza Felix),* which immediately sailed away. The crew being busy in embarking us, one hundred and eighty-seven in number, had no time to give us either breakfast or supper, and we, being unaccustomed to the motion of the vessel, suffered the whole of the day with sea-sickness, which rendered the greater part of us less fit to take any food whatever.

On the very same evening we were surprised by two English men-of-war, and the next morning found ourselves in the hands of war conquerors, whom we at first very much dreaded, they being armed with long swords. In the morning, being called up from the hold, we were astonished to find ourselves among two very large men-of-war and several brigs. The men-of-war were His Majesty's ships *Myrmidon,* Captain H.G. Leek, and *Iphigenia,* Captain Sir Robert Mends, who captured us on 7 April, 1822, on the river Lagos. Our owner was bound, with his sailors, except the cook, who was preparing our breakfast. Hunger rendered us bold, and not being threatened at first attempts to get some fruit from the stern, we in a short time took the liberty of ranging about the vessel in search of plunder of every kind. Now we began to entertain a poor opinion of our new conquerors. Very soon after breakfast we were divided into several of the vessels around us. This was cause of new fears, not knowing where our misery would end. Being now, as it were, one family, we began to take leave of those who were first transported into the other vessels, not knowing what would become of them and ourselves. About this time we six intimate friends in affliction – among whom was my brother Joseph Bartholomew – kept very close together that we might be carried away at the same time.

It was not long before we six were conveyed into the *Myrmidon,* in which we discovered no trace of those who were transported before us. We soon concluded what had become of them when we saw part of a hog hanging, the skin of which was white – a thing we never saw before, as a hug was always roasted on fire to clear it of the hair in my country – and a number of common shots ranged along the deck. The former we supposed to be the flesh and the latter the heads of the individuals who had been killed for meat. But we were soon undeceived be a close examination of the flesh, with cloven feet, which resembled those of a hog, and by a cautious approach to the shots that they were iron. In a few days we were quite at home on the man-of-war; being only six in number, we were soon selected by the sailors for their boys, and were soon furnished with dress. Our Portuguese owner and his son were brought over in the same vessel, bound in fetters, and I, thinking I should no more get into his hands, had the boldness to strike him on the head while he was standing by his son – an act, however, very wicked and unkind in its nature.

When one receives the favor of God, people around him or her would always come to his aid in whatever program or course he or she chooses to establish, so that the glory of almighty God would be made manifest to the understanding of everyone. Nature turned Ajayi into a marketing commodity that was being transferred from one merchant to the other until the day he met the Supreme Being he was to serve for the rest of his days. The great ordeal he went through as a youth was contained in the little note that he himself narrated in his own words above. He was humanly destined to either die on the voyage or survived it and reached the Americas like many of his own brothers and sisters that were captured and transported before him through the same route. But as fate would have it for him, he noted that at length, after two months and a half on board while the man-of war continued to cruise for slaves to be liberated they finally reached Sierra Leone on 17 June 1822, when he again set his foot back on African soil, this time as a free man and no longer as a slave. Indeed during his two and half stay on the sea with the sailors working in the Majesty's ship that now became his safe-heaven, it was said that Ajayi became a great favorite with the sailors as a lad of exceptional quickness and intelligence.

On his arrival at Sierra Leone, he was immediately sent to a missionary Schoolmaster at Bathurst, a town very close in distance from Freetown in the loving care of Mr. Davey and his wife. Remember that the best of Joseph in the land of Egypt did not come to open not until when he finally made his journey to the palace of king Pharao. So also the best of

Ajayi did not open as the flower of the sun not until when he reached the caring home of the Daveys. The new environment became very interesting to him as he now began his lessons in English alphabet with the help of another native boy who had been there before him. The story was told that after his first day's schooling Ajayi was so much exited and delighted with his new taste of knowledge that after the lesson, he ran down into the town to beg for half penny from one of the natives to buy to himself an alphabet card.

The type of passion and enthusiasm that Bishop Ajayi had for his new knowledge is always very similar to people of his age anytime such opportunities come their ways. They always grab it with all seriousness and alertness. I could remember what happened to people of his age as lately as in the 1940s when Western education was introduced into the villages and towns in my local area in the countryside of Yoruba nation. We were small kids with the golden opportunity to attend schools at our own tender ages which was then available to us. At this time, it became a matter of struggle between those of us who were in the ages of between six and ten years and those who were two or three times older than us in age. I had in my class as classmates some of my big uncles and ants of matured minds with serious passion for education. One of my classmates and a distant uncle in 1946 who later became a lawyer in the end was already married to a woman in the village and had a child of about one year old by the time he joined us in infant two class. Education during its formative years in the continent of Africa was one of the greatest opportunities to be bestowed on those that had the privilege and chance to grab it not minding the age, status or religious beliefs.

Bishop Samuel Ajayi Crowther could not forget those good and bad old days as it was told by those who were close to him that the memories of those days and moments kept flowing in him as a river would continue to flow through its natural course un-ceaselessly during its season and period recalling those scenes through a long vista of years. The opportunity afforded him here was not limited to learning alone but was as well extended to a skill that would add some taste to the meal now being prepared for him by the host of heavens and the new strong feathers for him to fly like an eagle in the skies of the universe. He was now introduced to another skill entirely under the pupilage of another Schoolmaster, Mr. Weeks who imparted in him the knowledge of carpentry, and from his wife more otepa in the knowledge of reading. Destiny is an unrevealed package to its owner as an unfinished contract that could contain a lot of miserable addendum.

In his apprenticeship under Mr. Weeks, the master did not know or could imagine that one day his pupil would wear the lawn as the Bishop of Niger and in turn, would direct the See of Sierra Leone where he served him as a pupil apprentice.

On 11 December 1825 Ajayi was baptized during which time he received his new name **_Samuel Ajayi Crowther_**, a name after a Venerable clergyman, the Rev. Samuel Crowther, Vicar of Christ Church Newgate street, London and who was one of the first committee members of the Church Missionary Society. To close this unique chapter in the life of the Bishop and with the brief historical retrospect, we cannot but appreciate his character and career, not only as a rescued slave, but for the reason that the moment he landed his feet back on the soil of his continent from the ship of man-of-war, one of the noblest battlegrounds of missionary conquest began to emerge. From all the precious annals of missionary enterprise in Africa, rich as they are in brave deeds, there is not more magnificent than the costly valor, which fought a good and wining fight for God and man on the sandy shores of Sierra Leone.

In Africa, the story of Christianity is inseparably linked with the emancipation of the slaves as the water and alcoholic substance are closely linked together. This degrading value of human being and quality of nature could only be seen and remembered as one of the penalties of our privileged age from the Supreme Being above in the sky. It can only be temporarily forgotten but always permanently remembered from generation to generation by the off-shoots of those victims that were directly and seriously connected to the inhuman actions of the economic masters of the time. How difficult it is for the peers of the victims of this deadly atrocity whose minds are filled with sorrows to forget what had been done to their national interests and capabilities to develop themselves without any hindrances from the policy makers from foreign lands.

But lovers of justice and nature owe their profound gratitude to those that began the battle of freedom for the slaves. The battle began when Granville Sharp was kind enough to give shelter in 1765 to a slave from Barbados because of his suffering conditions, and the wrong action brought against this kind man, won the famous dictum of Lord Mansfield that: "as soon as a Negro set his foot on English soil he was free". This action was followed by the advocacy of equal rights of man by Thomas Clarkson who was a philanthropist of purest type and William Wilberforce who with persuasive eloquence lit up the flashes of kindly wit that took the lead.

In the dangerous struggle of this issue which raged on with lots of enemies from the beneficiaries of the trade were loyal friends such as John Wesley and George Whitefield, the two great evangelists of their age, both who denounced the traffic in burning words.

It was on record in the books of history that the last letter ever penned by Wesley on his dying bed, four days before he died at the house near the Chapel in City Road, London, was addressed to Wilberforce, urging him to persevere in his "glorious enterprise". He urged him to "Go on in the name of God and in the power of His might till even American slavery (the vilest that ever saw the sun) shall vanish away before it". In the passage of time of the struggle, the Society of Friends, lifting through the darkness hours of history and an unquenched lamp, presented the first petition to the House of Commons asking that something should be done to ameliorate the shocking conditions of slaves. By parliamentary speeches, dropping of leaflets, and various addresses throughout the country, the horrors of the trade, with its wholesale waste of human life, were made known to the people at the grass root level. It was now difficult for any righteous thinking or barely honest man to oppose this merciful plea.

John Wesley

But the representatives of this carnivorous business were not without protests against the move of the right thinking people. They raised the commercial difficulty that there would occur a big downfall of Liverpool trade, that the public revenue would suffer beyond repairs, and dexterously standing on another foot asserting that the slave was happy in his lot quoting the sacred antiquity of the traffic from the Book they did not believe in. At last, on 25 March 1807, the Bill for the Abolition of the

British Slave Trade became law. The lessons gained from the history of all great struggles for the moral emancipation of men and women sufficiently thought everyone that any conflict with evil, means storming the rampart of self-interest accompanied with bloodshed, heartbreak, sorrows and tears. The first huddle was cleared but subsequent ones began to set in place through the activities of slave trade abolition opponents.

Chapter 8

Bishop Crowther as a Foundation Student of Fourah Bay College in Sierra Leone.

The acclamation of victory over the abolition of the British Slave Trade that became law on the 25th March 1807 was with a lot of obstructions from the enemies of the Bill. Its opponents endeavored to barricade all routes that lead to the streets of freedom for the slaves through the provisions of the statute. Initially the penalties for the trafficking were simply pecuniary and to the astonishment of the fighters of this deadly trade, person like Wilberforce and his friends in the struggle were made to know that the traders were ready

Old Fourah Bay College in Sierra Leone

to pay handsomely to square the penalties, and because of this the battle rebounded back again and this time with much vigor and zeal.

Lord Broughham then presented another Act in the House of Commons making the offence a felony, which must be punished with imprisonment with hard labor, but the final and last nail, was hammered down on the head of the Trade when the Act of 1824 was passed. This Act declared the Trade to be piracy and anyone caught in the act must receive a death penalty and not until this time that the law was respected.

The slave trade was now condemned, but the practice and system of slavery had yet to receive its legal deathblow. Wilberforce was now getting old in age and becoming weary in actions of the struggle. He therefore passed on the mantle of leadership and the sword to the younger hands of Mr. (later Sir) Thomas Fowell Buxton. Buxton was said to be an energetic, devoted and an upright leader whose leadership was well acclaimed throughout the land. People commented on the decision of Wilberforce to hand over this glorious endeavor to him as a wise decision. The new leader on assuming office declared a straight war by moving the historic resolution, "That the state of slavery is repugnant to the principles of the British Constitution and of the Christian religion, and that it ought to be gradually abolished throughout the British Colonies with as much expedition as may be found consistent with a due regard to the well-being of the parties concerned".

The firebrand speeches of Buxton on the struggle glistered the eyes of his former boss Wilberforce, as he was delighted and pleased with his choice. At a certain point, Buxton declared that, "the object at which we aim is the extinction of slavery – nothing less than the extinction of slavery – in nothing less than the whole of the British Dominions". At another time, Buxton declared while replying to some taunts of enthusiasm that, "there are such enthusiasts. I am one of them, and while we breathe we will never abandon the cause till that thing, that chattel, is reinstated in all the privileges of man". During this second season of struggle in the emancipation of the black slaves, the Anti – Slavery Society was established and the term "Abolitionist" was at once an honor and also a reproach.

After long years of struggle and conflicts, the victory was won and on the 7th August 1833, the Bill was passed; on 1st August 1834, every slave was free, and four years later the apprenticeships ceased throughout the Colonies while slavery roots and branches were uprooted and being cast into the burning furnace. People were overwhelmed by this glorious government decision and the event was seen as a replica of the English Magna Charta, which may be called the Magna Charta of the black man's freedom.

The freedom given to the blacks who, were now living in the English territory posed a bigger question as to what had to be done with the blacks now roaming the streets of London begging for foods and money because of lack of employment. As a result of this ugly situation, a plan was put in place to make a settlement near Sierra Leone on the grain-coast of Africa where the blacks and people of color can be shipped as freemen under the Direction of the Committee for Relieving the Black Poor and under the Protection of the British Government.

This arrangement received the blessings of the British Government while a little fleet of liberated Negroes, with some European women (who might have been spared too) sailed for the West Coast of Africa in April 1787 under the convoy of a man-of-war, whose commander, and on arriving acquired a strip of the Coast in the name of King George. Sierra Leone itself acquired its name from the contour of its natural mountains and, which was identified as the spot where the slave-trading vessels of Hawkins in the days of Elizabeth used to load their human cargoes. As time went by, the settlement was becoming very popular as other slaves from Nova Scotia, those that fought on the side of the British soldiers during the War of Independence in the USA began to join the first set of settlers there. The population of the settlement was now swelling and diseases, disorder, mutinies, and aggressions of the natives soon brought the place to early ruin. It was no longer an easy task to live in affluence in those days especially after the slave trading, which was the major source of economic power to those Africans and their foreign accomplices was abolished internationally.

Other carnivorous tactics were employed to destroy the settlement. At a point, the French masked by English uniforms and flying the Union Jack, invaded the town, laying all waste and carrying away the trading vessels of the Sierra Leone Company from the harbors as spoils of the war. But for the wise administrative skills, discipline and zeal of the then Governor of the Colony in person of Zachary Macaulay, father of the great historian and the founding fathers of modern politics in Nigeria, Albert Macaulay, order and prosperity were afterwards re-established. Sierra Leone became a Crown Colony, and from that moment the man-of-war started cruising in African waters to bring their captures of slaves into the Colony.

Under the direction of the newly formed African Association, which composed of Bishops and philanthropists, schools were beginning to spring up and the arrival of the missionaries here complemented the efforts of the Association. It was sad news to note that the first team of the missionaries to arrive here to bless the African land and her people were almost extinguished by the terrible attack of malaria fever. They came to this place with their hearts beating high with the faith and hope that one day, the fruits of their labor would be ripe enough for eating for them and their converts; but they could not spear themselves when the deadly attack began to consume their powers; they cried with tears of love as they lay helplessly when they were attacked; and when the host of heavens drew the curtain, in some cases on the land and often on the sea, the onlookers that were equally helpless whispered to themselves that "To die in this manner is certainly a gain indeed". The missionaries remained undaunted because of the strong faith they had in them. As others were fallen, so others were rushed to fill the breach.

It was on record that out of five missionaries that left Salisbury Square on the mission, four died in six months and two years later, out of seven, six died in four months. In the first twenty years of the missionary works in the West Coast of Africa, fifty-three of them with their wives had already died at their post. The climate was only one of the hindrances to the planting of Christianity seed in this part of the continent at this time. Others were the non-cooperative attitudes of the local chiefs, tribesmen and their leaders and the Mohammedans who were up in arms to make the soil very hard ground for growing the seed. The belief of the early missionaries was rested on the future younger generation of the natives whom they fervently prayed to God to raise up to become faithful disciples of the Great Master so that some of them may be raised up as instruments to proclaim the good tidings of salvation throughout the native land.

Their prayers were heard when the time came for God to diffuse the Gospel widely through the people and the nation. The great revival that spread across the Colony came when Rev. William A.B. Johnson, who was full of deepest interest, and whose conversion took place when he was a poor workman at a London sugar refinery was himself now a missionary worker in Sierra Leone. Rev. W.A.B. Johnson was astonished when one day in the Colony; the greatest revival broke itself up through the blessings of the Lord that had at last fallen upon His people. In one of his entries in his diary, he remarked that he entered the church and the: "**vestry, the gallery stairs, the tower, the windows were all full; some of the seats in the passages were over-weighted and broken down. When I entered**

the church and saw the multitudes I could hardly refrain myself. After evening service one of the boys wished to know if it were really true Jesus prayed for them. Many had been in the field to pray and did not know how. I spoke to them, and they went back with joy. It was a moonlight night, and the mountains re-echoed with the singing of hymns, the girls in one part praying and singing by turns. The boys had got upon a huge rock with a light. One gave out a hymn, and when it was finished another engaged in prayer.

From whence, the revival began. The breakdown of the health of his wife coupled with his own increasing weakness compelled him to travel back to England. On his departure the people crowded the shore to bid him farewell as they cried and wailed. He was so much loved by the people that if not because of the waters of the sea that could not permit them to go with him, they could all have joined him on his trip back to England. On his return from this journey, he broke the news of his wife's demise to the people and they all together mourned the passage of the kind woman.

Two years later, in total broken health, he again set sail homewards, but this time a voyage of no return that took him to the everlasting shore. One of the members of the crowd that assembled to see this devoted missionary embark for his last journey from the land was a black youth of about fifteen years of age with his school books and a Bible in his hand and to whom the Reverend gentleman bided good bye turning to him and said, "Crowther God bless you, my boy. Good bye." The sad news that came later was about the death of their hero in England. They all wept sobbingly and cried out their eyes but with the consolation that God took him away because they were looking more unto Johnson than they did looked unto the Lord Jesus and henceforth, they should concentrate to look more to the Lord for He alone can save them and that He alone is the light of the world. These words were part of the eulogy delivered by one of the converts when the news was broken to them. Bishop Crowther continued his studies with interest, passion and with the support given to him by his guardian and mentors especially Mr. and Mrs. Davey.

In 1826, the first signal of his journey to the top came to open when Mr. & Mrs. Davey told him that he was to join them on a short trip to England, their home country. One could imagine the type of excitement and joy that would fill the mind of this young lad traveling out of his home base to visit Whiteman's land not as a slave this time but as a guest. By this time Bishop Crowther had learnt much about English history and its people and his visit was to complement what he had learnt and heard about this country. In his diaries, he recorded these fascinating impressions of his visit to England for the first time: **I had the privilege of visiting your happy and favored land in the year 1826, in which it was my desire to remain for a good while to be qualified for a teacher to my fellow creatures".** It was also recorded that during his stay of about eight months he attended the Parochial School in Liverpool Road Islington and probably stayed at the house of the Rev. E. Bickersteth; and during his stay he was taken to the country home of the clergyman where he freely mingled with other boys and girls as part of them. It was really an exciting and interesting trip to him.

On his return to Sierra Leone, he was appointed as a pupil teacher (Schoolmaster) by the Colonial Government on a salary of One pound a month, which is an equivalent of N240 (Naira) in today's Nigeria currency in a village in the Colony. As an obedient person, he was full of thanksgiving to his masters for given him such opportunity to be part of the development of his people's minds. He specifically made a note of this opportunity in his diaries but also in the demand to meet any of his native people from Oshogun. He usually lamented down deep into his inner mind that he had not cast his eyes on his beloved father, mother, or any of his relations since he left his home town Oshogun, and this taught always wear him down and bordered him greatly.

When the doors of an opportunity to send a native to England for training opened, it did not cost Mr. Davey any moment to recommend Crowther for this noble course. In his memo of recommendation of December 25 1827, he wrote: **The only lad I could at present recommend as fit to be sent to England is Samuel Crowther. He would, I have reason to believe, prove a very useful instrument for carrying on the work in Western Africa. He has abilities far surpassing any I have met with before, and added to this he appears to be truly pious. Our only fear respecting him might be that he should be lifted up too much by a second voyage to England. He has improved very much under the assiduous care of Brother Haensel, and gave great satisfaction in the examination the other day.**

This letter opened many opportunity doors for Samuel Crowther especially the one to the African Institution later known as Fourah Bay College at Sierra Leone. The history of this Institution marked a turning point in the life of both the missionary works and the natives of Africa in acquiring knowledge and skills, which were used to open up the lines of development in the continent. Fourah Bay College was established as a result of that appalling death rate that had hitherto decimated the ranks of the first sets of European missionaries that were sent to the West Coast of Africa. In far-away England, the committee of the CMS decided that if Africa was to be evangelized it must be through the natives because her own sons must have had sufficient immunity to the terrible climate and diseases of the time. It therefore became imperative to begin to train the natives to become intellectually and spiritually sound for the high vocation. In any democratic process the world over, a decision of this strength and magnitude may not go down well without opposition. Some people in the committee almost distrusted the capacity and capability of an African to discharge the functions of a responsible ministry.

In anyway the CMS finally agreed to send the Rev. Charles Haensel to start this important Institution. Rev. Haensel was a young Lutheran missionary, a German by birth from the Basle Seminary and a man of sound mind and intellect. The building chosen for the beginning of this noble Institution was a disused slave house with an extensive grounds overlooking Fourah Bay. The building was of European taste because it was well far away from the natives and the surrounding villages to ensure the privacy and quiet of the students. Interestingly, this building was really an ordinary dwelling house but adopted to serve as all-in-one for this purpose. The young students were boarded and lodged on the ground floor, the principal and his wife on the upper floor while the verandah was used to serve as class room and lecture hall. It was really a simple and unostentatious beginning with wider future opportunities and programs for the education of the intelligent and pious natives for them to become Christian teachers among their countrymen and women.

It was placed on record that Ajayi Crowther was the first student to enter the doors of Fourah Bay College after many years as schoolmaster under the Colonial Government. Although he was still a youth but for his passion for knowledge, he made some sacrifice of present interest to do this by taking the bold step to leaving teaching to become a student again. Rev. Haensel the principal in his diaries noted some details of his daily round and the common but salutary tasks of those youthful students especially with a glimpse of Crowther who excelled himself as a future leader of his people. Rev. Haensel wrote: **It has been my endeavor to prevent any sudden rise in the outward condition of the youths. Coming out of Government schools, or out of menial employ, they have mostly brought scanty clothing with them – a couple of shirts, a pair of trousers, a hat and perhaps a jacket, with a book of Common Prayer,** and in some instances a Bible, constitute their entire possessions. I have in the first place, where necessary, added a Bible to their stock, a pair of trousers, and a shirt after a little while, a jacket, if necessary after a month or two, and another pair of trousers some time after that.

This for their full dress on Sunday and other particular occasion; at home they always go barefooted. Even Samuel Crowther does so at home, though his visit to England has raised him to the height of white stockings, a suit of blue cloth, a waistcoat, and a beaver hat on Sundays!

Their food consists of rice and yams (a sort of potato), plain boiled, with some meat or fish occasionally and palm oil, which they eat out of tin pans. The youths are their own servants; they sweep and scrub the schoolroom and sleeping room, clean the table, and wash their clothes. I send occasionally one or other on errands, just to remind them that they are not above carrying a basketful of rice or anything else on their heads. From Samuel Crowther I require only the inspection of these services. I have, however, pointed out to him the necessity of example accompanying precept in this as in all other branches of our work, and he follows my suggestions. When Samuel Crowther first entered the Institution he brought with him a mattress with which he had been presented when in England, but as this was too great a luxury I at once forbade its entrance, to which he readily consented. I wish for the good of his own soul to see him in that state of lowliness of mind which Africans so easily lose by visits to England.

The future Bishop after going through all the rigors of an Institution of learning, he too had his own personal opinion about the man who was at the head of the Institution he attended and who helped to mould and reshaped his future course of life. Now this was Crowther's opinion about his former principal and mentor, which he wrote after a lapse of forty years that he left the Institution: **Mr. Haensel was a peculiar person altogether; we could never find one to match him. He was so venerated by all the merchants they would all tremble at his presence if they did not act straightforwardly on honestly. He would tell you in language which was not offensive, but which you could never forget, and next time you saw him you would tremble to act in the same way, either by speaking inadvertently or by acting contrary to Christian principles. He was a man of very penetrating qualifications.**

Concerning the conduct and academic performances of Ajayi Crowther while in the college, his principal Rev. Haensel wrote these movable comments about him and all that surrounded his life a few months after he came into the Institution. "He (Crowther) is a very clever lad, and it is a real pleasure to instruct him. He advances steadily in knowledge and he is a lad of uncommon ability, steady conduct, a thirst for knowledge, and indefatigable industry". On his graduating from the College, he was appointed assistant master at Regent at a salary of (24) twenty-four pounds sterling a year – an equivalent of less that N500 (Naira) in today's Nigeria currency. In 1834, he came back to Fourah Bay College, this time as a regularly appointed tutor and at this time, he was working very hard on his Greek and Latin languages at his own leisure time and as well doing a good service as a parish assistant under the Rev. G.A. Kissling who had succeeded the Rev C. L. F. Haensel as principal. Bishop Crowther remarked in one of his notebooks that: "At my coming back to the Institution the second time, I looked at myself as a student rather on the one hand, while I endeavor to assist the pupils on the other, and I may humbly say through the ministry and private assistance of the Rev. G. A. Kissling I am greatly improved in many respects.

Throughout the long and eventful years that Crowther lived, he never stopped being grateful of all that the Church Missionary Society had done to him especially the way the Society tendered and cared for him during the early days of his career; when he was receiving instructions from the missionaries and Schoolmasters, which so much influenced him for good. To make this gratitude known to the people at Salisbury Square in London, he on the 19th of September 1829, wrote this letter of appreciation from the Christian Institution at Fourah Bay to the Secretaries at the Society's Headquarters: **Rev. and Dear Gentlemen, ... Your most humble and obliged servant addresses these few lines to you and hope that all what he says is directed by his God, in whose vineyard he desires to labor and be useful. I thank you for all the privileges which I have had, by and through you, in learning those good things which are very useful and pleasant in this life, and most of all in learning to know that one needful which none can take away from me.**

When I was brought to England by my honored master Mr. Davey, my chief desire was to learn something which may be good for me and my fellow creatures. When I was to be sent back home again, I begged very hard, not for anything else, but that I might remain there and learn something , that when I came back to Africa I might be a little help to the mission. But when I found that it was not God's will that

I should stop there any longer, I cast myself upon Him, because He knows best. He has not forgotten, He has sent a faithful servant of His to impart to me those good things which I was in need of, and not to me only, but to those to whom He sees fit to be employed in His vineyard.

I am very glad to say I am now engaged as the assistant to my faithful master Mr. Haensel, in the Christian Institution, yet this is not my chief desire, for I am desiring to be instructed by God's Holy Spirit that I may soon rise up and become a teacher to the others. I have that Africa will soon stretch forth her hands unto God, and that joy and gladness shall be found in her, thanksgiving and the voice of melody. I hope Iam not forward in saying I can and do bear all things if Jesus strengthens me. My earnest prayer is that my four brethren, who are yet with you, may have the same desire and pray with me and those that are here in the Spirit, that in future we may join in Africa as Christ's faithful soldiers, who come forth to fight for the soul's of their fellow creatures under the great Captain of our soul's salvation. Pray ye for Africa, that many natives may come forth and give themselves unto Jesus, to employ them in what He wants them to do.

My kind respects goes to all who care for the Africans. And I would comfort them that they need not be in despair that Africa shall not return. Though how few we natives may be that profess to be teachers, we shall try, perhaps God will hear our prayers and help us. Elijah was the only prophet that remained, as it is said in the 1st Book of Kings, chapter xviii. V. 22, in the days of Ahab; and the prophets of Baal were four hundred and fifty, yet God answered him, though he was the only one that remained, and his life was sought to be taken away.

Pray for Africa is the prayer of your most humble, thankful, and obliged servant,

SAMUEL CROWTHER.

Samuel Ajayi Crowther's love affairs, courtship and marital experience to his life partner were full of bunch of historical events. On his admission to Fourah Bay College, he was already on the threshold of manhood and he was then qualified to find a companion. It has been a fact that soon after Crowther landed at Sierra Leone there was also a little girl named Asano, who always sat by the side of Samuel to learn her letters. She was also a rescued slave too that was captured by His Majesty's ship called "Bann", under the control of Captain Charles Phillips, on 31 October 1822, and was brought to Sierra Leone in the same year as Crowther. She was now grown up and also made her mark in the field of learning. She was at this time acting as the Schoolmistress, and had changed her name at baptism to Susan Thompson the way her future husband did. The Christian lives of the people of those days were obviously quite different from what it is being practiced today. In those days, any marriage arrangement between couples especially those who were working in the vineyard of Christ, must be approved by the meeting of the Missionaries in Council. If not approved by this highest body of the organization, such a marriage would never be solemnized. Respecting this important issue in the case of Crowther and his wife, the only parents they both had in the colony were the missionary friends and brothers of different nationalities.

For the issue to be properly and administratively addressed, some body had to present the matter before the Council. The role now had to shift on the shoulders of the old and candid friend of Crowther, Mr. Haensel who drew the attention to the existence of this young lady at the very time when Crowther first came to Fourah Bay College as a student. The principal (Rev. Haensel), in sober terms and reflections now reported to his committee in March 1827, regarding this important issue in the lives of these young loving couples.

He wrote: **You will see by the minutes that Samuel Crowther is to be admitted into the Institution as a probationer for the present. This is owing to the information which is received of an attachment by him towards a girl who is schoolmistress at Bathurst. He says he will not let it interfere with his education and I am ready to trust in his sincerity, but it is to be doubted whether he knows himself sufficiently; and it will be easier to let him withdraw during this period of probation if he should feel it too hard to be separated from her after his full reception as a student.**

In any event Crowther's application for marriage with Susan Thompson was presented to the Council. The interesting and eventful application was approved at a meeting of the Missionaries in Council thus saying.

An application from Samuel Crowther, schoolmaster of Regent, for leave to enter into holy matrimony with Susan Thompson of Bathurst, having been submitted and a satisfactory account being received of the girl's suitableness for a fellow-worker with him, it was resolved that this meeting consent to the marriage of Samuel Crowther with Susan Thompson taking place.

The marriage was solemnized on the day that the minutes and the application were passed and approved and they were blessed with three sons, one being the Venerable Archdeacon Dandeson Coates Crowther and the others were laymen, and three daughters all married to African Clergymen. All of his six children were educated in England. His eldest son, Samuel was given scientific and medical training but later took up trading and became a successful trader of his time. Josiah received industrial training in Manchester and later settled down as a successful businessman. One of his daughters was the mother of Albert Macaulay, a man who was so much respected by his countrymen and women and who was regarded as the father of Nigerian modern politics. These members of the Bishop's family and others in the immigrant's camp with missionary training in Sierra Leone rallied together to resist the campaign mounted by Townsend who claimed that Africans were incapable of running their own affairs. The Bishop and his wife lived together a happy life in the providence of God for over half a century until his wife died at Lagos at a ripe age in 1881. They both saw three good generations of their bloods and bodies.

Chapter 9

First Niger Expedition of 1841

Jonathan Edwards, America's greatest theologian once remarked that: "Holiness was revealed to him as a ravishing, divine beauty. That his heart panted to lie low before God, as in the dust; that he might be nothing and that God might be all, that he might become as a little child". The combination of the intellect and peity that Bishop Ajayi received from the Christian Institution at Sierra Leone characterized his whole life and the turn around of the life of African continent. He was chosen to suffer; destine to be taken as slave; captured and later released; born to be a freedom fighter among his people; a true son of African continent who was ordained by God Himself for the salvation of his people's souls and to bring back the lost and stolen glories of his people back to their anointed lands and territories. His love and affections for his native land had no equal and can still not to be compromised in any small measure because his spirit would always walk throughout the length and breadth of his continent until there would be no more somewhere to be called the earth planet.

The colony of Sierra Leone that was founded by a coalition of anti-slavery interests, mostly Evangelical Christian in inspiration and belonging to the circle associated with William Wilberforce and the Clapham sect could be said to have been constructed mainly as the spiritual and intellectual development center for the growth and up-liftment of Bishop Crowther to the highest flight. Before anyone is lifted high in any community or society, the heavenly hosts must have been instructed by the Supreme Being to work and supply every necessary need that would grow such person up to the required height that the Holies of Heaven have earmarked for such person. Bishop Ajayi Crowther's case and situations were no exception at all.

When Bishop Crowther was growing in the little town of Oshogun, no one ever thought that one day he would be called upon to lead the delegation of people from different lands of the world to the hinterland of his continent in search of place of abode and economic sanctuaries. There was nothing at his birth or during his youthful years that suggested what he would become one day. Not even any prediction that he would one day become the first Anglican Bishop and the most famous African Christian of the 19th century. If God is on the side of a person, who then can be against such person? This was why calamity and providence alternated each other to put Crowther on that extraordinary path. Throughout his years of struggle, he himself did not think that he was using those struggling days to prepare himself for better tomorrow. The personality he was building up to himself was like a childish play to him and unknowingly he did not realize that such personality was also pointing the way to the top globally, continentally and locally.

The British expedition to the River Niger, which was ratified so rapturously at the Exeter Hall meeting in London in June 1840 in the presence of Prince Albert and that galaxy of distinguished public figures, did not happen magically. Although the purpose of the Exeter Hall meeting was to rally round a big support for the extinction of the slave trade in Africa and elsewhere in the world but it also preoccupied itself with intense moral values that were needed after the abolition of the trade. For this purpose, the Niger Expedition program indeed justified itself on purely Christian principles; but which could not devoid itself from the great Imperial excursion for the acquisition of British influence in West Africa. The effect of the missionary interest in West Africa was similar to those of the Association for Promoting the Discovery of the Interior of Africa, which had been established in London. This Association was organized by men of science who had resolved that "as no species of information is more ardently, or more equally useful, than that which improves the science of geography; and as the vast continent of Africa, notwithstanding all the efforts of the ancient, is still a great measure unexplored, the members of this club do form themselves into Association for Promoting the Discovery of the Inland parts of that quarter of the world". The primary aim of the Association was to simply find what the unknown region contained of.

By 1840, the Association had sent several expeditions from the North of African coast towards the interior, which brought back various degrees of success to England. In the Government circle a few wise men were well aware that behind the high moral purpose of the missionary societies and the anti-slavery lobby, lurked the anticipations of men who were not dedicated to an end of man's inhumanity to man in Africa just to satisfy their own economic interest in the trade. After Fowell Buxton, of the Church Missionary Society and the Society for the Extinction of the Slave Trade, had presented his great project for the Civilization of Africa, Lord Palmerston observed to a colleague that "No doubt the extension of commerce in Africa is an object to be aimed at, but I am inclined to think that such extension will be the effect rather than the cause of the extinction of the Slave Trade". Like all other government agencies in the world the then British Government, in its usual sidelong fashion, it became committed to a venture that really paid no more than very loud lip service to the course and ideas of the Christians. It did not even have to border its head in planning any program that would convert souls to God and rescuing savages from degradation because Fowell Buxton had already done this for Her Majesty's Ministers when he presented his proposals in 1839.

Fowell Buxton and his new society had no intention or program of opening missionary stations or starting schools in the Niger region at the present time, but they were asking the Government to back an expedition up the Niger for a variety of other projects. He particularly had in mind that the Government would use its machineries to start a survey of the leading languages and dialects and translate the most important ones into written scripts. He urged the Government to set up printing press in West Africa and initiate the local manufacturing of paper products to feed the press; that the Government should thoroughly investigate the climate in various places in the region with a view to introduce medicine to relieve the worst of the medical problems the climate was causing to the inhabitants. He was pressing it on the Government to take the first steps towards the engineering of roads and canals for transport and of drainage for health, and for it to share with the Africans any available knowledge of Agriculture and to provide farm implements and seeds, as well as advice on the best crops to grow for a world market. As a matter of a fact, Foxwell's ideas were astonishingly sophisticated and highly ambitious in the eyes of people of that century coming from a man starting out with the haziest information from the field in the middle of the 19th century.

In the end the Government made up its mind to pursue the loadable program and decided to back the expedition with the sum of Seventy-nine thousand, one hundred and forty three pounds being the initial estimated costs to run the expedition for one year. It appointed Captain Trotter RN to command the voyage with the instructions to report directly to the Admiralty. This expedition would begin its journey from Rio Nun, which was one of the estuaries of the Niger, which had been sighted by Mungo Park at the end of the 18th century. Interestingly the year 1840, which was the eventful year of Exeter Hall meeting, was also the year in which the Atlantic Ocean was crossed for the first time by a regular steamship service. For this expedition, the newly appointed Comptroller of Steam Machinery at the Admiralty was instantly instructed to prepare three steamships that were constructed of iron for the voyage. The three ships were named **Albert, Wilberforce, and Soudan.**

In the spring of 1841 on 11th of April, the expedition sailed out from England with the load of professional sailors and scientists in various fields. Some of the scientists in the voyage included a group of agriculturists, who were intended to establish a model farm along the route. Also in the expedition were only two missionary workers that were permitted to go on the trip by Her Majesty's Government. One was J. F. Schon who was chosen because of his linguistic abilities while the other was a very promising young Nigerian – Samuel Ajayi Crowther. These two men were stationed at Sierra Leone under the employment of the Church Missionary Society and they joined the expedition as the three steamships called at Freetown on 24th June 1841 with other natives who were to act as interpreters among the Niger tribes and to work at the proposed model farm, which was to be established. On 28th June, 1841 a church service was held for the members of the expedition at St. George's church by Rev. D. F. Morgan who was then the colonial Chaplain in Freetown. On the 3rd of July the expedition team left Freetown to continue their voyage. The Rev. J. F. Schon was placed in the ***Wilberforce*** while Samuel Crowther was in the ***Soudan.*** People back in England were curious about this expedition, which a substantial amount of public fund had been committed to and they were anxiously waiting for its results.

By the middle of August 1841, the squadron arrived at the *Rio Nun* and by the end of the month, they had sailed pass the dreaded delta without a single case of malaria on board. But by 4th September, the chief medical officer in charge of the expedition logged in his diaries that "fever of a most malignant character broke out in the ***Albert*** and in the other vessels. A fortnight later some people had died and the general situation of the expedition became worsen bringing Captain Trotter to a decision of turning his vessels round and make their ways back to the Sea. But instead, he decided to load ***Soudan*** with sick people and dispatched it down south with forty fever cases aboard. Two days later, it was recorded that ***Wilberforce*** followed ***Soudan.***

By the beginning of October the ***Albert*** was still forging ahead on the journey and had actually accomplished some of the programs of the expedition's instructions. They had already concluded two treaties with the tribal chiefs who promised that they would allow the teaching of Christianity in their kingdoms and also to forbid the traffic in slaves to the coast through their domains. In addition to the treaties made, the team succeeded in locating the site of the proposed model farm on the west bank of the Niger in an area facing the junction of River Niger with River Benue. By 3rd October, the captain noticed that the river was already drying because of the dry season that was setting in around that time of the year in the region, coupled with the serious malaria attack on the European members of his team, Captain Trotter submitted to the inevitable and put his little flagship about three hundred miles or so up the Niger. It took the *Albert* about two weeks to reach a relatively save place but no sooner that the ship turned south that Captain Trotter himself went down with fever. The ship was left in the weaker hands of Mr. Willie who was Trotter's mate. The sickening incident was fallen upon almost every European and very few of the natives in the ship and the three engineers on the voyage were now out of action, meaning that the navigation of the ship was now the responsibilities of inexperienced sailors and non-technical personnel of the voyage. Dr. Mcwilliam, one of the medical officers was now in the captain's shoes and uniform to navigate the ship through the little knowledge he had had through reading interest. The story had it that one of the engineers was too ill and fast loosing his wits; but managed himself, out of the strait-jacket, leapt into the river and was not seen again. Another officer Mr. Kingdom died and Rev. Schon buried him on the marshy banks of the River. Then Mr. Willie died and within one hour latter, the purser's steward was dead too, and after him Captain Allen of the marines.

Within the period of this week three other officers and a marine were also dead and buried by the weakened colleagues of the ship's company. The whole situation became panicking as the ship was now swinging and swerving downstream, getting out of control while its decks were filled with sick and dying men. Dr. McWilliam was doing his best to navigate the ship but he had to take care of the sick colleagues who were screaming in delirium too. So also Dr. Stanger who was now in charge of the engine room had to abandon his pistons and his pinwheels to do the job that he was trained. It was in this horrible and dangerous situation that the glorious Niger Expedition was met by the trading steamer ***Ethiope*** whose, crew helped them up to the shelter of Fernando Po.

The expedition was clouded with blankets of danger in the sense that out of 145 Europeans that took part in the voyage, no fewer than 130 had been attacked by malaria disease and 40 of them were now dead. In the past, Sierra Leone was known and called the white Man's Grave; but now it was the turn of Rio Nun to assume the new name of "Gate of the cemetery". Because of the disastrous end of this expedition, the African Civilization Society was discredited in the Government circle and was later dissolved by its members. Christian historians noted that when Fowell Buxton was on his way to the last meeting of the Association, he remarked that: "I feel as if I were going to the funeral of an old and dear friend". He was greatly disappointed by the outcome of the expedition and he was gradually becoming vegetative and weary. He rarely referred to the lost temporary battle for the rest of his life and he was able to survive the terrible shock for only three years before he was called back home. It was on record that "The failure of the Niger Expedition killed Fowell Buxton".

But the treaties and the farm established became destitute because of lack of thorough follow-up and supervision. Analyzing the failure of the expedition, J. F. Schon from his part suggested that the Society should not in the future contemplate a mission staffed by Europeans anywhere along the three hundred miles of the River that had been navigated, for no suitable sites had been detectable to accommodate them. The message that his observations were sending to the missionary authorities in England was that the training of the native Catechists to preach the Gospel in the areas with such devastating climate as it was then was the only best option. People advanced different theories on what went wrong with the climate of West Africa that caused such high rate of death and sicknesses to the Europeans.

Samuel Crowther had a different view altogether to the problem. He was inclined not to believe that the great casualty figures aboard the three ships had resulted from the storage of fresh and green woods for the boilers in the holds of the vessels, where they had decomposed into malaria germs.

Whatever any right or wrong reasons attributed to the death rate that occurred during the expedition voyage, the Africans that were recruited to work with the team did not suffer any malaria attack. Out of 158 black men recruited, only eleven of them were taken ill and not one of them died. The recommendations of Rev. Schon therefore went a long way in the new policies of the Church Missionary Society about the West African region. Rev. Schon noticed and observed that during the voyage of the Expedition, the liberated African slaves who sailed with them on the trip were warmly welcomed by their peers as prospective teachers; and from his experience in Sierra Leone he could promise the CMS that those freed slaves in the colony that had received training and employment around Freetown would be glad at the prospect of returning to their homelands.

Rev. Schon was seen to have been an advocator of the translation of the Bible into African vernacular languages so that the local preachers might take this into the interior of the continent to teach their people. His report was adopted by the CMS almost in its entirety and a special fund was lunched for the extensive of Fourah Bay College to accommodate the implementation of some of the newly formulated policies. Although the expedition of 1841 was a wreck but the spirit behind it started working on a new strategy to continue the important investigation of River Niger. Both the Government and the CMS saw the disaster as a temporary setback. The British missionaries believed that they had a divine purpose to fulfill in West Africa, and the British Government through the reports it received during the first trip was convinced of its temporal obligations in the area. Ever since the abolition of the slave trade the West coast of Africa had retained a special interest in the minds of the British nation. This region was seen as potential gold mines in the areas of agriculture, mineral potentialities, trade and industry and as such no temporary set back would make them abandon the exploration of the region to its logical conclusion. The important work of Sir Thomas Fowell Buxton titled "The Slave Trade and its Remedy" had actually pointed a path to the politicians that the extinction of the accursed trade should open doors of commerce and the development of the region.

These and other reasons were the motives behind the expedition of discovery of 1841 to ascend the Niger and obtain valuable information for the use of the Government. The Government's motive and intentions were clearly spelt out in the letter of Lord John Russell who was then the acting Colonial Secretary, which he addressed to the Lords of the Treasury on 26th December 1839 in which he expressed the objects of the proposed expedition:

> The Queen has directed her ministers to negotiate conventions and agreements with those chiefs and powers, the basis of which conventions would be, first, the abandonment and absolute prohibition of the slave trade; and, secondly, the admission, for consumption in this country, on favourable terms, of goods, the produce and manufacture of the territories subject to them – of those chiefs the most considerable over the countries adjacent to the Niger and its great tributary streams. It is therefore proposed to dispatch an expedition, which would ascend that river by steamboats as far as the points at which it receives the confluence of some of the tropical rivers falling into it from the eastward. At these, or at any other stations which may be found more favourable for the promotion of a legitimate commerce, it is proposed to establish British factories, in the hope that the natives may be taught that there are methods of employing the population more profitably to those to whom they are subject than that of converting them into slaves and selling them for exportation to the slave traders.

Samuel Crowther as it was earlier noted was placed in the **Soudan** ship. It was his first experience of the world beyond and behind the coast of the colony; and the tears of separation from his wife and the children were still rolling down his cheeks as he took up his pen to make the first and subsequent entries of the journey in his diary on board. He wrote about the beginning of the voyage as thus:

> Today about eleven o'clock the *Soudan* got under way for the Niger, the highway into the heart of Africa. She was soon followed by the *Wilberforce*, which took her in tow in order to save fuel. When I looked back on the colony in which I had spent nineteen years – the happiest part of my life, because there I was brought acquainted with the saving knowledge of Jesus Christ, leaving my wife, who was near her confinement, and four children behind – I could not but feel pain and some anxiety for a time at the separation. May the Lord, who has been my guide from my youth up till now, keep them and me, and make me neither barren nor unfruitful in His service!

On their arriving off cape coast castle they went ashore and at this place, he was glad to meet with that able Wesleyan missionary the Rev. T. B. Freeman, who received him with kindness and joy, and took him into his library and told him that he was free to use whatever book he desired from his collections. As he was roaming around the graveyard of the castle, he noted an inscription on one of the tablets erected to remember the good work of a native the Rev. Philip Quaque who was sent to England by the Society for the Propagation of the Gospel in 1754, baptized at St. Mary's Islington on 7th January 1759, and returned fully ordained as Chaplain to the factory, and died, after many trials and disappointments in 1816. The inscription on this tablet was a moving interest to Crowther that when the expedition was over he referred to the incident in a letter, in which he says:

Who the individual was I know not, neither have I ever heard anything of him, except from his monument. What attracted my attention was that he was a native of that place – sent to England for education, received Holy Orders, and was employed in his country upwards of fifty years!

Leaving this coast behind them, they continued their journey and day-by- day their troubles were increasing and whenever they had the opportunity to exchange notes with others in other vessels, it was to tell each other a woeful story as thus recorded by Crowther:

This morning the *Albert* and the *Wilberforce* came up to us where we were getting woods. Captain B Allen immediately came to his ship. He took all his unexpected afflictions with Christian resignation. I went with Mr. Sidney, one of the officers, to a village on the top of the hill, below which we were wooding. These villagers are refugees from the town of Addu Kuddu, on the right side of the river at the confluence, having been driven away by the Fulatahs. From the top of the hill you may see three other villages at the foot. The one on the top of the hill contains two hundred inhabitants the four together contain eight hundred, at an average. The people are Kakandas. As I could understand a little, I mentioned to them the design of the expedition, at which they were transported with joy. One of them was so confident that he wished to go with the white men altogether. I asked them whether they would like me to stay with them and teach them about God. They all answered in affirmative.

The chief of this village, an old man about sixty, had been sacrificing a fowl to his idol this morning. The blood he sprinkled on his forehead to, which were attached a few of the fowl's feathers. His idol is rather difficult to describe, as it was a mixture of some sort of grass or palm leaves, clay, and broken pieces of calabashes, to which feathers of fowls were fastened by means of blood. I shook my head, indicating that it was not good, at the same time pointing my finger to heaven, directing him to worship the only true God. He did not pay much attention. They all took fright at Mr. Sidney's instrument to take the distance, but their fears soon subsided. Their huts are built in the same form as those of Iddah – a circular form, and they are so low and close to each other that if fire should break out in one, the whole village of about sixty huts would be consumed in a moment.

As soon as **Wilberforce and Soudan** were instructed to sail back into the sea with the cargoes of human sick and dead people Captain Trotter in the **Albert** decided to push on a little further and here Crowther was able to join Rev. Schon to their mutual satisfaction. When they reached a place called Gori they went ashore and Crowther, in describing and the interview he had with the chief of Gori, he observed the curious custom of the king and he wrote:

We were led to the house of the chief, where the gentlemen of the expedition were seated on mats in the courtyard, about twelve feet by eight, and formed by five huts in the shape of casks placed in an oval form.

The chief is about seventy years of age. He appeared to have been so frightened at the sudden appearance of the white men that he could not speak a word, and was thought to be deaf and dumb. There was one who acted as his mouth (or speaker), who answered with great reserve every question put to him, especially such as related to the slave trade. He denied knowing the number of slaves brought to market to-day, or that they were the Attah's subjects. The heat from the crowd by which we were blocked up in this narrow spot was suffocating; besides, the noise was so great, not only from the spectators, but the headmen themselves, that it was almost enough to deafen anyone else. When one headman calls out for silence, it takes him nearly five minutes to complete his palavering with the people, and when he is on the point of holding his tongue he is never in want of three or four seconders who also must scold the people, so that instead of obtaining quietness both the headman and the people make more noice and create greater confusion than ever, till perhaps after a quarter of an hour there is silence for a time.

Throughout the journey, Crowther was the chief spokesman, and his kinship as a black person no doubt gave the people a certain confidence in listening to him. When they reached Egga, the captain and the officers of the expedition had an important interview with Rogan the chief who was a person of great authority. Crowther took some pains to explain to the ruler the objects of the expedition, from a commercial and religious standpoint. He wrote:

After a long walk through narrow and crooked streets we came to Rogans's palace, and in about half an hour's time he made his appearance. After a hearty salutation, by shaking of hands in the name of the king of the ship, and telling him the reasons why the ship could not then come near, I commenced my message:

That the Queen of the country called Great Britain has sent the king of the ship to all the chiefs of Africa to make treaties with them to give up war and the slave trade – to all their people in the cultivation of the soil, and to mind all that the white people say to them, as they wish to teach them many things, and particularly the Book which God gives, which will make all men happy. I added likewise that there are many Nufi, Hausa, and Yoruba people in the white man's country who have been liberated from the Portuguese and Spanish slave ships, that they are now living like white men, that they pray to God and learn His Book, and consequently are living happier life than when they were in their own country, and much better off than their country people are at present. To this many of them said that they could judge of their happy state merely by my appearance. I added, moreover, that our country people in white man's country had written a letter to the Queen who lives in Great Britain, expressing their wish to return to their country if she would send white men along with them; but the Queen, who loves us all as her children, told them to stop till she had first sent her ships to the chiefs of Africa, to persuade them to give up war and slave trade; and if they consented to her proposals she would gladly grant the request of our country people.

The malaria fever attack was now dealing ruthlessly with its victims on board with such a rapid strides that sickness and daily burial of the dead were the only sad achievements recorded at this period of the journey. The courageous Captain Trotter was at last taken ill and now being confined to his cabin; Captain B. Allen was also lying dangerously in his condition and the only officer left to navigate the ship was Mr. Willie who was just a mate. Dr. Stanger had to take charge of the engine. The record showed that at about ten o'clock one night, the Captain's Clerk used the advantage of the darkness to throw himself overboard in delirium; but he was rescued by a black sailor who swam after him, and brought him back to be roped down in his hammock.

The whole situation became darkened to everyone in the voyage as the ship was now running almost unguided down the swift current of River Niger with its decks strewn with dying and dead members of the expedition at terrific rates. The doctor who was the only one managing the engines from the experience he only got through the reading of a book on machinery which he founded in the dead Captain's room had to desert his levers to attend to his fellow sick men who were screaming in delirium. The whole situation became confused as the red light of tragedy was blinking and flashing around everywhere in the ship. As a matter of fact, it was Crowther alone that was not touched by the fever, and who kept his head as well as his health through this ill-fated journey. He was said to be working everywhere in the ship, and at anything, to save the ugly situation. Rev. Schon with his own afflictions throbbing with the fever managed to record these words in his journal:

Pain of body, distress of mind, weakness, sobbing and crying surround us on all sides. The healthy, if so they may be called, are more likely walking shadows than men of enterprise. Truly Africa is an unhealthy country! When will all redemption draw nigh? All human skill is baffled, all human means fall short. Forgive us, O God, if on them we have depended and been forgetful of Thee, and let the light of thy countenance again shine upon us that we may be healed!

Schon also made mention of a particular situation that would be gravely pathetic to every kind conscience that hears it. He said that when they read a quotation of "This piteous cry of a brave man is not to be wondered at" on a Sunday morning while conducting service on the quarter of the deck, he had the body of a dead sailor behind him and in front of him, the carpenters were busy making a coffin. And in the forepart yonder seven men were lying seriously ill with no assurance of getting healed. When this sad news reached England there was national grief and mourning throughout the land and the public opinion twisted anti-cloak wise immediately regarding this mission. It became serious debate everywhere in the land for upwards of twelve years before any other program could be drawn up for another attempt. The happiest part of the first expedition was that the Government acknowledged that the expedition had not been all failure, although it had claimed a toll of heavy human casualties. All agreed that the project had paved the way for other pioneers; and many lessons were learnt about how to prepare solidly for future trips of this kind to this particular region.

To the Church Missionary Society on its part, it used the information gathered through the experiences of their two representatives on the voyage – Rev. Schon and Crowther to map out their future strategies about the region and its native people and on how to establish missions along the routes covered by the expedition. The journey also enabled Rev. Schon to compile a valuable vocabulary of the different languages of the people that they met along the route and also added some new geographical discovery of one of the waterways of the world. Another thing to note from this expedition was the future of Crowther in the employment of the CMS. The journey actually brought a lot out of him especially in the areas of diligence, obedience, responsibilities, and leadership experience that he was acquiring for the future responsibilities that were to be laid upon his shoulders. The trip was supposed to be a pleasant voyage of discovery, but later proved to be a furnace of affliction to all concerned, yet it was an expedition of good and bad taste to fill or sense in the years to come for this region of the world.

Chapter 10

Second Niger Expedition of 1854

The temporary set-back cursed by the disaster of 1841 did not close the doors of further exploration of the Niger permanently because both the British Government and the Church Missionary Society saw a bright prospect coming out of the region in the areas of trade and commerce and extension of British rule over the land for a very long time to come. Initially the missionaries were busy working on the changing aspect of the people's culture while the Government was planning on the modalities to use in the taking over of the administration of the land from the hands of the monarchs and chiefs in all the kingdoms of the region of West Coast of Africa. By every standard of human behavior, the people of Africa have ever been known to be kind and hospitable people particularly to people of other nationalities of the world. This fact was contained in the report submitted by Samuel Crowther who represented the Church Missionary Society on this venture saying in his report that: "The reception we met with along from kings and chiefs of the countries was beyond all expectation". He had the belief that the time was ripe enough when Christianity must be introduced on the banks of the Niger and that the people are now willing to receive any person who may be sent to them for this purpose.

On Crowther's return from the ill-fated first expedition of 1841to Sierra Leone, which was his base since he was rescued from the slave traders and where he first experienced the blessing of Christian love, he was warmly welcomed by his many old friends and associates. He was now a very powerful preacher and an experienced man in the knowledge of his people's predicaments during the short period of time he spent in his trip to the interior of the continent with the first expedition team on the exploration of River Niger. His people back home in Sierra Leone were now ready to listen to him with rapt attention and dignity each time he rose to preach the words of God to them. Although his ultimate intention of destination was Abeokuta but he remained at Sierra Leone waiting for the time that such opportunity doors would be opened for him to make his journey back to Abeokuta one more time. More to his trip back to Abeokuta would be discussed further in chapters ahead. It was during this time that he was making all frantic efforts to interpret some of the chapters and important quotations in the Bible into his own mother tongue in order to please his Yoruba countrymen and women in the colony. In some cases, he would speak to them in English language from the pulpit, but the people were always anxious to hear him in their mother tongue, and afterwards, he would change the topic into Yoruba language to their pleasure and profit. This method actually promoted the sinking of God's words to the brains and hearts of his native audience either during the church services or during his visits to their homes. The people were proud to see that one of their own people was now so honored as to become a clergyman.

The doors of another expedition up River Niger were opened again through the public grace and enterprise of Mr. Macgregor Laird, who had been a long identified advocate of commercial development of West Africa. This time around, it was proposed to send a single vessel on the trip to explore the River Nun and the Niger to the confluence

Macgregor Laird

and moved further the Tshadda to wherever it could up the land. Dr. J. Baike was invited and gave the role of making fresh observations and notes of geographical value. Because of the important leadership role that Crowther played during the 1841 expedition that was clearly opened to the eyes of everyone in the voyage, Mr. Laird personally made an offer to the CMS of a free passage for Crowther, which was accepted with humor and gladness. This voyage was a complete success and very much unlike the previous voyage of 1841 that claimed many lives. The explorers penetrated two hundred and fifty miles beyond the limit of the first expedition and also recorded a clean slate of health without any loss of a single person.

This second expedition really brought out a lot out of Crowther's bank of knowledge and experience, which he had acquired over the years both at Fourah Bay and his visits to England at different occasions. This was the time that he actually brought to bear the advantages of his study and training under the beloved men and women of God. Crowther was highly rated as one of those that keep records of his daily life in form of journal. If not because of this attitude he built around himself, it would not have been possible for us today to know what he actually did and what his future thinking was all about concerning the continent and the people he so much loved and respected. His habit of indefatigable industry and careful observation of every important detail helped us to understand ourselves better and know much about our foreign friends of the past. His trips to Abeokuta and some other places inside the country were cut short because of the important role he had to play in the second expedition. He was given honorable good-byes at the gate of Abeokuta when he was leaving for Lagos to join *Pleiad,* the exploring vessel at Fernando Po.

At the shore of Fernando Po, Crowther, while waiting for his vessel made an important reference to someone who was a British Consul and an intrepid explorer, who had been of great service to West Africa and who once lived in this place. In his journal, Crowther wrote this about this great friend of West Africa during the dark-ages. **The people were very glad to see me, and expressed their regret for the loss of Mr. Beecroft, for he had made full preparation for the expedition and had engaged many intelligent natives who had been used to go up the Niger with him, and who were ready to go anywhere with him, they being mutually attached to each other, for he treated them as a father. It will be a long time before his place can be supplied by another who will take the same interest in the country and her people as he did.**

After breakfast, visited Mr. Beecroft's grave, which is on the point

of the cliff of Clarence under a large cotton tree, where he himself had directed he should be buried. Thus ended the life of this useful person, after twenty-five years of stay in Africa, during which period he had won the affection of many who knew his worth in the countries he had visited, and could not but greatly regret to hear of his removal by death. The chiefs of Abeokuta had sent salutations and messages to him by me, which he did not live to receive. As long as this generation lasts the name of Mr. Beecroft will not be forgotten in this part of Africa.

No sooner that the vessel arrived that it sailed on to the sea with a few mishaps ranging from the breakdown in the machinery to a rather awkward crossing of the bar outside River Nun and their mistake in choosing the right channel, through which they ran ashore on Sunday Island. The only CMS representative on this voyage was Samuel Crowther and he was all the while busy doing his job of preaching the Gospel to the people along the route. Interestingly a number of native canoes came alongside the ship to enquire from them whether they were "slave traders or oil dealers" to which they gave satisfactory reply about their journey. Samuel Crowther was no longer a strange person along this route because of his first expedition experience but he now noticed some changes, which had taken place since his last visit and he remarked in his journal the followings:

Soon after we had cleared Sunday Island traces of cultivation began to appear, together with land about three feet above the water's edge. As the water has not yet risen to its full height, it gave an entirely new appearance to the river from that it bore in August 1841. At that time only a few spots near the water's edge were under cultivation, and the whole was covered with water, as the river overflowed its banks. Not only old plantations showed a continual industry of the people of the Delta, but many newly-cleared spots in the midst of which numerous lofty palm trees stood, which were carefully preserved for their reach and valuable produce, showed further the improved state of the banks. About three hours from Sunday Island we came to inhabited villages; we induced two canoes to come off, from whom we learnt that the people between Brass and Aboh are called Uru. One of the people who came off, and who spoke Ibo language, was so confident that he offered to go with us to Aboh; and the people on shore never showed the least sign of opposition, but folded their arms and gazed at the steamer as she glided on.

Fewer traces of cultivation were observed during the day till we came to the village of Angiama. Brass people came here to buy palm oil, with large casks in their canoes, some of which they land as they proceed upwards. There is another striking changes in the habits of the people themselves. In 1841 very few of them were to be found with any decent articles of clothing. I spied today, among a group of about forty people, fifteen who I could distinctly see had English shirts on. This is an evident mark of the advantage of legal trade over that of men. The chief of Angiama, or Anya, came off and expressed his regret that we did not wait at his village as Captain Trotter did, and it was with some difficulty we could satisfy him by our excuses, but we hoped to be able to stay on our return. Dr. Baikie gave him a red cap and a looking-glass; but I could read in the countenance as well as by the temper one of his men manifested that if they had had it in their power they would have detained us in Oru, to reap all the benefits of the trade to themselves instead of allowing it to pass through their waters to the people of the interior beyond them.

The next place of stop was at Aboh from where they were told of the death of the old king Obi who had earlier on signed a pact of trading and peace with Captain Trotter during the expedition of 1841. The new king in his stead who was his son named Chukuma remarked that his father and his people had waited for the white man's vessel for too long a time, which never came. During their discussions, Mr. Baikie told the king and his people that in the name of the Queen of England and her people, they were so sorry to hear the demise of the former ruler of the land and that the Queen had desired him to visit them and see how they were doing and that they thought the new ruler would be of the same mind as the late king and that they from their own part still adhered to the treaty the old ruler signed with Captain Trotter.

He said that they brought with them this time a piece of good news that trade was now come to Aboh country. In his own reply, Chukuma the new Obi said that he was glad to see a large ship come to Aboh again, and that he and his other chiefs were particularly charged by the late Obi before his death not to deviate from the path he had trod respecting his friendship with the white men, and that they would act accordingly. His younger brother Aje, who was recognized by the people as someone with much more strong mind while taking actions than the king himself was not around as it was said that he traveled to Igara with a great number of chiefs on state mission. The king could not therefore give a decisive reply

The Journey of the First Black Bishop

not until the other strong men of the city had arrived from their journey. Samuel Crowther used this delay opportunity time to introduce the subject of a missionary establishment among them. He told them that they had come to see what they could do to establish a missionary station at Aboh, as they had done in his own country at Badagry, Lagos and Abeokuta and also done at Calabar and the Cameroons.

As soon as he finished his address, one of the Obi's daughters replied that they would not agree to an idea of the white men building houses in Bonny and Calabar, and not in Aboh. Crowther replied that the superiors in England had been nursing the idea for a long time, but now they were in earnest, and very desirous of sending some Ibo teachers to Aboh, to reside among them and teach those many things as long as they were willing to learn. Chukwuma thanked Crowther for the great speech he made hoping that all what the team told him would be realized as said. He said that he would not believe anything until he had seen them do what they proposed; that there was no problem on their part, nor need they fear any unwillingness to receive those that may be sent to them or learn what they may be taught, but that the fault rests on them if they fail to fulfill their own obligations. This interview showed the willingness and keen interest that the people had regarding their passion for acquiring knowledge that would enhance their life-style. The following morning, the Royal family was treated to a luncheon party in the saloon of the ship where Dr. Baikie gave some glittering presents to the little ones of the Royal family and the whole party returned home highly gratified.

The next day Crowther went ashore to pay a visit to the king, to get an opportunity to talk to him in privacy and detail on religious matters, and to introduce to him the benefits that such Christian doctrine would bring to his kingdom and he wrote this about the private discussions:

The quickness with which he caught my explanation of the all-sufficient sacrifice of Jesus Christ, the son of God, for the sin of the world was gratifying. I endeavored to illustrate it to him in this simple way. "What would you think of any person who in broad daylight like this should light their lamps to assist the brilliant rays of the sun to enable them to see better?" He said: "It would be useless; they would be fools to do so." I replied: "Just so." That the sacrifice of Jesus Christ, the Son of God, was sufficient to take away our sins, just as one sun is sufficient to give light to the whole world; that the worship of country fashions and numerous sacrifices which shone like lamps, only on account of the darkness of their ignorance and superstition, though repeated again and again, yet cannot take away our sins; but that the sacrifice of Jesus Christ, once offered, alone can take away the sin of the world. He frequently repeated the names "Oparra Tshuku! Oparra Tshuku! Son of God! Son of God!"

As I did not wish to tire him out I felt my discourse fresh in his mind. The attention of his attendants, with the exception of a few, was too much engaged in begging and receiving presents to listen to all I was talking about. I gave to Tshukuma a Yoruba primer in which I wrote his name, and left some with Simon Jonas to teach the children or any who should feel disposed to learn the alphabet and words of two letters.

The voyage continued and they were now approaching the confluence of River Niger and Benue and they were to pass through the site where the model farm was established during the 1841 expedition. Crowther observed a lot of changes that had happened in the area during the time he visited this place last and now. He noticed that some of the towns and villages that existed on the banks of River Niger during the first expedition were no more seen, while those areas that were covered with vegetations had now been turned into towns and villages. When he enquired about the sudden changes, he was told that it was as a result of warlike raid of Dasaba, who had swept down with his warriors to avenge the death of Mr. Carr- a white man that was killed by the people of the Delta area without any reason. The order to avenge the death of this white man was handed down to Dasaba by the Attah of Igala who urged him to punish the people of the Delta for the crime they committed for killing an innocent man who was to bring trade and civilization to his kingdom. About hundred towns and villages were destroyed and many people fled their homes for unknown destinations. It was said that Dasaba and his warriors drove and carried the inhabitants of those towns and villages away. The model farm that was established during the 1841 expedition was now covered with tall trees and shrub, as no one was available to continue tendering it. It was Mr. Carr who was originally intended to superintend the model farm established at the confluence that was killed for the sake of plunder. Mr. Carr was a member of the 1841 expedition and on his return from that crashed trip to Fernando Po, he was taken ill and when he was fit he now wished to return to the confluence on his recovery. He then set out in a canoe with some natives, but was never heard of again.

As slave trade was now dissipating rapidly in this region because of lack of international traders, the internal need for domestic services of slaves was still in operative. Crowther noticed this when they arrived at Ijogo and found that the people were very shy to come near the *Pleiad* for the purpose of trade, which was very unusual of the people they had met along the route before getting to Ijogo. Notwithstanding this odd attitude, some men from the interior still managed to come down to the shore to welcome the team. Interestingly among those people that came was a poor man named Asaba, from Rogankoto and whose one of his legs had been bitten off by crocodile when fishing.

The wounds had since been healed but he was hobbling about with the aid of a long stout stick. As the man was sighted in the midst of those that came near the ship by the two doctors in the team, they were touched internally about his suffering and they immediately set to find a way to improve his locomotion; with the assistance of Mr. Guthrie, the chief engineer, a wooden leg was set in manufacturing motion for him. When the artificial leg was ready and fitted for him, the man became a proud person when he got back to his town to tell his people the marvelous news of the new foot that the white men had given to him. They were all happy to see this wonderful invention and it gave them future hopes of more to come if they could maintain a very good relationship with them. And this singular action turned the people of this area to the side of Samuel Crowther in years to come.

Throughout the journey, they met with pleasant and unpleasant events and moments from the natives of different tribes along the banks of River Niger. Sometime they would meet with people that were armed to their teeth in readiness to protect their kingdom against the marauders and sometime they would meet with the people that would gladly accept them with open arms. To reference the unpleasantness of some people, Crowther made some reflections upon the common report of the hostility of the natives of Africa towards the Europeans. He pointed out that the people are always in such a state of alarm by reason of the tribal and marauding wars, that any stranger coming makes them fly to arms. He was of the opinion that the European explorers often overlook the fact that the natives are in constant fear of the treachery of their enemies. This makes them carry their weapons with them at all times, to be in readiness for any sudden attack by the enemies. He wrote about this as follows:

Though travelers fear nothing themselves yet they should endeavor to take due precautions to allay the fears of those whom they intend to visit, by previous communication, which will soon be circulated in the neighborhood, and then all will be right. A prudent man will not consider an hour or two wasted to effect this purpose, rather than risk the painful result of misunderstandings which may never be remedied. As far as I know, there is no place in Africa, uncontaminated with European slave traders, which Europeans have visited with the intention of doing good, where such an event not been hailed as the most auspicious in the annals of the country. Every chief considers himself highly honored to have white men for his friends.

The opinion of Samuel Crowther respecting the behaviors of Africans of the past may not be limited to Africa alone but to be extended to the entire world of the time. Even in recent times when civilization is known to be spread across the globe, we still hear of the same type of behaviors over the radio and on televisions from some countries in the Asian continent, Europe and other places where people are still being kidnapped or killed without any just reasons. His good advice will then never be out of date for travelers with good intentions. We cannot but refer to the intellectual reasoning of someone in the person of Buxton who initially argued correctly that the efforts of Britain to stop the slave trade through diplomacy in Europe and naval patrols on the Atlantic had not visibly shown any signs of reduction in the numbers of slaves exporting out of Africa; and that the only best way was to attack the trade at its roots, which was at the interior of the continent and the source of supply in Africa.

He then suggested that: We must elevate the minds of the people and call forth the resources of her soil. Let missionaries, the plough and the spade go together and agriculture will nourish; the avenues to legitimate commerce will be opened; confidence between man and man will be inspired; whilst civilization will advance as the natural effect, and Christianity operate as the proximate cause, of this happy change. In actual fact, the philosophy of Buxton was in latter years begun to bear fruits in the regions surrounding River Niger.

The second expedition journey continued amidst success and hardships. In some cases the team would meet with difficulties with their guide-men, who did not relish the hardships and risks of the expedition. Sometime they would have to unnecessarily anchor their ship when there would not be enough water to steam the boat and had to wait for when there would be enough water for it to sail. Crowther gave an example of his experience on his way to Hamaruwa that he was led astray onto different direction by the guide-man, when it became necessary for him to meet with the king of Hamaruwa whom he had sent a message to concerning a meeting between the two of them. He also spoke of times that they would abandon their ship and trek miles on the rough paths to meet chiefs and their people in the interior and in many occasions being paddled in canoes for hours and days before they would return to their ship. These are part of the experiences that nation builders face from time to time.

On their journey to Hamaruwa, Crowther narrated through his pen the troubles and mishaps they met on the way thus:

By the time we had traveled three hours the Krumen, who were as much deceived as ourselves, because very much dissatisfied and expressed regret that they had not returned to the ship instead of going such an unpleasant journey in which they had no interest. Truly it was unpleasant, inasmuch as we were deceived as regards distance, and the road was by no means enviable to walk in. We had not left Wuza half an hour before I was obliged to take off my shoes and roll up the legs of my trousers, as did Mr. Richards, to wade through the continual splash of water and mud we met with more than one third of the way.

At last they reached Hamaruwa a town which Crowther described as a fine town with nice and hospitable people. This town according to him was beautifully situated on a hill, from which a grand view of the river and scenery around are conspicuously seen, the long stretch of light green grass by the water's edge, then the darker green of the tree foliage, and beyond the blue ranges of Fumbina, with the lofty Mandranu mountain in Adamawa, and the Muri mountain in Hamaruwa. The houses were built with conical roofs on long public streets, with luxuriant trees representing the characteristic of most African town of that age. It was a delightful place according to Crowther, for it was built on a rock like the city of Abeokuta where the waters dries very quickly after it rains. They received a hearty welcome from the king, and were liberally supplied with food as it was reported in Crowther's journal: The king sent five sheep and lambs with a kid, six in all, and a large pot of plum honey for our entertainment, but unfortunately before the honey was delivered the pot broke and the whole was spilled on the ground, to the great grief of all present. Ibrahim with much sorrow to tell me of this great misfortune, and I must say I felt the loss myself, because it would have been very acceptable present to all the ship's company, considering that since the fourth instant we had been out of sugar. Butter and milk had been all consumed long before, and a pot of honey would have been an invaluable substitute. But travelers must take things as they come, and be content with such things as they have.

The Filanis use no lamps in their house in the evening; we had therefore to remain outside the house where we were lodged, seated in the dark, as they themselves did, till bedtime, when a few sticks were kindled, which gave out much smoke and little light, to enable us to ascertain the position of our bed, which was rough enough. Before we turned in Ibrahim requested me to take care of my sheep and goat in our room for fear of the wolves, with which the country abounds. I told him it was impossible to admit five sheep and a goat into a room already filled with eleven occupants, and he promised to take care of them until the morning. Ibrahim's yard was full of visitors going and coming, to whom he was relating the wonderful news of the Anasara's ship made of iron and moved by fire. Being tired with our journey, we left them to enjoy the story, and rested ourselves after we had offered a prayer of thanksgiving to God for our protection.

After their meeting with the king and their brief sojourn in Hamaruwa, they got back to the ship on a Sunday morning, and Crowther as usual conducted the service in the usual manner. The river was now running low very rapidly and it was felt that the engine of the *pleiad* should be turned homeward, if a complete success was to be recorded for this expedition. Before the final decision to go back home was taken, one more attempt was made by Dr. Baikie and Mr. May to further make additional observations about the river as they had to travel on a boat for three days journey on the investigation trip. Crowther confessed how fearful the rest of them left behind were at leaving these two men in such dangers, among an unknown and perhaps hostile people. Eventually on the third day, a big loud of cheers announced the return of the boat, with its two occupants. Everyone was happy and joyful for the safe return of the men into the ship.

During this trip, Crowther was able to make arrangements for the opening of many missionary stations at several places along the Niger route; preached the Gospel to a great deal of the natives and showed them how people of different nationalities and background can live together in peace and harmony through the love of Jesus Christ. For example, when they reached a little town down the stream he met a young chief, named Agbekun, who, being childless, and had been paying visits to "Aeo" where Chukwu, the great god of the Ibos reside, so as to plead with the god for a child. He told Crowther that he had gone through many ceremonies, and performed many rituals and sacrifices to Chukwu the god and he wanted to know Crowther's opinion about the powers of this god. Crowther said that he used this opportunity to speak to him about the true God, to whom he endeavored to turn his attention to look for blessings both temporal and spiritual.

This chief requested from Crowther to teach him how to pray to this great God he had just told him about. Crowther told him to do just as a little child would ask his father for what he was in need of. The chief further wanted to know from Crowther whether "There is no hatred in the white man's country as they are abounds in the black man's country"? Crowther replied and told him to see the living relationship between the three different nationalities standing in front of him as an example. Himself, a Yoruba by birth, Simon Jonas – an Ibo, and Dr. Baikie, an Englishman, yet they all live together as brethren, and so our God teaches all men to love one another. Crowther expressed his hope that very soon they would be able to teach them this love, which the chief was glad to hear.

On 6 November the *Pleiad* crossed the bar, and crowther held a Divine Service, expressing big thanks to Almighty God of all those on board for such a wonderful and favourable journey and he preached from the Book of Joshua 4 verses 6&7. He closed his journal with this note of praise:

May this singular instance of God's favour and protection drive us nearer to the Throne of Grace, to humble ourselves before our God, whose instruments we are, and who can continue or dispense with our services as it seems good to His unerring wisdom.

Samuel Crowther while reviewing the results of the expedition, he drew attention to several points, which were very crucial and encouraging to the authorities in England in the following order:

(1) The remarkable absence of any sickness to the European teammates and not a single life was lost during the voyage.

(2) That the time had come to introduce Christianity fully on the banks of the Niger because the people were evidently ready and willing to receive teachers among them.

(3) The utilization of the natives to spread the Gospel and civilization to their people. On this he said: let such workers go back to their countrymen as a renewed people, superior now to others, and whose walk and conversation would do so much to commend Christ and His Gospel in these regions.

The converted African was a special value in his testimony and he wrote:

It takes great effect when, returning, liberated Christians sit down with their heathen countrymen and speak with contempt of their former superstitious practices, of whom, perhaps, may now alive would bear testimony as to their former devotedness to their superstitious worship, all of which he can now tell them he has found to be foolishness and the result of ignorance, when he with all earnestness invites them, as Moses did Hobab, "Come with us, for the Lord hath promised good to Israel," and all this in their own language, with refined Christian feelings and sympathy, not to be expressed in words, but evidenced by an exemplary Christian life.

From the economic and commercial standpoint, the expedition team was rated very highly with great cheers of applause from the Government and the people; for Crowther took personal interest in the encouragement of cotton growing, and the development of trade through his initiative and persistency. Based upon his recommendations, a meeting of the friends of Africa was convened shortly after the return of *Pleiad,* where it was resolved that the British Government should be urged to establish a regular service of trading steamers between Fernando Po and the confluence of the Niger and Benue rivers. Because of the vital role that Crowther played during the expedition voyage, Dr. Baikie, at the conclusion of the voyage, addressed a very kind letter to Samuel Crowther, in which he gave the following well-deserved commendation:

After having been together for upwards of four months, closely engaged in exploring Central Africa, I cannot allow you to depart without expressing to you in the warmest manner the pleasure I derived from your company and acknowledging the information I have reaped from you. Your long and intimate acquaintance with native tribes, with your general knowledge of their customs, particularly fit you for a journey such as we have now returned from, and I cannot but feel that your advice was always readily granted to me, nor had I ever the smallest reason to repent having followed it. It is nothing more than a simple fact that no slight portion of the success we met in our intercourse with the tribes is due to you.

River Niger now became very important in the minds of the British subjects including the Government. This particular expedition was seen as a total success both from the commercial and missionary standpoint and this great waterway of Niger was now regarded as the gate to the heart of Africa. Samuel Crowther was known by those close to him to be a man of practical mind and it was this same mind that he used in working diligently with the Church and the British Government on any duties assigned to him. During the trip, he saw a future trade in palm oil and also foresaw that the trade would in less time eliminated the slave trade completely from the land of Africa with its accursed train of evils. On the advantages of the increase of palm oil trade Crowther wrote:

"Over that of the slave is so much felt by the people at large that their head chiefs could not help confessing to me that they –aged persons – never remembered any time of the slave trade in which so much wealth was brought into their country as has been since the commencement of the palm oil trade, the last four years; that they were perfectly satisfied with legitimate trade and with the proceedings of the British Government".

His economic intelligence was proved correct by the experiment of cotton growing he established at Abeokuta and his forecast on the produce that if the scheme was given a big push and a large area of land was cultivated, he anticipated no reason why the present export of two million tons from West Africa "might not quadruple itself in the next twenty years, if it be only protected until it has struck its roots a little deeper in the soil of Africa". He also pointed out that up to the present time he had only touched the coast only, and by allowing him to push further up the Niger, he might strike those great caravan routes of the interior and opened up a new world for investment, both in a business and spiritual sense. He therefore recommended a visit being made to Kano, which was then a rich province with its large and prosperous town to which Dr. Barth had already mentioned in his travels. Kano was then the seat of a most valuable cotton cloth industry in the whole black Africa.

Crowther's recommendations were seriously looked into by the British Government because, they all pointed to secured hopes of investment in the future. The Government immediately conferred with Mr. Macgregor, who was then the enterprising African merchant, as to what should be done. The Church Missionary Society on its part conferred with Mr. Laird, who again offered Crowther a free passage up the Niger the third time. Samuel Crowther thankfully accepted this opportunity again seeing it as an avenue to establish a Niger mission, where the services of the African missionaries from Sierra Leone and elsewhere might be useful. He gave many valuable suggestions especially on the intensification of commercial activities and he said: "The first five years the contract was to last should be the seedtime for introducing Christianity and civilization. When trade and agriculture engage the attention of the people, with the gentle and peaceful teaching of Christianity, the minds of the people will gradually be won from war and marauding expeditions to peaceful trade and commerce".

Chapter 11

The Third Expedition & Planting of the Seeds of Christianity along the Banks of Niger in 1858 by Samuel Crowther.

The year 1858 marked some remarkable events for the colonialists in Africa because in 1857, that indefatigable pedestrian and most famous explorer of the time named David Liningstone addressed an audience of young men in Cambridge's Senate House urging upon them an idealistic mission worthy of their attention in Africa. He was preparing to return there and told them, in the hope of making in-road into the continent in anticipation for commerce and Christianity because he wanted the young enthusiasts to continue with his work after his death or when he grows old. As the record showed it, David Livingstone's first involvement with the continent was purely as a missionary, who was sent out to South Africa in 1841 by the London Missionary Society. But in the course of his evangelical duties, he developed interest in other activities that was beyond the responsibilities assigned to him by his society. The challenge that first came to his mind and which actually inspired him was to establish mission stations further north into the unexpected interior of the continent.

This challenge actually opened the wide doors of the continent to him and allowed him to see clearly the source of the continent's slave trading activities where the victims are captured by their fellow brothers for sale to the Arab traders who will in turn dispatch them to markets on the coast. Livingstone was convinced that this pernicious trade will only be suppressed if other trading means or routes, along which European goods could reach the interior of the continent, would definitely provide the basis for new and different trading activities and thereby totally exterminated the human trafficking. He then thought it wisely that along such routes missionaries too will travel benefiting the African's spiritual as well as their material needs – hence "Commerce and Christianity". Before his ideas could be realized in finding such means and routes, it must require from the skills of people like David Livingstone, Samuel Crowther and others for which they all became renowned and famous.

Samuel Crowther and David Livingstone trod the same path in ideas and crossed each other very constantly. The reason may be attributed to an act of God or to the similarity in the background of both of them. Their early lives were in a small way not completely dissimilar. Crowther was rescued from the slave ship and given an education that opened an unprecedented new world for him. Livingstone from his own background was reared at Blantyre, Lanarkshire, in a Scottish industrial poverty and had raised himself to the threshold of greatness with the aid of his Latin grammer and dogged attendance at night school after his shift in the factory. Interestingly David Livingstone was sitting in the audience at the popular Exeter Hall meeting of 1840 in that summer when the expedition plans of 1841 in which Crowther was drilled to represent the Church Missionary Society upon the River Niger were made public with such a fervent flourish.

In the catalogue of African development, there was no one that matches Crowther and Livingstone in the breadth of their interests, or in their ability to write at length and with enormous detail upon African topography, linquistics, culture and people. David Livingstone in his own case was by far the most comprehensive source of information on South Central Africa. He was a very sound botanist, zoologist, medical doctor and great anthropologist. It was said about him that up to a few days before his legendary death at Ilala, he was still making his customary notes about new fishes, animals and plants he had just seen.

The third Niger expedition was not accidental. It was as a result of the success recorded in the second expedition of 1854 and the recommendations of Samuel Crowther about the voyage that prompted the British Government to set in motion this third expedition that was later to be labeled the "New era of commercial history of West Africa". In the immediate past both the British and French Governments had placed their interests in West Africa not on slavery business but on the ways to eradicate it. This common and joint agenda in this direction prompted the British Government to establish Sierra Leone as a settlement for freed slaves and similarly the French adopted the copy of the scheme with the same name in founding Liberville on the estuary of the Gabon River in the 1840s.

The time to reap the profits of their past labors had now come particularly the British when the results of the Niger exploration begun to show green light. On 29 June 1858, another vessel named *Dayspring* was put on this great river again to sail out from Fernando Po with the old colleagues and experienced explorers in persons of Dr. Baikie and Samuel Crowther. Dr. Baikie was appointed by the Government to head and lead the exploration while Samuel Crowther took the position of missionary head and leader of the missionary group of the expedition. Although the recent death of Bishop Weeks and the two other missionaries Messrs. Beale and Frey who were close friends and mentors of Crowther since he was rescued as a slave boy weakened his soul and body, but hence he had spiritual obligations and duties to perform, there was nothing he could do other than to pray to God to reenergize his spirit to the fullest in this mission. He gladly accepted the challenge and he was ushered into the ship with great cheers from colleagues and spectators on the shore. *Dayspring* pulled itself out of the anchorage and rolled into the waters and began its journey on the highways of the great African River Niger.

On this trip with Crowther was Mr. J. C. Taylor (later Rev. J. C. Taylor) another native clergyman, who was born in Sierra Leone to the family of a liberated slave from Ibo country. Also on the trip was Simon Jonas an old voyage colleague from the previous expedition and a trust worthy person. Crowther now being an experienced man voyaging along this route, he had already mastered every bit of the journey and quite able to map out his strategies and programs of where necessary to visit and who to meet. On this trip he wanted to extend his evangelical journey up the north to include such towns like Kano, Rabbah and Sokoto. He anticipated to face some problems in this direction because he knew that he was to cross the border of religious lines when he would meet and speak to the die-hearted Mohammedans of very many years of religious faith and wanted to introduce to them another religious doctrine quite different and opposite to their own belief. Crowther was always a prepared man who was ready to face any challenge of life that comes his ways and under any situation. On this particular issue, he wrote the followings in his journal:

I have thought it advisable, with a view of making favorable impressions on the minds of the Mohammedan population through whose country we shall pass to Sokoto and Ilorin, to engage Kasumu, a Yoruba Mohammedan and liberated African, who has been an Arabic teacher for many years, to accompany me on my travels. Kasumu has ever appreciated the benevolence of the British Government on behalf of Africa, nor less so the labors of the Church Missionary Society in converting the heathen from idolatry to the worship of the true God. Such a man will do a vast deal in softening the bigotry and prejudice of men of his persuasion. The beginning of our missionary operations under Mohammedan government should not be disputes about the truth or falsehood of one religion or another, but we should aim at toleration, to be permitted to reach their heathen subjects the religion we profess.

Crowther's way of approach to this delicate issue symbolized a great level of experience he had in his bank of knowledge. It was an issue that could tear down the already built walls during the previous travels if not carefully and wisely handled from the drawing table to the construction field. He was the type of man that could not be carried away on a mere wave of impulse and this character trait testified to his indomitable spirit of perseverance that always kept him going with his heart in stability and doing his things according to the dictates and instructions of the Almighty God he serves. Since he was captured as a slave boy, freed as a liberated person, thought in the direction of wisdom, and was able to know the type of peaceful mind endowed to a free man as compared to one living under oppression, he would have promised himself that whatever kind of opportunity he has to upgrade the lives of other African brothers and sisters still living under the oppressions of their masters or those living under the illusions of the dark-ages, he would do it with every power that lies in his hands. It was out of this philosophical thinking that he hoped to establish native churches in Africa, with native clergymen duly trained and equipped at their heads and minister to their own people in their mother tongues.

Crowther's attitude was similar to that of a Japanese man from patriotic standpoint of "How will this profit Japan?" instead of "How will this profit me alone?" Back home in Sierra Leone, Crowther, already perceived the bad odor of the meal of disunity being cooked on the stove among the various missionary societies that were fostering the evil of competition with each other. Whereas he saw the spread of the Gospel as something very important and helpful to the rebuilding of the dilapidated walls of unity that slave trading brought into the continent and ruined the growth of the people. As a great philosopher Crowther wrote this about this sort of cankerworm that was beginning to find its ways into the fabrics of the new converts:

At Sierra Leone this unavoidable evil has gone to a great extent, and it has been unhappily introduced into the newly established Yoruba Mission, where it has already begun to cause strife and disparagement of one another's church connection among the newly-converted natives belonging to the different missionary societies. This does no good in a new mission field either to the new converts or to the unconverted native population, and has caused us many sorrowful days and weeks.

It is the utmost importance that timely measures should be adopted by the great societies, whose sole and benevolent object is the conversion of the heathen to Christianity, and to do this effectually and with greater success than hitherto they should, and ought to, work separately for the extension of the Church of Christ. Why should not this generous-hearted proposal be as applicable to Christian missions as to the settlements of Abraham and Lot?

Is not the whole land before thee? Separate thyself, I pray thee, from me. It thou wilt take the left hand, then I will go to the right; or if thou wilt depart to the right hand, then I will go to the left.

Crowther did not allow the attitude of his people to give him any setback in his stride to move forward. The *Dayspring* was now well on her way and had touched at a village of the Brass country in the neighborhood of where it was believed that Mr. Carr and his servant were mysteriously disappeared some years back. In this region Crowther now noticed very rapid changes in the mode of dressing and the life style of the people compared to the last visit when the inhabitants were found to be much degraded. The effect of palm oil trading was significantly seen here from the wearing of Manchester made shirts to hundreds of Brass canoes loaded with palm oil produce paddling to and fro the great river for trading purposes. He was highly excited and delighted to see that the effect of legal trading was now gaining ground among his people and that the establishment of missionary posts here should no more be delayed further. For this purpose Crowther immediately begun to sort consultations and negotiations with the chiefs and the headmen of the region until he succeeded in securing land whereon the new mission would be built. The next place they reached was Ossamare where the people were happy to receive them with gladness and overwhelming joy and another mission post was established here too.

Progressively in the journey they reached Onitsha, which was an important trading town in Ibo country and where the people took sheer fright at the appearance of white men because that was the first time ever they would see white colored people in their life time. Crowther remarked that it took them some time to persuade them to lay down their defensive weapons and agreed to cordial and friendly discussions. Eventually he said that one of the people boldly agreed to lead them through the groves of bombax, coconut, palm trees and some plantations to the town itself, which he also described as a beautifully built and situated at about one hundred feet above the Niger level. Onitsha being a local commercial nerve center of this region in the past, the group decided to use the existing opportunity to establish a factory there. At the palace of the King where the monarch addressed his people for cooperation with the visitors, Dr. Baikie and Captain Grant requested for a factory site while Crowther mentioned his own request for a mission site.

He was happy to introduce to them Mr. Taylor who was of Ibo nation by birth as the religious teacher who was to teach the children how to read and write the English letters. And if they cooperate with him, many more teachers would be sent to live with them. The people were happy to see their own son being a teacher to teach them the new way of life and new religion that would improve and transform their standard of living and civilize them. At the palace and in appreciation to show the visitors of the people's consent to all negotiations and discussions, traditional guns (Muskets) were fired in accordance to the people's customs and tradition. To zeal up the agreement, a man stepped forward and said openly on behalf of the crowd that it was felt that the white men's proposals and the King's wishes were for the good of their country.

After the palace meeting, the party moved into the town in search of, suitable site for the factory, the mission house and a temporary dwelling place for Mr. Taylor to live. The dwelling houses of those days had different architectural designs and needs, as they were nothing to be compared with what we have today. In any case they were able to find a little square room at the price of six pieces of romal handkerchiefs at five shillings a piece totaling thirty shillings for an indefinite period perhaps for the duration of the time that the mission house would be built at its permanent place. The Sierra Leone cathechists on the trip and Simon Jonas were left behind to clean up this mud house for habitation to serve as Taylor's living place. On account of this success, Crowther wrote:

While they were doing this we took a stroll about the town, to know the extent of it, as well as to make acquaintances. We paid a visit to four groups of houses, the chiefs of which expressed their great joy at our establishments among them. The town of Onitsha is about a mile in length, if not more, which is divided into two sections. On either side are groups of houses, a little remote from the high road, and ruled by heads of familiar or inferior chiefs. Both sides of the road are either covered with bushes or plantations till you come to an open road leading to a group of houses further back; but some of the groups are close and open to the high road, where also a market is held occasionally. In the afternoon we returned on board, thankful for the success God had granted to us, though we felt fatigued after a few days exertions. The whole of yesterday and today was a very busy time about Onitsha; goods were landed, bushes were cleared, and sticks cut for the construction of the factory shed; the botanist and naturalist took their departments in the fields; while some of the naval gentlemen, not content to go out in the dawn of the morning to lie in wait for the hippopotami in their hitherto undisturbed hunts, pitched their tent in the immediate neighborhood of these amphibious quadrupeds, if possible to shoot one of them at the same time they were pursuing their nautical observations; but the mosquitoes, the universal pest of the rivers, did not leave them unmolested during their nightly watch.

A situation of remarkable interest happened when the visiting Christian party was going round the town to acquaint themselves with the people and the environment. They got to a place where they saw people dressed very gaily in their best jubilating and marrying and out of curiosity Crowther wanted to know what was going on. During his enquiry, he was told that the jubilation was to mark the final burial ceremony of a member of the family who had just passed away. Other information gathered revealed to Crowther that a human sacrifice was to be made at the end of the ceremony and this terrible act arouse the indignation of Crowther and in the presence of the crowd of people that was jubilating, Crowther protested against this horrible and barbaric act. The victim to be used was a blameless female slave.

During the dialog that ensued between Crowther and the head of the family, the head of the family requested that Crowther should purchase the woman for the price of a bullock they would use in her stead but Crowther declined and continued to talk to them why it should no longer be part of the people's culture to use human sacrifice for the final burial of an already dead person. He told them that the new religion just coming to them detested such barbaric custom and through his wise pleading and counseling, it was discovered that the poor woman's life was spared and she was loosened from her bonds. Before they left Onitsha, Crowther was sure that he received words of assurance from the King and his chiefs that human sacrifice of any form or kind would be stamped out completely and that they would absolve all visitors from the white man's country from the native laws, which do not permit any stranger to sit on any mat or wooden seats in the King's court.

Finally Crowther left with them Mr. Taylor, Simon Jonas and three young traders from Sierra Leone to now make Onitsha their new and permanent home where they were to begin the heavy works placed on their shoulders. He bided them goodbye with prayers that the blessings of God would be their joy and stay. It should be noted that this was the first seed of a purely native missionary establishment planted as the offshoot of the colony of Sierra Leone. For early economic prosperity and the safety of the Europeans coming to this part of Africa to settle for the first time and against an attack by the natives in the interior, they chose to place the Yoruba mission under the guidance and teaching of the Europeans while the interior mission was left to the Africans to manage. Because of this political gimmick, the African clergymen of this time saw the big burden placed on their shoulders as a challenge to find ways of how to rescue their people themselves. The challenge actually energized their both mental and spiritual intelligence and with the spirit of the Lord on their side, they actually succeeded. Their leader Samuel Crowther rejoiced in the spirit of the Lord that gave them the wisdom and who made it possible for him and his team to begin God's work from the interior and about this topic he thus wrote:

Mr. Taylor has to break open the fallow ground and to sow the seed of a future bountiful harvest among the people of his fatherland. May this be the beginning of a rapid over-spread of Christianity in the countries of the banks of the Niger and in the heart of Africa through the native agents! In parting with his colleague Crowther gave him much valuable advice. "Though we are about to separate for a season, dear brother, yet you are not alone. Lo, I am with you always is the faithful promise of the Lord of the harvest to His disciples; this will also be realized concerning us…….. Your ministerial duties will be very simple and plain. You will have to teach more by conversation when you visit the people or they visit you, at the beginning, than be direct service. Be instant in season and out of season. May the Lord give you wisdom to win souls to Himself! You will need much patience to bear and forebear with the ignorance and simplicity of the people, they are like babes……. Be not disappointed if you find the people do not act as to their engagement; it is rather a matter of surprise that they do so much. They must be taught the lesson of justice, and that by your own example."

With the strategic location of Onitsha among the Iboland, Crowther was quite right to have chosen this place as the headquarters of the Ibo missionary unit of his Society. He left the town with full realization of his call to duty and the *Dayspring* was now on its way to Idda where they were told of the death of the old Attah, which called for rivalry among the people claiming right to the throne. The people of this region had been fully epitomized in the religion of Islam and because of this the King – Attah was always shielded away from this new group each time an attempt was made to meet with him. During the previous expedition, the party leader Captain Trotter was not allowed to meet with the old Attah and this time again, Crowther too was barred by the head of eunuch who placed barrier on their way of seeing the new Attah.

Notwithstanding, this obstacle was removed by some string of royal notables who came to plead with the team in their ship the next day after the palava with the head eunuch at the King's courtyard and a new appointment date was reached for the team to meet with the King. During their interview with the young monarch, he promised the party that he would follow his father's footsteps regarding his friendship with the white men. What impressed Crowther most here was when they interviewed a number of Mohammedans and some portions of the Koran were read aloud fluently without reading those passages from the Holy Book but from memory by one of the Islamic scholars in attendance. Crowther's comments of this splendid rehearsal were as follows:

The further we go the more convinced I am of the necessity of introducing the study of Arabic into our institutions at Sierra Leone. What advantage it would have given if any one of the Christian teachers would also have stepped forward and read a few verses out of his Arabic Bible! Such capability would place the teachers of the Anasaras in a much more prominent position among these self-conceited people. Beside this, I believe in this part of Africa, where the knowledge of Arabic is so imperfectly known, the use of the Arabic character, combined with teaching in Roman or Italic characters in the native tongues, would be the means of counterbalancing the rapid spread of Mohammedanism among the rising generation. But so long as the use of the Arabic character is excluded from our schools and left to the use of the ignorant followers of Mohammed alone, they will take advantage of this to continue their deception upon the ignorant heathen by holding these letters as more holy than any others in the world; but by these characters being brought into common use their artful cheat would be laid open.

On 9 September 1858, the team arrived at the confluence of the Kwarra and Kaduna rivers and at sunset they anchored off the ruins of Gbara, the former capital of Nupe, which was reduced to a village of potters. This ruined city used to be the old home of Mr. Crook, the party's Nupe interpreter. When they got to his former city of birth, he was naturally very excited to be there after a long period of absence of forty-five years. One of the most crucial moments of the journey was about to come when they were approaching Wuyagi, the landing-place for the camp at Bida. This was the place that Crowther was to meet the great Fulani King, Sumo Zaki and Dasaba his war general, upon which interview with them lied the future of the mission enterprise around this huge territory.

On landing, some horses were sent for their use and they immediately made their ways to the King's courtyard to meet the King, Sumo Saki. The king was said to be a man of about forty years old, and of exceedingly cordial manner. His Majesty welcomed his visitors with warm handshake and treated them to sit on the special mats prepared for their arrival. In his welcome address, the Monarch expressed his joy and believed that their visit was not of his own making but it was God who directed them to visit him. He granted all the requests put forward to him by his visitors respecting trade and missionary establishment in his kingdom.

Dr. Baikie and Crowther narrated the purpose of the expedition to the Monarch in clear terms. Crowther told him that they had come to see the state and the population of the region for the purpose of establishing trade and the teaching of his people the religion of Anasara. The Monarch at once gave his full consent and said that he would provide them with a place at Rabba and they were permitted to trade in all parts of the river with his permission and protection as far as his influence and authority extended. After he was presented with the Royal gift specially prepared for him as a token of friendship, he was so much pleased and happy with the gift and requested them to see Dasaba in his own courtyard, which was said to be located at a distance of about half a mile from the King's palace.

Dasaba, the generalissimo of the territory was the half brother of the

King and when he was met, he was assumed to be a man of between forty and fifty years of age and appeared to be a person of lively disposition and humorous in manner. He welcomed them with open mind and great salutations. The party as usual narrated the intentions of their visit to their country and he was pleased with their explanations. He was quite agreeable to everything that his brother had agreed to, as he gave the first place to him and made his brother's wishes his own. At the end of the visit, he presented the party with a live cow; but when he had received the token present delivered to him by Dr. Baikie, he was so much excited and pleased that he added a sheep, lots of yams, and a port of palm oil to the previous cow he had given to them.

The visit did not go down well without negative reactions from people of fanatic religious belief. It had been circulated around the country and believed that as the Anasaras do not belong to the religion of Mohammed they cannot be friendly with the people of that faith, and that they cannot bear the sight of a Mohammedan praying in the name of Mohammed, whom his followers believed to be the true prophet of God. When Crowther was confronted with this question, he was glad to tell them the good and true relationship that had been existing between the Christian members of his team and people like Abdul Kadu, the Foota Toro interpreter and Kasumu, a Yoruba man, both of whom were Mohammedans and tolerable Arabic scholars in their company respecting the type of treatment they received on board.

Dr. Baikie

The Monarch and his council members were astonished to hear from these men of their own persuasion that they were treated with the utmost kindness, respect and none of them in the least put any obstacle in the way of their performing their religious obligations and rights. The open confession from these people wet down their appetites of confusion and hatred as they begun to reverse from their former opinions about the Anasaras. Crowther in the end contended that Mohammedans can never be brought round by his religion being quarreled with and abusively charged with falsehood and imposition, but by kind treatment he may be led to read and study the Christian's Bible, which by the blessing of God may lead him from the error of his way.

The journey continued until they reached Rabbah where they found out that the place was directly on the caravan route between Kano and Yoruba country, and as well the halting camp for those traveling to Ilorin, a great stronghold of Mohammedanism inside Yoruba Kingdom. One of the native members of the party - Joe died here of an illness connected with self-poisoned when he ate some roots mistaken for cassava and he was buried by Crowther on the high cliff. The following day they met with some Borgu and Yoruba traders in an area close to Jebba who were trading with Ashanti business people and who later told Crowther that they knew the spot where Mungo Park's boat was wrecked, and of which their fathers used to tell them that the boat was built of brass at the bow and the inside was full of sharp irons. This piece of information aroused the interest of Crowther and he began to entertain the hope that he would like to see this place, which was associated with this great explorer.

But unfortunately *Dayspring* was now running into a big problem when it struck one of the steep rocks that drifted it away from its course and thereby making it to leak rapidly. Very shortly the boat was now grounding to the bottom of the river. As there was nothing any one can do to rescue the ugly situation, they all waited to watch their devoted vessel wrecking and drifting down the river. All they could do was to collect those possible things and carry them to the shore, with the help of friendly canoes trading on the river. The story further had it that all of them passed the night under a very heavy tornado of wind and rain sweeping over them without shelter, except their rain coats and umbrellas. Every hope was now lost about the ship and the Captain decided to abandon it and sent a messenger down to the confluence to look for *Sunbeam* a ship that was suppose to follow them as a relief vessel and to tell the sailors of their present predicaments.

In the meantime, they were to live by the shore only at the mercy of the friendly natives who brings them food to eat. The doors to the outside world were now closed on them, as there was no information coming in or going out. But fortunately or miraculously for them, on one cool afternoon, they suddenly received a visitor who told them that he heard of their misfortunes through the native traders trading on the river and this visitor was an American missionary the Rev. M. Clark living around the area. On his way to them, he brought with him some sugar, tea, and coffee which Crowther said he regarded as the most valuable present they had received during this journey because since their misfortune begun, they had been living on parched Indian corn, sweetened with honey for many past weeks. It was at this temporary place of abode at the shore of river Niger that the members of the party spent the Christmas day of that year with the problems resting on their shoulders plus the faith that solutions to their problems would certainly come.

The spirit of the Lord was with them in their new location in the heart of Africa, as the sojourners had no alternative only to wait on the Lord to rescue them. In this land Samuel Crowther was effectively making use of every minute that passed in talking to the people either on the land or in canoes about the new religion of the Anasaras and the profits that it carried if embraced. As might be expected, the new religion had its own enemies and these were the slave traders who begun to circulate false reports about the white men, and doing their utmost to poison the minds of the Kings, the chiefs and the noble people that were still benefiting from the illegal business against this new religion. But instead, the work was progressing especially through the interests, efforts and commitments of the women folk in every community they had visited. Crowther noted in his diary that these women were the most industrious part of the population that had to suffer most, as well as work the hardest. His true picture about this subject plus the curious system that these women had when they had to pawn their children in order to escape slavery is worth mentioning here out of pity from his journal:

A great deal of labor is entailed on the women; on them solely devolves the care of the children, to feed and clothe from childhood until they are able to render their mothers a little assistance if they are females, or if they are boys, till the fathers claim their help in the farms if they be farmers. With such a charge upon them, without help, having to labor hard in bearing burdens – for they are the chief carriers of loads, grinding corn upon the millstones many times till late hours of the night, beguiling labor by their mill with songs, which labor is resumed at an early hour of the morning, preparing the flour into meal, retailing the same in the market, or hawking it about the town from house to house, and providing their husbands with provisions for it – it is no wonder that they are soon warn out, and a female of thirty years has an appearance of forty. The most distressing part of the whole is that in time of war, when these poor women are unfortunately enough not only to lose their own liberty, but also that of their children, the additional care of procuring a ransom for themselves and their children adds tenfold more to their already heavy burdens. During the war which terminated in the subjugation, Umoru and thousands of families had been brought into slavery by it, which added not a little to their painful toil. Very little is done by the husband to ransom so many wives and children; the consequence is every woman must see after herself and her children the best way she can to prevent their being sold into foreign service. Hence they have no other means but to have recourse to the system of pawning, as it is done in Yoruba. One example here will suffice. Fatima, the aged mother of our good friend Dagenna, the Galadima at Ghebe at the Confluence, was met here living in the village of Kawura, about a day's journey from Rabba. She had the misfortune to have three nieces under her care, who were cut during the Umoru war. Her son being afar off at the Confluence, she had no help; there was no alternative; these children were to be sold northward by way of the desert, or westward down to the coast, if they were not forthwith ransomed. In this dilemma she could not do otherwise that sell all she had that was saleable, and then have recourse to a loan of cowries to make up the amount required. Two of the children were put in pawn for 20,000 cowries each – their labor was taken for the interest till the principal could be paid – and she herself was pawned for another 20,000, for which she had to pay the interest of 30 cowries a day, making 210 cowries per week. Since we had been cast up here she had been actively at work, selling yams, rice, rice flour, and such articles as were needed, and by small helps from us she had almost cleared up her debts when I last saw her. We should have been glad to release her at once in consideration of the assistance we had so many times received from her son if our means could have admitted of so doing.

The people of the continent should pay special thanks to our mothers in the dark ages for the credible role they played in the upholding the dignity of the people and in the transformation system of our society in the past. We should always put them on the honors card in the historical shelves of every nation of the African continent. If not because of the role they played with their steadfastness, plus the love and the security walls they provided for the safety of their families and the nations, there would not have been any trait of peace and happiness in the land either yesterday or today. Honestly speaking the role played by our women of the past deserves a big applause of cheer from us all.

In October 1858, the long awaited relief vessel, the *Sunbeam* arrived at last and all the members of the party including Crowther were taken on board. But it was not an easy thing for Crowther and his men to depart just like that from the place where they took shelter for two years. He said a big thanks and welfare to the chiefs, the people, and the mission he established during their sojourn in this wonderland. In fact he was glad that not even a second had been lost because his stay here afforded him to know his people better than what he taught of them in the past. *Sunbeam* was now returning back home through which way it came and as it stopped at Onitsha, Mr. Taylor was happy to be rejoined with Crowther – his compatriot in the blessing of Christ. Taylor had been working very hard with marked success in his station. The new mission house was now completed and many converts were gained into the side of Jesus Christ, as they were anxious to learn new things from the missionaries. Crowther decided to wait behind at Onitsha to work with Taylor for sometime while others in the party left in the ship to the coast.

After his short stay at Onitsha, Crowther started his journey back to the Confluence in a native canoe where he had much difficulties with a crew he could not managed, but had to put up with him until he had a relief to himself when in the end he finally reached Idda. His trip from Idda to Rabba was an eventful journey to him because during this journey, he met with lots of difficulties and dangerous situations from the canoe-man and the weather; but his tact and courage stood him in good stead. When he got to Rabba, he was told that Sumo Zaki – the King had passed away and that Dasaba was now the new King of Nupe. But Dasaba was at this time fighting for his throne against the Gbaris and the internal rift in the territory curtailed the stay of Crowther in Rabba. Instead he started his overland expedition on foot from Rabba to Abeokuta. The story of this piece of journey had it that he was ill with dysentery, which he attributed to the long exposure and constant worry in open canoe on his journey to Rabba.

On foot, he made his journey from Rabba to Ilorin under such terrible condition of health and on reaching Ilorin, the King and the chief mallam warmly received him. At Ilorin, he addressed a large crowd of people on the subject of Christ being the only Son of God and that if the new religion is embraced, the benefits attached to it is over whelming. He left Ilorin on his way back to Abeokuta in the usual manner of trecking through the bushes that was abound in everywhere in the Yoruba country of that time. After a weary and tiresome journey, he reached Abeokuta in good health, spirit and he was met and welcomed by the Bishop and Dr. Baikie, who had just arrived from Lagos.

In his welcome address to the old and the new converts since he left Abeokuta for the glorious journey, he thanked God for the strength and skills that He had given to everyone in the mission for the good works they had done since he was away from them. He was very happy to see the progress made during this short period of time. It was actually a heroic welcome for him by his people in appreciation to the gallant courage and leadership role he had demonstrated during his trip to the countries of the Mohammedans. He did not stay too long with them here because he was eager to travel to Lagos to meet his wife and children he had left for almost three years.

Again Crowther was scheduled to travel back up the Niger in the summer of 1859 on board the *Rainbow* but disappointedly the passage was stopped at the Confluence through the message sent to the voyage leader by Dr. Baikie that no missionary work could be undertaken. *Rainbow* had to return to the coast. But on its way back from the Confluence, the vessel was shot at by some natives of the Delta; and two of its crewmembers were killed. This incident had to stop any voyage on River Niger for two years and during this period, all the stations that Crowther had opened along the route were left on their own to grow and suffer. Crowther had to stay at the mouth of the Nun waiting for the gunboat that was to be sent from England to punish the villagers from where the gunshots were fired at *Rainbow*.

In July 1861, H.M.S. *Espoir* sailed on the Niger to destroy those places where guns were fired at its sister vessel – *Rainbow* and Crowther was on board the vessel with two native helpers to replace some of those that were sent there during the last trip. While he was waiting for Espoir at the mouth of Nun, he opened a new mission station at Akassa and in the following season he prepared a large group of thirty-three native teachers, with their wives and children, for the Niger mission. This group led by Crowther was taken on board another gunboat, H.M.S. *Investigator,* which reached Onitsha on 5 September 1862, but he could not come out of the ship to see the mission works at Onitsha because of the timetable of the gunboat or by the instructions given to the Captain of the ship. In any event, he reached the Confluence and went ashore at Ghebe. The people were happy and overwhelmed with joy to see this faithful minister of God who first spoke to them about the only God in existence both in heaven and on the earth. It was at Ghebe that Crowther saw the first fruits of his labor in this region when he baptized eight adults and one infant in the new chapel and in the presence of a congregation of one hundred and ninety-two persons, who sat still with their mouths open in wonder and amazement at the invitation of their friends and companions into a new religion by a singular rite.

These nine persons were the first fruits of the Niger mission and they represented several tribes of large tracts of territories on the banks of the Niger and towns from Tshadda, Igaru, Igbira, Gbari, Eki, or Bann communities and even a Yoruba man was among them. Samuel Crowther had always been a successful person in winning the confidence of the native potentates. He always impressed upon them that the Christian religion was not war-like type but the type that teaches the truth and encourage the people, for their own advantage; to engage them in the trading relationship with the people of the outside world and to develop their nations along the lines of other developed nations of the world.

It was recorded in the book of memory of the people of Ghebe that when Ama Abokko, the King of Ghebe was on his deathbed, and was giving his last instructions to his head chiefs concerning his children and the government of the town after his death, he told them that he did not forget Crowther and his fellow helpers in the mission, saying, "suffer nothing to harm Oibo's – colored people; because they are my strangers". But unfortunately when the King died, his country was thrown into chaos, confusions and anarchy. In the midst of these confusions, the mission premises were entirely destroyed and this prompted the authority to move the mission from its site in Ghebe to Lokoja.

Chapter 12

Bishop Crowther's Missionary Works at Abeokuta:

The history of the city of Abeokuta – a city that was built under the rock is not the concern of this book but to be left to the great Yoruba historians of our time to tell. Almost all the cities of the Yoruba kingdom including Abeokuta enjoyed the devastating raids of the Foulah in search of slaves to be transported to the coast for an exchange for material produce from the white man's country. It should be noted that the cities that were located along their caravan routes suffered most because they incessantly carry out their raids on these cities and towns for possible catch if not on their way going but on their way back from the slave market on the coast. The devastating effect was that the houses built around this time were built with local materials of bamboo sticks, palm leaves and tall grasses, which would normally help to engulf the houses very quickly when, set on fire by the Foulas. This was what happened in the case of Oshogun Crowther's town that was rebuilt twice as a result of the destruction afflicted on it by the raiders making it difficult for anyone to identify the particular site of the place that was associated with his happy childhood's days. The effect of such raids left so many populous cities and towns of Yoruba country desolated and could never reappear again on the maps.

It is believed that the same situation prompted the Egbas to seek refuge under the rock of Olumo. During the time of any raid in any city, town or village, it was apparent that the natives would run hither and thither in order to escape from the slave hunters, and where ever they could possibly found themselves would now become their permanent place of abode and equally whosoever they found around them in these hidden shelters would also become their neighbors, families and friends. Abeokuta under this devastating situation was no exception. The story had it that the caves under the Olumo rock were formally used as a hidden place for notorious people of the time because they could not freely live among the peaceful people of the city. It is as well obvious that when the city was at its full swing, it was only the robbers or sane people that would ever think of hiding themselves in the isolated caves in the rock for protection.

But now that the raiders had waged war against the people of the Egbas, they had nowhere to run to except to hide themselves in the caves. They were living here until others from the neighboring towns and villages began to join the first inhabitants in the caves, sharing their hardships and their safety together. As time went by, they began to grow in population, strength and bravery; some brave ones among their men began to form themselves into battalion comprising many companies for the defense of their new territory. Sometime they would send out a company to travel to the nearest villages to buy little seeds of Indian corn for food and planting at the foot of the boulders of Olumo. In the course of few years later, a large community, comprising a number of tribes and clans began to emerge with its own war captain, judge, and code of laws brought with them from where they originally came to settle together under the safety shades of Olumo rock.

The caves could no longer contain them as they were rapidly increasing in population and the best thing to do for them was to come out of the caves and started building houses around the rock. Prosperity had now waited upon security, and soon they named their new place of abode Abeokuta – meaning under the rock/stone. The early Government of the new settlers was rested on the shoulders of a brave, courageous and an enlightened ruler named Shodeke, his chiefs or mayors called the Ogbonis, and the war generals called the Baloguns. For effective administration, these groups of authorities usually meet with the ruler at Ake palace, which was then the sit of the government with Shodeke presiding as its head. Progressively the city was expanding and growing in population and industries. The unity of interest among the people gave strength to the new settlement, and they were now able to organize themselves into such a formidable and strong military organization to defend their people and the city against any serious attacks from outside enemies.

Egbaland in the past used to be one of the popular slave trade routes to the coast and as such many of its sons and daughters were an easy target for the traders to capture. But during the reign of Shodeke, the slave trading was now abolished internationally and the British war ships with the big guns mounted on them were now cruising on the sea to capture any vessel carrying human cargo abroad. As a result of this British action, news were reaching Abeokuta that some of their sons and daughters that were formally sold into slavery were now being rescued and living under the British protection in Sierra Leone. From both sides there arose fervent longings to meet each other again, but how this meeting was to become reality was a misery to everyone. Incidentally in 1839, some group of liberated slaves now trading legally in Sierra Leone bought an old slave ship from the Government and laden it with goods and sailed to Badagry, which was the nearest port to them.

At Badagry, they met with so many of their Yoruba kin and kiths and it was a happy reunion for those who could still recognize each other. Some strong minded adventurers in this group carried on their trading adventure further down to Lagos while the Egbas amongst them decided to travel on foot for many miles under strenuous conditions to Abeokuta through flat lands that were covered with thick jungles, swampy or marshy areas covered with tall grasses, and sometime through fairly large rivers. On their journey, they would reach the undulating region that was bright with flowers and shaded with groves of palm trees and large trees. They would sometime stay under the large trees to rest or do same after crossing the rivers or streams.

They would now pitifully pass through the blackened ruins of the towns, which the enemies had destroyed during their raids. As they approached Abeokuta they now noticed signs of cultivation and industry, farms with poultry, and men quite busy with their individual professions everywhere. Once again these people would pass through the beautiful banks of their respected Ogun River with its luxuriant foliage that would usher them into the gates of their glorious city for the first time after they had left their home base. On entering the gates, they all raised their voices in high spirit to thank their God, raised their hands in jubilation to greet their city with shouts of joy. This was how the exodus of the liberated Yoruba citizens living in Sierra Leone started their journey back home in earnest.

Inside the city everyone of them was eagerly busy looking for their relatives and friends they had left behind; and where ever it was possible to meet with any, they would clasped unto each other and began to tell their wonderful and astonishing stories about the ordeals they went through either when they had their shelter under the Olumo rock, in the slave markets, or in the slave ships. After the emotional cries and joys the visitors would promptly jump unto the discussions about the missionaries that saved them from the hands of the slave traders and who taught them out of the book of God concerning the true and the only God that abounds in heaven and throughout the universe. The exodus of the Egba natives coming back to their native place ignited two major areas of issue concerning the early development of Christianity in this region.

The first one was that this new group of liberated slaves that had been taught by the missionaries in the culture of their crafts and the Gospel propagation about Jesus Christ helped to expand the scope of the new religion amongst their people by the way of seeing their lifestyle as practical example to others. The second one was the fear entertained by the missionary authorities themselves in Sierra Leone thinking that by means of this mass transit of people to Abeokuta, the people they had spent time and money to develop might possibly relapse again into the dark practice of heathenism and this new situation was fraught with danger.

On account of this suspicion, the Sierra Leone church authority sent a petition to their headquarters in London asking for spiritual leaders to accompany them on their journey back home. As a result of this request, Mr. Henry Townsend who was then a very promising and an articulate young missionary was asked to visit Abeokuta on fact finding enquiry with his party composed of the members from Sierra Leone church organization. The journey from Sierra Leone to Abeokuta around this time would take several days or weeks with many untold hardships and sufferings both on waters and on the land. The travelers would only be too lucky to find a place of shelter when the night came in and when there was none, they would have to make a shift bed mostly under the foot of big trees in the jungle or on flat places over the rocks.

This was part of the suffering situations that the early missionaries that brought Christianity to us in this part of the world faced. Mr. Townsend reported in his journal about the evangelical discussions he had with a large group of natives that gathered to listen to him during one of his evening service he held at a stopping place along the route on his way to Abeokuta. He thus reported: I said, "Do you know the true God who made us all and preserves us day by day?" The people answered "No, but we heard about ten years ago that white men knew Him, and we have wished they would come and teach us." He asked, "Do you want to know Him?" They replied, "Yes." "Then you must ask God to send you teachers, and He will send them to teach and lead you in the right way of God." They arose, and lifting up their hands saying, "O God, send us teachers to teach us about Thee."

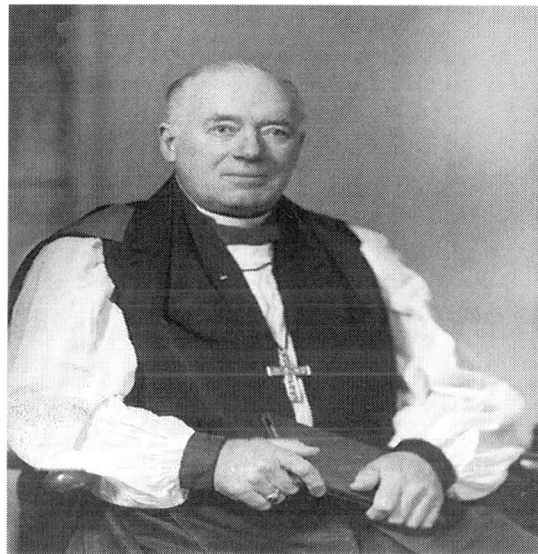

Townsend

One thing that is certain is that if in actual fact that it is God Himself that sends one an errand, He will definitely provide every needed materials to use in accomplishing such errand to the amusement of every generation. This was happened to Mr. Townsend and his team when they arrived at Abeokuta after a very strenuous and unpleasant journey. The party was warmly received with great kindness and joy by the king – Shodeke and his chiefs. Shodeke as part of his own contribution and security of the visitors allowed his palace to be used as a place of worship where the missionaries started their church services in Abeokuta. In addition he promised them of his moral support, land and hospitality to any number of missionaries that they might wish to send to them in the future. In 1843, Townsend returned to Sierra Leone with good report and afterwards traveled to England where he was ordained as a priest by Bishop Blomfield and sent back again to Abeokuta to establish a mission there.

The beginning of Abeokuta mission received the blessings of both Sierra Leone and England from the spiritual side to financial support. On Rev. Townsend's return to Sierra Leone, he began to prepare a strong and large missionary party that would accompany him on his mission to Abeokuta. In this party were two Europeans – the Rev. C. A. and Mrs. Gollmer and Rev. Henry and Mrs. Townsend; The Rev. Samuel and Mrs.

Crowther, with their two little children; Mr. Phillips, a school master; Mr. Mark Willoughby, the interpreter, with his wife and three children; four carpenters, three laborers and two native maids. The team sailed out on 18 December 1844 and spent the Christmas Day at Monrovia, and reached Badagry on 17 January 1845. It was in Badagry that they learnt of the death of King Shodeke whom they had built great expectations on the promise he made to the missionaries during Rev. Townsend's last visit to Abeokuta. Despite the sad news about the death of Shdeke, they still received messages of goodwill from the chiefs at Abeokuta telling them that they still stood firmly by the promise of the deceased King.

Although the sad news weakened their spirit and morale but their save journey from Badagry to Abeokuta was another news that would handicapped and disabled their planned trip to Abeokuta. The news reaching them at Badagry was that the roads between Badagry and Abeokuta were by then infested with robbers and their safety could not be guaranteed. They had no alternative other than to remain in Badagry for as long as the roads were to be cleared for safe passage through them. In the usual manner and habit of the missionaries, no minute was wasted in organizing themselves into preaching groups and arranging services and visits to people on evangelical discussions.

As it was described about the people in this region in the past, the natives were the Popos of the Dahomean type, steeped in degrading and cruel superstition and utterly demoralized by the vile rum which the slave ships had been in the habit of supplying them in exchange for their brothers and sisters in slavery business. It was as well said of this time that human sacrifices were common among the inhabitants especially when one was suspected of witchcraft. At this time that the party arrived Badagry was the time that Kosoko, who was the nephew of the King of Lagos, had conspired against him and when the plot failed, he fled to Badagry and made the town his temporary revolutionary place of abode. Kosoko, through the history of this time was known to be a cruel and merciless slave dealer who was responsible for many massacres and even made attempts to seize Badagry and threatened Abeokuta. It was also during their sojourn at Badagry that the party suddenly lost Mrs. Gullmer whose body was laid to rest with much solemnity and mourning including the natives that were witnessing Christian burial ceremony for the first time.

Rev. Samuel Crowther wrote in his journal that the scene of that day was witnessed by a congregation of about 150 persons while the chiefs having been informed of their mournful bereavement, sent their messengers to express their sympathy with them. He also reported of the successful meeting they had with chief Ogunbona who was a notable personality in the community and the lodging facilities he provided for them when they were in his area in the Badagry region. He remarked that chief Ogunbona's reaction to the missionary's intentions was very astonishing especially when he saw people of his own race and clan reading the Scriptures and talking in white man's language, translating all that were said by the white men to him in his native language. He was very supportive and helpful to the establishment of the mission station in Badagry. Gradually the Gospel work was gathering momentum with great success. The Sunday school class of forty children the first of its type ever to be seen in Badagry was formed and thus became a popular feature of their work.

To return to the main topic of this chapter, after several months of stay in Badagry, Crowther was able to make tremendous progress in his translation of the Scripture book into Yoruba language, and had also translated the lithurgy into his native Yoruba language for the use of the congregation in the service. No one could tell whether because of these valuable works for the progress of the Gospel that God made them to remain in Badagry for such a lengthy period of time.

It is only God that is able to turn around any situation at will and to which nothing will obstruct His decisions of doing so. The progress of the party's movement to Abeokuta was retarded but providentially expedited by the interposition of an enemy. There are situations where God will use an enemy to resolve national, community or personal entangled problems. This was what happened in the case of this party's journey between Badagry and Abeokuta. During this time, there lived a notorious slave trader of Porto – Novo named Domingo who had sent presents to Sagbua at Abeokuta, promising him that he would clear the roads of robbers if he Sagbua would allow traffic in slaves to be established in his kingdom. The missionaries getting wind of this message from those sent to Sagbua in Abeokuta immediately sent with the embassy an appeal to Sagbua, telling him of their urge to come to his city to establish missionary works and trade among his people.

Domingo knew very well that the moment the missionaries were allowed to gain ground in Abeokuta, his slave trading business would suffer indeed. When Domingo's messengers arrived at Sagbua's palace at Ake, Sagbua was already having in his hands the message of the missionaries. Considering the two messages, he told Domingo's messengers that he was not going to be so easily deceived. He told them in clear terms that, "We can ourselves tell who are our best friends – those who rescue our children from their captors and send them freely to us again, or those who bring goods to purchase them for perpetual slavery and misery. The English are our friends, and you people at Badagry take care, for if any wrong is done to them in your town, you must answer to us for it."

Sagbua's threat and stern warning to Domingo the slave dealer opened the way for the Christianity works to move forward and on 27 July 1846, during the raining season, they decided to make their move towards Abeokuta without further delay. They wanted to beat Domingo into his own game of whether he might change his mind again and block the roads. The Christian team had no weapon of any sort to defend themselves against any human attack if it happened not to talk of any attack from the wild animals during the journey, but with strong faith the journey was made successfully. Though it was full of misfortunes, difficulties and all sorts of hardships and terrible moments, which no one could talk about other than those that were involved and for first hand information about the trip, Rev. Crowther wrote a fellow missionary at Sierra Leone after they had arrived at Abeokuta of their woeful plight on the journey through jungle, rain, marshy land and with little children in the party. His letter to a friend regarding the full account of this journey was dated 12 November 1846. Please come on board with me and enjoy reading it along.

The first day we traveled about twenty-five miles, with an escort of twenty-five men from Badagry to accompany us till we passed the most dangerous part of our journey. Being pelted by rain all day, we were glad to rest ourselves in our tent, which we pitched, after we had cleared away the bush, in the middle of a large forest on the bank of a stream, which we had to cross in a bathing-tub the next morning, because it was unsafe to carry anyone across the stream. The tub was brought with us all the way to Badagry, that this stream might not be an obstacle to prevent our proceeding to Abeokuta.

The next morning we crossed the stream with safety in our bathing vessel, navigated by two men as they waded to the middle in the water, the bottom of which was full of roots of trees, which grow in it. Our second day's journey was still more difficult than the first, because the road was so badly cut by rain that our horses could scarcely go on, and there was no way to turn on either side, which was high, bushy, and slippery. There were also many trees, which fell across the path, around which travelers must go if it cannot be crossed, in doing which our horses and carriers found it very wearisome. Mrs. Crowther was nearly thrown down by her carriers, because they could not keep on their feet on account of the slipperiness of the path; she had to walk nearly all the way to Abeokuta, which completely knocked her up. Our children, Juliana and Dandeson, were carried on the back according to African fashion; there was not much trouble on their part, but the poor little children did not like traveling in the dark forest, besides which they were beaten by rain, the path even not admitting the use of an umbrella. When we halted in the forest the second day we were obliged to catch rain-water for our use, there being no water near where we could pass the night with safety.

Rev. Samuel. A. Crowther.

Within days the party was welcomed into the city of Abeokuta by the chiefs and Sagbua with the traditional greetings and entertainment. From the side of the missionaries, they presented to this great man Sagbua a large mirror that had miraculously survived the hectic journey between Badagry and Abeokuta. The immediate action of Sagbua towards this valuable present was highly commendable because as against the rare pattern of behavior of the native public figures of this time, he turned the mirror over to the Town Hall or Council Room where it would excite the envy, but not jealousy of the chiefs. Soon after the traditional greetings and exchange of presents, a public was summoned where Rev. Crowther talked to the people in their mother tongue and the purpose of their coming. The people were very excited and happy to listen to him and also paid rapt attention to the story he gave about himself and others that were fortunate to be rescued by the white men on the sea with their huge gunboats and gave to them new lifestyle that could be seen by the eyes of everyone in the crowd.

He told his people that the mission had come to teach them about the true God, the legal trading methods with which they themselves would be able to develop their country, change their environment, train the minds of their young children and be proud to be recognized by the developed countries of the world. Towards the mission works, the people were happy to donate generously some variable amounts of cowries - the currency of African countries of this time, ranging from 1000 cowries from the chiefs and notables in the community to 20,000 cowries, which were donated by Sagbua himself as the chairman. A piece of land was allotted and all hands were on deck for the construction of the Lord's house. The women's role in the construction work was recorded as very excellent because they were the ones carrying the mud clay with which the builders used in the construction of the building for a daily wage of three pence per person. It came to a certain period during the construction time that many people volunteered to work for free thereby making the managers to reduce the wages from three pence to two pence a day and later to one penny as the supply of labor was actually becoming more than the demand. The magnificent building of its type in the country during this era was completed with good finishing with glass windows, smooth boards for flooring, and generally considered as good native handiwork and nice workmanlike finish.

The working system of God greatly differs from that of human beings in the sense that it was He Himself that has in stock the providence of a man. It was during this ordained visit to Abeokuta that Rev. Crowther received an intelligence report that his mother and his two sisters that their father had asked to escape and run for the safety of their life the other years when the Foulas attacked their town in search of human commodities were still alive and living in the neiboring town of Abake. Crowther could not believe this story neither could the mother and the sisters too when they received a message from Rev. Crowther that they should travel down to Abeokuta for a happy re-union. When this information was passed on to him, he wasted no time in sending some people to bring them forth if actually it was a fact that they were still living. When the messengers got to them and delivered Crowther's message the whole episode looked freaky to them that his two sisters would not bulge or agreed to follow them.

No matter what anyone may call it, I still believe that mother is always a mother and with this type of believe and faith in that old woman's heart, she agreed to go and set for Abeokuta in the company of one of Crowther's half brothers whom the mother was now living with. The result of this meeting could be anybody's guess but please read on as it was described in the words of Rev. Crowther himself and feel for you the type of faces that both of them, the mother and the son were wearing after a gap of twenty-five years of not seeing each other or talk to each other.

The text for to-day in the Christian Almanac is "Thou art the Helper of the fatherless." I have never felt the force of this text more that I did this day, as I have to relate that my mother, from whom I was torn away about five-and twenty years ago, came with my brother in quest of me. When she saw me she trembled. She could not believe her own eyes. We grasped one another, looking at one another in silence and great astonishment, while the big tears rolled down her emaciated cheeks. She trembled as she held me by the hand and called me by the familiar names, which I well remember I used to be called by my grandmother, who has since died in slavery. We could not say much, but sat still, casting many an affectionate look towards each other, a look, which violence and oppression had long checked, an affection, which twenty-five years had not extinguished. My two sisters, who were captured with me, and their children, are all residing with my mother. I cannot describe my feelings. I had given up all hope, and now, after a separation of twenty- five years, without any plan or device of mine, we were brought together again.

It is a great and moving opportunity for me to have access to the materials that I used in writing this book especially those ones from Rev. Crowthers journals, which in actual fact served as a plum cake of life to me that has rich raisins and currants in it. The story of how Rev. Crowther met his loving mother, his two sisters and his half brother touched not only me to my bone marrows but as well as the teaming population of my readers I believe. The story had it said written that the mother told the son of her sorrowful ordeals since circumstances of slave trade separated them. She told him that after Ajayi had been taken to the Coast, herself and the two sisters regained their liberty and went to live with the half-brother who had redeemed them. As fate would have it for them, the two sisters got married, but one day as she was in the company of the older sister on their way to the market, they were both kidnapped, and her daughter had to be ransomed by her husband leaving her to be dragged from place to place, exposed for sale in the market place like wares and in the end she became a domestic servant to her master. At another day the poor woman was sent to the market in Abeokuta as usual by her mistress, and again she was captured on the road, sold into a very bitter and hard bondage. At last her daughter made available sufficient cowries worth about four British pound sterling and ten shillings to buy her back. Crowther instantly decided with his wife to offer a place to his mother for living with them at Abeokuta to which she accepted willingly.

The poor old woman had a heavy burden in her heart that she had not known anything about the God that his son was now serving but gradually she was being introduced to this God through the preaching of his son and the teachings she was taught of by her little grandchildren and their mother. In a lesser time, his mother came to know the true God after an illness that she survived and after her recovery, she confessed to her son that if she had been left alone to herself during the sickness time, she would have attributed such an illness to the handiwork of this or that deity, and should have made much sacrifices accordingly; but now she had seen the folly of so doing and that all hopes have to be rested in the Lord Jesus Christ whom now she served. On hearing this testimony from his own mother, Rev. Crowther was so happy and on the 5th of February 1848, Crowther baptized her mother with the meaningful name of Hannah. It was recorded that the mother lived to be over one hundred years and saw her children's children up to her fourth generation.

Undoubtedly the missionary work in Abeokuta was rapidly advancing and progress was being recorded on daily, weekly and yearly basis. Within three years of hard work more than 500 constant attendees were in the church and more than 200 candidates had been registered to be baptized. Rev. Crowther and his family at this time made Abeokuta their home place because his influence among the Egba people carried much weight to be reckoned with in the realm of evangelism and the administration of the new religion. While he would be busy with the young kids teaching them the English and Yoruba alphabets in the classroom with the help of other Sierra Leone trained teachers that came with him for that purpose, his wife too as a trained teacher would be occupied with the same task in the class of the girls teaching them how to hold needles to hem, make stitches and how to cook delicious meals. Both of them were partners in progress in the development of their own people.

Every stage of development in any community has its good and bad moments of its own, and Abeokuta was no exception in this regard. The bad moment of this community came when the news reached them that the army of Dahomey was ready to pounce on them just because the miscreant King of Dahomey taught that Abeokuta was standing on his way in his slave trading business and as such he was ready to deal with them decisively, if possible crush them, shred them into pieces and make an abrupt end to the ongoing developments that the missionaries were making at Abeokuta. Immediately the missionaries arrived at Abeokuta, the city's lifestyle had changed from war tactics to peaceful co-existence among the people of the city and their neighbors according to the tenets of the new religion they had just adopted. Because of the new lifestyle, no one was expecting any attack from any where by the time the Dahomean army attacked Abeokuta. Initially, the situation looked as if the Egba people were helpless and was at the mercy of their attackers. The city that they were steadily building with hard work, patriotism and great sacrifices from its citizens plus the mission work peacefully advancing with great success was to be wiped out amid a wholesale slaughter of its inhabitants by the aggressors.

After the coming out of the Egbas from the caves under the Olumo rock, they had formed themselves into a very powerful military units that were ready to repel any outside aggression at will; but that the new religion had now told them to live in peace with everyone, they had

The Journey of the First Black Bishop

to lay down their military weapons and face the direction of modern development and because of this temporary slow down in military action they could not instantly hold back the insurgents at the ford but were able to retreat back to the walls of their city to defend it. After a long period of time at the battle field where both sides exchanged musketry fire, much to the advantage of the defenders, the Egbas made a sortie and the Dahomean army had nothing left than to turn tail and fled. Many of the Dahomean war generals were killed and many were captured. The defeat of the attackers at the battlefield was a glorious victory and great deliverance for Abeokuta. History recorded the defeat that on the following day that the Dahomean army was booted out of the Egbaland, Rev. Crowther traveled to the battlefield where he was greatly grieved when he saw on the side of the enemy line almost as many women slain as men. Rebuilding of Abeokuta city and its bordering towns had to start all over again.

Rev. Townsend was to return home on account of his wife's ill-health, and Rev. J. C. Muller and Crowther were to be joined by another missionary the Rev. D. Hinderer, who was said to be a valuable helper. On Townsend's way back home, The Council of Egba chiefs had addressed a petition through him to the Queen of England saying in part that they had seen her servants - the missionaries, whom she had sent to their country. They were happy to tell the Queen in the letter that they agreed with all that the missionaries were doing so far, which included the building of the house of the Lord, the teaching of the people and their children the words of God and the speaking and writing of the English and Yoruba alphabets. The contents of the petition pointed to the sorrows of slavery that was still going on around them; and implore the great ruler to summarily deal with the people on the coast at Lagos who still thrived on the traffic in flesh and blood. The Queen of England's reply to this petition was very gracious and was delivered at a meeting of the Council of Chiefs at Ake palace at the instance of Sagbua, Crowther and other church dignitaries. The letter was accompanied with presents of two beautifully bounded Bibles from the Queen and a steel corn mill from Prince Albert. Rev. Crowther translated the contents of the letter in these words:

The Queen and people of England (he explained) are very glad to hear that Sagbua and the chiefs think as they do upon the subject of commerce But commerce alone will not make a nation great and happy like England. England has become great and happy by the knowledge of the true God and Jesus Christ. The Queen is therefore very glad to hear that Sagbua and the chiefs have so kindly received the missionaries, who carry with them the Word of God, and that so many of the people are willing to hear it.

The present and the message from the Royal family from England were warmly accepted by Sagbua and his Council members especially the steel corn mill, which Prince Albert had sent to them for their use. The crowd was highly charged and astonished when some Indian corn was put in the mill then turned on the handle, and fine flour poured out of it. Their delight knew no bounds because that was the first time for the people to see such a magic machine grinding corn into flour powder as against their on method of producing the same result only on the large flat grinding stone with much labor and strain.

To turn around the lifestyle of a human being is not an easy thing to do as it takes a lot of perseverance, methods and long patience to achieve. Though the people had begun to see tremendous changes in their ways of living but yet their hearts were still dominated by the heathen believes and methodologies. Rev. Crowther reported, that one day after the meeting where Sagbua was presented with the Bible and the corn mill, he was talking to him in his court yard and he Sagbua curiously asked him whether it would be necessary and appropriate for him to offer sacrifices to the beautiful presents which he had just received from the Queen and the Prince of England. Crowther then enquired of what present and Sagbua promptly replied "The Bibles". The man of God then read some portion in the Bible concerning idolatry to explain to the King why such sacrifice was not needed and at variance with the teaching of the words of God. The explanation gladdened Sagbua and went down deep into his thinking faculty. So also was chief Ogunbona who was at the courtyard during this discussion time. In his own case he even took the explanation much more to heart than Sagbua for he instantly told Crowther about the deep impression that his explanation had made on him and confirmed to him that in six years time Christianity would become the national faith of the city of Abeokuta.

During this period of time Lord Palmerston was the British Foreign Minister and at this period also Rev. Crowther visited England where he had the opportunity to be interviewed by the Government Minister. During the interview he had with the Minister, Crowther explained to him the political situation of the West coast of Africa and especially that of Abeokuta. He told the Minister point blank about how the King of Dahomey was not only an unscrupulous slave trader, but someone who was injuring the interest of civilization, development and trade on the coast.

After this political and commercial briefing given to the Government Minister by the only person that the British Government relied much upon if the Government was to succeed in their interests in Africa, the Minister on the 18th of December 1851 addressed a letter to Crowther expressing his pleasure and delight at the interview he had with him saying that:

I am glad to have an opportunity of thanking you again for the important and interesting information with regard to Abeokuta, which you communicated to me when I had the pleasure of seeing you at my house in August last. I request that you will assure your countrymen that Her Majesty's Government takes a lively interest in the welfare of the Egba nation and of the community settled at Abeokuta, which town seems to be a center from which the lights of Christianity and of civilization may be spread over the neighboring countries.

While Crowther was still in London and surprisingly one day, Lord Wriothesley Russell invited Crowther to accompany him to Windsor Castle where he was unexpectedly met first with the Prince Consort who was glad to discuss with him the interesting political and commercial situations of the West Coast of Africa and then the Queen of England later on. The visit was really a moment of surprise altogether but spiritual elevation to the heart of this African Reverend gentleman who was walked into the castle by a Government representative to sit and discuss the problems facing his people with the Queen and her husband. It was really a great honor done to him and his native continent Africa.

Windsor Castle

Chapter 13

Bishop Crowther's Meeting with Queen Victoria & Prince Albert at Windsor Palace.

The greatest honor to be bestowed on any foreign dignitary visiting England is to be asked to meet with their monarch in any of the royal palaces located at various places in the country. It is the culture and traditions of the English people to place valuable honor and respect on the throne of their monarch and who occupies the throne because he/she is at all time the head of their Government and the people. For example, in London, one can only be allowed to view the beauty of the Buckingham Palace building from a distance or walk on the lawn surrounding the building if permitted but what is inside the building is restricted from the view of every Tom, Dick, and Harry except one is specially invited to go in there; so also the various palace buildings at various locations including Windsor.

The first Niger expedition of 1841 that ended tragically never go down well with the people in the Government especially each time they remembered those human volunteers that lost their lives through the deadly malaria attack in the voyage. They were conscious to take every precaution to avoid any similar occurrence should there be any need in the future to embark on such expedition again. And before the Government can address such issue again, it wanted to know for sure that it had enough information about the region of West Africa and from whom was in a position of authority to give them the required first hand situation report that would include the people, ecological problems and economic development.

It was on the basis of this information tapping that prompted the interview that Rev. Crowther had with the Foreign Secretary – Lord Palmerston some few days back while he was in England on a visit. With all honesty, Rev. Crowther was not expecting to meet with any person in the Government circle nor aim at meeting the head of the British Government – the Queen for any discussion or demand on this trip or in the future. He was only in England in his usual administrative duties to report to his superiors at the CMS Headquarters in London about the progress made so far as his evangelical duties were concerned and nothing more. But something with greater distinction came his way when Lord Wriothesley invited him to accompany him to Windsor Castle where he was to meet with the Queen and Prince Albert sitting down together to discuss on the future of what is today known as West African region that grouped many strong countries in Africa together for economic development, trade and commerce.

Windsor Castle

Prince and Queen Victoria of England
Reign from 1837- 1901

Findings about Crowther's character trait revealed that he was a copious diarist and a revealing one for that matter. He was such a man that could not conceal or attempt to distort anything of his own feelings and that he was far too uncomplicated person. These were the testimonies written about him by those who worked with him and new him in person. These people went further to say that whatever he wrote was revealing of the fundamental awe and gratification of his feeling not only of his English superiors but everyone inclusive. It was this attitude that he carried with him into the Windsor Castle on the 18th of November 1851 at 4.30p.m where he grasped one of the greatest opportunities of his lifetime to meet with the Royal family of England and the head of the British Government.

Greatness of the people of this time was also extended to Rev. Samuel Crowther because of the job well done on this day when he excellently won the hearts of the Royal family members and her Government on a number of issues concerning his native continent - Africa. Being an articulate and a diarist person, he graphically recorded every facet of the discussions and interview of that day; and to those who preserved the graphic of the text about this great visit for our generation to read and assimilate, "I say bravo and thank you all". The text of the visit is herewith given, word for word, just as Rev. Crowther himself told it:

Through the kind recommendation of the then Hon. Secretary of the CMS., the late Rev. Henry Venn, on the slave trade question agitating the minds of the Members of Parliament at that time, on 18 November, 1851, at 4.30 pm, Lord Wriothesley Russell kindly took me to the palace at Windsor. On our arrival there Prince Albert was not in; the servants-in-waiting went about to seek him. While we were waiting in a drawing –room I could not help looking round at the magnificence of the room glittering with gold, the carpet, chairs, etc., all brilliant. While in this state of mind the door was opened, and I saw a lady gorgeously dressed, with a long train, step gracefully in. I thought she was the Queen. I rose at once, and was ready to kneel and pay my obeisance;

Prince Albert

but she simply bowed to us, said not a word, took something from the mantelpiece, and retired. After she left Lord Russell told me that she was one of the Lady-in-waiting. "Well", I said to myself, "if a Lady-in-waiting is so superbly dressed, what will be that of the Queen herself!" Soon we were invited to an upper drawing -room more richly furnished than the first. Here we met Prince Albert standing by a writing–table. Lord Russell made obeisance and introduced me, and I made obeisance. A few words of introductory remarks led to conversation about West Africa, and Abeokuta in particular. The Prince asked whether we could find the place on any map, or thereabouts. I then showed the position in the large map from the Blue Book, and brought out from my pocket the small one which Samuel [his eldest son] had made on the section of the slave trade influence, with the different towns and seaports legibly shown. About this time a lady came in, simply dressed, and the Prince looking behind him, introduced her to Lord Russell but in so quick a way that I could not catch the sound. This lady and the Prince turned towards the map to find Abeokuta and Sierra Leone, where the slaves are liberated. All this time, I was in blissful ignorance of the Great Majesty before whom I stood and was conversing freely and answering every question put to me about the way slaves are entrapped in their homes, or caught as captives in war.

On inquiry I gave them the history of how I was caught and sold, to which all of them listened with breathless attention. It was getting dark, a lamp was got, and the Prince was anxious to find and define the relative positions of the different places on the map, especially Lagos, which was the principal seaport from which Yoruba slaves were shipped; and when the Prince wanted to open the Blue Book map wider, it blew the lamp out altogether, and there was a burst of laughter from the Prince, the lady, and Lord Russell. The Prince then said, " Will your Majesty kindly bring us a candle from the mantelpiece?" On hearing this I became aware of the person before whom I was all the time. I trembled from head to foot, and could not open my mouth to answer the questions that followed.

Lord Russell

Lord Russell and the Prince told me not to be frightened, and the smiles on the face of the good Queen assured me that she was not angry at the liberty I took in speaking so freely before her, and so my fears subsided. I pointed out Lagos, the particular object of inquiry, and told them that I with others were shipped from that place, and showed the facility which that port has, beyond all the other ports, as a deport, being much nearer, and the port of the highway to the interior Yoruba countries. The Prince said: "Lagos must be knocked down, by all means; as long as they have the lake (Lagoon) to screen them, and the men-of-war outside, it is of no use."

"The Queen was highly pleased to hear this. Lord Russell then mentioned my translations into the Yoruba language, and I repeated, by request, the Lord's Prayer in the Yoruba, which the Queen said was a soft and melodious language. Lord Russell informed the Queen of my having seen Sir H. Leeke who rescued me and others from the slave ship many years ago, which interested her very much. She was told that Mrs. Crowther was recaptured in the same way that I was, and she asked whether she was in England, and was told no. She asked after Sally Forbes Bonetta, the Yoruba African girl rescued from Dahomey. After these questions she withdrew with a marked farewell gesture." And before Crowther returned to Africa, he was invited to address a large audience of the students of the University of Cambridge where he appealed to them with touching earnestness for more missionaries to preach the Gospel to his people in Africa. In his closing remark he said:

St. Paul saw in a vision a man of Macedonia, who prayed him to come over to his assistance. But it is no vision that you see now; it is a real man of Africa that stands before you, and on behalf of his countrymen invites you to come over into Africa and help us.

Samuel Crowther gave many lectures, talks and speeches and many of its kind were given in honor of the valuable work he was doing at his native land during this trip to England. The most moving and spectacular of them all was that of the 5th of December 1851, at the old parochial schoolroom in Church street, Islington at the scene of a very sizeable gathering, where Crowther and his wife said good-bye to their hosts on their journey back to West Africa. The Earl of Chichester who was then the President of the Church Missionary Society presided over this important farewell meeting arranged in honor of the August visitors – the African missionaries. Also in attendance was a well-known friend of the cause of eradication of slave trade and establishment of missionary works in Africa, Rev. Daniel Wilson the excellent Vicar of Islington. At this meeting, Rev. Henry Venn, the Administrative Secretary of the CMS gave the short but memorable speech, which contained an admiring and fine eulogy about Rev. and Mrs. Crowther whose attendance conspicuously attracted the greatest attention, where they sat with their eyes suffused with emotion, the only two black eyes amid a concourse of white men.

The Secretary rose and thanked God for all He had been doing in the Yoruba mission since the past eight years that the mission works there began, particularly how He had delivered Abeokuta from the hordes of the King of Dahomey. In his closing speech, he charged the outgoing missionaries to be "harmless as doves" in the midst of the people. He then congratulated Crowther upon his outstanding wisdom he had been employing in dealing with the chiefs, and urged him to be more tactful when dealing with their enemies, especially the slave traders, the Mohammedans, the native priests, and the ignorant heathen.

Turning to the future, Revernd Henry Venn appealed to them and asked them to remember that the future character of the Christian Church in West Africa was at stake, and that their policy and individual actions would influence the success of the religion. He advised them not to see their sphere of labor in comparison with what was going on in India or New Zealand where other missionaries had been on the ground before; and that theirs were completely different in the sense that they are not only to spread Christianity on the Niger but to fix its character, organize the native churches, create a Christian literature and lay plans for the days to come. He reiterated that they should aim at self-government, self-support, and to put the Bible in the hands of the people. He then commended the efforts of Samuel Crowther for his translation into Yoruba language of a great portion of the Holy Bible and the Lithurgy.

It was at this meeting that the CMS authority charged the outgoing missionaries to start an educational institution at Abeokuta for the benefits of the young men and women of their native land. He then turn to Mrs. Crowther and expressed the feelings of the people of England towards the great assistance she was given to her husband and how heartily England welcomed her as a great helper and team player in her husband's game team. He said that his people in England felt happy with the role and position she was carrying as the first Christian mother in Abeokuta, and they gladly rejoiced that her own children were also an example to others. Before the standing ovation from the crowd, Rev. Venn said all these concerning this great woman:

May she return with a double blessing to her country-women! May she indeed be a mother to that spiritual Israel in the wilderness of Africa! And may the native church, once confined to the house of Samuel Crowther, become a national church, but still retaining its character as an aggregation of Christian households bound together by one common tie of love and union with Christ in whom all the families of the earth are blessed!

An eye witness account of this meeting reported that when Crowther rose to speak, his heart was very full of emotions, and amid of deep silence for a moment, and then told the audience that eight years ago when he and other missionaries began their exploration works in Abeokuta, he first entertained much fear and trembled. His fear centered on how it was going to be possible for them to obtain an entrance into a community that the slave trade had rendered so difficult to penetrate into; but the promise of Him who said, "Lo, I AM with you always, even unto the end of the world," had been fulfilled and made manifest. He was grateful to God who in His infinite mercy had been supporting the work in Abeokuta and especially helping him with the translation of part of the Scriptures into his native language for the use of the converts. He was happy and delighted to inform the authorities with confidence that his people were now making the translated script a topic of conversation in their homes, their farmlands, and its influence had also been felt in the war camp.

General improvement about his nation, he told his audience how industrious they were and how anxious their throats were thirsty for the waters of legal trade and commerce. He spoke of how the people were completely weary of the slave traffic and sighed to be relieved of it and that the trade was the greatest enemy of his people. He then urged the support of the British people and its Government to remove this enemy once and for all and as soon as this was done, there was nothing to see as an obstacle to the course of Christianity on the Niger. He assured his audience that these natives are quite ready with a reason for the truth as it is in them, and can stand their ground bravely. He referred them to the fierce days of persecution at Abeokuta when the converts were required to renounce Christianity, and they were enabled to reply with boldness and told their chiefs that: "You elder chiefs admitted the teachers without consulting us. When you did so, they told you that they were going to teach, and that they had no cloth, no tobacco to give. You gave them admission. Then why do you now hinder us from going to them? The Book and the religion, which they teach we consider this as our share. When they came we had no part of the gifts, which you received from them. When you promised them that they should have children to teach, we had no share of the presents. Now this instruction is our share".

These natives are quite ready for employment in the cultivation of cotton in the country, of which I have hopes that a real trade will be one day established. Brethren, believe me, these Christian natives of Abeokuta do not wish to keep the Gospel to themselves alone. Already they had promised that teachers should be sent to other towns; nor do they fail, wherever they go, to speak of what they know. I am going back to my own land with great hope in my heart; feeling much blessed and encouraged, and has only to ask that my many kind friends in England will continue to pray for me and for the salvation of my people.

At the close of this meeting, it was said that people gathered round Crowther and his wife to wish them God-speed and mercy journey back home. A few days later, they were once again on the boat back home to continue with their God sent jobs with new zeal and vigor. The trip opened up a wide diplomatic way between England and the West coast of Africa in the areas of development of trade and commerce, education, health program and modern town planning which still stands up till today as monuments in many cities of the modern countries in West African Region.

Chapter 14

Consecration of Samuel Ajayi Crowther as the First Black African Bishop of the Church of England.

The African generation of the past, presents, and in the future have reasons to acknowledge the intellectual and spiritual abilities of people like William Wilberforce, Henry Venn and hosts of others at the CMS Headquarters in London for their long ending predictions and venerated ideas they had for the converts of people in both Africa and Asia of their time. In particular was that of Henry Venn who was a Prebendary of St. Paul's Cathedral, a member of the Clapham sect, son of one of the CMS founders, John Venn and the secretary of the CMS for thirty years from 1842 – 1872. During his tenure of office, he formulated series of policies and mapped out a lot of strategies for the development of the church particularly those that were to be coming up on board from Africa. It was he who decided that the converts from Africa and Asia should slowly be persuaded to pay for their ministers instead of accepting them as a charity from England. He also made it mandatory for the churches in these two continents that as soon as they reached this level they should be organized into a native pastorate, to be staffed by African or Asian ministers who must have been carefully trained and selected for the job.

And as soon as this was done, the white missionaries should hand over such pastorate to the natives to manage and move to some other green areas for the continuation of their duties. He was in-fact proposing future autonomy and self-government to the churches in these continents so that they would be totally independent of England as the case is today. Henry Venn was actually a great visionary who used the far-sightedness of William Wilberforce ideas and thinking to achieve a honorable goal for the church and the converts as well. He also sent strong instructions to his missionaries in the field particularly in Africa asking them to exercise their will-power and to respect African customs and traditions which were clearly marked as very opposing to the standards of Christian's faith. By virtue of his position as the administrator of CMS, he initiated at the earliest opportunity the native African church considering its size and economic opportunities that it had to offer. To achieve his objectives and goals, Samuel Crowther had to be invited to London again and at this time to be consecrated as the first black Bishop in the Church of England.

This important occasion in the annals of the Church of England and the native Church in Africa drew the attention of both Church recorders and journalists to this moment as the beginning of good things to come. The glowing optimism of the moment in CMS circle was carried by one of its journals as the day of the ceremony drew near. In this journal, the writer wrote that "Already the African Christian has shown himself not only capable of understanding and receiving the truth of Christianity, but of communicating it to his fellow-countrymen. On him the African climate exercises no malign influences to him, the language of Africa present no impediment…….. The moment had come for the African native, already raised to the ministry, to be further elevated to the episcopate, and the initial choice had fallen on one man and this was Rev. Samuel Ajayi Crowther" (see full text below).

People in the Government and the church circles clearly saw it that Crowther's fond idea of Africa for the Africans could only be accomplished when the Africans are given the opportunity to demonstrate their skills and knowledge about how to develop themselves. As regards to this, the foundation of a native church had to be erected and it was now seemed within sight of realization. An article that appeared in the Church Missionary Intelligencer in May 1864 clearly defined the steps that led to the new departure of creating a native Bishopric in West Africa. The writer of this article discussed this question from both official and authoritative sources to bring his point nearer home when he analyzed the evils of the slave trade and the unavoidable danger that the climate of Africa as at then created and he wrote:

[But these difficulties have been, in a great measure, overcome; the power of the slave trade is broken, and although it still lives, yet, like a venomous serpent, which has received a mortal injury, it is in its death throes. The insalubrity of the climate no longer presents the same hindrance that it used to do to the progress of the missions, and that because the European missionary is no longer alone in the work. A native church has been raised up on the peninsula of Sierra Leone, with its well-ordered congregations and its native ministers effectively discharging the high responsibilities imposed on them. This native Church, in a great measure self-supporting and self-ministering, is now girding itself up to enter upon its duties as a missionary church and send forth its evangelists into the heathen and Mohammedan countries which lie around it. Already the African Christian has been tried in this service. He has shown himself not only capable of understanding and receiving the truth of Christianity, but of communicating it to his fellow-countrymen. On him the African climate exercises no malign influences; to him the languages of Africa present no impediment. Although few in number, compared with the multitudinous inhabitants of that great continent, yet the first-fruits of Africa to Christianity is in a remarkable degree multilingual, and thus the services of a large proportion of the tongues of Africa are clearly placed at the disposal and are ready to be engaged in the services of Christianity

The opportune moment thus appears to have arrived when the native Church should be still further empowered to go forth and with a holy freedom do the Lord's work in Africa, and as the native Christian has been raised to the ministry so the native ministry be permitted to culminate in a native episcopate. The question is can one among the African clergyman be found to whom so great a responsibility can with safety be trusted? And this question the Church Missionary Society has ventured to answer in the affirmative. Nearly twenty-one-years have elapsed since the Rev. Samuel Crowther was ordained a deacon by the late Bishop of London.

The Lord has given him grace during the period, which has since elapsed to continue humble, consistent, and useful. He has made full proof of his ministry. The new missions on the Niger imperatively require Episcopal superintendence. They are so remote from the Bishop of Sierra Leone as to be placed entirely beyond his reach. The native catechists who have been instrumental in raising-up congregations at Onitsha and Ghebe require prompt admission to Holy Orders, that they may duly minister to their flocks and, as well by the teaching of God's Words as by the due administration of the Sacraments, promote their growth. Our Christians on the banks of the Niger need to be as quickly as possible brought forward into activity and be utilized in missionary effort among their countrymen. To delay any longer the native episcopate would be unduly to retard the development of the native Church.]

Without mixing words the content of this article clearly showed that there was no one among the natives of West Coast of Africa that was capable of wearing this garment of honor and responsibility at this time and moment except Samuel Ajayi Crowther who had the capability and capacity that was needed for the position as he had been tested and proved to be sufficiently equipped both morally and intelligently. Furthermore many achievable successes had been recorded for him both in the ministry and in the field, which had already attended his labors among his own people. He had also laid a solid foundation on which future blocks could be securely placed upon until the structure is brought to roof level; and because of this, he was called to head a diocese which he had himself created. Crowther had in quiet manner, unostentatious, and unmistakable ways proved in himself the latent qualities and capacities of the African intellectual ability, and, in a lesser degree, the profile of his attitude was equally seen in the native agents he employed along the banks of the Niger, which were wholesomely his own making. Unequivocally, everyone agreed that his selection to the highest position in the Church was nothing more than the greatest honor bestowed on the native church, the people of his continent, and himself.

The wonderful event was scheduled for 29 June 1864, on St Peter's Day at the Grey old Cathedral at Canterbury and this day was said to be one of the red-letter days in the annals of the Cathedral. Document of records of event for this day that was preserved showed that the event was no ordinary occasion. It was said that special trains were run from London and some other suburbs to the site of the occasion at Canterbury, and as early as eight o'clock an unusual crowd were seen at the morning prayers in the Cathedral. It was an ordained day when Crowther's friends and mentors gathered together to witness the first-fruits of their labor in him since he was rescued as a slave boy very many years back in the mid Atlantic ocean of his native continent.

Among the dignitaries that occupied the front seat rows in the Church that was capable to contain thousands of worshipers were the two important persons in the life of the new Bishop elect. One was Admiral Sir H. Leeke who attended this occasion in his naval uniform, and who was the young Captain on board H.M.S *Myrmidon* to lift up Crowther's hands out of the slave ship that was taken him abroad when attacked by his gunboat off the coast of Lagos. Interestingly, here was the boy of the other day who now was to be consecrated as a Bishop, but Crowther never lost sight and contact of this friend, who this day, with many thankful memories, formed one of the congregation at the ceremony.

Cathedral at Canterbury

The second person was now an old lady who slowly made her way up to the front seat, where she might clearly see and hear every moment of the occasion. It was said about this woman that the Churchwardens challenged her at first and reminded her that where she was about to sit was especially reserved for a dignitary with a ticket. She turned around and quietly told the Churchwardens that: "I think I have a right equally to this seat, because that black minister to be consecrated Bishop this morning was taught the alphabet by me". The Dean and the Churchwardens on hearing this begged the visitor to remain in her seat. This was the widow of Bishop Weeks of Sierra Leone.

The historical service was about to begin after the Archbishop and other prelates had taken their places. The Bishop of Lincoln was slated to read the Epistle while the Bishop of Winchester was assigned to read the Gospel; the sermon to be preached by the Rev. H. Longueville Mansel who was a Professor of Philosophy at Oxford University. He carefully and intellectually selected his preaching from the Book of 1 Peter, chapter 5, verses 2 & 3, which says:

[Feed the flock of God, which is among you, taking the oversight thereof, not by constraint, but willingly; not for filthy lucre, but of a ready mind.

Neither as being lords over God's heritage, but being ensamples to the flock.]

After the sermon the choir sang the melodious song of "How lovely are the messengers" and the two Bishop-elect walked to the vestry to put on their rochets, and on their return they took their oath of office that says: "We do by this our license under the Royal signet and sign manual, authorize and empower you the said Samuel Ajayi Crowther, to be Bishop of the United Church of England and Ireland in the said countries of West Africa beyond the limits of our dominions."

Later Bishop Crowther was walked up to the Archbishop by the Bishop of Winchester to introduce the African prelate to him. At this point the choir again sang Wise's anthem, "Prepare the way of the Lord", while the Bishop-elect were kneeling with their heads bowed, the "Veni Creator Spiritus" was beautifully sung to Tallis music. Then with hands outstretched, the Archbishop gave the apostolic charge saying:

"Remember that thou stir up the grace of God, which is given thee by this imposition of our hands, for God hath not given us the spirit of fear, but of power and love and soberness." At this impressive moment Crowther took from the hand of the Archbishop his consecration Bible with the words: Take heed unto thyself, and to doctrine, and be diligent in doing them: for by so doing them thou shall both save thyself and them that hear thee. Be to the flock of Christ, a shepherd but not a wolf, feed them and devour them not. Hold up the weak, heal the sick, bind up the broken, bring again the outcasts, and seek the lost. Be so merciful, that you be not too remiss; so minister discipline, that you forget not mercy: that when the Chief Shepherd shall appear you may receive the never-fading crown of glory: through Jesus Christ our Lord".

The ceremony was concluded after the newly consecrated Bishops had taken their places within the Alter to partake in the Holy Communion Service to which many people in the congregation waited to attend. This occasion was indeed a memorable and eventful one that Bishop Crowther himself would not find easy to forget throughout the days of his life. Throughout the solemn occasion with its impressive prayers, the pealing music, the cadence of the singing, the hush of the consecration vow, and the moment of sweet communion, the heart of the new Bishop was focused on his homeland Africa and the people he left behind that were yet to know the way forward. The public opinion about this occasion was written and echoed by the press in one of the papers, that it was a good and promising step in the right direction. An article in the "Record" had these few words to say concerning the elevation of a Negro to this high office as against the findings and opinion of some people of this time about the cerebral development of the black people.

We might dwell on the practical refutation afforded by Dr. Crowther's merited elevation to the episcopate to the taunts of certain professors who maintained that the cerebral development of the Negro shows that he is disqualified for intellectual pursuits, and that he cannot be lifted out of his congenital dullness; but we pass on to entreat the prayers of our readers for him and his diocese. He will need much wisdom, peculiar grace, and constant strength. Humanly speaking, the future of the native Church depends on the manner in which its first Bishop shall administer its polity and organize its laws. It will be necessary also for him to exercise great discrimination in conferring Holy Orders on his brethren, and to take heed that he magnifies his office in the estimation of all by the exemplary consistency of his life and the holiness of his conversation. That he will do so we are assured of past experience, but the slightest consideration proves how much he needs to be supported by the sympathy and prayers of the Church.

On 24 July 1864, Bishop Crowther left England and arrived at Sierra Leone on 10 August where he was met by friends in the missionary and large crowd of people from the colony, who displayed the love and affection they had for him particularly as one of them who was now elevated to the highest position in the Church. The next day he was escorted to his beloved institution – Fourah Bay College where all the clergy, catechists, and school masters had gathered to give him a befitting reception and to congratulate him on his new achievement and also to let him know that they were ready to support him in whatever form he might need their joyful hearts in the course of his new assignment and duties. The new Bishop was presented with two different addresses; one was from the body of the college where he was a foundation student and teacher and the other one was from the whole body of the Church Missionary Agents and the native pastors. The first address that was presented to him came from his missionary colleagues and signed by over thirty-six dignitaries of the Church expressing in it the amount of love they had for him and prayed for him that God Himself would grant him abundant grace, strength and support throughout his tenure of office as the Chief Pastor in the black African region. The extract of the address and the Bishop's reply that were preserved for our generation and the ones coming indeed testified to the happy mood of everyone present at that occasion on that day:

[We regard your consecration as a token of God's favor to the Church in Africa, and would unfeignedly rejoice with you in this mark of His distinguishing love, believing it, as we do, to be an earnest of richer blessings which are yet in store. In reviewing your whole past career in this colony, and subsequently at Abeokuta and the Niger, we thank God for the abundant grace bestowed upon you and for the measure of success granted you in your missionary work, and we trust that the same grace may be vouchsafed to guide and comfort, to strengthen and support you through all your future course in the high office to which you have been called.

It will be a source of comfort for you to know that prayer meeting were held in every district in the colony on the day of your leaving England that God would protect you from the dangers of deep, and you may rest assured that prayer will constantly ascend, that under your wise and judicious culture the thorn and thistle may be uprooted and the Rose of Sharon and the Lily of the Valley may be seen along the whole banks of the Niger. May the Spirit of the Lord rest upon you, the spirit of wisdom and understanding making you as a chief pastor of the flock of Christ in Africa, of quick understanding in the fear of the Lord, so that you will judge not after the sight of your eyes, nor reprove after the hearing of your ears, but ruling and superintending all things according to truth and love.]

By the time the Bishop rose to reply to this address, it was said that he was under a great deep of emotion and his voice thrilled with feeling but expressed his thankfulness to his fellow brothers and colleagues for the love and support they gave to him in the course of his service in the missionary. He in fact took everyone back to the good old days when he said:

[When we look back to the commencement we find the mission took its beginning among a heterogeneous mass of people, brought together in the providence of God from many tribes of this part of Africa, out of whom, through the zealous, faithful, and persevering labor of the early missionaries, arose devout congregations of faithful and sincere Christians. After a time the mission produced a native ministry, then a self-supporting native pastorate, and latterly, out of the native ministry an humble step outward was taken in faith to introduce a native episcopate in missions beyond Her Majesty's dominions. Here we pause and raise our Ebenezer of God's praise. Hitherto the Lord has helped us.

This onward progress seems to be an indication from God, beckoning to us to come forward, put our shoulders to the wheels, and ease our

European brethren of the great work, which they have so nobly sustained alone from their predecessors for fifty years, many of whom had sealed the testimony of their zeal with their lives. Their graves at the burial grounds are existing monuments of their faithful obedience to their Master's command: "Go, and teach all nations."

Whether called to their rest or whether beaten back from the fields of their labor through ill-health and forced to retire, or whether still laboring among us, it is our bounden duty in gratitude to remember and esteem them highly in love for their work's sake, of which we are the fruits.

We must exhibit a missionary spirit ourselves, and encourage it among our congregations, if we are imitators of missionary enterprises; if, like as Timothy knew Paul, we also have known their zeal, we should endeavor to preach the Gospel in the regions beyond the colony. To extend our line of usefulness we must seriously impress on our Christian countrymen the necessity of exhibiting a spirit of liberality, after the example of the mother Church, whose spirit we should imbibe, not only to support their own pastors and school teachers, keeping in good repair their churches and other buildings made over into their hands, but also contribute, according to the means God has blessed them with, to send the Gospel into countries beyond them which are yet destitute of the blessings of its light.

But above all, we must be followers of Christ the Great Shepherd of His flock and the example of His apostles in the habit of prayer for help from above. This is the weapon, which prevails most in the work of the ministry. When we feel our weakness and insufficiency for the work to which God has called us, we must constantly go to the Throne of Grace for divine aid. We are better fitted when we feel our incompetency to change a sinner' heart. This will drive us to apply to the Fountain Head for a quickening spirit from above, which He has promised to all who ask Him; then we shall be encouraged to go on in this our might. Has He not sent us?]

The College address was presented to the Bishop by the Principal of the College and signed by him, the tutors, and the students all in appreciation of the honor laid upon the Bishop, in which they all shared together. Copy of the address was preserved in the College till today but a brief extract from the greetings of his Alma mater on this day reproduced below demonstrated their love and loyalty to him:

[We thank God for the grace bestowed upon you, enabling you to labor so faithfully for the past thirty-five years in His service. This Institution at one time enjoyed the benefit of your instruction, but of late years the

Jacob Oluwatayo Adeuyan

Yoruba and the Niger missions have been the fields in which you have labored. Notwithstanding this we have not been unmindful of you; your name has been familiar as a "household word" among us, and you have ever been held up as an example to our youth.]

The traditional characters and behaviors of students no matter where they are located when they assembled together for a meaningful purpose was what was being demonstrated by them this day at one of the lecture theaters of their college, which was the venue of the meeting where they joyfully greeted their fellow colleague and former master. Record of this event said that when the Bishop got up to reply to their address, he was received with boisterous applause from his fellow-students. He told the audience in his speech about some of those things that happened in the college during his own student days and a little bit about his journey in the missionary and I wish you acquaint yourself with the narratives of his speech and out of his own words: He told them that he left the college in 1841 to join the Timmance Mission, which was then established under the superintendence of Mr. Kissling, but he was shortly afterwards detached for the field of labor to join in the Niger Expedition. He then entered into a narrative of bitter taunts and ridicule from his friends, some of whom styled him a fool for joining the expedition without any guarantee for good pay like the Europeans. He said he told them that the Society had promised to supply him with necessaries, and subsequently he should not want. He told them that he was subsequently connected for ten years with the Yoruba mission, where he gathered, under God's blessing, a very promising and much attached congregation. He dated his connection with the Niger since 1854, from which period he had been literally moving to and fro. To a friend inquiring at the same time whether he did not mean to rest, he answered: "I shall only rest when I have no more work to do." It was his firm conviction, from what he had witnessed from traveling to and fro along the coast, that the difficulties, hardships and deprivations of missionaries are nothing in comparison with what many merchants suffers for a paltry gain. A missionary should be jack-of-all-trades, one ready to put his hands to work and to do in a legitimate way anything that might tend to advance the cause of Christ. In conclusion, he called the attention of the students of the college, who were all present, to the fact that though they were but six in the reopening, yet that number was greater by two than what they were when the college was first established in 1827. They had all the brethren before them as an encouragement, whereas he and his fellow-students then had none to look up to.

He trusted that he had succeeded in his attempt to deepen their hearts in the work, and prayed that every one enlisted under the banner of Christ should never fail to prove himself a good soldier of the Cross.

At the end of the occasion, the Bishop prayed for everyone and soon afterwards he was on his way to Lagos, which he reached on 22 August 1864, and when he held his first ordination service, he admitted Mr. Lambert Mackenzie to deacon's order. He later took a passage on board the *Investigator* and traveled up the Niger again to continue his Episcopal duties.

Apostle J.A. Babalola
1st Gen. Evangelist

Pastor D.O. Odubanjo
1st Gen. Superintendent

Archbishop Longley

Bishop Townsend

Chapter 15

Crowther as the First Bishop of His People:

Hellen Keller once said that: Someone's success and happiness lies in his or her resolve to keep happy, joy, and then he or she shall be able to form an invisible host against difficulties. We may agree that this quotation that surfaced over a hundred years after the existence of Bishop Ajayi Crowther matched his ways of life when he was actively participating in the building up of the present nations of the West Coast of Africa in the 19th century. His role in the Niger Expedition of 1841, 1854 and the subsequent trips up the Niger; the important part he played in the translation of the Bible into his mother tongue; his efforts of being the first to write book on Igbo nation; his diplomatic knowledge of accurately dealing with the Mohammedan chieftains of his time to agree with his principles and understandings of trade and industry to the advantage of all citizens made him a great person of all time. On the Mohammedan sector of religious belief of the people of his time, Crowther understood how Islamic practice could merge with traditional views of power. In this regard, he found a demand for Arabic Bibles, but was cautious about supplying them to the wrong hands unless he was sure they would not be used for other unholy practices.

In discussions with the Muslims, Crowther sought common ground and found it at the nexus of Quaran and Bible where the two holy Books accepted Christ as the great prophet, his miraculous birth and angel Gabriel as the messenger of God. He enjoyed courteous and friendly relations with the Mohammedan rulers and his writings mentioned various discussions he had with those he came in contact with, especially the rulers, their courts and clerics of various religious beliefs including that of the African religion. In his opinion and through his many years of experience in dealing with these groups of people, he concluded that the Bible, which is the word of spirit, must be left to fight its own battle, by the guidance of the Holy Spirit. He supported an idea that the Christians should defend Trinitarian doctrine, but they should be so mindful of the horror-stricken cry of the Quaran while doing this. He also queried that "Is it possible that Thou dost teach that Thou and Thy Mother are two Gods"? In other words Christians must show that the things that the Mohammedans fear as blasphemous are no part of Christian doctrine.

Crowther was never an Arabic Scholar but he developed an approach to Islam in its African setting that reflected the patience and the readiness to listen to religious critics that marked his entire missionary regime. He avoided denunciation and allegations of false prophecy, but respected what the Quaran says of Christ, and effective knowledge of Bible. During his time, it was a fact that the Muslim rule of faith was expressed in Arabic while the young Christian religion had begun its expressions in Hausa, Nupe and Yoruba, which produced different views and understandings of how faith was to be applied in life.

His personality was all the while pointing the way to the development of his African people whom some Europeans of his time had written off as human beings. His intellectual ability and passion for industrial activities to lift up his brethren were part of his hands-on approach that showed a good sign of his becoming a leader. The missionaries in England recognized his dignified humility, which commended him to the planners of the First Niger Expedition of 1841. Though this mission was intended as a precursor to a larger program through which the humanitarians expected the trinity of Christianity, commerce and civilization to wipe out the slave trade in the region of West Coast of Africa but ended up in tragedy from the loss of many lives from the villain of malaria that killed 40 Europeans and incapacitated many.

Yet this man of honor volunteered himself to risk all the dangers associated with traveling up and down the River Niger of this time when the technology was at its infancy. His ability to organize the liberated brethren in the colony played a great role in whatever positive outcomes there were in the history of the region. These brethren knew the language, they understood the terrain and they did not succumb to the malaria attack.

Crowther had now become a tower of strength to both the missionaries and the legitimate traders from Europe at the outcome of the expeditions he made along the banks of River Niger. His published journals about the first and the second expedition became grist for the mill of policy makers in England. Everyone in the British Government and in the C.M.S. began to passive the sweet odor coming out of him because of his outstanding ability, his instinctual understanding of human psychology and a strength of character in him that would do honor to every mankind. In quick reaction to the passive qualities in him, he was sent to the C.M.S. Training College at Islington in London and was ordained by the Bishop of London in 1843, thus becoming the first native Anglican priest from Sierra Leone sect.

When he came back to Sierra Leone, he was engaged in the missionary works doing many things at a time simultaneously. He was a preacher, a writer, a teacher and a translator. In the area of preaching, he was said to be a great orator and a strong preacher. He used both languages – English and Yoruba languages to preach to the admiration of his audience and to the rapture of his hearers. Best of his glorious services to mankind was the translation of several books of the Bible, in some instances by himself alone, and in others with the collaboration with some European Scholars. He was a sensitive and sage translator and because of his insistence that the Yoruba version of the Bible must sound and reflect the Yoruba speech, he carefully listened to the rhythms of the elders talk. He noted the key words used by specialists of the traditional religion or Moslem expounders of the Quaran.

He was deeply aware that the proverbs of Yoruba language were full of wisdoms distilled from them and as such, the tribal myths and legends from the storehouse of African theology fascinated him so much. He brought all of these to bear in the Yoruba translation of the Bible, which took forty-five years in making, and being regarded as a genuine and Herculean achievement. The translation has endured and inspired a large extension of modern Yoruba literature. His services at Abeokuta, in the heart of Yoruba country with his foreign missionary colleagues – Townsend and Gollmer opened up the way to modernization and industrial activities, which were to be the model for future missionary establishment and modern government set-up throughout his country- Nigeria.

It was in this city that Crowther would be seen each morning addressing his people under the tree in fluent and riveting Yoruba language about the Words of God and ways forward in life. When Abeokuta became the bone of contention between two warring Kings in the region, because one of the Kings was to reopen and continue in the slave trade that was being abolished internationally, it was Crowther that went to England in 1851 to persuade the British Government to send military aid to the city's defense. His visit to London at this time was organized by Henry Venn, who was then the General Secretary of the C.M.S. after he had convinced himself that Crowther had all the necessary skills to achieve this fit. This visit made great impact on the British Government while the people of England respected his engaging eloquence as he always carried every day of his engagements either with the Government officials or at any other public meetings where he would be made the guest speaker. In the end of this successful trip, the British Government bolstered the defense of Abeokuta by the dispatch of Gunboats and the city was saved from the slave trade Guru of the region. Crowther's immense knowledge of the geography and cultures of his native Yoruba people plus his commensurate humility made a deep impact everywhere even at those places he was unable to visit during his lifetime.

True to the fact, it was said that Crowther had never at any time wanted the office of the Bishop. But Henry Venn true to his character, administrative experience and evangelical vision was known to be a man who does not take "NO" for an answer. He always stood by his philosophy that African Church would be incomplete without an African Bishop and therefore he was not going to be swayed by the arguments of those white C.M.S. missionaries in the field who were against Crowther becoming a Bishop. One of such was Charles Townsend who was Crowther's keen competitor to this high office. Townsend did everything possible and in his capacity to undermine the integrity of the lonely African son in the midst of the high hierarchy of the C.M.S. His statements against Crowther were damaging and destructive that if they were to be measured by today's political and social standards, people would crown him as racist; but notwithstanding, the Church leaders stood firmly by their decision to have an African Bishop that would help them to move the wheels of their faith forward in that continent.

During this power tussle between Crowther and Townsend, it was noted that at a certain time, Townsend's views were evolved to such a point where he accepted a proposal to make Yoruba land a diocese separated from Crowther's – with an African as Bishop but unfortunately for him the proposal never saw the light of the day for many reasons advanced by the authorities of the C.M.S.

By the license given to Samuel Crowther to practice his Bishopric duties, he was made the Bishop of the countries of Western Africa, which was beyond the limits of the Queen's dominion; and in those years, the Queen's dominions only consisted of Sierra Leone, the coastal area of Ghana and the Island of Lagos. In effect, he had a vast portion of African land to cover and to evangelize and this alone gave a challenge to Crowther rather than probing queries and tiny quarrels against anyone. During his tenure of office, he doubled the number of missionary stations along the banks of River Niger and he was deeply respected by many of the Muslim potentates of the upper Niger region because he preferred to enter into dialogue with them rather than confronting them with the preaching that would denigrate the religion of Islam. His approach to interfaith dialogue revealed how knowledgeable he was about the Quaran especially about those parts of the Holy Book that honored and referred to Jesus as a great prophet.

During the years between 1864 and 1889 when Bishop Crowther reigned as the Bishop of his people, his high office recorded many transformations in the Church, he established many missionary stations, built many schools, trained teachers, catechists and improve the life of his people tremendously. His Alma Marta – Fourah Bay College in Sierra Leone never disappointed him to supply trained teachers and catechists to staff the missions and the schools he established. The fear that may have been entertained in some quarters of the C.M.S, that as soon as he became the Bishop, he would rush around to ordain his fellow black brethren without the most careful preparation and perfect discrimination was however, groundless. It was recorded that in his first seven years as a Bishop, Crowther turned only eight Africans into the position of priesthood. Regarding mobility, Crowther was known to be the most mobile Bishop of his time than any other Bishop ever known in that century because he always made use of every traveling opportunity that came his ways especially when there was a Government steamer going towards the direction of his itenarary.

Crowther's idea of Africa for the Africans was seen by his detractors at the later part of his life, as a torn in the flesh of the European missionaries and as such every means were employed to undermine his authorities and got him disgraced out of office. But one important thing was amiss in the thinking faculty of human beings and this is that "God is always on the side of his anointed people". No matter how formidable or large a group of people might be that gathered themselves together against an anointed man of God, all that is mapped out to net or trap him would always be loosen by the host of heavens and in the end they themselves would be caged in their set net.

It was around this time that the politics in the canister began to emerge in Africa and the breaking or partitioning of the continent was to be the primary aims and objectives of the Europeans either coming from the Government side or from the Missionary organizations. Scrambling for territories became the order of the day and possible tactics were employed to achieve this fit. The cordial relationship that formally existed between the European missionaries and their African counterparts was now tearing apart as dictatorial principles were being introduced into the missionary agenda in Africa. Referring to the good old days, we saw that it was Henry Venn that made a new sphere of leadership for Crowther, and also made him an outstanding indigenous minister of God in West Africa. He did not stop at this point but moved on to secure for him in 1864, a place of honor as a Bishop of the "Countries of Western Africa beyond the limits of the Queens dominion", a title that reflected some constraints that were imposed by Crowther's European colleagues and the peculiarities of the relationship of the Church of England to the Crown. His influence over those dominions were now seen as a threat to the new program of colonization kept in the pouch belt of his friends in England; but Crowther as a genuine humble man was never moved and Venn himself never stopped supporting his ideas and philosophy for the African continent.

To successfully produce this wholesale product, his diocese that was supposed to represent the triumph of the three-self principles and the planting of the indigenous seeds on the ground of the episcopate now changed gear and was reflecting compromise, rather than the full expression of those principles. We should not forget that around this time nearly every needed modern product for human consumptions were being manufactured and imported into the new region through England only including educational materials for the newly established schools. In a way the region was totally subservient to the British authority. Colonial tendencies were gradually creeping into all the spheres of African life and the European missionaries were being brought into the new missions to take over its administration, brushing aside the old Bishop and suspending or dismissing his staffs so that they could perfect to its fullest the program of their masters back home.

Notwithstanding all the pre-programed set-backs, contemporary mission account praised the Bishop's personal integrity, graciousness and godliness. Among his people of Yoruba race, his influence had been irenic and blessed with many strong personalities raised as pillars of modern Nigerian politics, Government, trade and industry, education and health services. In England, Bishop Crowther was recognized as a cooperative and effective platform speaker and an orator to the fullest. The people still remembered him as someone who was capable of holding his audience spellbound each time he rose to speak. Yet when the turnaround program started, he was not only labeled as a "weak Bishop" but drew the moral that "the African race" lacked the capacity to rule. This was part of the strategies mapped out to undermine the intellectual ability and integrity of a black man by some of the Europeans in Governments and industries and even their missionary brethren of this time with a view to support their home Government's ideas of taking over the rule of African continent.

The complete take over of the Church administration by our past missionary friends in disguise through their Government's machineries did not go down well without a resistance from the African clergies of the post Crowther's regime. Some legacies of this period still remained un-erased by the action taken by one of the sections of the Niger mission, that of the Niger Delta when it organized itself into financially self-supporting unit within the Anglican Communion but outside the C.M.S. Declining the European take over, this mission maintained a long separate existence under Crowther's son, Archdeacon Dandeson Crowther. It grew at a phenomenal rate that it became so self-propagating and the evangelical works under his leadership were reported to be excellent and ranked as one of the best in the old colonial empire of the time. The refusal to appoint an African successor to Crowther, despite the availability of many African clergies that could succeed him marked the beginning of new African native churches we see today. The treatment given to Bishop Crowther in his last days coupled with the question of who was to succeed him gave a close focus for the incipient nationalist movement of which E.W. Blyden was the most eloquent spokesman. But un-disputably, Crowther has his own place in the martyrology of African nationalism, which is too difficult to be removed, taking away or brush aside by any generation of the land.

The economic development of the Yoruba people under the Bishopric regime of Bishop Crowther is worth mentioning here for prosperity purpose. The American War of Independence gave rise to the price of cotton in British market and for such purpose; there was the need to look for cotton production elsewhere from which the product could be made available for British industries at a cheaper price than what was available from American cotton growers. The shift in both political and economic gains of the British people in the American continent now began to move towards Africa, as much money was already spent on the expeditions of River Niger by the British Government in the recent past years. African continent was now seen as a safe heaven for the British traders after being defeated in the American market.

E.W. Blyden

Therefore by 1860 the supply of cotton from Abeokuta, though relatively small in quantity when compared with what the American continent was supplying in the past, was still being regarded as significant in the English market and a good beginning. Before the blown out of the American war, Clegg who was the pioneer and the principal cotton merchant of Abeokuta had been consulting with Crowther about how to expand and improve cotton production in other regions bordering Abeokuta especially having Ibadan axis in mind. In 1858, cotton production in Ibadan was rapidly gaining ground and attracting merchants like Madam Tinubu of Abeokuta buying from Ibadan market and taking it to the cotton gins at Abeokuta. Subsequent years particularly in 1859, Edward Gurney, the Quaker banker and philanthropist, was said to have given the C.M.S. 1000 pounds sterling for industrial establishments in Yoruba land particularly for the growing of cotton at Ibadan so that the industrial activities now going on at Abeokuta could be extended to Ibadan.

Under the industrial development program in the region, another group of English merchants and philanthropists headed by Lord Alfred Churchill, MP, formed an organization called African Aid Society with the primary aim to target the persecuted Negroes in America who wished to go to West Africa and grow cotton. For this purpose two delegates, a

Jacob Oluwatayo Adeuyan

Canadian Negro, Dr. Delany and a Jamaican, Robert Campbell visited Yoruba land in December 1859 and signed a business treaty regarding the settlement agreement of the Negroes with the Alake of Abeokuta in which he promised to provide the land and other privileges to the settlers they intended to send. What these arrangements were pointing to was to prove the administrative capabilities of the Bishop's regime about the best way to industrialize his people both from the coast and from the land.

Crowther must have followed the Chinese principles of teaching one about how to catch fish rather than to supply it in his education policy. The introduction of schools where people would learn and develop their knowledge was his chief method of evangelism. Wherever a mission was established, a school must also be built there so that both establishments would work in good harmony to the overall development of that area. In those days and up till the time of our generation in the 1940s, his idea of persuading the Kings and the chiefs to own schools in their names worked wonders and helped to accelerate the speed of education in almost every locality in the Yoruba land. The schools owned by the Kings and chiefs were the ones taken over by the Local Government Authorities when self-government system was introduced in the Western region of Nigeria in the 1950s and called them Local Authority Schools maintained and funded by the public funds.

Between 1861 and 1878, missionary stations on the Niger had been doubled but the constraint facing these missions was adequate funding as the C.M.S. was not prepared to pump money into those establishments. Everything was left on the shoulders of the Bishop as the head of a self-supporting and self-propagating church. To salvage this helpless and hopeless situation, Henry Venn who had at all time stood by the Bishop through thick and thin in 1864 instituted a special endowment fund, called the "West African Native Bishopric Fund", for which he appealed to Christians all over the then developed countries of the world for financial assistance to help grow the young native diocese of Niger. Responding favorably to this call were the congregations from England, Madras, Quebec and Bucharest. The European and African traders at Lagos, in the Delta and in Sierra Leone contributed immensely to the covers of this fund, which was described as being at the disposal of the Bishop for the commencement and encouragement of local missionary efforts and to support the native teachers and school masters as far as their emoluments were concerned.

It was placed on record that apart from the mission stations at Onitsha and the Confluence for which the C.M.S. were responsible, all other stations elsewhere particularly in the Delta area solely depended on Crowther's ability to survive through the Bishopric Fund. Education of the children of the natives had now been seen as a workable weapon to pull the adults and elders of the community to the side of the Christian faith and as such efforts and emphasis were placed on the development of educational programs in each community. Community efforts were used to build classrooms and places of worship in the cities and in the rural areas. Where the community was unable to build two separate houses – one for the school and the other for the church, a single building would be built for the two purposes. The fairly big building would be used to serve as classrooms from Monday to Friday partitioning each class with local mat materials and on Sundays these local mat materials would be removed to accommodate the worshipers for Sunday service. The people of my generation still met this arrangement in the 1940s and not until towards the end of this decade that noticeable improvements began to surface and Church buildings were no longer used as classrooms.

In October 1864, Bishop Crowther went to Bonny to negotiate with King William Dappa Pebble and his chiefs who had earlier on asked the Bishop of London for a missionary station in their Kingdom and promised the Bishop that the Kingdom was ready to pay for the half of the cost of a mission school and house while the remaining half of the cost be met from the Bishopric Fund. A clause in this agreement referred to payment of school fees for the children of two classes of citizens in the community. For those who belonged to the elite group, their children were to pay two pounds a year per child in the lower grades and three pounds in the upper grades. The children of poorer people would be accepted at a lower rate. The fees to be collected from the parents were to take care of the emoluments of two school-masters while the C.M.S. would be responsible for the maintenance of the catechist and later ordained priest of the mission. When King William Pebble died he, was succeeded by his son George; who was an ardent Christian and had his education in England. His reign witnessed many credible transformations in the life of his people and the advancement of Christianity faith in his Kingdom. The Bonny mission soon became a model to the neighboring states for emulation. By an agreement similar to the one at Bonny, Crowther moved to the Brass in 1868 and Kalabari in 1874 to pioneer the method of the village school and self-support system that rapidly expanded his missionary visions in Southern Nigeria during the period of 1891 to 1914.

The uniqueness of Crowther's vision about the social transformation of his people was now bearing bountiful fruits and between 1871 and 1875, he attempted to try similar methods of self-supporting and self-propagating missionary system he had established in Bonny and Brass in Warri when the European traders there were willing to sell off their business houses for cheaper prices because of decline in their business ventures. But unfortunately there he found Chief Nana Olomu who was the ruler as being too conservative and distrustful about the social effect that his education program would bring to his Kingdom. The Bishop waited for a while to catch on the fastest opportunity to be made available for business better climate and improvement on the Niger and then to introduce the method of self-support and self-propagating into the mission there. As it was then, the economic situation of the whole region around this time was unstructured and was mainly in the hands of the foreigners and some few scattered natives who were being regarded lucky to have moved closely to these foreigners and employed as their agents.

The programs of the Bishop were inadequately funded and in some instances, he had to squeeze himself up to meet with some of these programs, while others would be left to die a natural death. For example, the only college in the whole land mass of West Africa where people could be trained for the needed expansive work was located at Sierra Leone and most beneficiaries of this college came from the neighborhood of that place and only few scanty numbers of students were able to join the student's population at Fourah Bay. After graduation, the bulk of job opportunities for these young graduates were mainly in the up-land of the region i.e. along the banks of River Niger and we should not forget that the only solid means of transportation to get to the up-land as at then was through the traders steam ship trading on the Niger. The movement of the ships was seasonal because it was only during the raining season lasting for about only four months that the ships could sail safely on the River. The priests and the evangelists that were to be employed to work in the new stations up-land were to come from Sierra Leone and in most cases if they are married, they had to leave their families behind to first of all go on their own to face the music of the new environment before ever thinking of asking their family members to join them.

Another important thing to note here was the salary structure of the category of workers in the missions as at this time. For example, the salary of a trained evangelist was thirty-six pound sterling of that time per annum while that of a trained and ordained priest was between fifty and sixty-two pounds sterling. We should not also forget to note that during this time, there was no restriction on the number of children a family could raise and as such some of these workers had between four and six children in their family structure to feed and catered for. Because of this terrible condition of service available then, most of the highly qualified men of the time preferred to stay at Sierra Leone or Yoruba mission rather than to move to out-stations where they could be stranded forever.

To cap it up, the policy of the C.M.S during this time was that all volunteers for the Niger mission must consider themselves emigrants and could not expect passages to be paid for them to come back to Sierra Leone for their annual vacation if at all there was any one to visit their families left behind. Where it became very expedient for any of them to visit Sierra Leone for any urgent or personal matters, Crowther would make a special grant from the Bishopric Fund for such visit.

Much of the problems facing the first crops of African missionaries during the religion formative years centered on "inadequate financial resources" to keep both body and soul together under the same spiritual roof. Those that chose missionary work as their profession then did this under the banner of Christ's love and for the rapid transformation and civilization of their people. Different from what we see prevailing today, where people go to missionary works just for the love of the money first and then that of Christ next. Some of the people of today in the missionary services all over the world see it the way an industry or business entity is viewed for employment opportunities where any one can apply to and get what he/she wanted easily. Those of us that grew up in an environment where traditional religion is being practiced would testify to the fact that it was not an easy thing to penetrate into the borders of the practitioners of this religion with a view to either convince them or educate them to change from the practice of their religion to any other one.

To work with the heathens of this time, the Bishop laid down to his agents some management tactics and approach that would help them to face the challenges of their duties. He told them that, "it was impossible to try to understand or deal with the rulers and some notable people in the community except one learns how to respect some aspect of their way of life." Thus, as the Bishop seriously supported and depended much on the education and on bridging the gap between the Mission and the old world, he continued to emphasize the value of civilization and seeking what is good in the old society and cultivating it. Based on this philosophy, he had to ponder over the Yoruba equivalents of God, Devil, priest, and much more native words in the Yoruba version of the Scriptures we enjoy today. On the issue of nationalism and the Church he once wrote:

Christianity has come into the world to abolish and supersede all false religions, to direct mankind to the only way of obtaining peace and reconciliation with their offended God.... But it should be borne in mind that Christianity does not undertake to destroy national assimilation; where there are any degrading and superstitious defects, it corrects them; where they are connected with politics, such corrections should be introduced with due caution and with all meekness of wisdom, that there may be good and perfect understanding between us and the powers that be that while we render unto all their dues, we may regard it our bounden duty to stand firm in rendering to God the things that belongs to God.

He further wrote in this memo that the native Mutual Aid Clubs should not be despised, but he cautioned that where there is any with superstitious connections, it should be corrected and improved after a Christian model. He accepted that amusements are acknowledged on all hands to tend to relieve the mind and sharpen the intellect. If any such is not immoral or indecent, tendering to corrupt the mind, but merely an innocent play of amusement, it should not be checked because of its being native and of heathen origin. Of these kinds of amusement are fables, storytelling, proverbs and songs, which may be regarded as stores of their national education in which they exercise their power of thinking. Such will be Improved upon and enriched from foreign stocks as civilization advances.

Their religious terms and ceremonies should be carefully observed; the wrong use made of such terms does not depreciate their real value, but renders them more valid when we adopt them in expressing Scriptural terms in their right senses and places from which they have been misapplied for want of better knowledge. This policy could be seen as perfect one that enabled Christianity to grow in our community faster. The Rev. J. C. Taylor (later Bishop) of Onitsha diocese in the 1860s sanctioned the policy and said that he did not see anything sinful in converts taking *Ozo* titles – which were comparable to those that were members of the *Ekpe* Society in Calabar or the *Ogboni* at Abeokuta. But today we see a lot of killer clubs in nature of which most of them have their roots deeply planted either in the Churches or in the Mosques, yet we pretend to harbor them as being holy and un-sinful.

To the same degree as Henry Venn had said on many occasions that so long as Europeans retained control of a Church abroad, it would never become a fully national institution. This assertion was correct and right because the signs that began to show its ugly faces towards the end of Bishop Crowther's Bishopric regime confirmed the true intentions of the European missionaries on the Niger and else where in the continent.

But it could be said with clarity that Samuel Ajayi Crowther and his co-African missionaries built a solid foundation for the Church in the West Coast of Africa. He envisioned a Church that would be deeply African in governance and spirituality, and richly Anglican in doctrine and worship. We commend his efforts and salute his gallantry that the foundation and the vision flourished over the years and up-till today in Nigeria, the Church there is one of the fastest growing and one of the most dynamic Churches of the Anglican Communion with close to 100 diocese or more and an estimated number of worshipers close to 20 million or more.

The journey of the missionaries up to where it is today in Nigeria was too far from what could be called a smooth passage. It was full of lowlands, high hills, and range of Rocky Mountains, large and wide rivers, muddy grounds, and plain terrains and so on; but the role played by this unsung hero of the Anglican Communion and of the Christian world is now beginning to come into play after being buried for so many decades by his friends and foes alike. Statutes, monuments, institutions of higher learning, long and popular streets in our cities, airports, river badges and ships and all others have been dedicated to the beneficiaries of the efforts and struggles of this single man, yet his name has been forgotten in the history book of our nation and even in the books of the region of West Coast of Africa, which he suffered a lot to bring out to see the light of the day.

Crowther's colleague in England, France, Portugal, and other nations in the world, and, even those that received training as missionaries under his tutorship were being given places of honor in their respective nations. Why then ours become different and difficult to do? Is there anything that goes wrong somewhere? I think the time has come when the off-shoots of the people he sacrificed his time, labor and energy to improve their lives, to civilized them as may be called, to set up industrial machineries for their nations, to evangelized their souls and educated their children to demand for an explanations on why it took so long a time from 1900 a year after his death up-to-date to recognize the valuable works of Bishop Samuel Ajayi Crowther as the first native builder of our modern nations in West Africa.

Chapter 16

Bishop Crowther – The Atlas of Modern Nigeria Economy and Government:

Bishop Samuel Ajayi Crowther believed that industry is "the true secret, the grand recipe for felicity". And for his people to apply themselves to the new style of education he brought to them and to master the techniques of the newly introduced work training, they would certainly need some trades that would keep them going if really they would become self-reliant according to the numerous programs he had for them. One of his programs was to equip them through the development of their individual talents that could make them enjoy life to the fullest. His philosophical belief was that industry makes people worthy members of civil society, because it enables them to be of good service to their neighbors and that there was never a great Man that was not an industrious Man; likewise never was a good Man that was a lazy Man. This philosophy helped him greatly to build up the very strong pillars that held the structures of our educational fortresses together.

He had the believe that the only foundation for a useful education in a society is to be laid in religion because without this there can be no virtue and without virtue there can be no liberty, and liberty is always the object and life of a good government. He therefore proposed to his people an idea that supported the truth of the Christian revelation, which declares that all its doctrines and precepts are calculated to promote the happiness of a society, and the safety and well being of civil government. He contented in theory and practice that a Christian cannot fail of being a good representative of his people in government, for every precept of the Gospel inculcates those degrees of humility, self-denial, and brotherly kindness which are directly opposed to the pride of other forms of religion and the pride of the rulers of the kingdoms of this era at their courts.

A Christian cannot fail of being useful to the public he serves, for his religion teaches him that no man "lives to himself" and he cannot be wholly inoffensive for his religion teaches him to do unto others in the likewise manner he would wish others do unto him. The foundation of our early education and economic policies were virtually built in all parts of African land on the Christian rock of faith and this confirmed that what all agreed upon is probably right; but what two disagreed upon is most probably wrong. Life itself is an object to be improved upon from time to time and from generation to generation. Therefore what is to be done tomorrow must start its course today.

It was a fact that the exit of slave trading must usher in a better and civilized way of trading that would bridge the gap between the entire people of Africa and their monarchs and noble men who were in the past years the slave trade magnates and lords. Walking through the first half of the 19th century, one would notice that private chartered companies and various association had had very serious impact and contact with the native of Africa from the North down to the South of the continent for trade and in missionary works. But throughout this period, the interest of the British government in setting up budget for the cost of colonial administration of territories that might fall its way was virtually non-existent. Reason for this move may be attributed to such barriers created by the hostilities of the natives as well as the physical dangers of disease.

Instead of the government to pursue this line of action, it restricted itself to combating the slave trade, which it had outlawed in 1807 as well as seeking ways to persuade the African rulers to cooperate with the government in eradicating and destroying the fortresses of the deadly trade pattern throughout the continent. In its activities to stamp out the trade, the government of England provided a naval squadron off the West African coast fully armed with sophisticated war equipment to deal immensely with the slave traders attempting to sail out of the territory with their human cargoes. As time went by, the British government began to sponsor expeditions into the interior, mainly by the explorers and missionaries to find more facts about the continent and its people; not only to facilitate the anti-slavery activities promoted by the mission societies but also to help discover sources of raw materials that her private merchants might exploit through commerce with the natives.

This noble intention gave birth to various expeditions on the full course of exploration of the Niger River, a task that took 36 years of hard work coupled with loss of men and materials. The project at the end bore bountiful fruits for the government and people of England for it led to the establishment of trading and mission stations in the interior of West Africa. It should be borne in mind that the many requests of the traders for their home government's protection of their trading facilities inevitably drew the British and some of their European counterparts more and more into the internal affairs of the whole continent.

The following document is an extract from the instructions issued by Lord John Russel, British Colonial Secretary to Her Majesty's Niger Commissioners (Jan. 30, 1841) clearly showing the position of the British government on this topic when he wrote:

…..**O**n your arrival at each native settlement, you will ascertain the proper mode for opening a communication with the Chief: and …you will take care that you are treated by him with proper respect; and you will not neglect, also, to treat him with the respect which is due to the rank which belongs to him.

You will tell the Chief that you are sent by the Queen of Great Britain and Ireland to express her Majesty's wish to establish friendly relations with him; and to settle and agree with him for the extinction of the Foreign Traffic in Slaves in his dominions; and for the substitution instead thereof of a full and free intercourse and barter of all articles of innocent trade between the subjects of Her Majesty and those of such Chief, for his profit advantage, and for the mutual use, comfort, and benefit of the subject of both countries…. You will inquire what further articles of native growth, or produce, or manufacture his country can supply as articles of useful export with Great Britain; and you will encourage him the cultivation or production thereof, by expressing generally the readiness of this country to take off his hands, on fair and reasonable terms of barter, all such articles of useful trade for this country as he can supply, in return for all such articles of use, and comfort, and advantage to himself as he requires.

You will show him the advantages of putting down the Foreign Slave Trade, and building upon the lawful and innocent trade. You will say to him, that his subjects will thereby be induced to cultivate the soil, to value their habitations, to increase their produce, and to behave well, in order to keep the advantage which that produce will give to them; that they will thus become better subjects, and better men, and that his possessions will thus become more full of what is valuable. You will impress upon him, that he himself will no longer need to make, or to keep up, quarrels with his neighbors, or to undertake distant and dangerous wars, or to seek out causes of punishment to his own subjects, for the sake of producing from the odious Trade in Slaves an income for himself. You will explain to him, that the people of his country will, out of the produce of labor in cultivating, gathering, and preparing articles for trade, bring to him more revenues, and be consequently more valuable to him.

You will tell him, that Her Majesty…proposes that, upon his abolishing the Slave Trade, not only he and his subjects shall have this free and advantageous commerce; but that he himself shall have, for his own share, and without any payment on his part, a sum not exceeding [5 percent] part value of every article of British merchandise brought by British ships and sold in his dominions; such proportion to be taken by himself…. You will not fail on all proper occasions…. To impress upon him the impolicy as well as the injustice of slavery, and to acquaint him with the abhorrence in which it is held by Her Majesty and the people of England.

You may further remind him that every man naturally works harder for himself than for another, and is more economical and more careful of his own property; consequently, that the produce of his country would be much greater by free labor. You may further intimate him, that a compliance with the wish of Her Majesty's Government and her people, in this respect, would certainly increase Her Majesty's interest in his welfare, and enable her Majesty and her people to render much greater assistance and encouragement in improving the condition of himself and his people, than would be afforded them during the continuance of a system of slave labor. But you must always bear in mind that the main object of your commission is the extinction of the Foreign Slave Trade, and all other points must for the present be considered subordinate.

You will, at the proper time, exhibit the presents with which you are furnished from Her Majesty, as proofs of the desire of friendship with the Queen entertains towards the Chief, and as samples of the articles, with which, among others, this country will be glad to supply himself and his subjects in as great a quantity as they want and wish, on fair and reasonable terms of barter.

If, after discussing this mater with the Chief, you shall find that your arguments have not so far prevailed with him, as to induce him to enter into this Agreement for the Extinction of the Foreign Slave Trade in his dominions; and if he shall resolutely resist your suggestions and the wishes of Her Majesty to that effect; you will entreat and urge him to reconsider this matter, you will ask him to assemble his elders or head-men, and consult with them, before he finally rejects the proposals made by you.

While you describe the power and wealth of your country, you will, in your entire interview with the African Chiefs, and with other African natives, on the subject of the suppression of the Slave Trade, abstain carefully from any threat or intimation, that hostilities upon their territory will be the result of their refusal to treat. You will state that the Queen and people of England profess the Christian Religion; that by this religion they are commanded to assist in promoting good will, peace, and brotherly love among all nations and men; and that in endeavoring to commence a further intercourse with the African nations Her Majesty's Government are actuated and guided by these principles.

You will make allowance for the motives of fear, of distrust, of jealousy, of suspicion, by which native Africans, unaccustomed to treat with Europeans in this formal way, may, at first, naturally view the overtures made to them; you will make allowance also for misunderstanding, either of language, of manner, or of conduct; you will also allow for any hardness of feeling you may witness in them on the subject of Slave Trade, a hardness naturally engendered by the exercise of that traffic, and, perhaps, in some cases, increased by intercourse with the lowest and basest of Europeans….. You will on no account have recourse to arms, excepting for purpose of defense.

If after all your attempts to attain the immediate object of your commission, you shall fail in it, you will conclude by telling the Chief and his head-men, that Her Majesty is bound to use all her naval means… to endeavor entirely to put stop to the exportation of Slaves from the dominions of every African Chief; and that the Chief and his subjects will, when perhaps too late, see cause to regret their conduct….

It is considered desirable by Her Majesty's Government to have power to erect one or more small forts on the Niger, from whence, and by means of which, to watch over the due execution of the Agreements, to assist in the abolition of the Slave Trade, and to protect and further the innocent trade of Her Majesty's subjects.

Bearing these views in mind, you will, in your course up that River, select one or more appropriate spots for the erection of forts for the above mentioned purposes; and you will make with the Chief of the country a conditional bargain for the land, stating the purpose for which it is intended; you will pay down a small portion of the price, as security for the purchase and permission....

If at any place, in an independent State within the range of your commission, it shall appear to you to be desirable, that a resident agent on the part of Her Majesty, shall be immediately appointed and enter on his duties, you are empowered to leave at such a place provisionally, as British resident agent, any one of the gentlemen [normally a military officer] of your commission...

[*Ref: British Parliamentary Papers, 1843, Vol. xlviii(472)*]

On reaching the continent, the British Admiralty further issued other instructions for the guidance of its officers in their negotiations with the local Chiefs in forwarding the suppression of the Slave Trade from coastal Africa. In furtherance of this, it issued the following sixteen guidelines on how to approach the issue in order to get achievable results.

1. The suppression of the Slave Trade may be materially assisted by obtaining the cooperation of the Native Chiefs of Africa in the object, you are therefore authorized to conclude engagements for this purpose with the African Chiefs; but you must strictly adhere to the regulations herein laid down on the subject.
2. You will procure the fullest and most correct information as to the state of those parts of the coast in which Slave Trade is carried on, so as to enable you to determine, with what Chiefs it may be expedient to enter into negotiations for the conclusion of Engagements.
3. With this in view, you will endeavor to ascertain the power and influence of the several Chiefs; their personal character, and the habits of the people; the extent and force of the country; the sources, amount, and description of the legitimate trade carried on.
4. You will endeavor to obtain the most accurate information as to the Slave Trade; its present extent, and whether it has recently increased or diminished.
5. You will investigate the means whereby the Slave Trade may most effectually and speedily be extinguished, and you will enquire into the inclination and the power of the Chief to carry into effect an Engagement for that purpose, and the means, which Great Britain may have for enforcing it.

6. When you shall desire to open negotiation with any African Chief, you will, after taking every proper precaution for the safety of yourself and your people, at the same time avoiding giving offence to the Natives, obtain a personal interview with the Chiefs, and endeavor to induce them to conclude an Engagement.
7. Every opportunity is to be taken of impressing the minds of the Native Chiefs and their people with a conviction of the efforts Great Britain has made for their benefit, and of her earnest desire to raise them in the scale of nations. It is most desirable to excite in them an emulation of the habits of the Christian world, and to enable them to make the first practical step towards civilization by the abandonment of the Slave Trade.
8. Special care must be taken not to offend the prejudices of the Natives; and every respect must be paid to their peculiar usages, so far as the same are not of an inhuman character; and allowance must be made for any jealousy or distrust that may be shown by them.
9. Threats or intimidation are never to be used to induce the Native Chiefs to conclude the Engagement: on the contrary, forbearance and conciliation must be in all cases the rule of conduct; and if the Native Chiefs refuse the Engagement, every means must be taken to encourage in them feelings of confidence, and to leave a favorable impression that may facilitate the renewal of negotiations at a future period.
10. Immediately after the conclusion of the Engagement, you will require the Chiefs to proclaim a law to their people by which its stipulations shall be publicly made known.
11. In case the Slave Trade is actually carried on within the jurisdiction of the Chief at the time the Engagement is concluded, you will then require that all the slaves held for exportation shall be delivered up to you to be made free at a British colony.
12. You will also demand that all implements of the Slave Trade, such as shackles, bolts, and handcuffs, chains, whips, branding irons, etc., or articles of Slave equipment for fitting up vessels to carry Slaves, shall be given up to you, or destroyed in your presence.

13. You will also insist on the immediate destruction of the barracoons, or buildings exclusively devoted to the reception of Slaves, and, if necessary, you will enforce all these demands.
14. You are not, without the signed consent in writing of a Native Chief, to take any step upon his territory for putting down the Slave Trade by force, excepting when, by Engagement, Great Britain is entitled to adopt coercive measures on shore for that purpose.
15. You will cause a vigilant watch to be kept over the proceedings of the Chiefs, until you are satisfied of their fidelity to their Engagements. After which, you will visit the Chiefs in person, or send a Commander of one of Her Majesty's Ships, at least once in six months, to see to the due execution of the Engagements on the part of the Chiefs.
16. In the event, however, of ultimate failure of the negotiation you will finally state to the Chief that every civilized Naval Power in the world has declared that it has abandoned the Slave Trade; that most nations have united with Great Britain in endeavors to put it down; that Great Britain will not allow the subjects of the Chief to carry Slaves for sale to or from any places beyond the limits of his territory, and that Her Majesty's Officers have orders to liberate Slaves when found embarked in boats of his subjects for that purpose.

The suppression and end to transatlantic Slave Trade did not come to a total end not until the 1860s. As soon as this fit was achieved, the illegal trade was replaced by other means of trade in commodities such as palm oil business to start with. This shift in trade now had serious economic and political influence and consequences in the interior of Africa, which led to increasing the British intervention in the internal affairs of places like the Yorubaland, Niger Delta and some other areas of the coastal plain of the continent. In the regions of Yorubaland and the Delta for example, the instability created by the Yoruba wars and the activities of other European powers made the British government to move cautiously toward colonial domination of the lower Niger Basin.

In the decades that followed the abolition of the Slave Trade, British diplomacy wove fabric of treaties with the Kings and the Chieftains of these areas seeking for their cooperation in suppressing the traffic as well as establishing their trading facilities and interests which occasionally dictated armed intervention by the Royal Navy and by the Royal Niger

Company Costabulary to protect their legitimate commerce and a way to maintain peace among the inhabitants of the region where these trading facilities were established. Furthermore the missionaries too cried out for protection and assistance in stamping out slavery and other barbarous practices associated with indigenous religions. To encourage the new movement, the British government through the Foreign office posted out consular officials to serve the increasing amount of trade in the ports of the Bights of Benin and Biafra thereby increasing the influence of the British inland.

The British influence would not have come to fruition at the time it occurred if not for the motives of rival European powers, especially France and Germany that were scurried to develop overseas markets and ambition to annex territories. The intentions of the various European countries to divide the continent among themselves now became obvious especially when an idea of allotment of exploitation areas were put before the Berlin Conference of 1885, where the European powers attempted to resolve their conflicts of interest in the continent of Africa. In this Conference, dual blank cheque of free access to the continent for trade and also providing African people with the benefits of Europe's civilization were issued. The Conference acknowledged and recognized the influence of Britain in the Niger Basin but for this to be legally recognized, effective occupation that would secure full international recognition was the best option and in the end, pressure through France and Germany's attitude hastened the establishment of an effective occupation of the British in the regions of the Niger Basin.

One of the major successes of the British occupation of the Niger Basin was the establishment of a trading company called the United African Company (UAC) that was founded by George Goldie in 1879. In 1886, Goldie's Consortium was chartered by the British government as the Royal Niger Company and granted broad concessionary powers in "all the territory of the basin of Niger". As the few Nigerians that could read, write and digest the English language as at this time were those that were trained by the missionaries, the concessions granted to this company only emanated from Britain and not from any authority in Nigeria. An advantage of this situation was taken for granted in so many areas of our development around this time.

For example, if we go through the contents of the form used as pro-forma treaties by the Royal Niger Company in the 1880s and which our Kings and Chieftains tumb-printed as a legal document on-behalf of our

The Journey of the First Black Bishop

people, one would be amazed and clearly observe that this document contained a lot of rope-in statements on the part of the Natives and these statements were obviously forced on the people by their trading partners. The following is a true copy of the pro-forma form of this time:

TEXT OF BLANK PRINTED FORM USED FOR PRO-FORMA TREATIES IN THE 1880s.

We, the undersigned Chiefs of ………………….., with the view of bettering the condition of our country and people, do this day cede to the Royal Niger Company (Chartered and Limited), for ever, the whole of our territory extending from…………………….

17. We also give to the said Royal Niger Company (Chartered and Limited) full power to settle all native disputes arising from any cause whatever, and we pledge ourselves not to enter into any war with other tribes without the sanction of the said Royal Niger Company (Chartered and Limited).
18. We understand that the said Royal Niger Company (Chartered and Limited) have full power to mine, farm, and build in any portion of our country.
19. We bind ourselves not to have any intercourse [i.e., transactions or communications] with any strangers or foreigners except through the said Royal Niger Company (Chartered and Limited).
20. In consideration of the foregoing, the said Royal Niger Company (Chartered and Limited) bind themselves not to interfere with any of the Native laws or customs of the country, consistently with the maintenance of order and good government.
21. The said Royal Niger Company (Chartered and Limited) agree to pay native owners of land reasonable amount for any portion they may require.
22. The said Royal Niger Company (Chartered and Limited) bind themselves to protect the said Chiefs from the attacks of any neighboring aggressive tribes.
23. The said Royal Niger Company (Chartered and Limited) also agree to pay the said Chiefs…………… Native value.
24. We the undersigned witnesses, do hereby solemnly declare that the ……………… Chiefs whose names are placed opposite their respective crosses have in our presence affixed their

crosses of their own free will and consent, and that the said ………………….has in our presence affixed this signature.

Done in triplicate at……………this ……….day of……………, 188…

Declaration by Interpreter.

I, …………………..of…………………, do hereby solemnly declare that I am well acquainted with the language of the ……………….country, and that of the …….day of ……… 188…., I truly and faithfully explained the above Agreement to all the Chiefs present, and that they understood its meaning.

History cannot not be overlooked or silenced concerning the role that was played by Sir George Goldie - an English administrator in the building up of a modern entity called Nigeria during its formative years. Goldie was born on the 20th of May 1846, which was the year that Bishop Samuel Ajayi Crowther was consecrated as the first black African Bishop. He received his education at the Royal Military Academy, Woolwich. He first visited the country of Nigeria in 1877 during which time he built up an idea of adding something significant to the British Empire out of the regions of the lower and middle Niger. For over twenty years, his efforts were directed and devoted to the realization of this motive. The method by which he was to achieve this objective danced around the revival of the British government's chartered company's idea that was once buried with the East India Company of the first experiment. His first step in this direction was to combine all the British commercial interests in the Niger and he accomplished this fit in 1879 when the United African Company was formed and later in 1881 granted charter by the Imperial government.

Goldie and his ideas were never without opposition especially from the French traders that established themselves on the lower part of the River, thus making it too difficult for the newly formed company to obtain large territorial rights; but tactically the French traders were bought out of the area in 1884. In 1885 at the Berlin Conference on West Africa, Goldie who was now being regarded as an expert on matters relating to Niger River was able to announce that on the lower Niger the British flag alone flew. More speed was added to annexation of more territories by the British along the Niger coast through their trading agents under the protection rights. Within a very short period of time, over 400 political treaties drawn up by Goldie were made with the Chiefs of the lower Niger extending to the Hausa states. In July 1886, the National African Company transformed into the Royal Niger Company with more powers had Lord Aberdare as its first governor and Goldie as vice-governor; and on the death of Lord Aberdare, Goldie automatically became governor of the company, whose destinies he had guided throughout.

Like in the case of Nigeria and other nations along the Atlantic Ocean coastline, the building up of these nations as either British or French occupied states had similar structures and organs as they were carried out in the face of difficulties raised by the interests of other European countries. Most of the countries in Europe of this time were now becoming conscious of the political powers to be enjoyed if it were possible for them to carve out territories to themselves in the continent whereby it would be possible for them to dominate the trade, government and the natural resources of such territory.

The French travelers worsened the situation when they coupled their trade mission to this part of the continent with serious political ambition at the back of their minds. From the third frontier were the German's strenuous efforts to secure for Germany the basin of the lower Niger and Lake Chad, which posed a dangerous threat to Goldie's scheme of empire than the ambitions of France. Of particular interest in the game here was the activities of Prince Bismark of Germany who was a persistent antagonist to British successes in this region and because of this reason Herr E.R.Flegal who had traveled in Nigeria during 1882 – 1884 under the auspices of the British company, was recruited in 1885 by the newly-formed German Colonial Society to secure treaties for Germany, which had established itself at Cameroon.

Unfortunately, Flegal died a year after in 1886, leaving his assignments to be continued by Dr. Standinger, who was his companion in this program. The German strategy was to burst up the charter of the Royal Niger Company by stirring up trouble in the occupied portions of the company's territory. The person who was at the head of this strategy was Herr. Hoenigsborg but unfortunately for him, he was arrested at Onitsha, tried by the Royal Niger Company's supreme court at Asaba, and expelled from the country.

Prince Bismark continued in his efforts to establish German interest in Nigeria and he therefore sent out his nephew, Herr. Von Puttkamer, as Gernam Consul General to Nigeria on orders to report back to him the general situation concerning the aborted plans of Flegel and his co-plotters, and when, this report was published in a White Book, Bismark demanded from the Royal Niger Company heavy damages. His other demand from the British government through constant pressure was for the British government to compel the Royal Niger Company to give up a larger part of its trading influence in the country to German traders and administrators. If this had been granted, it would amount to the British government loosing a third, and most valuable part of the company's territory in the new set-up. But too bad for Bismark, he fell from power in March 1880 and in the following July, Lord Salisbury concluded the famous Heligoland Agreement with Germany, which ended the aggressive ambition of Germany in Nigeria.

As noted above, the French and German ambition to have their share of the pie continued endlessly. Immediately after the Heligoland Agreement, the door was opened for a final settlement of the Nigeria/Cameroon frontiers. This Agreement that was initiated by Goldie was a way of stopping the advance of France into Nigeria from the direction of Congo and as part of the Agreement, a long but narrow strip of the territory between Adamawa and Lake Chad was conceded to the Germans.

Meanwhile French efforts at aggression were also made from the West of the country especially from Dahomeyan side despite the previous Agreement that was concluded with France in 1890 respecting the Northern frontier. As the Royal Niger Company was facing problems from both West and North-East frontiers, hostility of certain Fula Princes led the company to dispatch in 1897 an expedition against the Mohammedan state of Nupe and its other neighboring states. This expedition was organized and personally directed by Goldie himself and it was a successful operation with resounding victory. In the following year differences with France regarding the frontier line became acute, and this called for the British government's intervention.

On the negotiation table, Goldie who was instrumental and vocal at the talk was able to secure for the Great Britain the whole of the navigable stretch of the lower Niger. During this time it was impossible for chartered company to hold itself against the state-supported protectorates of France and Germany; and because of this on the 1st of January 1900, the Royal Niger Company transferred its territories to the British government for the sum of Eight hundred and sixty five thousand pounds sterling (865000 :00 pds). The ceded territory together with the small Niger Coast Protectorate

(Lagos) that was already under the imperial control was formed into two protectorates of Northern and Southern Nigeria we see in existence today.

The various semi-accidental events primarily the extinction of slave trade and the introduction of legal trade created the final placing of the French and British pieces in the African board game. The role played by the missionaries of the early twentieth century in the colonization of Africa was considerable and enormous in terms of cultural and political domination of the people. It was this organ of the colonial master's program that changed the entire culture of the people from its original model into adulterated and diluted cultures in the continent today. Although the missionaries task was to make people accept the Bible, its teachings, principles and philosophy, but Christianity was turned into an ideology which was used to convince the people not to resist the white domination based on the doctrine that the reward of the people's labor is awaiting them at the gates of heaven while the colonialists were busy taking away the treasures and the wealth of the continent to build their countries in Europe into modern cities with magnificent fortresses, well paved roads, nice holiday results, world class universities and other reliable economic projects. The continent that produced the wealth with which all these things were achieved was left empty without good and reliable roads to connect the countries of the continent for economic development, solid economy to absorb the graduates from institutions of higher learning, stable electricity and water supply, effective land and waterway transportation system, and even food for the people to eat.

The power of religious doctrine was enormous that its ideological bargains were used to legitimize, sustain and even promote political division, tyranny and oppression, as well as in other areas of the people's life for reasons of political liberation of the people. Outwardly, the missionaries could lay claims that they regarded themselves as opposition to the colonial ideology but inwardly they were part of the colonial structural agents that brought with them into the land the type of religions beliefs and practices, which were alien to the land. Father Wolf Schmidt was therefore correct when he asserted that, "the early missionaries did not differentiate between their faith and their own culture".

The missionaries were at no time been forgotten in the apportionment of the continent. Article 6 of the Berlin Act, actually stipulated that "Christian Missionaries"….. shall likewise be the subject of especial protection". And from now on the hazard of their life in Africa would be progressively diminished. There would be an increasing population of European soldiers and police to protect them; to safeguard their converts against the reprisals of their tribesmen who may feel betrayed by their change of heart and faith, or merely envious of their present position in their community because of their enlarged material opportunities. Therefore the actualization of colonial intent in the continent largely depended on how strong the missionary's religious tendencies were deep-rooted into the hearts of the members of the community they serve.

It should be noted that it was out of the early converts that the colonialists used as members of the early governments in the land because of their proximity and obedience to the foreign administrators who were carefully selected for their positions with the recommendations and approvals of the church strong men either in England, Portugal or France. By gradual methodology, prodded by the already mapped out strategy of annexation of Africa, the Foreign office in England for example and the British traders connived together to turn the table of events in Nigeria to suite their purpose.

Before 1914, the church was the center of the social, spiritual and political aspirations of educated Africans and illiterate converts. Those that were educated through the efforts of the Church Missionary Society (CMS) constituted the bulk of the elites that the country was able to produce as at this time. They formed the mouth organ of the people on how best their country could be governed and their resources be managed to the advantage of the populace. The advocacy of a parliamentary system of government for Nigeria was made not only by these educated Nigerians in the 19th century, but had started agitating for this through Legislative Council procedure from 1886 to 1914 by the ardent churchmen and their ministers.

It is a pure fact that in any computation of the role played by the press in the struggle of the nationalists, much credit must be apportioned to the Christian Church and educated Christianized Nigerians. It was not either gain saying or an accident that it was Dr. Dikko, a Christian trained medical doctor from Birmingham University by Walter Miller and his friends, whose ideas played a key role in the formation of the strongest political party ever to be emerged from the North of the country – Nigeria known as the Northern Peoples Congress (NPC).

Without misappropriating words here, the fact would ever remain that the first generation of educated Nigerians wherever geographical location they may come from were pre-eminently equipped for a nationalist task by their learning and the foundation of the educational programs that Bishop Samuel Ajayi Crowther and his Nigeria partners (people like from James Johnson to J.C. Taylor and others) laid down from the beginning of event. The philosophy of the Bible that the foreign missionaries brushed aside because of their nationality gains, i.e. its notion of equality, justice and non-racialism were the containers of the weapons employed by the converts during their nationalist struggle against their oppressors. It was easy for the nationalists to attack their foreign masters and dealt a big blow on them below the belt because they had the full knowledge of their master's custom and clearly saw every inch of their movement on daily basis and furthermore they were the Natives working directly with them in their offices and trading facilities.

More will be said about the activities of the Nigerian nationalists in the preceding chapters but for the meantime, the philosophy of Henry Venn, which was continually being echoed at every occasion in the meetings of the C.M.S was true and strong to its tap-root. He said at various occasions, "that so long as Europeans retained control of a church abroad, it would never become a truly national institution". It can be said with pure clarity that Bishop Samuel Ajayi Crowther who was a direct beneficiary of this philosophy and his followers built their churches on this solid and strong foundation in Nigeria. With sensitivity in church doctrine, more of the 20th century than 19th century, he envisioned a church that would be deeply African in governance and spirituality, and richly Anglican in doctrine and worship. That foundation and vision of Bishop Crowther are today still seen and flourished in all the areas of Nigeria economy, trade and industry, government, education, health, and in all the churches of the land.

For example, the Church of Nigeria is one of the fastest growing and one of the most dynamic Churches of the Anglican Communion with large dioceses and an estimated twenty or more million members. His education policy based upon the charity of others he enjoyed during his captivity as a slave boy to his independence days was what developed his mind and that of his fellow African nationalists into a larger form of picture in existence today throughout the continent of Africa. We should not forget that it was through the hospitality and generousity of the church that his people became whatever they were, whether traders, businessmen/women, teachers, clerks in offices and trading facilities, evangelists, pastors, doctors, lawyers, engineers and so on. His policy in cooperation with the church made it possible for these professionals to fulfill their whole being, and by the involuntary monopoly of his education program, the destiny of their children was gloriously placed on their hands. I beg to quote from the speech of Pastor Mojola Agbebi in 1892 when he said these words concerning the future of his people:

When we look for no manifesto from Salisbury Square, when we expect no packet of resolution from Exeter Hall, when no bench of foreign Bishops, no conclave of Cardinals, 'lord over' Christian Africa, when the Captain of Salvation, Jesus Christ Himself, leads the Ethiopian host, and our Christianity ceases to be London-ward and New York-ward but Heaven-ward, then will there be an end to Privy Councils, Governors, Colonels, Annexations, Displacements, Petitions, Cessions and Coercions. Telegraph wires will be put to better uses and even Downing Street [will] be absent in the political vocabulary of the West African Natives.

By Mojola Agbebi, 1892.

Chapter 17

Early Missionary Activities on the Banks of River Niger:

The consecration ordinance and the license given to Bishop Crowther in 1864 stipulated that his Episcopal authority and powers extends beyond the Niger Mission or Niger Territory, and it includes the "countries of West Africa beyond the limits of the English dominions", that is the territories of West Africa from the Equator to the Senegal, with the exception of such places like Lagos, Gold Coast (now Ghana) and Sierra Leone, which were placed under the British administration and called them the British Colonies. Documents from the Church Missionary Society's records clearly revealed the jurisdictional territory of Bishop Crowther's diocese approved by the Archbishop of Canterbury just to silence the doubts of the Salisbury Square's white missionaries who were antagonists to Bishop Crowther's consecration as a bishop. The white Bishop's authority in such places called the British Colonies of the time i.e Lagos, Gold Coast and Sierra Leone was intended to be for a temporary period only meaning that as soon as there could emerge enough Africans to manage those stations effectively, Crowther's Bishopric duties would annex those areas to give full legal authority and meaning to the territories covered in the Bishop's license. Furthermore, it would cover the true interpretation of what was meant in Venn's keynote address during the Bishop's consecration, which he called the "full development of the Native African Church". While he was the Bishop of Niger, he was as well the Bishop in-charge of the American Episcopal Church of Liberia as revealed in a report of visitation he made to Liberia and sent to Rev. J. Kimber who was then the Secretary and General Agent of the American Church Organization resident in New York on the 12th of February 1878.

When Venn was at the helm of affairs at Salisbury Square, his administrative strategy for the Niger Mission was quite different from that of others in key positions in the C.M.S. organization including the members of its Board of Directors. Venn, in May 1860 declared that the fundamental principle of the Niger Mission "is not to be Native agency and European superintendence or vice versa. Both were to work together to achieve the ultimate goal of the new religion going to Africa but people with different perceptions, intentions and goals to achieve at all cost manipulated the whole original concept to mean a different language interpretation. There is no doubt about it that some people are born into different geographical locations in the world and into different races of the world with dangerous in-built attitude and self-arrogance. One of such was Rev. Charles Townsend who by his manipulation of things in Africa prevented any European clergy to work under Bishop Crowther and his Niger Mission.

The opposite figure of this man was Rev. Venn whose administration at Salisbury Square deserved credit for being able to contain the pressures mounted by the white missionaries that were afflicted with the doubts that African Missionaries were inferior to their white counterparts. The whole thing that were going on in the missionary circle of the time looked like magic to some of the reactionaries in England when it was discovered that the African Missionaries were able to catch up with their white colleagues at such a fast speed and even pass them over in many areas of evangelical works and studies. Example is what we shall touch upon later about the achievements and the architects of those achievements on the banks of the Niger in the early days of its evangelical history.

The churches in Yoruba land were supposed to be superintendent by Crowther being his native place of birth but the strategic location of Lagos, which was much more easier for the European Missionaries to operate from in terms of the only available place at the time where they can easily communicate with their home government through European vessels and also being protected by the Naval war ships and the advantage of material supply they needed through the merchants made them to sit tight in Lagos and occasionally visiting the neighboring towns of Ibadan and Abeokuta which they called outstations.

But at a certain time and due to the expulsion of the European missionaries from Abeokuta and Ibadan made the Bishop of Sierra Leone to hand over the control of those two important missionary jurisdictions to Bishop Crowther to supervise. The record showed that although his control over these mission stations was not seen as being really complete, because he was at this period only asked to supervise those stations so as to allow the tension between the Natives and the Europeans to cool off; but all the while he was the controller Bishop of other Yoruba missions especially the town of Otta and those places that were not occupied by European Missionaries while the transfer to him permanently of the problem places including Lagos was being regarded as imminent. What pre-occupied the mind of Bishop Crowther as the first Bishop of his people was not sectional but very broad in outlook. The establishment of churches in Yoruba land was not a problem to him as such but that of establishing new ones in the interior of the country more so on the banks of the Niger was the program that conspicuously engaged his attention. Reason being that he had traveled to the interior part of the country and had seen every necessity for the Gospel to be taken there at all cost so as to save the teaming population of his people from total destruction and out of darkness and degradation. This was one of the main reasons why the Bishop concentrated much of his efforts on the new churches that are to be established on the banks of the Niger in the interior parts of the country.

Bishop Crowther saw slavery in action, he experienced slavery in its totality and swam in the oceans of slavery and this was why he was in a better position to testify to the true meaning of what the free encyclopedia says about the word "slavery" as thus:

> *Slavery is a condition of control over a person, known as a slave that can be enforced by violence or other forms of coercion against his or her will.* Slavery therefore occurs for the purpose of securing the labor of the slave and put such a person under the total control of his or her master/mistress. A specific form of slavery known as chattel slavery is the type whereby the owner of a slave has absolute legal ownership on his or her slaves, including the legal right to buy, sell or exchange them for whatever commodity that is available at the time of negotiation. It was under this chattel slavery condition that the Bishop was exchanged for a horse and

a bottle of gin when he was in the camp of slavery during his formative years.

Now that the Bishop had become a free man, it was too difficult for him to brush aside such conditions that he himself underwent each time he met similar situations still very much alive and prevailing in the interior part of his own country during the time of his previous trips to the banks of the Niger. It was a fact that he had now acquired sizeable power and authority to unleash his people from the bondage of slavery and degradation and what was left for him to do was to hasten that opportunity to open every available doors and channels that can be used to perform that task.

As difficult as it was in those days, problem of communication was the biggest thing faced by the missionaries because they only depended on the traders for passages, freight, provisions, mails and their daily supplies. Interestingly the salaries of the missionaries were usually paid by bills of credit issued on merchant stores in form of taxation for the goods imported into the countries of the Niger. Trading vessels had only the raining season period to navigate on the River and if by chance they are caught in the web, they had no alternative but to stay put at where they are until the next raining season comes in. Not this alone, the native pirate groups had now emerged in the Delta attempting to crack down on the merchant's vessels trading on the River for beads, cloths, tobacco, salt, rum and gin to steal. The journey on the banks of the Niger River was now becoming hazardous because of the impediments mentioned above.

The expedition of 1854 that opened up the success of its team to navigate for another 300 miles on the Niger River to Lokoja and found the confluence at which River Niger and Benue met was to them only a scientific achievement as trading along the route was under estimated. Now that the rate of European mortality in Africa had been reduced through the invention of quinine, more European traders were willing to trade on the River. Furthermore, those rescued slaves that were resident in Sierra Leone and, the Natives there were now being encouraged to immigrate to the banks of the River to join hands with the missionaries in their efforts to rescue their brothers and salvage their father land. The insecurity of trading activities along the route prompted the traders to request from their home government adequate protection of their businesses and the traders themselves.

Under this arrangement, the Foreign office agreed to provide warship to protect all the vessels navigating the Niger for lawful commerce. As said earlier, the missionaries were at the mercy of the trader's vessels for everything they needed for the progress of their work. The Bishop too was not exempted from this charity gesture of the traders and he himself like all other Native Missionaries of this time faced the music of discrimination and doggedness of the white traders who own, ran and control the trading vessels on the Niger. For example in 1857 when Bishop Crowther planted his first missionary stations at Onitsha and Igbebe, trading activities on the Niger were then at its infancy stage and no one was sure of its future successes, and as such transportation of men and materials through the land to the new area was virtually zero. The waterway transportation system in existence was to carry humans and few of their merchandize with small canoes and nothing more.

When the steel boats were brought as new method of transportation to move goods and human by Europeans, its navigation period was limited by season and time. Sometime when the boats were not available to transport the missionaries to their respective stations or when the River would not be full enough to move the vessels, the alternative means to get to the interior for the workers and their families including their little children is to trek on foot across the hazardous terrains of the jungle or to use the small wooden canoes where the demand is necessary or inevitable.

On one occasion in July 1860, Bishop Crowther was said to have gathered a large group of missionaries in McGregor Laird's Rainbow vessel (the only merchant trading on the Niger during this time) for a trip to the interior of the country at the Nun entrance of the Niger. They carried with them a pre-fabricated iron house meant for Onitsha mission station, saw gins for cleaning cotton, food and provisions meant for consumption on the journey and other missionary materials which included Bibles, slates, pencils and papers. But when the warship that was to escort the vessel failed to arrive and Rainbow could not sail freely on her own, the missionary agents of about sixty five of them had to return to Sierra Leone and the trip for that year was ended leaving the evangelists already stationed at Onitsha and Igbebe and Dr. Baikie at Lokoja without any supplies of foods, mails and other essential materials for that season.

The missionary work on the banks of the Niger was being regarded as experimental in nature to actually test the intelligence and abilities of the Africans on how best they can organize and manage their affairs themselves. In actual fact, some white opposition to the consecration of Bishop Crowther were all the minutes of the day exhibiting their anger and protest on the corridors of Salisbury Square in order for them to be victorious in their belief and wicked philosophy championed by someone like Charles Townsend concerning the competence of an African Native holding such a high office in the missionary set-up that was mainly established by the Europeans. By today's management skill's interpretation, it will not be too much for one to label Townsend as a professional destroyer because he did not only attempted to destroy the credibility and intelligence of Bishop Crowther alone but also that of all other African clergymen that were marked for promotions in their different areas of calling during this era.

For instance, in 1851 when Venn issued his first paper concerning the organization of the Native church, Samuel Crowther was the only native on the scene who like Townsend was ordained in London in 1843. The turn of the tide in the relationship between the two started when Crowther was appointed on the first Niger expedition of 1841 and ever since this time, he saw Crowther as a rival. In that year Venn proposed that by the time the new Bishop of Sierra Leone moved to Abeokuta, two more Africans would be ordained. The two Africans to be considered were T.B. Macaulay (the father of Albert Macaulay) and Theophilus King. The two men had a good record of achievement and they were both qualified for the post they were to be considered for. T.B. Macaulay had recently returned from the C.M.S. Training Institution at Islington, where both Crowther and Townsend had been trained. Theophilus King who had distinguished himself as catechist to the ill-fated farm settlement at Lokoja in 1841, was a product of Fourah Bay college and he was Crowther's able assistant as translator of the Bible into Yoruba language. The following is what Rev. Townsend wrote to oppose the ordination of these two African natives:

> "I have a great doubt of young black clergymen. They want years of experience to give stability to their characters; we would rather have them as schoolmasters and catechists".

On similar footstep, when the C.M.S publication had reported that at the last anniversary meeting of the society, the Rev. H. Stowell had made a distinctive proposal for the erection of an Episcopal see at Abeokuta, to be occupied by a black bishop, and Townsend learnt that Samuel Crowther had been invited to London, his doubts became a nightmare. He immediately summoned his European and African staffs to find out how many of them would serve under a black bishop. In the petition he submitted to oppose the move, he was able to obtain the signatures of both Hinderer and Golmer who were not fond of Episcopal form of government but an ordinary accomplice to his negativity of progress.

The politics he played in his petition never reflected his true thoughts on the matter as his argument in the petition was not that an African fit to be a bishop could not be found, but that an African bishop, however worthy, would lack in the country the respect and influence necessary for his high office. He noted further that Native teachers of whatever grade have been received and respected by the Chiefs and people only as being the agents or servants of white men...... and not because they are worthy...... our esteemed brother Mr. Crowther was often treated as the white man's inferior and more frequently called so, notwithstanding our frequent assertions to the contrary.......

> Finally in his petition, he dived very deeply into the trouble waters when he wrote that: There is one other view that we must not lose sight of, viz, that as the Negro feels a great respect for a white man, that God kindly gives a great talent to the white man in trust to be used for the negro's good. Shall we shift the responsibility? Can we do it without sin?

Venn must be commended for his administrative capabilities and skills in defending his theory and principles to the end concerning the Native Churches in Africa. In the end of it all, under Venn, Townsend remained an ambitious but frustrated leader of the opposition. Against his wishes, Macaulay and King were ordained when the Bishop of Sierra Leone reached Abeokuta in 1854 and in 1857 three other Africans were ordained. A lesson to learn here is to recognize the reward that both Townsend and Crowther received as benefits of their attitude towards their assigned responsibilities and to the authority that assigned those responsibilities to them. It was on record that while Townsend was seeking for position with all the strategies he mapped out and falling just short of attaining it, Venn was calling Crowther to posts of more responsibilities and power than Crowther himself bargained for.

What impressed Venn most in Crowther's way of life was that during the bickering and struggle of Townsend for power, Crowther did not show any desire for office but was busy mapping out his strategies on how to evangelize his people and take them out of the clutches of heathenism. He was so much endowed with great tact, remarkable knowledge of human psychology and ability to feel for others, understand their plights and, when necessary knows how to manage them effectively. His humble spirit and wise judgment in dealing with sensitive matters made him to excel among his counterparts and peers.

There is no doubt about it that Bishop Crowther in the face of persecution and hatred of the Negro race of which he himself became number one victim in the end, he did not change his attitude and loyalty towards Salisbury Square. In the 1880s, Bishop Crowther was really pushed onto the walls when the white missionaries were first introduced to the purely African Mission of the Niger only to undermine his authority as the Bishop of the place. The interior of the country no longer pronounced death verdict for the Europeans; and as such the white missionaries were now being injected into the banks of the Niger by Edward Hutchinson with whom in the past the Bishop clashed over the anti-educated African policy of the Royal Niger Company.

Bishop Crowther and his missionary team suffered a lot for transportation of their men and materials along the banks of the River because they had to rely mainly on the vessels of the merchants for their trips to the interior. When they could no longer stomach the constant insults from the traders, Bishop Crowther had to ask for a missionary steamer, which was purchased for him by his admirers in England for missionary works. The Bishop's plan was to place the steamer in the hands of an African merchant who had great knowledge of shipping and who knows every bit of the River since their day one in 1841. He was of the opinion that the steamer would pay off its cost in five years and at the same time helped the missionaries greatly to fulfill their evangelical obligations along the banks of the River. But instead of Hutchinson to follow the Bishop's plan, he went ahead on his own to appoint one J. H. Ashcroft who was an ordinary layman and another James Kirk to be in charge of the steamer.

As part of Hutchinson's program to destabilize the work of the Niger Mission and its men, he asked Ashcroft to take over the "temporalities" of the mission, including the finances of the mission. Ashcroft who was now in-charge of the steamer had on a number of occasion denied the Bishop of the use of the steamer for Episcopal visits that the machine was originally intended for and he was now extensively trading with it along the banks of the River his own ways. Discrimination at its highest level arrived into the mission's activities as large number of African Agents was dismissed by Ashcroft and Kirk without prior notification of the Bishop. At an occasion, Ashcroft informed the Bishop that his authority was now limited to the spiritual sphere of the mission only.

This model of insult was becoming too much for the Bishop to accommodate from rat-like persons of Ashcroft and Kirk and the next thing he did was to protest to Hutchinson but instead of the later to reproach Ashcroft and Kirk for dragging the dignity of the office of a Bishop in the mud, Hutchinson's letter to the Bishop was decidedly disrespectful. The unpleasant situation in the Niger mission continued unabated. Negative reports concerning the activities of both spiritual and temporal in the mission from the European merchants and Ashcroft were flying about all over the corridors of Salisbury Square, which prompted Hutchinson to appoint a Commission of Inquiry into the Niger Mission.

As there was no evidence to substantiate the allegations levied against the Bishop and the Mission, Hutchinson discovered that the reports were malicious and complete false. Nevertheless in 1880, he appointed one J.B. Wood to report on the Niger Mission. The Bishop as a clean man of God asked his staffs to cooperate fully with J.B. Wood, because he believed he had nothing to hide. He was unable to present physically at the Inquiry sittings because at this point in time, his wife was mortally ill in Lagos. The outcome of Wood report was said to be a damaging report that Hutchison's remark about it was that the first reaction of anyone who read the report would be to write off the Niger Mission instantly.

The reaction of the Bishop about this report was nothing short of an intention to "smash up" his Mission by the white boys. The C.M.S. decided not to act upon such report until Wood was able to prove all the allegations contained therein to the satisfaction of the authority, beyond every reasonable doubts and show them facts on how he collected those evidences he used to arrive at his conclusions. Finally a deputation under the leadership of the pro- African J. B. Whitting was sent to meet with Bishop Crowther, Henry Johnson and Wood himself at Madeira but it was on record that Mr. Wood never showed up at this meeting. The Bishop was at this meeting able to rebut all the allegations made in the report and asserted that much of the report was premeditated and untrue. The final judgment of C.M.S. highest authority on this matter was that "in several instances the reports circulated respecting the Native Agents had been shown to be unfounded and in some others much exaggerated". Ashcroft and James Kirk were dismissed for their un-Christian, high-handedness in their treatment of the Africans.

Wood was reproved for the manner with which he collected his evidences and his final opinion in the report. Wood protested against this reproach while he saw the rejection of his report as vote of no confidence in him and all the white missionaries. He was reminded at once that any one who read the report would not escape the conclusion that he had made up his mind to "smash up" the Niger Mission and he and his European colleagues were repudiated to work with the Society for the same cause,

"African for Africans". No sooner that the report was made public that Hutchinson himself resigned and Bishop Crowther and his missionary team on the Niger Mission became Victorious.

There was much difficulty that beset the path of missions among the natives of the interior of the country than expected especially when it comes to the expected relationship that was to manifest between the pagans, converts and missionary workers. There was a solid and thick barrier of a long-established customs of the people that binds them together for millenniums, a religion that touches every detail of their human life and the vested interests of its priests, soothsayers and witch-doctors, who were ready to raise again the old cry of "Great is Diana of the Ephasians" in an entirely different language and to similar god in nature. The people living in these communities too have their secular power vested in their Kings and Chiefs who were clothed in a little brief but very despotic authority, which was interlocked at every point with native customs and regards for the custodians of these customs. It is a fact that all these things were not clearly documented in form of writing them down in their books of law but their traditional memories never failed them from generation to generation.

To deal with such situations, it is obvious that the missionaries would depend much upon their tactics and abilities to swindle the beliefs of the people around in order to gain entrance into their soul and spirit. The inevitable complications that followed the coming-in of the new religion began to appear in the wake of the march of the legal commercial interests. Each time there was a commotion between the natives and the foreign traders on matters of little rift, the natives would receive as judgment to them severe and great reprisals from the white man's government. This particular move to punish the natives on matters directly affecting the two communities i.e. the Africans and the Europeans clearly showed and testified to the old African adage that says "where two elephants fight, it is the grass that suffers most" is true.

When there was a little misunderstanding between the two communities in any area of the interior, it was always the downtrodden people of the affected area that suffers most in terms of human displacement and property loss. Reason being that the power in the white man's guns would descend on such community with impunity and in a matter of hours, the whole community built up with bamboo sticks and palm fronds would be raised down into ashes not minding the inhabitants especially the aged people, the sick and the children. These were part of the problems that the natives on the banks of River Niger suffered and experienced from the hands of the early traders and their government back-up team of destroyers in the 1880s.

Most of the actions taken to undermine the abilities and integrity of the Natives were taken at the back of the Bishop who was then the only lone tree in the desert. But when the whole thing blows up on the perpetrators of the evil-deed, the Bishop would be the one to be contacted to help them repair the damages caused. We all know that he was by no means a diplomatist but his presence saved a lot of situations of this nature not only for the time it happened but, as regards the safety and success of the future. Most oftenly, the Bishop found himself standing between contending tribes to act as a peacemaker facing some blood thirst Chiefs, and like another Elijah, denouncing the barbarities of his African Ahab, and warning him of the Divine wrath and judgment. Those who know him in person and left behind prints about his personality remarked that he was a man without idle moment and he always had a knack of knowing what to do in an emergency situation. He was always free from fear, patient, tender to the utmost and never seemed to lose his heart. One of the glorious attribute that can be bestowed on a person of his mark and status was that he knew his converts as none other person did, and, like a true shepherd and leader, cared for and did his best for the development of his flock, knowing very well that most of them were so weak and tender sheep, who needed the crook to preserve them from the perilous pastures.

Bishop Crowther was known to be in anxiety for Lokoja, fearing it might be abandoned because Masaba who was then the King was an unfriendly human being to the course of missionary work in his Kingdom and about this particular situation, the Bishop noted in his journals that the Lokoja situation could be likened to Nehemiah's ejaculation before King Artaxerxes concerning the Jews that had escaped from Jerusalem and which were left in captivity to suffer for the offence of their religion and faith. In the Book of Nehemiah, it is neatly recorded the concern of Nehemiah over the desolate situation of the city of Jerusalem and the afflictions meted out to its inhabitants.

Chapter 1 verse 3 of the Book has this to say: *And they said unto me, the remnant that are left to the captivity there in the province are in great affliction and reproach: the wall of Jerusalem also is broken down, and the gates thereof are burned with fire.* In verse 11, Nehemiah went into serious plea with God concerning this issue and he said: *O Lord, I beseech thee, let now thine ear be attentive to the prayer of thy servant, and to the prayer of thy servants who desire to fear thy name, and prosper, I pray thee, thy servant this day and grant him mercy in the sight of this man. For I was the Kings cupbearer.* God sitting on His Throne in heaven heard the supplications of Nehemiah and granted him favor in the eyes of the King Artaxerxes: In the same manner, God listened attentively to the plea of the Bishop concerning Lokoja situation, which was similar in nature to that of Jerusalem in the Old Testament and granted the Bishop favor in the eyes of Masaba the King.

To see how God answers prayers, when the Bishop had put the case of Lokoja and the converts there before God with a very strong plea, he set up his journey to visit Egga, a town that its annoying filthiness made people hate it as at then, the Bishop reached Bida where to his astonishment and joy he was told that the King had adopted quite another attitude, and had himself suggested that the mission should remain in Lokoja, where better order amongst the people shall be established. On this subject matter, the Bishop had this to say in his journals:

[We were agreeably surprised to hear this difficult subject matter solved by the King himself before we had time to broach it. Thus the dark gloom, which overshadowed the prospects of Lokoja was blown away as the morning fog before the rising sun, even before we had opened our lips to protest against the order. Thus we have been relieved of our anxieties and doubts. This is an instance of an answer to prayer: "Before they call I will answer; and while they are yet speaking, I will hear." The Lord has graciously interposed in behalf of His own course. The clouds we so much dreaded have broken in blessings on our heads. "The King's heart is in the hand of the Lord, as the rivers of water. He turneth it withersoever He will." How often has this His prerogative been pleaded at the throne of grace in this case! He has shown His readiness to help in every time of need, yet we need again and again to pray: Lord, increase our faith.]

The missionary work at Onitsha was neither free from disasters, obstacles, ups and downs. In this part of the country, the Bishop in his usual habit of taking full account of different customs of his people in the interior, he gave some interesting details respecting the rules and customs that hedged around the dignity of a King as thus:

> His visit to Onitsha at one time coincided with when the community was on a great yam festival holiday when the King usually makes his annual appearance to his people publicly. According to the custom of the people of this time, His Majesty is never allowed to pass beyond a certain limit from the day of his coronation till his death; otherwise a human sacrifice would

be offered to appease the gods. The prescribed area does not go farther beyond the walls of his palace court, which means that after he is crowned as King, he may not know to which extent the problems of his people are regarding their social status and physical expansion and development of his Kingdom.

As the Bishop humorously pointed out he described him as a harmless animal in a zoological garden, roaming inside his fence at pleasure, but no further. The Missionary Station at Onitsha was at this time thirteen years old and the King had never seen any of the structures erected on the premises, neither house, church, store nor the steamer that navigates on the great river that run across his kingdom. It was at this time against the native law that the King should see the flowing of a river, or a boat or canoe, which may resemble coffin, lest it should hasten his death. This was the erroneous assumption and belief of the people of the time. Because of the un-necessary restrictions that the law of the land placed on the King regarding his free movement, the palace aids and the Chiefs took advantage of this situation to manipulate the King their own ways. They influenced him easily against the work of the missionaries in his Kingdom.

There are always two sides to a coin. As some people were trying to shield-off the King from the advantages and benefits he could enjoy from the presence of the Missionaries in his Kingdom, God was busy using some of the King's house hold members especially some of the chief ladies in the palace, including his own daughters to raise the hands of the Bishop up right in the palace court yard without the knowledge of the King. Only God Himself knows whether the King was aware or not that those who were his confidants and important staffs in his courtyard had been baptized and converted. The Bishop used this underground opportunity to later on preach the Gospel in the Royal apartments and pump into the heart's of the King the truth of the Bible that were to turn his life around for better in the future.

Soonest, Bishop Crowther opened the new church at Onitsha amid simplicity and frugality. The available local materials for construction around this time were bamboo sticks, clay-mud and palm fronds and these were the materials with which the first church building and other mission houses were erected at Onitsha just like in all other places too. The only source of light for church service both in the evening and night came from candles stuck into an iron cask hoops to produce little brilliant illumination that may be enough for the catechist, pastor or the Bishop to read from the Bible at every evening services. The collection from the faithful consisted of a small piece of tobacco leaf, a bunch of trade beads, a reel of cotton, some fishhooks, and silk pocket-handkerchief. Inside the mud-wall building with the light of those twinkling candles, the Bishop in his usual character would preach, pray and sing melodiously unto the Lord without any musical accompaniment. The whole thing seemed little and insignificant in the eyes of the people, but it was a little light shining in a very dark place and such little light sustained the Igbo community until the day light came to show them the path to salvation and industrialization we acknowledge today.

The missionary work on the Niger banks was now expanding steadily amid all odds and confrontations from both the Natives on one hand and the foreign merchants on the other. It would amount to a very serious oversight if nothing is mentioned about the two notable personalities who stood thick and thin with the Bishop when the ground of missionary field was being cleared. The first to recognize was Francis Langley. Langley was a faithful native helper to the course of Christianity along the banks of River Niger. He was equally a liberated slave like the Bishop himself, landed at Sierra Leone, where, he worked for a trading merchant as an apprentice, and who taught him how to read and write, with the additional aid of the Sunday-School and evening classes until when he was able to gain a fair education. The story recorded it that he later secured a good and rising position in Government service at Freetown. But when the call for Missionary workers in the Niger Mission was made, he gave up his promising and lucrative job in the Government for the evangelization of his heathen brothers and sisters in the interior. In due course, he and his family member became the solitary representative of the mission at Onitsha at the time when the station was at its worst stage of persecution.

His life was threatened on several occasions and one dark night, an attempt was made to kill him and for a very long time, he became the night-guard to watch his family members at night sleeplessly. This man was said to be a kind-man to the core and was friendly with everyone including those who were looking for a way to exterminate him for no reason other than he stood on the ways of their native religion. At a time when a terrible epidemic broke out when he was working at an outstation, and everyone from the villages made their ways to Onitsha for the security and protection of their lives, Langley and the members of his family stuck to their post, exposed to enraged cannibals, and for many weary months gave his best to those who sought help from him as their only friend. In spite of his impaired health, Langley kept working with consecrated persistency until he gave up the Ghost. Concerning this beloved man of God, the Bishop wrote this testimony about him:

> *Through faith in Him whom he believed to be the only Friend of sinners he trusted for pardon and forgiveness. From Him whom he so faithfully served here on earth we may hereby express our belief that Francis Langley had received the approbation: "Well done, good and faithful servant: thou hast been faithful over very little things: enter thou into the joy of thy Lord." Oh, that this were the ardent desire of us all laboring in this mission, to spend and be spent for the salvation of the souls of our heathen countrymen! Half a dozen men of like mind as that of our dear departed Francis Langley would be inestimable boons to missionaries among our heathen brethren according to the flesh.*

The second person in line to mention here was the son of the Bishop – Dandeson Coates Crowther who was the capable companion of his father in his missionary journeys. If space permits, much will still be said about this industrious, faithful and an articulate nationalist human being of his time in the preceding chapters but for the meantime, we shall mention in passive just a little bit about him. Dandeson Crowther was well known as the Archdecon of the Niger who received his ordination at the hands of his father – Bishop Crowther on 19 June 1870 at St Mary's Parish Church, Islington. The event was so unique because it was the first time that a black Bishop would ordain his black son into the service of God. The occasion pulled a very large crowd of worshipers and friends all over England, and the church was full to its capacity. An important event of the church that coincided with this ordination was the annual Church Missionary Society's Aid day. It was reported that the service was followed with deepest attention and re-assurance of God's promise on the suffering people of Africa.

The Bishop in his sermon solemnly committed to his son the responsibility and yet privilege of waging a brave warfare against sin under the banner of the cross. The ceremony was a touching spectacle especially when Rev. T. Green, the principal of the Church Missionary College rose up to present Rev. Dandeson to the Bishop. Inside the rail to assist the Bishop for this grand occasion was Rev. Daniel Wilson, the aged vicar of the church. When all was over, large number of spectators carried with them in their hearts a sense of gratitude to God that there was yet another sign and promise that "Ethiopia shall stretch her hands unto God". Young Crowther who was ordained this day was destined to be his father's partner in progress to move the wheels of the missionary vehicle forward in the

Jacob Oluwatayo Adeuyan

interior part of his own country and continent. He was also destined to take up the sacred inheritance of his father's labor as well as his name when the old Bishop was gone. He faithfully and diligently served under the Bishopric of his father and the Lord in his capacity as the Archdeacon of the Niger Mission.

Bishop Crowther on a number of occasions experienced some nasty and rough moments when he was building up his Niger Mission. These moments of occasion were so numerous that if a whole book has to be devoted to this subject matter, volumes upon volumes of such book will be published and yet much will be left on the desk of the writers. Here, we are to remark about a particular moment during his stay at Onitsha in 1874 when a plague of smallpox killed many of the promising converts in the city. The plague was a deadly type that actually devastated the city of Onitsha leaving no mark of respect to any class of people residing in the city. Several of the children of the native missionaries too died of this deadly disease and the sorrow, which visited the town of Onitsha was shared by nearly every family clan there. Such a calamity did not go without having superstitious strings attached to it by the native doctors and juju priests who used the incident to advance their own ends, and also attributed the disaster to the anger of the offended gods.

It was during this malady that King Idiari died and his death brought a confusing situation among the Chiefs and his subject. A section of the town was pointing accusing fingers on the other whom they believed to have brought a chaotic and confusing situations into their country, killing their King, and, staggering number of people of all ages and class. Moments later, a new theory surfaced, which attributed the presence of the disease to a well being dug on the mission premises fourteen fathoms deep into the ground that aroused the anger of the deities; and to appease these deities, a human sacrifice had to be made, and the body of the victim to be thrown into the well. This sort of request could have been possibly met if it were to be in a different location in the city but in the present location – the mission compound, such a request would be too impossible to meet. There was a big talk, arguments and persuasion before the decision could be averted. During the town meeting where the final decision on the issue was taken, there arose a young convert who stood between the parties, and said to his people: "My friends, I have listened to all that you have been saying about the well at the Mission compound. I will join you in filling it up, only if you can promise me that, after it is done, there shall be no more death in Onitsha".

As no one in the judgment bench ever expected this sort of challenge, the question of filling up the well was dropped, and the attention of the perpetrators was shifted from the Missionary compound unto the elderly women in the city, whom they accused of having be-witched the people, and thus brought calamities unto them. Some twenty of these elderly women were seized and made to drink droughts of poison. The end result was that half of these women died in agony but we should not forget that in the African set-up of this time, this type of sanctions, judgments or orders were so prevalent in the native courts of the land.

Despite all the stringent and cooked-up measures adopted to avert this deadly disease, it did not abate; even the destruction of their domestic animals like goats, pigs and sheep, which was erroneously believed to have contributed its quota to the calamity could not prevent the spread of the hell disease. There was chaos everywhere including the new church organization where its meetings for worship were deserted. During the on-going course of this affliction, a member of the church came up to reveal the dream he had in which their old pastor Mr. Langley appeared to him in his dream, and seriously warned him that if he continued to slight the offer of mercy now made to him and to all the people of Onitsha, they would all go to hell after death. This message was taken very seriously and set the tide to flow in another direction as people began to return into the mission this time with full force and zeal. The church began to overflow with new members. Interestingly, the plague was stayed leaving its great ravages on Onitsha.

There was no doubt about it that the Bishop had a very great desire to improve the condition of the people of the Niger by encouraging trade and industry. Bishop Crowther was known to be a rigid Anglicanism to the core, but he still believed that the Christian faith could forge ahead in the continent of Africa only if it can work in harmony with the culture and religion of the people. He had great respect for African customs, laws and national assimilation that have no conflicting jurisdictions with the principle and laws of his new religion that was to abolish and supersede every other false religion. His policy here was that where degrading and superstitious defects occurred, Christianity must correct them; and where these defects were connected to politics, then a different approach would be needed altogether. Under such condition, he asserted that care and caution must be employed "with all meekness of wisdom, that there may be good and perfect understanding between the mission and the state.

During the Episcopal reign of the Bishop, which was around the time when human sacrifice was the order of the day in the interior of the country, Crowther abhorred and totally condemned this barbaric practice in clear terms each time he visited his outstations on the bank of the River. For example, on his missionary visit to Kippo Hills in 1880, he openly condemned the killing of twin babies when he said this:

> [*To convince the people of the wickedness of this natural barbaric practice which is to them a time-honored custom and mark of high rank….. so as to give it up for a new and strange religion, is not a day's work. They must be convinced of the errors of their religion through the inward teaching of God's Holy Spirit.*]

On one of his previous visit to Idda in 1867, he had a confrontation with the Attah of Igala on the issue of human sacrifice that when a popular person dies in the community, living persons were to be buried alive with him so that those buried with him might act as servants for him in the world beyond. Crowther's objective point to this practice was that: If such attendants were necessary, they should be plentifully supplied from those dead who "were better circumstanced to know the wants and the management of affairs of the invisible world" than those buried alive who would be "perfect strangers" over there. He greatly believed that effective preaching from the Book of Truth – the Bible would gradually make such practice to cease in communities and his method actually worked wonderfully in exterminating such practices among the heathens of the time.

Bishop Samuel Ajayi Crowther was a great man of his time and beyond. He pioneered many economic developments of our land through his inflammable national spirit. The political as well as the commercial interests on the Niger and the rest of the country owed him a great lot of thanks. He was always ready to use his ideas and personality in state matters and his correct judgment on matters affecting his native people always pleased the British authority and the local Kings and Chiefs. In 1874, when he accompanied the merchants to Bida to introduce them to King Omoru, he as their interpreter and commercial strategist pulled a very strong trading string between the merchants and the King with his Chiefs. It was recorded to be a successful and profitable bargain as regards future trading in this region. He used the opportunity to read to the King and his Chiefs a letter from Governor Berkeley, which accompanied the Queen's presents and congratulations on the accession of King Umoru to the throne of Masaba. The following is the role he played during this negotiation:

> Amongst other things, I informed the King of the visit of the Shah of Persia to England, his kingly reception, and the impressions made on his mind so favourable that he could not express them in words, but in ardent request that England would be kind enough to consent to construct railroads in his dominions for the facility of communication and commerce; that while such a mighty Mohammedan monarch did not spare himself the trouble of such a visit, nor did he think his Kingdom was beyond improvement, how much more should African Kings desire a foreign power to improve their countries by their wealth and skill. I then showed him a lump of coal, which Captain Croft had kindly given to me on asking, as the fuel with which steam work is done in England, and that he should show it to his subjects; perhaps they might come across such a thing as that in the country one day, to report it to him. This was a piece of curiosity.

King Umoru was one of the Kings of the land around this time that the Bishop ever spoke very highly about during his personal contact with him and his Chiefs along the banks of the Niger and elsewhere in the continent. Crowther saw this King as someone who was well read in Arabic Books, which had come to him across the desert; he was a man of considerable knowledge, open-minded and a reasonable person to deal with. The Bishop remarked that he was able to write a very sensible letter to the English Governor, sending his messages of thanks to the Queen for the present she sent to him. He assured the Queen and her subjects that while he remains in authority, all English subjects shall be adequately protected. Bishop Crowther accompanied this letter with his own clean opinion about King Umoru through his pen and he wrote:

> King Umoru is an educated Mohammedan, and is well read on subjects relating to civilized nations in the north; the quickness with which he entered into the idea of any information on such subjects at once proved his superior intelligence to his late predecessor. Taking all these into consideration, together with his own express wishes to be led and advised by wiser minds, and also the extent of countries over which his influence is felt. I feel persuaded that if Her Majesty's Government would continue to show their recognition of his earnest wishes to promote the interest of trade and more extensive cultivation of produce suitable for

European markets by a moderate annual remuneration. I believe good benefits will accrue from it both to commerce and Christian civilization of this extensive portion of interior Africa.

This kind of intelligent report and sound opinion about a King who controls a large portion of land in the interior of Africa in 1874 concerning his proficiency, education and commercial interest showed that those who formed different opinion about African development in the early centuries must have something heavier at the back of their minds which followed them to their graves. The question that demanded an immediate answer from everyone of us now is that "between Bishop Samuel Ajayi Crowther a son and Bishop of the land and Sir George Goldie a merchant that came to trade in the land in the 1880s, who is better qualified to be called the father of Nigeria amongst the two?"

Chapter 18

Bishop Crowther and Episcopal Crisis

It may not be too far from the fact that Bishop Crowther knew why he and his men were acting not only for the people of his Episcopal jurisdiction – the Niger Mission but for the entire people of the African continent as well. It was up to the Niger Mission to show to the world that native government in the church is a viable alternative to the despotism and tyrannies of the past when the then few churches of the land were being controlled from a distance of over five thousand miles away. The program of annexation of the whole country was already on the table right from the time Lagos was forcibly annexed and made a colony of the British Empire. But to fully carry out this program was a thing to be looked into with every care and thorough planning. The planners were then waiting for any available atmosphere under a very good climate to catch on the slightest opportunity for them to position themselves at the head of the table. Another important factor was the implacable hatred for the educated Africans and their activities, which were becoming derogative to the status of a white man both in the missionary and the public service. It should be borne in mind that there was never a time in the history of the European presence on the soil of Africa that this type of arrogance from their people were not noticed but this time around, it was really getting out of hand and climbing up rapidly to its climax.

In the sixties, it was placed on record the unfriendly activities of people like Burton Winwood Reade and T.J. Hutchinson who were then classified as anti-missionary and anti-Christianity works in Africa when they openly castigated the educated Africans and Negro race without much effect. It was impossible for these group of people to carry their plans to fruition because of the heavy intervention and the presence of someone like Henry Venn at Salisbury Square and who was throughout his life-time a good and sincere friend of African evangelical program and an organization such as African Aid Society founded by Lord Alfred Churchill in 1860, which was all the time a very strong defender of the African course both in the British Government circle and in the Missionary set-up. From the beginning, the tendency of the British Government and the Protestant missions in West Africa was to use African agencies to carry the message of the Gospel to their people because of the close affinity, language and cultural ties that binds them together. But towards the end of the nineteenth century notable figures such as Joseph Thompson, the explorer, Consul H.H. Johnston who deposed King Jaja of Opobo and Miss Mary Kingsley, an anthropologically-minded British explorer in West Africa severally or jointly turned the table around to suit their nefarious intentions and those of their god-fathers that were sitting behind the curtains. Interestingly, it was the single view of the lady among them in 1869 that the Negroes were altogether depraved and as such they are different creation from the whites because they belong to an intermediate stage between men and beasts that have no souls and incapable of being raised.

Consul Johnston in his own case never saw anything good in the characters of Africans. At a certain time he declared his opinion about the converts in West Africa as "drunkards, liars, rogues and unclean livers" of West Africa and they were Christian adherents. He observed further that throughout the whole West Africa, hardly could twenty genuine Christian could be found. About the Niger Mission Agents, he described them as "a bad ally" to European missionaries and went to say documentarily that: I regret to say that with a few-very race-expectations, those African pastors, teachers and catechists whom I have met have been all, more or less, bad men. They attempted to veil an unbridled immorality with an unblushing hypocrisy and a profane display of mouth religion, which to an honest mind was even more disgusting than the immorality itself. While it was also evident that the spirit of sturdy manliness was present in their savage forefathers found no place in their false cowardly natures.

Certain allegations made against the administration of the Bishop in the Niger Bishopric Mission were made without giving room for their defenses

The Journey of the First Black Bishop

from logical point of view. In the first place, the Bishop and his agents were the ones facing the problems emanating from transportation system of this time, the health hazards and communication problems. He was accused of operating his administration from Lagos, which was a distance of about 200 miles away from the nearest post in his mission's territory and that if he had stayed right in the interior, things would have worked out well for him. People forgot that the type of developments we have around us today including all the facilities here and there were never in existence then. We had mentioned the ordeal the Bishop and his agents faced in the hands of the merchants regarding transportation and communication. The only place he could stay to communicate effectively with Salisbury Square then was in Lagos, which had been declared British Colony and the center of the British Administration in West Africa. Definitely if Bishop Crowther had been too far away in the interior from the seat of the Government of this time, he would have been forgotten there completely. We should not also forget that the Archbishop of Canterbury or Henry Venn of Salisbury Square did not leave Canterbury or Salisbury Square, London to come to live in West Africa before they were able to coordinate and supervise the administration of their respective organizations in West Africa or elsewhere effectively. We all know that there is no perfect administration without its full and half measures of fault and as such no one could certainly guaranteed that if the Bishop had been staying permanently in Lokoja or at Onitsha, the enemies of his missionary course would not have taunted him the way they did in pulling him down.

Number two point that was raised against the Bishop was that he did not promote self-support program in the churches in his Mission and possibly making the C.M.S spending too much money to support the agents. Crowther was never known to be an active nationalist and as such he was not in the Niger Mission to promote either politics or fund raising activities. Therefore, there was no need for him to become one all of a sudden. The main job that was supposed to pre-occupy his mind was the way to win the people to his own side and this was what he was doing with the help of his agents. This Bishop was known to be a humble man to his masters and always listened to their views and opinions even when the tide was changing directions at Salisbury Square. Moreover the natives of the Niger Mission that were supposed to support the churches financially were not of viable economic stock because the major trade of the merchants of this time was mainly alcohol, which the church vehemently go against.

Those that were close to the foreign merchants and who later became their agents with little money in their pockets were mostly the non-natives per se because this set of people came from Sierra Leone, though of Yoruba stock but yet considered foreign Africans with their own programs and economic interests to take care of. As such begging for money for total support of the churches at this point in time was clearly difficult for any one to do lest for the Bishop. The senior partners in business of this era were the whites who were not interested in the development of the native churches at the expense of their trade. There were only very few of them that attended the local churches if there was any on important ceremonial days all because of their complex arrogance. All that pre-occupied their minds was the profits from the sales of their goods and quick return to their respective basis in Europe. Where then is the money to fund the local churches, pay the emoluments of the agents as it was being done in Lagos diocese where the money was coming directly from the common pool of the Government in form of subsidy to evangelical works and funds from parent body in England?

The third accusing finger being pointed at the Bishop was his tender ways in which he handled his agents anytime there was allegation of any misdeed against any of them. It was morally and evangelically correct for a person of his status and in his shoes to act sometime the way he acted as a father and leader of a new group that was looking for people to join his new religion in the face of open persecution from the natives of this time. His actions on this topic sometime were in similar line with what was going on in the circle of the white missionaries in Lagos diocese or elsewhere. By his faith it was difficult for him to come to the church with the Bible on the right hand and a rod on his left hand to shepherd his flock.

Above all, people like G.W. Brooke actually saw the qualities being planted in the Bishop when he remarked in his journal about his true opinion about Crowther as thus:

[He is a charming old man, really guileless and humble, I like him more each time I see him.] This is where the Yoruba proverb that says: Because of trait I have four hundred friends. If two hundred of them go against me, the other two hundred would support me fitted-in concerning the personality and characters of the Bishop. As some white men of his generation who came to Africa for exploitation purpose either in the clergy dresses or merchant jackets condemned the intellectual abilities of a Negro or African people, a lot of them still had the time to pour out their clean minds about what an African man was in the real sense of it.

The adversaries of the Niger Mission were on their heels to run the race of total destruction of the work that the Bishop had used substantial part of his lifetime to build just in a number of days to come. Between 1887 and 1890, the European Missionaries began to arrive at the Niger stations in their determination to put into effect the growing idea of the dominant race that had being brewing for years especially to dislodge the Bishop from his nominal episcopate. The agents recruited to carry out this program were the young, industrious, over-zealous and visionary Englishmen mainly from Cambridge University, who under the pretence of good Samaritans wanting to make their mark in the field of evangelism; and who believed that it could be possible for them to turn the whole world over to their side just during their generation. They were absurdly idealistic and romantic with their quixotic beliefs. The type of evangelical movement they set-up to achieve their goals later became a laughing stock for the people of high intellectual abilities and even to their fathers-in-support in England as well. It was said of them that before they started any work in Nigeria, they condemned the methods of all Christian Missions in Africa. They saw human beings through their outward look only and never had the strength and experience to look beyond the language that the inner minds in them was pointing at. One of their target places in Africa was Sudan where they thought that they could easily evangelized the Moslems there by adopting part of their culture in dressing mode, food and lodging but after sometime their program crashed.

Among this new crop of missionaries was a particular figure J.A. Robinson who was the General Secretary of the Niger Mission from 1887 – 1890. He was well educated but contemptuous of the relative academic insufficiency of the African agents in the Mission as well as having the worst opinion about the black race where ever they could be found on the planet. This dangerous attitude of Robinson in 1887 pushed him to declare to the C.M.S that it was wasted effort to evangelize the Muslims and that the Niger Mission should not extend beyond the geographical boundaries of Onitsha. He therefore recommended to Salisbury Square that the Bishop should be asked to retire honorably from the labors of his many years of hard work in building up the Mission where he was only for two years. In his usual manner of destructive attitude, it was said of him that he always liked to choose anti Negro choruses and in a sweeping sentence to destroy the Bishop and his Mission in one of his numerous writings where he declared that the Negro Race shows almost no sign of ruling power.

This is true in Sierra Leone, Liberia, West Indies and equally on the

Niger. Another person whose name is to be mentioned here was a good comrade of Robinson in this premeditated program and his name was Graham Wilmot Brooke who was possibly born a traitor. He was hell-bent on converting the Moslems in Sudan at all cost and for him to gain entrance into this part of Africa, he had to use the Niger Mission as a point of contact with Sudan in 1888. His journals revealed his unbridled efforts to turn the Sudanese dervishes to Christian Crusaders. He was referred to as a genuine Christian, extremely able, highly devoted and prepared to die a martyr but with all these spiritual qualifications he came to have fanatical hatred for educated Africans, particularly the Sierra Leonians, who according to him their pretensions, hypocrisy and dissoluteness filled him with disgust.

The only person he saw as a genuine Christian in West Africa was James Johnson while he described in an unmeasured language that the Niger Mission was a "den of thieves and the sort of lying and robbery going out there is shameful". He described the Sierra Leonian people in the Mission as "swarms of ragamuffins" and their Mission a "charnel house". The on-going hatred extended to the Mission station at Lokoja where they branded the converts there as adulterers and harlots and even went as far as dismissing the Church members until they were forcibly made to confess their iniquities one after the other. They labeled the Christian converts there before their Muslim brothers and sisters as infidels and unclean beings.

To confirm what the secrets of their intentions were and what they set out to do, the opinion of Brooke in one of his journals testified thus:

We came out here hoping to carry on and expand the works of twenty years in the place, and now after two months we are driven to admit that there is no hope of success until we have first taken down the whole of the past work so that not one stone remains upon another. What he meant in this message was that all the pastors of the Niger Mission must be changed including the messages they were preaching, the time, mode and place of worship, the school children and the course being taught in the schools. The so-called reformers plunged their hoes and diggers into every available land in the Niger Mission for destruction. In the last week of August 1890, the meeting of the Niger Finance Committee was called where the two races – the Africans and the Europeans were equally represented. The African team in the meeting composed of the Bishop who was the nominal chairman, Henry Johnson and D.C. Crowther, while the Europeans were represented by Robinson, Brooke and Eden. It was in this meeting that the

Bishop was unnecessarily humiliated and charges of cheating, falsehood, inefficiency, slave holding, immorality, drunkenness, robbery and others were preferred against the agents and the converts in the Mission.

Archdeacon Crowther was himself charged with an offence of deliberate lying and robbery. The Bishop was insulted and called a liar; his mission, they remarked, was of the Devil because it was built with money collected from merchants engaged in the liquor trade. Archdeacon Crowther and the Rev. Charles Paul who both had served the Mission with clean records for close to thirty-five years were suspended by F.N. Eden who was on no account had the administrative power to do so. The position of the Bishop in the Finance Committee was described as follows: To see him (the Bishop) at his age and after so long a period of earnest service for the Master, placed in the position he occupied at our last Finance Committee was I felt at the time, a cruel, though inevitable wrong.

This dangerous impression was carried to the Parent Committee in Salisbury Square with a view to buttress Burton's past school of thought concerning the non-intellectual abilities or capabilities of a Negro or African people to organize things perfectly. In their petition, they described the Sierra Leonians who were mostly the agents in the Mission as the worst species of the African races because they were the descendants of people sold into slavery by their tribes just because they were the scum of their races. They blamed Henry Venn and those that were responsible for making Samuel Ajayi Crowther a Bishop for the allowed zeal to outrun discretion and sentiments to have greater weight than sober facts. Hamilton, who was the General Secretary of the Niger Mission from 1885 to 1886 declared in his own remark that the evangelization of the Niger territory by African agencies was exclusively accidental and the appointment of Bishop Ajayi Crowther was unintentional and regrettable.

The issue has now been blown into Inquisition level and its proceedings became known to everyone in the Niger Mission and in England particularly the ultramontane administrative views taken against the Bishop by the reformers. Something closer to total break down of law and order in the Mission was making its appearance felt throughout the whole of West Africa. National feelings in support of the Bishop ran to the height that was never seen in the history of the Mission and its outburst became universal. As James Johnson described the situation in his own words, he said that it was Africa that was on trial and it behoved all Africans whether Christian, Muslim or Pagan to rally round the Bishop and his agents in the Mission. Petitions of protest that were never seen before were running up and down between Bonny, Brass, Lagos, Sierra Leone and Salisbury Square all signed by the editors of the Nigeria newspapers and people that matters in the society of this time.

Among the important signatories from Sierra Leone was Sir Samuel Lewis who was then a very popular lawyer in West Africa. It was said that the Emir of Bida from his Kingdom reacted sharply and promptly to the call of the nationalists by asking David Makintosh who was the Agent General of the Niger Company during this crisis time to send away the white missionaries from his territory. In the Delta area of the Niger Mission, the chiefs and the converts swore that if either Brooke or Robinson should venture to come to their territory, they would club him to death. This outburst gave the nationalists the opportunity to tell the Africans in the Niger Mission and West Africa about similar treatments that the Negroes in America were under-going in the hands of the whites there.

At the wake of this highly charged atmosphere, Edward Wilmot Blyden who was a popular person since in the sixties through his prolific writings and sensational speeches about the type of treatment being meted out to the Africans on the soil of their continent by visiting foreigners was well received in Lagos. He had been known to be a supporting figure in the course of native Christianity programs in the Niger Mission as the only permanent hope for the growth of the religion in West Africa because the whole affairs there were singularly in the hands of the Africans. While in Lagos, Blyden gave a lecture on "The Return of the Exiles" in front of the Glover Hall where he solicited for the formation of an African Church that was being made necessary and now ordained by God Himself so that it might be easy for the natives to take upon themselves the responsibilities of the church not only in the supportive areas of the Gospel but in the extension of it to the regions of Africa. He believed that Lagos that has been placed at a strategic position in Africa possessed far greater advantages more than elsewhere for the purpose of the proposed indigenous church. Blyden's parental background was believed to have come from Hausaland but he was born in the Danish Island of St. Thomas in West Indies in 1832. In 1849 he had a scholarship to be educated in the USA but because of the racial discrimination going on then he was unable to use it; but remained an ugly memory that lived with him throughout his lifetime. As an alternative, he transferred to Liberia College where he excelled himself as a great scholar. He distinguished himself in languages, particularly in

Classics and Arabic, which later earned him fame among the Muslims in the interior of Sierra Leone.

People taught that because of his knowledge in Arabic studies he would be a strong Muslim person that would oppose Christianity faith but instead he was himself a missionary in Liberia, in the employment of the Presbyterian Missionary Society of America. Blyden in 1871 had problem in Liberia and then moved to England where Henry Venn appointed him as a missionary with all the facilities being enjoyed by his white counterparts. His main task was to render the Scriptures into many languages particularly the Fula, to teach Arabic at Fourah Bay College and carry missionary enterprise into the interior of Africa. He did not stay too long on this appointment before he was dismissed because the news of his trouble in Liberia reached England. He was alleged to have a case of immorality with the wife of the President Royes, hence he could not continue with the C.M.S. but as a person he was much loved by Henry Venn. It should be noted that Blyden did not advocate an African Church for political purposes like the Nigerian nationalists.

He advocated for an African church that could stem the tide of Islam and completely destroy it. Because in his biography, he confirmed that Mohamed himself had prophesied that "in the last times the Ethiopians shall come and utterly demolish the temple of Mecca after which it will be rebuilt again for ever". Blyden's type of African nationalist was purely on the cultural plane rather than the political side. It should not be forgotten as well that his writings on the topic of African nationality and personality influenced such Nigerian nationalists of their time in persons of James Johnson, Mojola Agbebi, J. O Payne and Dr. O Johnson who tailored their own nationalist pattern in a different form to include political awareness of their people.

All eyes and ears were being directed towards Salisbury Square for their decisions on the Niger Mission crisis and the future of its agents. The Salisbury Square of the beginning days was now being eroded because many waters are now passing under the bridge moving tons of debris to unknown destinations. From the European side, their revolutionary missionaries would not want any modification of their recommendations whether in principle or in detail; likewise from the African side, were determined not to take anything less than unreserved apology to their beloved Bishop and demanding for a commission of Inquiry to investigate and substantiate the charges brought against the African agents. The scenario became very charged and confrontational in size and nature.

On the overall the C.M.S. decided in favor of the Europeans as they were commended for the war they were waging against the "Satan". Brooke, Battersby and Eden were given the opportunity to state their case before the Parent Committee while the African agents that were dismissed without knowing the reason for their dismissal were denied privilege to defend themselves. For the final row, a special Sub-committee to look into the whole crisis was put in place by the authority in December 1890 and it comprised the following Africans J.B. Whiting, Dr. R.N. Cust and Sydney Gedge whose voices in the deliberations were being drowned of silenced. The Committee as expected accepted and used all the unfavorable documents from the Wood's Report of 1880 and the current ill-garnered accusations of Robinson and Brooke in its proceedings as authentic exhibits. The outcome of the Sub-committee was not a surprise to the African natives because of its composition and the documents it accepted and used to form its opinion.

Finally the report was out officially and it upheld all the principles that the European missionaries had been fighting for since 1887 except that Bishop Crowther could not be removed which may not be too far from political gimmick employed to avoid further problems from the natives. The Niger Mission was labeled in the Report as corrupt to the core and to salvage it was only to take the white missionaries there to clean up the mess and those native agents that were to be retained would agree to work under their superior white agents. The dismissal of most of the African agents that were recommended for outright dismissal by the reformers were ratified while only very few left were put on probation for one year under the supervision of the white missionaries. Archdeacon Crowther was said not to be guilty of the charges preferred against him but notwithstanding he was reduced to become the pastor of St. Stephen's in Bonny under the superintendence of a new white missionary. The tone used on the role of the Bishop was "unacceptable" with no apology of any kind given to the old honest man.

The main epitome of the reformers and their cohorts in Salisbury Square had now been achieved. The Report of the Special Sub-committee had spoken the minds of the white missionaries and had at the same time branded the Africans as incapable, fraudulent, adulterers and people of low or no intelligence to man an organization of such magnitude as that of the Church Missionary Society. The tone of the Society's journal on this issue was decidedly anti-African and the letters that were addressed to the West African Churches were not in any form seen to have appealed to the minds of the people concerned especially the nationalists. Based on the outcome of the Report, the nationalists retaliated with fire for fire. The *Lagos Times* in its forty-eight pages of pamphlet titled [The Niger Mission Question] refreshed their memories with the history of the American Revolution.

The dismissed agents were at serious war with their former masters with the tale of wrongs that had been inflicted on the Negro race in general. The hysteria was well expressed by Mojola Agbebi in an address he delivered on September 20 1891 titled "The eve of a crisis" when he remarked among his words that "The feathers of revolution are beating the air, and revolution is prolific of results….. and the car of Jehovah has unloosed itself…….. and in its onward progress through the length and breadth of this country, willing as well as unwilling men who obstruct its pathway will be reduced to atoms". The burning flame of the trouble was clearly seen everywhere in the land because the nationalists were seriously fanning the producing fire with whatever available fans at their disposal.

James Johnson who had been known for his uprightness and a fearless leader emerged as the leader of the nationalist movement that revolted against the C.M.S. on the ground of white missionary's cruelty to the person of the Bishop and his African agents and their attempt to seize the Niger Mission from the hard working Africans that began the work at the expense of their sweat and blood. James Johnson was now convinced that the time had come when the Delta Mission Churches should become independent of the C.M.S so as to repudiate the European control. He now observed that the missionaries had failed to prove holiness and equally failed totally to exhibit the "Spirit of the Great Master of the loving Jesus, the Jesus of the Bible who would not break the bruised reed nor quench the smoking fax" but now decided to destroy all the achievements of the purely African agency in the Niger Mission; practically using the new breed reformers to keep Bishop Crowther in the cooler; when the outcome of the Report of their Special Sub-committee failed to uphold justice, which was the intended reason for its establishment and where a fair and impartial enquiry could not be obtained without considering racial profile. Johnson's patience was pushed to the extreme and he now blew up at Salisbury Square openly accusing them of "fanning up the flame of race antipathies".

Under the leadership of this great nationalist, the educated Africans met in Lagos on 17 April 1891 to pass two Resolutions regarding the ongoing crisis. The first Resolution was a call to the Bishop to declare the Delta churches independent; and the second one was the one concerning financial backing in form of grant for five years. About this time too, the nationalists in Sierra Leone also threw in their financial support for the proposed independent church in the Delta region. Anxiety was building up around the people as everyone was waiting impatiently for the reaction of the Bishop, which they saw as crucial and necessary to the future of the churches in the Niger Mission, in West Africa and the sustenance of the nationalist movement that championed this course. To keep the flag flying for the nationalist movement, Bishop Crowther's decision here must be positive otherwise the whole efforts would collapse and become meaningless and its rubbles would be thrown into the Atlantic Ocean. Finally to the joy of everyone, the Bishop accepted the proposals of the nationalists without modification. He considered the suggestions made to him as a product of "mature deliberation" as well as putting into effect the Henry Venn's scheme and he concluded in this tone that, "the way to prove failure or success is to make a trial for a time and watch".

The Bishop's new line of action by accepting the nationalist's move came as a surprise and serious problem to Salisbury Square in the sense that the way they had been riding too high on his humility and loyalty in the past was no longer possible for them this time around and they now began to see the hand writing on the walls being written with red chalk. The message that this decision sent to them clearly showed that they had somehow met the waterloo type of answer they asked for in their destructive bid they had been asking for since 1879. It was now most welcomed that he who lives in a glass house does not have to form the habit of throwing stones to those walking on the streets otherwise he would be asking for a serious dent to his house when the street man returns throwing stones back at him.

When the white missionaries were hauling bricks at the Bishop, he never cared to defend himself with the natural gift that God had endowed him in terms of his kith and kin as well as the people that surrounded him; they forgot too that they could only be equated to a simple drop of water out of the Ocean's water volume. He had been accommodating all sorts of insults from all sorts of degrading people in the suits of clergymen but this time around he was rallied round by his people to throw off the arrogance of the mafia boys who saw themselves as dominant race in the Bishop's territory. Because of his humility that had always been taken for granted, he accepted the recommendations of the Special Sub-committee and when the people of Niger Delta including their Chiefs and noble men were burning with rage because of the insults passed on to the entire

African race in its Report and the verdict of the Parent Committee on the issue, the Bishop still asked Salisbury Square to send a deputation to the region to appease his people.

He was all the while a humble man to the course of his belief and to the fact that he never at one time bit the fingers that fed him. He kept the sacred thing that binds the British people with him and always remembered all that was done for him by their people from his rescue days as a slave boy to his Bishopric glorious day when he was put on that golden stool in 1864 at the Cathedral of Canterbury. All these the Bishop carried at the back of his mind into his grave. If he had had the minds of the new generation of the white missionaries of this crisis time, he could have utilized the nationalist forces that rallied round him to breakout completely with the Church Missionary Society but instead he allowed the spirit of his Master to take control of the whole issue.

At the peak of the crisis, in January 1891 the Bishop wrote a pathetic memo to his youngest son Archdeacon Crowther in this form telling him that: *Patience is a gift which the Giver of all good things has given me; it may appear that I exercised it too long, and, perhaps, to my own disadvantage, but the result of it will be that the* **Director** *of the course of Providence will never err.* One could judge correctly the type of person the Bishop was during his lifetime and how grateful a person he was to those that lend help to the building up of his life. He was actually seen to be patient enough in dealing with every situation that came his ways both in the spiritual and physical realm. Concerning the issue of Independent Delta Churches, Bishop Crowther presented concrete proposals that seemed workable with strong promise for immediate take-off. He fixed 1st of January 1892 for the formal inauguration of the Independent Delta Church with a program to have James Johnson appointed as his Suffragan – Assistant Bishop, with the hope in mind that after his death James Johnson would step into Bishopric stool. The date and the ceremony could not take place because of the deposition of Jaja of Opobo but the chiefs and the converts of Bonny, Okrika and new Calabar were solidly behind the Bishop's decision and assured him that no amount of persuasion from the C.M.S that would make them yield from the determination to establish independent church of the Delta region. They told the Bishop in clear and strong terms that they would not draw back and embitter his last days by supporting those that proved his life work a failure as stated in the Report.

Apart from the destructive program of the Sudan Party, the young missionary reformers activities in the Party were now proving a total failure, as they were unable to lure or win a single convert with their modern missionary weapons, techniques and lousy program. Record revealed that they did not live in native houses depicting their arrogance and when illness began to fall upon them they gave up eating African foods. Their medical skills failed them too as they began to drop either by dying, invalided at home or resigning one after the other. By August 1891, it was only Brooke that remained and the following April he too kicked the bucket.

As the nationalists were digging their hole differently so also the Salisbury Square was planning about how they could win the African elites and converts back into the fold again. In this regard a deputation was sent out consisting of the Rev. W.A. Allan and Hamilton; both of them who had had enough experience in the past in resolving such a tight and naughty issue between the Africans and the whites. Hamilton in his capacity as one time Archdeacon of Lagos diocese and Allan at a time in the past weaned Africans in his desire for an African Bishop of Yorubaland in 1887 arrived Sierra Leone in the middle of December 1891. The delegation met with only few numbers of Anglicans that showed up out of the large numbers that were invited because the others boycotted the deputation.

The delegates managed to patch-up things at its surface and moved to Lagos for the second round of their talks with the natives. On reaching Lagos around Christmas time the deputation's optimism calm down at once because James Johnson's influence was supreme everywhere they went. Regarding the Bishop's position, no amount of persuasion would make him change his stand and course as the deputation observed that he had lost every confidence in the C.M.S. At the meeting convened James Johnson and Otunba Payne spoke for Lagos and the former elaborated on how the credit of Africa was being placed at stake and it would take sometime if not years to repair the damage already done to the personality of the African people. He also said that an African must succeed the Bishop after death must have silenced him; and that the C.M.S must accept responsibility for paralyzing the growth of the churches in Sierra Leone and Lagos by withholding independence from them too long. Otunba Payne spoke extensively on the indignities heaped on Bishop Crowther; he then called for the immediate withdrawal of the white missionaries from the Delta region and move them to places like Lake Chad region where they could effectively practice their super missionary knowledge and demonstrate their unbroken flow of experience among the people there.

Finally he lectured Allan and Hamilton on the policy of Henry Venn and his hopes for the Africans.

Unfortunately the Bishop of his people was now getting to the end of his journey and the last hour for him to give up the ghost was fast approaching and eventually on 31st of December 1891, on that glorious and anointed day our illustrious son and beloved Bishop of his people went home peacefully in Lagos. Whatever program Allan and Hamilton might have in mind for detailed settlement of the dispute came to an end abruptly. It may not be too far away from the truth and the assumption of the people that it was the C.M.S, which in a way was responsible for the death of their Bishop at this particular time. Because when the crisis was at its peak, the Bishop was already an old man who may no longer had the strength and stamina to uphold the amount of pressure and stress that were associated with such huge crisis. This was naturally the time of his life when he was supposed to sit back at home with his blessed children and grandchildren to enjoy the fruits of his labor, but, the opposite was planned for him by his adversaries and men of different Christian souls and minds in the organization he helped with all of the energies in him to move to a prominent height. In Lagos, where he was buried his funeral service was attended by a very large crowd of personalities that included Governor Carter, Major Macdonald of the Oil Rivers Protectorate and the then Colonial Secretary. The funeral service was conducted by James Johnson who in his oratory eulogy delivered a very powerful and touching speech about the journey of the Bishop on this earth planet which, the African adversaries of the time later labeled as too much of "racialism". The struggle for his successor emerged immediately as the West African Press demanded that no other person could step into the vacant stool of the Bishop other than James Johnson.

Chapter 19

The Brave and Fearless Nationalist Missionaries after Bishop Crowther

This chapter is specially dedicated to some of the past founders of our nation and those men and women who worked on the highways as well as the marshy roads of our country carrying with them their learning difficulties, passion and their senses of honor on both their heads and hearts for a single purpose that you and me may have the fullest right to walk as a free person, organize ourselves into various groups of our own choices without outside intervention, control our resources and use them for the betterment of all and be a free man and woman to exercise our Constitutional rights in the realm of political arrangement. Part of what they fought for with the last drop of blood in their veins and the last drop of water dripping down from their eyes and running through their cheeks was that "All Africans" can see both of their patrimony and their basic obligations to keep the continent save and to hold all of its purposes high in any form, where relevant and what it would take to achieve this task.

Our past founders believed that institutional arrangements either in the church, mosque or in the government would be central to the success of our modern men and women and we should be rightly proud today that their dreams are gradually coming to the day's light after several centuries of its lying waste in the bed for an endless deep slumber. The founders remembered all the travails of their ancestors before the partition of their beloved continent; how both the religion and government of the old had, in time of colonialism, been destroyed by convulsions and upheavals, by vice and decadence. From their study of human behavior and nature, they were acutely aware of man's self- interestedness, his selfishness and self-greediness when they were at the war front, but yet they designed African freedom to take all these into account.

The nations that fought this type of war before them and won especially the America saw the reason why it was necessary to solicit for the absolute support of their people which they presumed would be necessary to do much to re-channel and curb the individual selfishness and discourage political convulsions in order that their society may be stabilized and move in the right direction for total liberation and survival. Our founders too bought this idea when they faced the music of the war that quenched many of them either through death, persecution, incarceration, extermination or permanent disablement. As John Adams one of the founders of modern America and the 2nd president of the USA put it at a time of the struggle in America and said: "Human passions unbridled by morality and religion...... would break the strongest cords of our Constitution as a whale goes through a net".

One of the areas of our culture that was taken away from us either inadvertently or out of our carelessness was the particular one that formed the basis of our today's mistakes. Before the art of writing was introduced to Africa, we always trusted our retentive memories to record accurately the events that happened in our lives and we do not easily forget ourselves, our history and our great men and women of excellent virtues in their respective callings and their contributions towards the development of our continent and people. How can Nigerians or Somalians for example fully know their countries and themselves without knowing at least a little about the men and women who pledged and risked their "lives", "fortunes" and "sacred honor" for the blessings of liberty the citizens of these two nations enjoyed today? It is a living fact that the Lord gave our continent a name and standing among the continents of the world but why then have we decided out of our own volition to drag the beauty, the glory and the blessings of the great continent, in the mud?

My prayer and hope is that the gratitude in the hearts of our founding fathers may be expressed by proper use of those inestimable blessings that God has endowed us, with the greatest exertions of patriotism, and by taking serious attitude and support for the institutions that would cultivate human understanding so that we may expect greater progress of the Arts and Science, by establishing laws for the support of peity, religion and morality so that we may be able to once and for ever extinguish the light of greed, selfishness and other dangerous virtues that beclouded our progress. By now Africa is supposed to be operating on the same level with other continents of the world in those areas of social, public and private virtues that gives dignity to people. The aim of our founding fathers was that by now we should totally be a free person with all virtues attached to people and that the gains of our economic productivity must remain in the soil of the continent for the development and expansion of trade and industry. But where is the position of Africa in the committee of the continents of the world today?

Those that laid down their lives, shed their bloods and ran down sweats through their foreheads for the emancipation of our people throughout the land of the continent were so numerous to mention in this text but nevertheless few of them are to be referenced because of their outstanding, remarkable and astonishing contributions which could not be easily forgotten or overlooked. In the preceding chapter we had talked about Blyden who initiated the nationalistic ideas into the heads of the educated Africans of his time. Though his own format of nationalist movement ideal may differ from those of others who copied from his thoughts, yet credit must always be given to this great scholar for his early initiatives, consciousness about his race and stupendous move in the right direction and at the right time.

James Johnson – 1839 to 1917:

The next person in the hierarchical order of nationalist activities of the early time was James Johnson, who was born to Yoruba parents that had been taken in slavery but recaptured and released by British antislavery patrol and settled in Sierra Leone. Johnson who was born a twin at the village of Waterloo in the colony at the time when the birth of twins was an abomination in the land of Africa due to heathenism belief of the time owed his survival solely to the time when he was born and to his place of birth which was under the protection of the British flag; otherwise Johnson would have been killed as others were being killed during this time elsewhere in the interior of the continent.

Because of the freedom enjoyed by the inhabitants of the colony, Johnson's early life was thus spent in an environment that was self-consciously Christian. In 1847 the young Johnson entered the C.M.S School in St. Mathews Parish, Waterloo where he was thought the Scripture passages, hymn singing, catechism and other subjects in the School curriculum of this time. He was known to be an intelligent independent minded, envincing a deep spirituality beyond his years while still in the elementary school and because of this gift, people began to notice him as being destined for a career in the church. In 1851 he gained admission to the C.M.S Grammar school founded in 1845 to provide secondary education for boys from the new middle-class families of the colony similar in curriculum to its contemporaries in England except from the daily stints in farming and a course in Navigation that was added as an opportunity and future advantages to the boys in their chosen career. On June 1, 1857, Johnson entered the Fourah Bay Institution, which was also founded by the C.M.S in 1827 for the purpose of training the "native" ministers in West Africa and in December 1858 he was duly graduated and took up a catechist position at Kent, a Southernmost village on the Sierra Leone Peninsula, which was some twenty-five miles away from Freetown.

Johnson said of himself that one day when he was reading the book of Zechariah while he was preparing for his lesson on the 3rd and 4th chapters of the book, the Lord spoke to him as his Savior and within that week at Holy Communion Service he found Salvation. And from then on the joy and gladness of personal salvation led him to offer himself to God that He might send him out as a missionary among the heathen people of his continent. This transforming experience became the mainspring of an enduring religious fervor and his unshakeable commitment to Christian service. The reason bred in him a fanatical peity and diehard dogmatism that both attracted, repelled and tended to polarize Johnson's acquaintances into either staunch supporters or antagonists. As a young man, his appointment to Kent actually signaled his future career and lifelong dedication to the organization he so much respected and loved. From Kent, he was transferred to his Grammar school where he was a tutor for almost three years and during this short period his star in the missionary work was already coming out. He was ordained a deacon in March 1863 and took up the curacy of the prestigious Pademba Road Church under the superintendence of a European missionary. He was connected to the church for eleven years and his stay there marked the second major turning point in his life.

It was said of the Parishioners of this church as "purely heathen" worshiping in a veritable center of non-Christian practices because majority of them there were Shango (god of thunder) worshipers. Johnson embarked on a crusade against the evil around him with unconventional and confrontational zeal. Among the fruits of his evangelical labor in this district was the conversion in October 1863, of King John Macaulay (of the Aku) a prominent Muslim man who was seriously known as reveling in immorality and heathen practices. In December 1866, Johnson was elevated to priesthood and because of high-mindedness of being antisocial, he refused not to marry at all not until when he was in his late twenties that he eventually met a lady worthy enough for him to marry but unfortunately the lady died in England in 1868.The death of his wife was a severe blow on him to an extent that for another twenty-seven years, Johnson remained without a wife. Eventually he was either persuaded or out of his own volition married another lady – Sabina Leigh who was a daughter of a prominent Yoruba businessman.

While Johnson remained a missionary in the service of the C.M.S in Sierra Leone, he was not directly affected by the native pastorate scheme that was being anticipated by some group of radicals in the colony as at then but the experiment of the scheme coincided with the beginning of African nationalism spawning "Ethiopianism", and Johnson became one of the earliest and most aggressive advocate of the ideology. "Ethiopian" ideology was to extol African identity, defend African capability, anticipated to turn the whole continent into Christianity and ultimately acquire political goal, which its rhetoric focused primarily on racial equality and ecclesiastical independence. Arguably its demand and emphasis went much further on the road than Henry Venn's program, which in a sense was hijacked. Johnson was so much entrenched into this ideology that he remarked in one of his writings that "we see nothing around us which we can call our own in the true sense of the term; nothing that shows an independent native capacity excepting this infant Native Pastorate Institution".

Johnson believed that the establishment of an independent nondenominational "African Church" would make the African people see the good qualities that were contained in Christian religion. Along with many others in his thinking faculty condemned the inimical effects of European missionary enterprise on the African identity and heritage. Therefore the desire to have an independent church would go a long way because we are a distinct race, existing under peculiar circumstances and possessed peculiar characteristics. He further argued that the arrangements of foreign churches were made to suit their own local circumstances and hardly could such arrangements be expected to suit our own in all their details. He demanded that the immediate upgrading of Fourah Bay College into West African University would be the best idea because it would put Africa on the map of the world in the field of education; and secondly that the African pastorate dependence on C.M.S for financial assistance would always ensure the continual domination of European missionaries which would totally negate the original program of Henry Venn of self-supporting churches in Africa.

The Ethiopian ideology was embraced by nearly every educated West Africans of his age if not all as they saw it as an in-road into the development of Africa by the Africans and Johnson became the undisputed champion of the native pastors and the leading figure in the propagation of the ideology in the areas of ecclesiastical independence. His brand of Ethiopianism animated clergy and laity alike and crossed denominational barriers but the clamor for the scheme was seen as premature at this time and for this reason, it met with strong opposition of the powerful European missionaries especially that of the newly appointed Bishop Cheetham and some discents from the ranks of the native pastors. Because of the relentless efforts and agitation of Johnson and people of his like-manner in the struggle, challenging the entrenched European structures and attitude without break coupled with the sympathy it evoked at the C.M.S headquarters in England, Johnson was summoned to England in 1873 for talk.

The authority at the C.M.S Headquarters in England saw clearly that Johnson was becoming a big problem for them at Sierra Leone and all they could do was to transfer him to the Yoruba Mission but the ideals he had championed had already made far reaching consequences on the organization. The C.M.S now resolved that Africans should join the staff of Fourah Bay College, which was soon to be elevated to a fee-paying University that can admit any well recommended Christian African to study for vocations other than the Bible studies. The move later led to the institution's affiliation to Durham University in 1876 and changed the direction of the C.M.S policy with regards to Sierra Leone Mission where much emphasis were now placed on African leadership and the systematic withdrawal of all foreign support. In 1875 a Sierra Leone Missionary Society was established under intense C.M.S. pressure and by either cajoling or coercion, the C.M.S ceded most of its missions to the new body. It was said that seven years after Johnson had left the colony, the Sierra Leone Anglican Church was distinctively filled with African personnel both in its administration and polity and the only office occupied by a European was that of the Bishop.

In June 1874, Johnson was transferred to Lagos and the center of gravity of his Ethiopean movement now moved with him to a more hospitable environment than Freetown. When he got to Lagos, he immediately identified himself with the vigorously pursued nationalist movement that was already on the ground there and he became its leading and most outspoken figure. Johnson was placed at the Breadfruit Church, which was the home of the most ardent nationalists among the population and also being the wealthiest and most important church in Lagos of this time. He was an influential figure among his Parishioners and the Society to such a high level that he was nominated as a member of the Legislative Council from 1886 to 1894 and enjoyed a pre-eminence among Nigerian Christians, which would have been difficult for him to attain had he stayed in Sierra Leone where there were better qualified and educated colleagues than himself. In fact it was only Bishop Samuel Crowther that was much more popular than him in Yorubaland. In Lagos he worked very hard to win converts from among the populace, which was predominantly Muslim population and strove very hardly to learn Yoruba language which was the mother tongue of the majority of his congregation and the people of Lagos. People's reaction to his energetic leadership and fanatical Ethiopianism tended to divide along racial lines.

To the native Christian, Johnson was an inspiring figure as he was eulogized as Holy Johnson, but among the European missionaries his influence and proclamations provoked deep apprehension and resentment. As he was when he was in Sierra Leone, so he is now in Lagos or even more tougher and harder than that. His rhetoric whipped up considerable anti-European feelings and more than ever before, African nationalism and racial outcry singled out Johnson among his colleagues and defined his attitude, activities and relationship with the whites around him and those that were far away from him, who were in the position of authority in the organization he served but wanted to remain dominating race on the soil of Africa. A year after Johnson's arrival in Lagos, the C.M.S established Lagos native pastorate based on the Sierra Leone model and in the face of strenuous European opposition. The affairs of this new pastorate was dominated from its day one by Johnson as he was now recognized as an experienced person in the administration of native pastorate through the knowledge and skills he had acquired in Sierra Leone on similar and identical project.

Johnson's first administrative strategy was based on the experience that Sierra Leonian project had taught him that self-support for the churches is the key to ecclesiastical independence and in this regard he made sure that his Breadfruit church became the pastorate's financial backbone. Johnson's record at Breadfruit church revealed that his Lagos pastorate, which he was its prime mover superseded that of its counterpart in Freetown in inspirations and innovations. Africanization and self-government formed its over-reaching objectives, and "Africa for the Africans" slogan became a thing of reality. It was during this time that the "indigenous White-cap Chiefs" in Lagos were embraced by the Breadfruit community, and the prayers for the Native Kings replaced the previous prayers for the Queen of England in the prayer book. When the white missionaries saw the on-going evangelical surgery being undertaken by Holy Johnson, they were alarmed and were predicting secession and in truth his militancy was already pointing to facts and reasons to allay such fears. In 1876, Johnson was made the Superintendent of all the stations in the interior of Yorubaland, which was a great tribute to his outstanding ability and to further test his creative abilities in the leadership position if he were to be considered for one in the future.

In the West African Church Organization, Johnson was now number two and next after Bishop Crowther of the Niger Mission. Apart from his nationalistic tendencies, the C.M.S faith in Johnson's capabilities was to make him a Bishop "exercising jurisdiction in Abeokuta and the Yoruba country". Although his two older bosses- Bishops Crowther and Cheetham, thought that he still needed more experience, but neither of them doubted that he was destined for that office one day into the future. His superintendency in Yorubaland lasted for only four years amidst of controversy that ended in his removal. His aggressive evangelism produced many surprising results especially in the area of growth for the churches in his jurisdiction and tremendous progress towards self-support and self-government in those churches.

Upon his losing the superintendency of the Yoruba Mission, Johnson went back to his Parish at Breadfruit church where his image and popularity never diminished among the African Christians and the society. In the West African axis, the Sierra Leonian leading clergmen including the European principal of the Fourah Bay College were putting pressure on the C.M.S that Johnson should be appointed archdeacon of the Sierra Leone church to provide leadership for the native clergy there. The need for another native clergy to be elevated to the position of Bishop in West

Africa was being demanded for both in Sierra Leone and in Nigeria and the call for this demand was incessantly knocking at the doors of Salisbury Square. But the Society was only in favor of the issue of Yoruba bishopric with an African incumbent. On Johnson's visit to England in 1887, he made a powerful statement in a memorandum he presented on the West African Native Churches and Missions & Native Episcopacy concerning an argument for a native Bishop and native self-government; the document focused on Sierra Leone and asserted that over seventy years of C.M.S labor in that colony, the natives had not been given a place of supervision.

The presentation was admitted as eloquent and brilliant but the C.M.S determined only to approve the Yoruba bishopric as an option setting aside the intention of Johnson. In the event, the move toward a native Bishopric was hindered by a violence of conflicting opinion, resurgent racial tension, stiff European missionary opposition towards Johnson's candidacy and more decisively, the financial obstacle. On the long run, in 1888 Johnson was appointed a member of the Lagos based C.M.S Finance Committee instead of given him the high office of the Bishop because Salisbury Square knew much of his activities and successes in the area of money making for the church. On the other hand the white missionaries saw the vision of Henry Venn of self-supporting for the churches as very premature because of the security of the positions they occupied in West Africa and the quality of life they live compared with what would have been their lots if they were to be in England.

In the face of racial tension that cut across the 1880s into 1890s especially the disillusionment and uniform umbrage at the treatment meted out to the aged Bishop Crowther fueled secessionist sentiments. Johnson was called into renewed efforts for an independent African Church. Unfortunately he did not found one but instead he threw his considerable weight and influence behind the separatist movement in the Niger Delta. The Niger Delta Pastorate that came into existence in April 1892 after six years of promising existence faltered and returned to the camp of the C.M.S. In this wise Johnson's vision of an independent African Church that would be headed by an African Bishop vanished into the oblivion and thin out into the air. Meanwhile a European was already appointed to succeed Crowther and what could be called a compromise agreement of his ideals, Johnson now accepted the position of assistant Bishop of the Niger Delta in 1900 the position he held till the end of his life. As popular as Johnson was within the rank and file of his Breadfruit church, in October 1901 two thirds of his congregation seceded on his behalf to form the independent Bethel African church, but he denied them his leadership, thus making him to throw away the golden opportunity to implement his Ethiopian program. Himself being in opposition to European customs, dress, and names for the African church, neither changed his own name nor abandoned the vestments of the Western church.

Unfortunately Johnson who was an inspirer of so many secessions from the Anglican Church remained its loyal servant despite the fact that his trust was often betrayed. But perhaps it may be correct to judge or view Johnson as a transitional figure who embodied the contradictions of his times but being blind to the inherent contradictions at the heart of his vision. The rest of the years of James Johnson were being spent as Assistant Bishop of Western Equatorial Africa with various missionary activities until he died on May 18, 1917. Many great Nigerians both in missionary works or other trades owed their beginnings and achievements to the standard of nationalism that this great man set not for his own generation but generations yet unborn. His philosophy seemed to have worked for the Africans because he believed that Christianity was practically the only benefit Europe could offer to Africa and that the importation of their culture would be ruinous. He battled fiercely for government financial support for African churches, and for the establishment of an African University and industrial education program.

Rev. Samuel Johnson – 1846 to 1901

The second person to be referenced here was one of the famous Yoruba churchman and historian the Rev. Samuel Johnson of Oyo dynasty traced to the popular Alaafin Abiodun of Oyo Empire. His father was Henry Johnson, one of the Saros, the people that came back to their country of origin from Sierra Leone in the 1840s having lived there as "re-captives" – those taken off slave ships by the British Navy or as children born to such people in Freetown. Henry Johnson and his wife Sarah were blessed with several sons all who became famous in Nigeria through their chosen careers. The family moved to join the Church Missionary Society in 1857 under Rev. David Hinderer at Ibadan. The eldest son Henry became a famous archdeacon in the service of the CMS. The second son Nathaniel worked for the same organization as a teacher and catechist, while the third son Samuel was also a clergyman and historian. The fourth son Obadiah was the second Nigerian in the country to be qualified as a medical doctor.

As noted earlier, Samuel Johnson was born at Hasting, Freetown, on 24th June 1846 and moved with his family into Yoruba country. His stay at Ibadan was longer than as planned because of the Ibadan – Ijaiye war of 1860 – 62, this war was one of the many recent wars among the Yoruba Kingdoms after the one of 1820s. From 1863 to 1865, Samuel moved to Abeokuta to complete his education at the C.M.S Training Institution there and from 1866 he was in the employment of the C.M.S. as a schoolmaster at Ibadan. In 1867, he was promoted as an assistant to the popular Ibadan teacher, schoolmaster and Deacon at that time- Daniel Olubi.

Later he became the Superintendent of the Anglican Mission's Schools (known as Education Officers as at then) at Aremo and Kudeti in Ibadan, and in 1873 he visited Oyo, his ancestral homeland for the first time. In 1875 he became a catechist and also involved in the Yoruba conflicts of the time. In 1877, the greatest of all the wars that Yoruba nation ever fought among its states broke out – the Ekiti Parapo war that lasted for sixteen years according to Samuel Johnson. This war involved Ibadan, which was then the dominant military power in Yorubaland, the Egbaland and the Ekiti states, all joined together to form a military company called Ekiti-Parapo.

The few educated Yorubas of this time who were from the mainstream of the Saros were equally involved to serve as mediators or peacemakers. In the case of Johnson, he played the key role of peacemaker among the tribes. In 1881, he was the one who carried letters of understanding to Lagos as an agent of his people from the Alaafin of Oyo suggesting British intervention to restore peace in the land; although his efforts failed but himself and others continued their peace efforts until some light of peace began to be seen and in 1885 five years later he became an official British Government mediator between Ibadan, Ijesha and the Ekiti states. Through his efforts, the war extinguished in some parts in 1886 and in 1889, the whole land returned to peace. The intervention of the British Government to restore peace actually paved way for the annexation of Yorubaland by the British.

In 1880, Samuel Johnson became a Deacon and in 1888 ordained a pastor at Oyo to spread the Christianity faith to his people. It was during his time at Oyo that the Training Institution formerly at Abeokuta was moved to Oyo and renamed St. Andrew's College a popular Teacher's college of its time where many important Yoruba teachers were trained. In Oyo, Johnson had access to rich sources of Yoruba tradition and by 1897 he had carefully completed the remarkable manuscript of the history of the Yorubas and its traditions. Unfortunately the first manuscript that was sent to the C.M.S Headquarters in London for publication got lost without any trace. The loss of this vital document was glaringly suspicious but his brother Dr. Obadiah Johnson was kind enough to see that the efforts of his senior brother on this project did not go down into the drains. The mysterious loss of the manuscript moved Dr. Obadiah to re-compile the book from his brother's notes and luckily enough the book was finally published in 1921 by George Rouledge and Sons a year after his death in London as a ***History of the Yorubas from the Earliest Times to the Beginning of the British Protectorate,*** with Samuel Johnson as the author and edited by his brother Dr. Obadiah Johnson.

The book was recognized as a pioneering historical study of Yoruba country and its people and also ranked as of high quality that ensured Samuel Johnson's fame. What inspired this great son of Yoruba race to write the book was mainly from patriotic motive. He remarked that the educated Yoruba people of his time knew the history of Britain, Greece and Rome in both their heads and hearts, but they hardly knew anything about their own country and people. What an awesome nationalist and patriot he was to the core? Does this type of our great son deserves a place in our memory and a space in our land to show our gratitude and appreciation for his love and gesture at the time when the dominating race wanted to kill and wipe off our culture so that they would substitute our with theirs? I think this great son deserves both?

Mary Ibeso 1856 – 1945

Here is the name of a woman I stumbled into during the research of materials for the writing of this book and her name is Mary Ibeso who hailed from the Ogbe Onodi quarters of Emu Uno in the Eastern region of Nigeria. She was born in 1856 and lived up to 1945 making a good journey of eighty-nine years altogether on our planet amid sadness and joy. Her early stages of life were mixed with both joy and sorrow. She lost her only daughter one year after the death of her husband and the whole world became so miserable for her to live in. On the death of her husband many overtures were made to her by the Christian unbelievers in her community but she despised them outright and because of this she was hated more by the men-folk as well as the women, calling her all sorts of degrading names in her village and beyond. But she was so much loved by her Christian brothers and sisters who admired her virtues. Her close intimacy with the church gave her the laughing title of **Nne Uku** (mother of the church) and for this reason she decided to develop a spectacular custom of wearing white cloth as a symbol of purity and she closely attached herself to Jesus Christ the same way a faithful wife would attach herself to her husband. She was even fond of calling herself a wife to the Lord.

In actual fact Mary was the first Christian mother of St. Peters Anglican Church at Emu Uno and a woman teacher to instruct the young women converts of the church. She was a woman of hard prayer and often seen around the church praying for countless hours for everyone in her community. Those who knew her recounted how she would pray ceaselessly for the spread of Christian faith in her community and for the people in her neighborhood to be abundantly blessed both in spirit and materially so that there would be enough money for the propagation of the Christian religion in her place and beyond. Her whole lifetime was devoted to intercession for the growth of the church as she often prayed that the good reports she was hearing from other lands such as Isoko, Urhobo and Abraka also become a reality in her own land too.

Mary was so much glued to her own style of evangelism that the married men in her community reportedly warned their wives to stay away from her for fear that she might lure them into Christian religion which the majority of her people did not accept during this time. She would always carry her faith and belief in Jesus Christ with her to wherever she went. She was so much proud of this belief that at the cassava mills, in the village market places and from house-to-house, Mary was never ashamed of talking to everyone about Jesus Christ – the Savior. She was the type of women leader that always make herself readily available to assist the new women converts in any form that would make them stay comfortably in the church and more serviceable to their community as mothers. It was said of Mary that she was fond of a very good evangelical follow up each time a new convert arrived at the church as well as getting herself involved in such woman's life until she would become a committed and strong member of the church.

On Saturdays, she would lead the women in the cleaning of the church in preparation for the Sunday service. In those days when the use and manufacturing of paints were only limited to either Europe or America alone, the local materials that were being used to decorate the mud houses of the time were clay materials, talc and chalk. The women folk of the time were the main specialists in the decoration of the mud buildings with such materials and when it was necessary to do this art work, Mary would lead the other women on foot to some distance of three to four miles away to fetch these materials to rub the church walls and the mud benches with cocoyam leaves because of its quality to retain color and free from staining clothes when dried. Her labors in the service of Christ did not go in vain as she was taken care of by the Anglican converts at Emu Uno during her old age until she died in 1945.

Prophet Garrick Sokari Marian Braide:
Prophet Braide will be the next to talk about because of his evangelical impact on his people through the gift of anointing he received from above. Braide was a prominent healer and prophet of the Most High God with a new dimension of anointing in the spread of Christianity in Africa. He lived for only thirty-six years from 1882 to 1918 amidst strains, stresses and remarkable walks with God both in spirit and physical. He was one of the originators of the African Independent Church Movement when he became an Anglican catechist in the turbulent years following Bishop Crowther's crisis of late 80s to early 90s in the Niger Delta Pastorate. Braide had a gift of healing and this gift in him prompted many people to come to him for cures and prophecies in the areas of bareness, bad-luck, chronic diseases and material blessings.

He was so good and accurate in his prophecy predictions that whatever he told the people seeking his healing audience for counseling would always go back to their homes satisfied and because of this, he became very popular among the Christian converts in his community and beyond. He believed in the powers of God only and there was a time that he was said to challenge the traditional religion priests in a rainmaking contest and when the contest was over, he rendered them useless as he won the contest by invoking the Christian God. The people from thence began to call him Elijah II and he took this title to honor the powers of Almighty God in him. He was known to be a strong praying prophet, a talented preacher of peace and reconciliation and someone who loved to enforce Sunday observance.

Prophet Braide so much hated the use of alcohol by his people that when he was seriously preaching against it, the profit on alcohol imported into the country fell drastically and thereby reduced the Government revenue in excise taxes on the commodity very greatly. This was one of the offenses charged against Braide when the British colonial authority in

Nigeria moved on him in fear of his growing influence. By 1915, Braide was said to have attracted many people to his side in the rough estimate of over one million followers. He had now become the focus of a cult and over two thirds of the Delta congregation in the Anglican churches abandoned Bishop Johnson for Braide and this prompted the Bishop to turn against his protégé. His organization was proscribed for heresy and Bishop Johnson asked the British colonial authority to investigate him.

Based on this request he was placed under the close surveillance of the colonial authority and when he made a statement that was against the government that power was now passing from the whites to the blacks during the World War I, he was apprehended and sent to prison for sedition. During his absence in the prison, his followers severed links with the C.M.S to form a new denomination called the Christ Army Church. The organization was one of the first African Independent Churches founded in total African reaction to foreign domination. Unfortunately Braide could not carry the new organization farther down the road as he died of an accident in 1918 and his movement broke into many factions out of which some continued his Christian morality while others adapted Christianity that honored African customs. They predominantly settled in the South Eastern region of Nigeria.

Dr. Kato Byang Henry 1936 – 1975:
Next in line and possibly the last to reference in this text because of space is Dr. Kato Byang Henry who hailed from Sabo Zuro clan of Kwoi in Kaduna state, Nigeria and was born on June 23, 1936 into the family of Heri and Zawi. In the early stages of his life, his father dedicated him to a local deity called Pop-ku as was the custom of the people of his community by then. He was instructed in the practices of this deity as a young child and in the company of his age group all participated actively in the rituals of the deity. Soon after Kato underwent the traditional Jaba initiation rituals, he came in contact with one Ms. Mary Hass who was then a missionary of Sudan Interior Mission (SIM) whose evangelical mission took her to the village of Kato to speak about Jesus Christ to the children in her very difficult language of Jaba.

From here Kato who was among the children who often listened to Mary Hass had the opportunity to attend the Sunday school and the primary school established and run by SIM. Kato's father never saw anything good that his son would benefit from attending this sort of school more than the prosperous gains awaiting him as a farmer like himself and because of his negative thinking he vehemently opposed the new move that would better the life of his son. There was another missionary named Ms. Elsie Hendenson who went in company of an elder in the church to plead with Kato's father to release him to attend school. Fortunately they were able to convince the father and he agreed to send Kato back to school only on one condition that he was not going to be responsible for his feeding and clothing. This in a way depicted his outright rejection of the plea, which he was keeping to himself alone but pretending to be a nice and agreeable father in the presence of the old man and the foreign missionary agent.

Something interesting about Kato's life happened when his teacher was teaching the pupil in his class about the salvation in Jesus Christ, with the illustration of Noah's ark, the teacher's expression on this topic so much thrilled Byang that he immediately desired to enter Christ's Ark of Salvation and he made a public declaration of faith in Christ before his mates and the teacher. This declaration got his father more furious with him as he was very livid at his son's decision and he finally decided to stop paying his school fees and he withdrew every other support he had to attend to his son. As a result of his father's action, the missionaries decided to take up his responsibilities by given him employment in the mission that enabled him to pay his school fees, buy his clothes, books and took care of his little needs. Despite his father's refusal to provide for his needs in his school project, Kato would still help his father in the farm in the morning and attend classes in the afternoon until he completed his primary education with excellent grade.

The only post-primary education opportunity opened to him was the Bible College at Igbaja, which he attended and graduated from the institution in 1957. He was immediately assigned to teach in a Bible school located in his village Kwoi on a monthly salary of $15 :00. While teaching, he was taken correspondence courses from England to prepare himself for the external General Certificate of Education (GCE) and at the end of it all, he made this examination in flying colors. It was also during this academic strivings that he got married to his beloved wife Jummai in 1957, a lady that also came from a Christian home whose identity bonded the two of them together in hard prayer and commitment to each other. They both became prayer warriors and devoted Christians.

In 1959, Byang was transferred to Lagos to serve on the staff of "Today's Challenge" and from there he received some training in journalism. In 1963 he enrolled at London Bible College and graduated in 1967 with the Bachelor of Divinity degree and in the same year he was appointed to the office of the General Secretary of the Evangelical Church of West Africa – the ECWA being the first person from Northern Nigerian to hold that position and he moved to the organization's Headquarters in Jos. His academic pursuit made him to enroll for his post-graduate studies at Dallas Theological Seminary where he had his doctoral degree Th. D in May 1974. The topic of his dissertation "Universalism and Syncretism in Christianity in Africa" was later published by the Evangel Publishing House in Nairobi – Kenya under the title of Theological Pitfalls in Africa and became a popular academic textbook. On finishing his doctoral studies, Byang was unanimously chosen to occupy the position of the General Secretary for the African Evangelical Association being the first African to hold that post. He was also appointed to serve as the Executive Secretary of the Theological Commission of the ECWA. His service was so much in demand both in Nigeria and at abroad especially in the areas of preaching and teaching.

He was one of the keynote speakers at the International Congress on World Evangelization held in Lausanne in 1974. He also served as a member of the Lausanne Continuation Committee on World Evangelization and a member of the Executive Committee of the World Evangelical Fellowship and the Chairman of its Theological Commission. In 1975, he attended the fifth General Assembly of the World Council of Churches held in Nairobi. While on one of his international engagements, he decided to go with the members of his family to the seashore at Mombasa for some rest, reflection and relaxation. It was during this trip that he met his untimely death on 19 December 1975 when he drowned in Mombasa River under mysterious circumstances. His body was recovered a day after his disappearance. His death was seen as a tragedy and a big loss to Africa particularly when the continent was expecting a big reward from the talents he had acquired over the turbulent years of his life.

The people of Kwoi, his hometown did not part with his death without such an indirect allusion that someone must have either attacked him or was responsible for his mysterious death. Others believed that the powers of darkness must have cast spell on him forgetting that there is no other power that can withstand the powers of Almighty God in him while others proclaimed exhaustion. Up-till today the death of Byang still remained a mystery to everyone. His contributions to Evangelical development in Africa and the world were seen as significant strength that pulled so many strings that were already pulled out of the center of African Theology together. During his lifetime, he was not scared to address such issues concerning the social and political status of his African people.

In one of his popular lectures, he spoke in a way that many of the readers of the paper or listeners of the lecture would found him uncongenial when he said: "We must appreciate the call for a kind of socialism because capitalism has become a real curse in Africa and the gap between the haves and the have-nots continue to widen. In Africa, today, you will find many millionaires but also many people who go to bed hungry". In some other papers, he condemned the past oppression of African peoples when he said that "enslavement of Africans by the whites is probably the worst evil done by one class of people to another".

Chapter 20

Early Political Trumpeting in West Africa

Undoubtedly the result of slave trade of the eighteenth and nineteenth centuries in the continent of Africa left large scars and wounds on the bodies and souls of the people of the continent irrespective of their places of origin and the clan they belong. The suppression of the slave trade, which was initiated by the British; who was then a big partner in the business in 1807, and whose some of its people were of slavery by itself in British possessions in 1833 could not stop the trade outright. Its efforts and trials in this direction only opened more avenues for other nations who were not in the business before to rush into it and took over the business from where the British left it off. Between 1807 and its total collapse in 1861, the trade flourished as it never before; but through the hard-driven attitude of the British government concerning this illegal business backed by its nations industrialists, humanitarians and missionaries, the burning flame of the carnivorous and inhuman trade was finally extinguished.

   A British naval squadron for this purpose was stationed off the coast of West Africa to seize all ships carrying human cargoes and set their commodities of human beings free in Sierra Leone, where the missionaries could teach them Christianity, the art of modern technologies that were available as at then in the areas of trade and industry, which would later transform their lives and ways of living from the type they had been living before their ordeal in the hands of the slavers.

The political game played by the British industrialists in supporting their government's scheme was not far-fetched in the sense that they wanted to paralyze most of the American and French sugar plantations in the West Indies by denying them the required labor, and as well to encourage the Africans to labor in Africa at planting and harvesting palm-oil for the factories in Britain. It was equally part of their program and hope, that West Africa would eventually become the British supplier of raw cotton as well as palm-oil and thus free her from dependence upon the United States for such raw materials. For this purpose, the remaining able bodied people of West Africa that were left behind in the continent were now being encouraged to began planting cotton seeds as well as palm trees for the take-off of the new trade that was to usher in both the European type of government and living styles. The climate of West Africa being too harsh on the Europeans made them not to directly exploit its resources the way they had done in the West Indies. Instead, they used the African Kings as their agents to organize the palm-oil trade and left the development of the cotton wool industry into the hands of the few experts that were abound in some scattered local areas of the region.

On another direction, the British hoped and relied on the activities of the missionaries to produce a class of Christian and educated African merchants that would become British partners in trade and would be competent enough to supervise the growing, collection and preparation of raw cotton for British traders who would bring back the finished product to England to feed their cloth manufacturing industries. Other European nations such as France and Portugal at this time had few industries that would require the supply of cotton and palm-oil on regular basis. Because these two nations were mainly making their profits from the slave trade and as such they ganged up to mount a campaign of hypocrisy against the British asserting that the British was trying to enhance her own prosperity while trying to destroy theirs under the mask of humanitarianism.

For some time the slave trade business was actually going on without a proper check on these nations who were now developing new methods and tactics everyday. The British on their part was busy negotiating and employing diplomatic arrangements at different levels with the stubborn nations who were behind the screen to motivate the continuation of the trade. Treaties and series of agreements that were mostly unfulfilled were signed between the nations in the business. Most of these agreements were actually becoming useless as most of the terms in them were being violated without any recourse to the importance of those terms and the future lives of their victims.

Between 1841 and 1850, the British tried another method to suppress the trade when their navy forced the Kings along the West Coast of Africa to allow it the right to forcefully seize the slaver's vessels loading human commodities in the ports located within their territories. This was an attempt to blockade the major slave ports along the coast; but such ports like those of Kalabari, Nembe or Quidah, located on a maze of creeks with numerous outlets, could still be used to load the slaves and slipped away unto the sea without anyone's knowledge.

The suppression of the trade dragged its feet for so long a time until when it finally died a natural death toward the end of the nineteenth century. The rest of the story about this degrading business venture that ravaged and partitioned the whole continent into meaningless fragments will be left to the historians to tell into details. All we can tell about slavery and the slave trade for now is that it contained a lot of emotional chapters and subjects and even in its mildest form it has always been a social evil that left its ugly foot print on the soil and body of every continent of the world irrespective of their culture and geographical locations.

The basis and ideals of democratic principles of governing people has never been the making of a singular nation rather it is a combination of ideas and practices of all nations of the world modeled to serve people at different levels of their development. Generally speaking, no one imported an idea of democratic form of rule into the soil of Africa, the Portuguese explorers that first came in contact with Africa in the 15th century met and confirmed to the whole world about the superior form of government they met in the Congo and Benin City areas in Africa. They were even proud to tell the truth that they went back to their home country to perfect on the superior model of the government of people they met in these two areas in Africa. Part of the things they went back home with in the 15th century still remained with them till today.

West African states are often divided into two broad groups according to their geography and culture. One group comprised of the Western Sudan, which occupied the area of Savannah vegetation and usually distinguished by their proximity and attachment to Islam that followed the religious revolution of the nineteenth century. The other group belonged to those of the coastal kingdoms that are situated in the tropical forest of the region, which placed much value on their native religion, beliefs and organization of their society. Like all other parts of the world, the people of this region had close affinity with one and another in their religious beliefs and style of government. Their Kings were recognized as the head of their government and the chiefs as the ministers, head of government parastatals and advisors, which is the replica of what is on the ground today under any form of government.

Certainly nothing new has ever been invented to counter or totally wipe off the system that had been in existence either in the dark or light ages of the past. All that has always been happening is the type of dance we dance around the system in form of breaking it into different units and to remold them back into its original form and give it a new name that will suit the yearnings and aspirations of the generation of its time. The best example of this scenario still exist till today in the native governments of any city or town in Yoruba nation be it the ones located in the Savannah or forest land of the country.

The Yoruba country for example and like others in the region of the Western Sudan was profoundly influenced by the Islamic revolution in the Hausa states which was inspired by Usman dan Fodio and which brought them closer to the ranks and files of the political and spiritual sphere of the Sokoto caliphate. At the same time, the Yoruba people were equally influenced by European activities on the Guinea coast especially when the change from the slave trade to palm-oil trade, the presence of guns and its powder, the missionary doctrine and European mode of dress and its culture emanating from Sierra Leone, Liberia, Europe and America began to find their foothold in their society.

When the British navy decided to deal seriously with the slavers along the coast of West Africa, the colonist new settlement of Freetown became its headquarters where the re-captives settled to begin a new life. This little colony then began to receive an annual influx of people in hundreds and thousands. Record showed that the population of the colony grew rapidly from 2000 in 1807 to 11000 in 1825 and to 40,000 in 1850. The new settlement became one of the great cultural "melting pots" of the world; its population was a blend of diverse people with different customs, religions and languages originating from every race and nations in West Africa from Senegal to Angola. It was from this settlement that the first sound of modern political trumpet in West Africa began its journey.

Governor Charles Macarthy (1814 – 1824), who was the first Governor-General of the colony, used the available opportunity at his disposal at this time to spread Western education and Christianity among the re-captives that had been forcibly uprooted and cut off from their original society. The idea behind this scheme was to prepare the re-captives for a beneficial purpose of new model in trading activities of the Europeans and to be used as an instrument of British government to derail the existing culture and system of the people's government in order to install theirs in its place.

For this reason, the British government was to provide the money while the missionaries were to be used as agents of the cultural and religious changes. Before the arrival of the re-captives, settlers drawn from the cream of unwanted slaves of all nations from the homes and streets of England had already been deposited in the new colony for a purpose. The settlers who had been closely associated with English life-style were to be models of educated Christians, which the re-captives were expected to imitate and copy.

Governor Macarthy

Governor Marcathy systematically began to settle the re-captives in the villages where schools and churches were established. Most of these villages were already given English names such as Leicester, Regent, Bathurst, Charlotte, Kent, York and Wellington. The few places left for the remembrance of African people and culture were in Kissy area (named after Kissi people) such as Kru and Congo Towns. The settler's attitude towards the re-captives was left in absolute doubt as they oftenly look down upon the re-captives as crude and illitrate heathens. Because of the ugly reactions of the settlers to their sentiments and quality of life, the re-captives on their own took to education and Christianity with zeal and vigor. They began to leave the village farms and moved into Freetown and started building their mud houses alongside the elegant storey houses of the settlers.

At first, they took to such petty jobs such as pedlars, hawkers, tailors, barbers, carpenters or masons to make their living worthwhile, and very soon, they began trading in the interior, competing seriously with the settlers in the buying or building of storey houses like them. By 1860, a great percentage of children of school age were attending schools in Sierra Leone than in England. This great effort was achieved through the solid cooperation of their government, the missionary society and the *Creoles* (the natives), many of whom went into debt to educate their children. In 1845, the secondary schools for boys and girls were established to supplement the teacher training college (Fourah Bay) founded in 1827 and which in 1876 was elevated to university college status.

The educational system in the colony was now pouring forth a stream of teachers, clergymen, doctors, lawyers and writers who later formed the "firsts" of the professional class of West Africa. Among them were the followings: John Thorpe (the first African lawyer –1850), J. B. Horton (the first medical doctor -1859), S. Ajayi Crowther, and the first Bishop 1864, Samuel Lewis (the first Knight –1896 as well as the first newspaper editor, owner and the first to be granted Cambridge and Oxford degrees). In the church and government *Creoles* pioneered the path which future generations of West Africa would follow as they formed the nucleus of the government of the time in both Sierra Leone and other districts of the colony.

In 1872 it became clear evidence that the *Creoles* had held almost half of the senior civil service posts of the colony, which prompted Governor Pope-Hennessy to remark that there were now enough qualified *Creoles* to replace the entire European staff. Based on this Gospel truth, Freetown was made a municipality having its own mayor in 1893; and by the end of the century the *Creoles* had formed an educated society that was proud of their achievements in the development of their society. They were now able to voice out their views with confidence in a vigorous and flourishing press and sit at prominent places in the churches and secular government. The group became so powerful that as the British expanded their empire in West Africa, they were dependent upon the *Creoles* to fill both the junior and most of the senior civil service posts in the regions they occupied.

For example they sat in the executive and legislative councils of Ghana, Gambia and Nigeria. In Ghana *Creoles* were Judges of the supreme courts, colonial Treasurer, Solicitor- general, Postmaster-general, Chief Medical Officers, District Officers and once Acting Governor. In Nigeria too the Registrar of the Supreme Court, Colonial Treasurer and Postmaster-general were *Creole*. Gambia and Liberia were no exception; two successive Chief Justices of Gambia, the Mayor of Monrovia and another, President of the

Republic were *Creoles*. Under the Niger Company and in Lagos and Dakar they held responsible positions in Marine engineers while in Fernando Po one of the *Creoles* prospered as cocoa plantation owner.

Along the coast, they were the first to be reckoned with in the clergy, law, medicine and newspaper owners. As late as 1925, the record showed that forty-four of Nigerians fifty-six barristers were of *Creole* descent. Because of the great achievement of the *Creoles*, Freetown became the hub of the West Africa where every citizen of the region looked unto for prosperity and achievements.

Could the glory achieved by Freetown city and its *Creole* children over the years be seen as permanent or short lived one? The glory was actually short lived for two reasons. The first reason was the role of the British government, which stipulated that only Englishmen should administer the interior. The colonial office thought that *Creole's* influence was to be put at check and if possible kept out completely. Cardew's policy was to keep the *Creoles* out of the protectorate completely as he rejected J.C. Parkes plan for a scheme of indirect rule to be supervised by the *Creole* officers. He purposely stagnated every sphere of development from education to commerce and his policy made the *Creole* merchants to lose their place in the economic sector of the territory.

European traders too were not spared from Cardew's policy. They were quietly replaced by large European firms, which no one from the *Creole* group or from the European small traders could compete with. Reason being that these large firms who were originally whole-sellers were now advised or instructed to open their retailing departments with their huge resources to stiffen the small retailers up. Eventually the small retailers were driven out of the business especially the *Creoles* that controlled this sector of the economy for seventy years. From all economic indications, things were becoming too difficult for the natives in Freetown and in the interior they were treated as foreigners and even forbidden to invest in land, which was the customary starting point of any commercial class.

As soon as the partitioning of the continent was complete, the French and the Germans began to expel the *Creole* traders from the colonies apportioned to them in the West coast on the flimsy excuse that they were British sympathizers and because of this reason the *Creole* merchants in the Northern rivers – Guinea, Togoland, Dahomey and the Cameroons lost their businesses. In the middle Niger too the Royal Niger Company began to eliminate the *Creoles* who had for ages were their great partners in their businesses as independent merchants as soon as they introduced the licensing laws of the company.

In the missionary, they faced the same music. The Anglicans and the Methodists were replacing their *Creole* archdeacons and superintendents with Europeans. For example a European succeeded Bishop Ajayi Crowther in the Delta and no African clergy was considered qualified for that post for sixty years. The second reason was the issue of malaria attack on the whites, which was now put under control. In the past years, West Africa was known to be "White man's" grave as the record confirmed that 109 Anglican missionaries were killed in twenty-five years. The Europeans can now come to West Africa to live high and cool on their reserved mansions on top of the mountains or hills above the cities of the coastal areas as well as in the interior.

In 1892 fifty percent of the senior service posts in the colony were held by the *Creoles* but by 1917 the percentage had been reduced to ten. What pre-occupied the minds of the whites now was to sit in their mansions to talk about imperial mission and shunned social mixing of their body and soul with that of the black people. Nearly all of them could be seen as one who was above the laws of the land. If there was any official need for any of them to appear before the court of law where the *Creoles* were members of the jury, they would flagrantly absent themselves and nothing would happen to them. They were actually living above the law as this attitude was the order of the day for a particular group of people throughout the territory of West Africa and elsewhere in the continent. By 1902 close to twenty of the Africans had already qualified as medical doctors but unfortunately none of them was absorbed into the government medical services; equally by 1911 all the Africans occupying high seats in both the judiciary and executive council of any of the British colony were removed without any reason.

With all these things happening around the community of West Africa, the people would not forever fold their arms, close their eyes and seal up their lips waiting for help to come from heaven. They now began to realize that if care was not taken and if actions were not put in place, they would one day wake up to see that their father's compounds had been taken away from them. For this reason, a large number of Africans began to embark on what the white Christians did ever since Martin Luther pasted his ninety-five theses on the church door of Wittenburg in 1517. They began to organize breakaway groups from the parent bodies of their churches which seemed indifferent and hostile to their growth both in faith and as human beings, and which demonstrated their attitude of subjection to their color and creed.

Throughout the length and breath of West Africa of this period, it was noted that Nigeria in particular had been the scene of a growing nationalist movement that was so bitter on the way the European priests and their counterparts in the government had reduced the dignity of the Africans to nothing better off than a trash bin. This movement under the name of Ethiopianism was closely connected with the spread of Christianity in Africa. Its ideological slogan was paradoxically in line with the principles enuciated by Henry Venn of the CMS for Africanized churches many years back. The leaders of the new movement was drawn mainly from the church and they belonged to the group of African intellectuals that were trained by the missionaries and given a vision of the future by the missionaries, and who on the final analysis found out that they were being regarded by the same missionaries the way that young Samuel Crowther had been marketed by his old teachers in Sierra Leone; as nothing better than useful instruments of an alien tool.

It was from this group called "Ethiopians" that the great support came for Bishop Crowther when the Bishop was deserted by the CMS. The group also brought to light the philosophy of Henry Venn that had either been killed or silenced by the Salisbury Square all these years. They now realized that the code of conduct of Christianity, which the old patrons of the CMS organization laid down concerning African Christianity at the start of the African missionary journey, had clearly been wiped out of the slate.

Contending leaders of Ethiopian movement included nearly all the big African names of the time out of which the followings were notable within its rank and file.

(1) **Edward Wilmot Blyden:**
Blyden who was an ardent preacher of Pan-Africanism in the West Indies lost a scholarship to an American college because of racial discrimination, and also because of sex scandal with the Libarian President's wife lost a teaching job with the Presibytarian Missionary Society of America.

(2) **James Johnson:**
Johnson was in fact the leading Ethiopian advocate who later became an Anglican Bishop and who in 1900 preached the annual sermon of the CMS in London amidst a large crowd of diverse missionary interest about the future of Africa. He received

the same honor that was bestowed on his predeecesor Bishop Ajayi Crowther when he was received by Queen Victoria in her palace but who was marked as a perpetual thorn in the flesh of his white English patrons. Before he was wooed with all the brandishments at the disposal of his masters in London, the then Archdeacon holy Johnson expressed his feelings and those of his colleagues in the movement in a letter he wrote to a friend in London titled thus: "You in England". In the letter he said that......

We cannot fancy how some of those who come here inflated with the idea that they are the "dominant race", do treat with something like contempt the natives of the country. The truth is that they regard us this day in pretty much the same light as our forefathers were who were received from the ironpangs of slavery by the philanthropists of a former generation. We are not over sensitive, but at the same time we are not unduly pachdermatous (thick skinned)....... But does anyone think we have no feelings at all, or no rights, which are to be respected? Having educated us, you will not allow us to think and speak and act like men.

In the course of the Ethiopian struggle, many changes were effected through the formation of the Society for the Promotion of Religion and Education in Lagos. One of the agendas of the Society was to supplant the missionary educational machinery, which had impeded the African development for years and provide the right teaching that would equip the Africans for social equality with their fellow European counterparts in every field. In this direction, they revised the Book of Common Prayer in those Delta Churches that had gained its semi-autonomy through Crowther's last creative efforts as Bishop. The prayers for the Queen in the prayer book were excluded and substituted it with that of the local Nigeria King of the city or town where such churches were established.

Those who were formerly bearing the English master's names began to change them to those ones that their African ancestors would easily recognize. Among those that changed their names were the Rev. J. H. Samuel who thus became Adegboyega Edun, Joseph Pythagoras Haastrup became Ademuyiwa Haastrup and David. B. Vincent became Omojola Agbebi. Unfortunately James Johnson himself who was the senior advocator of this change was contended to maintain his English names for reasons best known to him. It was on record that Agbebi led the first native church that seceede from an established parent missionary body- American Baptist Mission.

Agbebi in his capacity as a strong leader in the movement organized the revolt that rented the air all over the place because of the arrogance and display of superiority of the white missionaries posted into the interior over their native colleagues. By training Agbebi who was a journalist by instinct and craft, editing at one time or another every newspaper that was published in Nigeria between 1880 and 1914 made his mark with a number of pamphlets and articles regarding the unbalanced state of affairs of his people.

It was he who argued more volubly than others for the retention of native names, native dresses, harmless native customs and habits and who demanded that native languages should be used to worship in the native churches. He remarked in one of his write-ups that English Prayer Books and Hymn Books, harmonium dedications, Pew construction, supliced Choir, the white man,s style, the white man's names, dresses, and other imitations are so many non-essentials, so many props and crutches affecting the religions manhood of the Christian African. He asserted further in this write-up that the principles of Christian religion centered on the belief that the lame walk, the leppers are cleaned, the deaf hear, the dead are raised up, and the poor have the Gospel preached unto them.

What Agbebi's write-up strongly denounced was, moreover, inseparable in his views from much greater dangers to the dignity and respect of the African thinking. It strongly noted in this paper that since the missionaries had led the white man's exploitation of his continent, there had been an established threat to African survival, which was now apparent to any black man who has his/her senses intact. He envisaged that the time would come when the Africans will no longer look for no manifesto from Salisbury Square, When we shall not expect any packet of resolutions from Exeter Hall, when no bench of foreign Bishops, no conclave of Cardinals, "lord over" Christian Africa, when the Captain of Salvation, Jesus Christ Himself, leads the Ethiopian host, and our Christianity ceases to be London-ward and New York-ward but Heaven-ward, then will be an end to Privy Councils, Governors, Colonels, Annexations, Displacements, Partitions, Cessions and Coercions.

Telegraph wires will be put to better uses and even number 10 Downing Street will be absent in the political vocabulary of the West African Native states. Agbebi being a fearless nationalist traveled extensively both within his own country and outside of it. He preached his cultural philosophy of nationalism to many ears and souls of people of diverse nationality all over the world and he stood firmly to his belief till the end of his life.

At a time when Agbebi was invited to the United States a land he was most critical and always attacked, he lectured on African customs and the fashion of Christianity that was brought to the land which was the counterfeit type of Christianity. His lecture, which was applauded by the Negroes of upstate New York as a blood brother and a black hope for the future was reported back to the Lagos Standard and hailed by his people all over the country. In London he addressed a Universal Race Congress at the University Senate House in 1911 where he defended the African secret societies and culture to the conviction of his audience. The black brothers and sisters of upstate New York promised that the occasion of his visit on 11, October, should forever be observed and remembered as Agbebi Day in remembrance of Africa for the Africans and to his own role in spreading this important Gospel to the Africans wherever they may be throughtout the world and under any condition they may find themselves.

(3) **William Wade Harris:**

Others to be remembered in this noble course and crusade will certainly include a man called William Wade Harris, who was a teacher in the schools established by the American Protestant Episcopalians in Liberia and who was imprisoned on a number of times for political disturbances. In his own case he was a preacher whose theme of preaching centered around idolatory and the ugly and inhuman treatments meted out to his people by the so-called white boys. His teaching and organization known as the Twelve Apostles became even more popular than the immigrant Catholic organizations that he met on the ground in making converts.

(4) **Simon Kimbangu:**

Congo produced a Baptist catechist named Simon Kimbangu who on several occasions had a series of dreams and visions and out from which at one particular time from the occasions he was left unconscious for days after a kind of fit. By his spiritual healing powers, it was reported that his reputation soon became such that the mission hospitals in his area found that their supply of patients became dried up because people prefer to see Kimbangu for their health problems through spiritual means. His village soon became a pilgrimage center for all kinds of ailments and problems. When the missionaries and Belgian civil authorities saw that Kimbangu was becoming a distinct threat to their stability, he was arrested in 1921 and sent to prison for thirty years where he eventually died in the hands of his captors.

Unfortunately for the perpetrators of his arrest and imprisonment, his church of Christ on Earth, which they waged war against was now flourishing as never before in the wake of what his followers saw as a mathyrdom. A couple of years after Kimbangu's death in the prison cell in Elisabethville, His organization had more than three million followers, and had received the highest accolade of twentieth century Protestantism in affliation with the World Council of Churches. On and on, the list of the early participants in the revolution that brought about the changes to the entire continent is inexhaustible. The growing concern of the early educated Africans as to what the future has in stock for the unborn African children was so paramount in their hearts and this made them to collectively agreed to keep the burning flame of the revolutionary fire on course no matter what it was going to take them to achieve this fit.

We all agree that not every necessary inch of the land from Casablanca to Alexandria, from Senegal to Ethiopia, from Khartoum to Kinshasa, from Kano to Lunanda, from Nairobi to Lusaka, from Kampala to Harare and from Maputo to Mogadiscio have totally been free from the clutches of the same old enemy. The beautiful African rivers – Senegal, Niger, Nile, Zaire, Cubango, Orange, Benue, Zambezi and host of others are yet to be fully utilized as far as modern navigation and energy supply are concerned. Lakes Chad, Nassar, Victoria, Tanganyika and Malawi that were once recognized and respected for their lovely and beautiful role they played in the lives of their people before the advent of the white merchants are completely ruined as of today.

The Sahara desert, an endowed large parcel of beautiful land that is rich in mineral contents, the Atlas mountains of the North Africa, the Ethiopian Highlands, the Jos Plateau, the Adamawa Highlands, the beautiful hills around Bulawayo, Mount Kenya, mount Cameroun all have been waiting impatiently for their bonefide owners to fully utilize the treasures in their baggages for the development and beautification of the continent where mother nature established them. The economic development of the land that the nature had endowed with millions of tons of assorted mineral contents is yet to shoot up its head from the ground.

The people itself who are supposed to stay back home to monitor every sphere of the economic development are instead living in almost all the poorest countries of the world. They are found in thousands in Europe, Asia and America in most cases roaming the streets in search of all sorts of gainful employment from cleaning of offices or factories to semi-labor jobs. The universities in the continent have never stopped producing tons of qualified men and women in various fields annually; but where is the planned economy to absorb them after finishing their course of studies like their fellow colleagues in Europe or America?

The industrialized nations of the world always include energy program in their bid to achieve their development goals but ours in Africa is always a failure because of the reasons best known to the leaders in the continent. Cheikh Anta Diop was quite right in his opinion regarding the African Energy problem when he cited the example of the rights granted under the International Law of the Sea to such tiny landlocked or semiarid states such as Rwanda, Burundi, Zambia, Niger, Upper Volta and the Central African Empire. He intellectually analyzed the problems that these semiarid states would face within the shortest time possible after the mineral contents such as iron, aluminium, copper, uranium, zinc, manganese and cobalt would have been extracted by their so-called present foreign business partners, which covered themselves up with sheep's wool but having the heart of wolves.

He continued his argument that these states have the right to prospect for mineral contents under the Sea but where is yet the technology and equipments to carry out the required geological investigation and the mining machines to extract them. We should all agree with his opinion that "A right which one has no material or technical way of using it is just a dead letter". He further querried that how would states barely as large as one section of Paris or New York – even if their populations grew – be able to run the risk of sending expeditions on their own into the abyssal depths to secure urgently needed supplies of raw materials? He was again right in answering this question when he said that it would be just for a legless competitor to compete in races at the Olympic Games and equally just for an African city of Gabon to transform itself into Kuwait in less than sixty years, which in his own views will be an empty shell. Cheikh Diop's analytical expressions concerning the present energy problem that the continent of Africa is facing is detailed in his book on Black Africa (English Edition) published in 1978 and grabbing a copy of it could be wonderful.

All hopes are not yet lost especially in the area of energy supply as we are now moving gradually unto the era of solar energy system. The on-going research throughout the world has been showing positive results and saying that if there is reduction in the cost of solar cells, this will allow us to have operational solar power plants (known as land or space heliovoltaics) at cheaper prices to build. If not for heavy industries for the moment, solar energy to power home utilities and other lighter facilities around our homes and streets should be considered ideal when the solar receptors could be produced cheaply in the continent. The organization of African Union has the biggest role to play in this developmental endeavour if really it has genuine agenda for the total liberation of the continent.

Chapter 21

The Scramble for Africa's Enormous Wealth.

As it is oftenlly remarked in the African history notebook by our writers, it is true that the scramble or partitioning of African continent is a testimony of the fact that "The forcible possession of our land took the place of forcible possession of our persons". By the early to middle period of nineteenth century, it can be observed that the powers of the native tribal Kingdoms were similar in nature and content and uniform in their applications throughout the land of Africa. The influence of the Europeans was then limited only to the coastal areas of the Atlantic Ocean where their trade in slavery was flourishing. The transformation that took place upon the map of Africa between 1879 and 1891 is a thing of remarkable event ever to be recorded in the history book of a continent. Around this period the area of Turkish suzerainty (feudal power) stretched from Tunis across to Cairo and down to the edges of Abyssinia.

The British occupied substantial part in Cape colony at the foot of the continent and relatively small areas around the West African coast. The French had already established their interest in Algeria, Senegal and the Gabon. The Portuguese that first opened their trade route to Africa from Europe in the fourteenth century now took firm control of Angola and along the East Africa at Mozambique. By 1891 the picture had changed enormously because of the physical interference of the European nations that were now freely moving up and down the borders of the continent annexing every available space they could. The only space left for the Turks was a strip of the coast in Tripoli. The Portuguese strongly held their territories and remained as they were. The French expanded their own territory from Senegal down to the Ivory Coast and moving toward Congo. In the case of the British, they were gradually moving out of the West Coast of the continent where their influence had been established for years into the interior. Their holding in South Africa was fast growing and they have huge stake in East Africa and had now occupied Egypt.

When other European countries saw how it was easy and cheap to acquire territories outside the borders of their own nations and get away with it freely, they too joined the bandwagon of the original colonists. The Italians for example took to themselves a large slab of territory on top of the British East African territory. The Germans took their root in East Africa, South-West Africa and the Cameroons. The Spanish dropped their anchor opposite their Canary Island. In the Congolese territory, there is a colossal piece of land which was labeled Congo Free State but not free in the real sense of it but a wheedle, and this portion was the private estate of a Belgium King. The tribal Kings and chiefs were now being encircled and their authorities were rapidly being stripped away from them.

It was not that the Africans of this time did not protest in their own right but the powers of automatic machine guns from the boats brought by their captors silenced the move they could have made. At this time, one notable African ruler - the Matabele who was the ruler of Lobengula told one London missionary stationed in his territory Mr. C. D. Helm just what the Africans felt about the on-going process. The King in one of their discussions asked him whether he –Helm had ever seen how a chameleon catches a fly. The missionary answered No. He then narrated the chameleon's process of catching fly to him thus: If a chameleon wants to catch a fly the chameleon gets behind the fly and remain motionless for sometime. Then he advances very gently, first putting forward one leg after the other. In the end when the chameleon is well within the fly's reach, he darts out his tongue, and the fly disappears into its mouth. He was trying to equate this analogy to the British tactics of annexation that he the King was well aware going on in the countries within his own region. At the end of their discussion he confessed to the missionary that England was the Chameleon and he the King the fly.

The urge for territory grabbing in Africa was not far-fetched. Immediately after the death of the slave trade from which African people were substantially the victim, the partners in the trade sought for alternative means of living. Legitimate trading in household commodities from Europe and exportation of raw cotton and palm-oil from Africa to feed European factories became necessary for both people. The larger part of the trade pie obviously went to whichever partner that provided the finance and technical know-how to keep the business going and in this regard the white partners who came with the cash in hand and the know-how in their heads took almost 75% of the profit from the enterprice back to Europe. The remaining 25% was left for their African agents and the farmers in the field to share.

By the end of the nineteenth century, just a mere fifteen years after the Berlin West African Conference, the whole continent was almost shared out between the European powers. All that was left unshared was the small portion of territories bordering the Sahara. But by 1912 these territories, which included Mauritania, the Central African Republic, Chad and Morocco were absorbed by France and Libya was taken over by Italy. During this rapid process of colonization, Africa had been penetrated and appropriated through three distinct geographical developments. After the Berlin Conference, the Germans secretly annexed the large territories between the coast and Lake Tanganyika in East Africa; a piece of large territory that was rather loosely claimed by the Arab Sultan of Zanzibar.

During the year 1884 this piece of large territory was visited by an imperialist explorer named Karl Peters who also was the founder of the Society for German Colonization in Berlin. To avoid the attention of the Sultan's agents, peter persuaded the local chiefs to enter into vague treaties with the imperial Germany. When the news came to the knowledge of Bismarck just after the end of the Berling Conference, in his new imperialist mood, he granted a charter to Peters to establish a German Protectorate in East Africa. Bismarck's arrangement became big news to other European powers that had just concluded the German Conference.

They now began to realize that Bismarck was already claiming a forth slice of the continent but in the end, the case was said to have been settled amicably amongst Germany and Britian with scant regard for the Sultan's supposed claims over the territory. In 1886 the colonial interest of the two countries (Germany and Britain) over the territory was demacated by a line from the coast to Lake Victoria. The German side stretched to the South, which in 1891 became German East Africa (subsequently Tanganyika). It was further extended west to include Rwanda and Burundi in 1899. From the British side- north of the line, Britain established the East African Protectorate in 1895, which later became Kenya and in 1896 Uganda. In

1890 the British also imposed a Protectorate on the Sultan's rich trading Island of Zanzibar.

The second geographical development was the British pressure northwards from Cape Colony. They began their expedition by making impressive start from the southern end where they established Southern Rhodesia (now Zimbabwe) in 1890 and Nothern Rhodesia (now Zambia). Their ulterior motive was to continue their corridor from the Cape of Good Hope to Egypt without any hinderance. Along the line, the Boer War of 1899 – 1902 brought into the waiting hands of the British the intervening Republics of the Orange Free States and Transvaal.

The third geographical development was that of the French activities in North-West of Africa. It is worthy of mentioning here that France was the only European colonialist that aquired a vast contiguous African empire, stretching all the way from the Mediterranean down to the Bight of Benin and the estuary of the Congo River. In 1886, the French added Gabon and Chad to their territorial control while in 1910 the Central African Republic fell to their side. Eight of their territorial jurisdictions were grouped administratively to form the French West Africa while the other four were grouped to form French Equatorial Africa.

The German Empire in Africa, which was rapidly gathered together than any other empire was also the first to be dismantled. The reason was as a result of the outbreak of the First World War in 1914. The War gave rise to the sudden end of its empire in Africa because all the German territories were submerged under the threat from troops from the neighbouring French and Brirish Colonies. As early as the first quarter of 1916, the whole of German territories were already in the hands of the allied forces.

At the treaty of Versailles in 1919, Germany gave up all of her imperial claims in Africa. The League of Nations handed the responsibility of part of Togo and Cameroon to France while the other part of the two territories and Tanzania went to Britain. Belgium took over the responsibility of Rwanda and Burundi and to South Africa – Namibia. With this arrangement, the European presence in Africa was finalized and settled. The physical administration of the whole continent now belonged to the foreign colonial masters. Orders were now being mailed or wired to the continent from foreign lands while the living conditions of the African people (the son of the soil) now depended on the decisions taken by only one person possibly of lower intellectual ability to that of the sons of the soil in those frightening titles such as the District officers, the Resident Officers, the

Regional Governors or the Governor-General who now represents the interest of the imperial Kings or Queens of the master nations.

To assert their imperial authorities and connections in the states they had forcibly acquired, trading companies were formed and endowed with Royal Charters that allowed them to do whatever they like unabated. The first of such company to come from the British side was the Royal Niger Company in 1886 followed by the Imperial British East Africa Company in 1888. Initially most of the Imperial powers were excercised by the authorities of these companies in their trading territories. The British merchants were fastly pressing inland from the coast, moving up the Niger River in search of economic ventures to replace the dead slave trade. The result from both regions was now increasing the British government's involvement at an official level under the pretence that they were protecting the interests of the legitimate traders, their commodities and to discourage the clandestine activities of the slavers.

The Royal Niger Company was founded by George Goldie in 1879 under the name of United African Company and later became chartered in 1886. Under the Royal Charter, it was granted broad concessionary powers in "all the territory of the basin of the Niger". It should be noted here for a particular purpose that these concessions were granted from Britian and not from any authority in Nigeria. The terms of the charter specified how trade should be free in the region but this principle was systematically violated as the company later became so difficult to control. Its monopoly program to forestall trade interest of other nations of Europe especially France and Germany became so glaring to everyone. The company would flagrantly disrespect the customs of the people and get away with it unchecked by the British authority.

For reasons of tight control of the interior and political game of this era, the company established its headquarters far inland at Lokoja, from where it pretended to assume responsibility for the administration of areas along the Niger and Benue rivers where its depots were built. The company maintained a very strong security unit around itself and on many occasion it interfered in the territorial welfare of the natives along the Niger and Benue banks. It sometime became embroiled in serious conflicts when it's British-led native constabulary intercepted slave raids or when they would attempt to protect their trade routes. The company was powerful enough to negotiate trading treaties with the big cities along the cavalry trade routes of the North especially with Sokoto, Gwandu and Nupe. These treaties were interpreted to mean exclusive guarantee for an access to trade in return for the payment of annual tribute. As time went by, the officials of Sokoto Caliphate began to read untenable meanings to those treaties that looked tenebrous in content to them considering them to be coax in nature. From their own perspective, they believed that the British were only granted extra-territorial rights that did not prevent similar arrangements with the Germans and the French and more importantly that those treaties were not meant to be seen as if they had surrendered their sovereignty to the British.

The official take-over of the territories that were acquired through trading treaties did not take place not until when Britain in 1849 accepted a more direct involvement in the West African affairs. This was the time when a Consul, based in Fernando Po was appointed to take responsibility for the Bights of Biafra and Benin in the person of John Beecroft. In one of his first assignment in office, he undertook direct negotiation with the King of Lagos, which was then the principal port from which slaves were being shipped to the America. But when the talk broke down in 1851, Lagos was attacked and captured by British forces and the King of Lagos – His Royal Highness Akintoye was forcefully deposed. As a result of this action, the people of Lagos were divided into various opinion groups. From one of the strong groups emerged the King's powerful nephew named Kosoko who was a leading contender to the throne. The belief of his group was that the missionaries were "spiritual intruders" and warned their followers and people at large not to embrace their doctrine and teaching.

From Akintoye's point of belief, he and his supporters though he was now banished to Badagry supported the missionaries and thought that the missionaries were going to be his best instrument to be used for his return to the throne of Lagos. He therefore threw all his weight behind the missionary expedition particularly in Lagos and beyond. As said earlier, the society was now divided into two major camps. One camp was pro-missionary while the other was anti-missionary. The two waring groups were predominantly noticed in Lagos, Badagry and Abeokuta and each of them would not see eye to eye and in most instances they would engage in direct conflict with each other on the streets and at such occasions such as funerals, marriages, or when performing traditional rights that may go against the religion, custom or belief of either of the group.

The group that supported the missionary stay in the land had their reasons for being advocators of their philosophy. The inter-tribal wars that really devastated the Egbas when they had conflict with Dahomey were a case study to buttress their reasons. The Egbas owed their gratitude to the missionaries who's through their intervention, the British came to their rescue and they defeated Dahomey at the foot of their city walls in Abeokuta. In Badagry, the frequent appearance of the British navy on the Sea gave the pro-missionary group the confidence of peace in their neighborhood and the right to expel the anti-missionary leaders from the town, which they did in 1851.

Alake of Egba Land

Alafin of Oyo

As could be seen from all evidences, the missionary propaganda in Nigeria was not just a religious invasion but as well associated with political invasion. Strongly behind the Christian doctrine was the secular arm of Britian, which could be invoked at will and when needed. The secular arm of the British we are talking about here was seen being used by the missionaries where there was the need to use it on Badagry, Lagos and Old Calabar. Understandably the motive for the missionary involvement in Yoruba and Efik politics was not far-fetched. Their objective had always remained constant – the Christianization of the Nigerian pagans. But they equally believed that this goal might not be achieved until certain conditions prevailed in both Yoruba and Old Calabar. Among these conditions were peace and stability, the abolition of the slave trade, the evolution of money economy, and creation of modern Nigeria society, which would be strong in industrial activities and which will produce civilized people similar to their contemporaries in Europe and elsewhere in the globe.

The second half of the nineteenth century winessed what could be called the beginning of the revolution that later extended to all other parts of the continent of Africa. This was the time when those who had interest in Africans believed and advocated the doctrine of the trinity of the three Cs – Christianity, Commerce and Civilization. During this time and strongly behind the doctrine were notable missionaries such as Thomas Birch Freeman who urged George Maclean of the Gold Coast to protect the Christians in Badagry, and called on the British to aid the Egbas against all their enemies; The Reverend Gollmer of the CMS who in 1856 asked that the Ijebu be attacked; when the bombardment of Lagos was seen as God's interposition for the good of the Africans; when Charles Phillip, the educated African pioneer of Christianity in Ondo, called upon a "national calamity" to befall Ondo township and people so that they might become Christians. These people should not be mistaken for ideologists but people who were working for their spiritual belief, which they felt would help the salvation of the people and make their material well-being stay on line.

The pro-Christianity group was now growing thick feathers especially in the Egba land and equally becoming a thorn in the flesh of Egba authorities. For security reasons, the incessant harassments of the Dahomeans placed Egba under heavy obligations to the British government. But as soon as the Dahomean menace was over in 1851, the Egbas joined the missionaries in pressing for Kosoko's removal in Lagos. Thus the bombardment of Lagos in 1851 was not an isolated case but the denouement of the first phase of the British involvement in Yoruba politics and territorial acquisition of Nigeria.

The bombardment of Lagos, the refusal of the British to destroy Whydah – Dahomey's chief port, and the request for an end to importation of ammunition to Ibadan through the Ijebu territory now began to send unpleasant messages to other areas in Yoruba land. These reasons aided the Egbas to lunch war against all their enemies – Dahomey, Ibadan and Ijebu. Egba's war with Dahomey prompted them to shift relationship from the British to the French authority thereby making it mandatory for them to offer their territory to France because of military assistance against their enemies.

From 1861 onwards, the anti-British and anti-missionary feelings were gaining ground among the Egbas and those other Yoruba nations that sympathized with them. The Yoruba chiefs were now beginning to doubt the type of friendship that the missionaries who had been courting their favor with such exciting articles such as silk umbrellas, looking mirrors, velvetine clothing materials, sugar and biscuits were making with them. In the same year, King Dosunmu who succeeded Akintoye as Oba of Lagos was forced to cede Lagos to the British authority. He at last signed away his authority over the land and became a pensioner under the arrangement. Much were to be desired from the members of the pro-missionary group who were now drifting away from the churches and every religious gathering in their domains. They no longer wished to see the British established any project in any part of the Yoruba country. The general fear of the people was that what happened in Lagos could as well be extended to other parts of the Yoruba country.

As to the opinions of the Egba people who first embraced the Christianity doctrine, they began to regret that they had in the first instance allowed them to come into their territory and blaming themselves as to why had they granted the Saros any audience when they came first. The opinion survey of the people of Abeokuta around this time revealed that the white men are not to be trusted for they come to take their country, to coax them and by and large they will take possession of their land as they did in Lagos. The next twelve years saw fire of hostility between the Egbas and their missionary visitors. In 1867 a long anticipated occasion when the two forces were to meet face to face was provided by Governor Glover's aggressive anti-Egba policy he issued. In an answer to the Governor's move, the Egba's cumulative rage that had been looming around over the years descended on the white missionaries in Abeokuta. Their properties were either destroyed or looted in this rage.

The Egba's action now sent messages across to other white missionaries in other stations especially in Ogbomosho, Ibadan and elsewhere in the Yoruba country where they voluntarily withdrew their services and moved back to Lagos which they believed to be their save heaven. This antagonist attitude of the natives continued for an indefinite period of time until the chiefs came to think that the educated Africans whom they lumped together with the whites were their own children. The reverse in their action was now the case as they taught it wisely that the educated Africans would not betray their father's land and they could be trusted better off than the whites. They went back to them for the employement of their advice, wisdom and guidiance in their enforced contact with Lagos. The educated folks were now respected and esteemed and by gradual process, sanity began to flow into the Yoruba country. The Egbas now shifted their confidence to their Saro educated brothers who were now admitted to their native councils and have large votes in all national matters.

During the remainder of the nineteenth century, the consolidation of British trade and British political control goes hand in hand. In 1879 George Goldie worked out a program with the British trading enterprises on the Niger to merge their interests in a single company, which later became the Royal Niger Company with the seal of the British Royal Government. In 1893, the Delta region was re-organized and to be called Niger Coast Protectorate. The difficulty encountered in the administration of the vast and complex region of Nigeria persuaded the government that the upriver territories, thus far entrusted to the Royal Niger Company to manage now needed to be brought under central control and to achieve this, the company's charter was revoked in 1900.

Britian now assumed direct responsibility for the region from the coast to Sokoto and Bornu in the far North. Noting the existing degree of British involvement in the entire country, the above-mentioned areas (Sokoto and Bornu) had been readily accepted at the Berlin Conference of 1884 as fallen to Britain in the scramble for Africa program. Though there had been one dangerous tension between Britian and France over drawing Nigeria's boundary with the neibouring Dahomey but this issue was later settled. The next sixty years 1900 – 1960 is to witness the merits and demerits of the British administration in Nigeria. The period covered an era of tumultuous events that lead the country unto the destination we found ourselves today. This period was also characterized by frequent re-classifying of different regions for administrative convinience and purposes. They were symptomatic of the problem of uniting us as a single entity.

Chapter 22

The Hassles of the Colonial Administration in Nigeria

Colonial administration in West Africa and particularly in Nigeria had its merits and demerits. Part of its merit was the preparation of the minds of the educated Africans/Nigerians of the time for the revolutionary groundworks and actions they took to achieve their goals and objectives. Immediately after the exit of the slave trading and at the turning in of the legitimate trade, the coastal merchants that had been the barons of slave trading had no alternative other than to shift their trading position. Among them were the big cocks that were ready to swallow the little ones alive. Furthermore the big names in Christian circle along the coastal line were becoming too big for the people to handle and because of this reason, the devout Christians, both clergy and laity, cautiously welcomed British colonialism as a substitution of Christian for non-Christian government. Others who did not have the same faith in the virtues of Christianity were angered at those who supported subjection as a step to conversion. The missionaries themselves possibly suffered the greatest abuse, because much was expected from them from the moral point of view than the traders and the consuls who definitely belonged to the other side of the isle as in tune with the parody of a Christian hymn in a Gold Coast newspaper of the time which thus indicated.

Onward Christian soldiers unto heathen lands,
Prayer books in your pockets rifles in your hands;
Take the happy tidings where trade can be done,
Spread the peaceful gospel with the gatling gun.

As the partitioning of Africa was rapidly moving on its track, the educated Africans faced a great dilemma for they were absolutely helpless as there was not much they could do to stop it. In the partitioning race, while Britian was holding back for some reasons, French was already running the race as if they were contesting for the world gold medal in 100m race at the Olympics. They met the British half way and in less than seconds, they overtook them to reach the final line as champion. The feeling of the British educated Africans was obvious. They were thinking that if Africa should fall, it would be better if it fell to the side of the Europeans they understood and whose language they spoke. The Lagos government was actually in trouble and fearing for French encirclement, which could happen without much notice to prepare. Confirming the state of the Lagos government at this time, *Lagos Weekly Times* moaned, **"We now find ourselves on the treshold of the fate which has befallen Sierra Leone and the Gambia – a colonial failure and a political ruin".**

The situation was now getting out of hands and the only option left was for the English educated Africans to come out openly for their total support for Britian against the French and the German foreigners. They began to do what it takes to feel their cultural affinity with the British and mounted a very strong campaign in favor of the British culture they had been living with in the past and which had favored them considerably. The slogan of their campaign was **"We back Englishmen",** whom we have been so benefited by their benevolence and justice. We cannot sit still and see her (England) robbed of the well-earned fruits of her sagacity, enterprise and goodwill. This was the kind of support that the Africans of this time gave to the British people in their own land and which the later intruders did not consider when they brought them back again into the higher level of slavery labeled *colonialism*.

While the silent war of where to pitch their tents in Africa between the European nations was going on from one side, the nationalist Imperialism emphasizing European racial superiority was brewing its offensive anger from the other side. Blyden, who was one of the advocators of such anger pointed out at one time that the European brought to Africa " **his prejudices, his faith in a natural inequality and his profound disbelieve in any race but his own".** He concluded that the hypocrisy of

Europeans in claiming that everything they do was in the best interest of Africans and because of this they were subjugated, was the greatest anger that aroused the resentment of the Africans. Also Herbert Macaulay with the same humour of bitterness pointed out in 1905 that *"The dimensions of the true interests of the natives at heart" are algebraically equal to the length, breadth and depth of the Whiteman's pocket.* The reactions of the Africans to European hypocrisy and their national tendencies in Africa contributed immensely to the thoughts of the natives over which way to follow between the slave trade and the scramble. There were mixed feelings over the faith of the future generations of Africa throughout the land and particularly within the educated Africans from the group where people became confused and were in the mood of despair rather than anger. In 1891 the situation prompted an editor in Lagos to express his opinion when he summed up the scramble, partition and subjugation of Africans thus:

A forcible possession of our land has taken the place of a forcible possession of our persons.

On February 16, 1885, there was a debate organized by the educated Africans at St Paul's Breadfruit school room in Lagos on the following topic: *Are the present efforts of European countries to acquire and increase their possessions in Africa and to develop their commercial interests therein, calculated to be an advantage to Africa and the African race generally?* Numerous of such lectures were organized by this group in form of protests and agitations regarding the behaviors of their visitors from Europe. To move the vehicle of their protest forward, there had been a need to establish a native government at Abeokuta, which would at least be at equal level to the forcefully established British government in Lagos. The natives were in dare need of those who would form the membership of such government among its educated African class and those who would be advisers to the illitrate chiefs on how best a modern government could be run.

Basorun of Egbaland whose task was to bring up a formidable group to form this intended government was then having difficulty in this mission because most of the highly educated folks at Abeokuta belonged to the missionary group under Reverend Townsend whom he himself was looking for political and bishopric leadership of Abeokuta. Basorun had no alternative better than for him to start wooing Townsend opponents among the emigrants from the group that had fallen outside the church and seeking political advantages as advisers to the chiefs. Those that belonged to this group were not as highly educated as those in Townsend's group and most of them were young and do not command much respect in the society. In 1865 this group was able to acquire a leader named George William Johnson who had been a tailor in Sierra Leone, and had had an adventure on board a merchant ship, as a foot-plateman and also a member of its band. This advantage gave him a chance to visit England.

The first native government to be formed at Abeokuta with Johnson at its head was to be a government of the traditional rulers, which would have a powerful civil service of educated Africans as officials and advisers. This government was to be an adaptation of European style of government to the situation on the ground at Abeokuta. The arrival of Johnson from Sierra Leone in 1865 to Abeokuta was without any notice to anyone but some few months later, Reverend Townsend observed and wrote that some of the Sierra Leone people who are jealous and ambitious of becoming chief advisers and writers of letters from the chiefs here to Lagos have arrived Abeokuta. They have been forming a company to accomplish their purpose and have so far won over the Basorun to allow them to write.

By April 1866, Townsend announced again in an attempt to discredit the new native group of Basorun that: "The Sierra Leone men are thus forcing on civilization, and English customs, teaching the people the use of writing and printing and bringing about adoption of written laws. They are doing what we cannot, for we cannot use the means they do to accomplish their purpose. I am trying to influence them, I cannot command them". Before the end of the year, it was again reported as rumours that there was a proposal by the natives to drive away the European traders and missionaries from Abeokuta. This was the kind of local politics on ground at Abeokuta during the formative years of modern local government in Nigeria. Townsend believed that such rumours were the handiworks of the emigrants in an attempt to create an air of trouble in the town and that they were using the reforms of Governor Glover in Lagos to play upon the fears of the people of Abeokuta.

According to Professor Biobaku's views in his book *"The Egba and its neighbors (p.79)",* he explained in details that "the Egba United Board of Management of which Johnson, was its Secretary and another emigrant its President was more than an empty bureaucracy pavading sovereign pretensions and issuing largely idle threats". It was never intended to be a "proper council representative of the traditional, sectional and immigrant elements in Abeokuta". The purpose of the Board was not to replace the traditional rulers but to be their chief advisers and writers of letters so that the old chiefs while providing as they think for the safety of the town and its institutions would at the same time be introducing great changes. The E.U.B.M won over Basorun who was then the Regent, Akodu the Seriki and Asalu who was the head of the Ogboni group. This first native government of its day as part of its responsibilities formulated policies; seek the cooperation and backings of the traditional chiefs for the execution of their policies; seek for better language and understanding of the diplomatic trickeries of the Lagos government and to systematically impose custom duties in place of arbitrary tolls.

The native government in Abeokuta was well placed and honored by the Lagos British government. It established a customs house at the Aro gate of Abeokuta and later on the river Ogun-South of the city to blockade those merchants who might wanted to smuggle out their goods of cotton and palm-oil through the river thus by-passing the Aro customs house. The decision to open this new customs house was reported in the native newspaper *(Iwe Irohin)* in June 1867 and the Lagos government's action regarding this decision was communicated to Abeokuta government in the letter of the governor Glover of 8, July 1867 where His Excellency wrote that "he considers this a fitting occasion to call the attention of the Egba government to the undefined condition of our respective frontiers. He therefore requested for a defined treaty on this subject".

Under the present territorial demacation, the Egbas claimed the land from Abeokuta down to the coast and recognized only the Island of Lagos as being annexed by the British. They did not see where custom officers violated British territory replied Johnson. He re-iterated to the Governor that the Egba government would and has the right to set up customs houses, appoint its officers in Abeokuta to man those posts in those territories which are recognized to be quite free from the Island of Lagos. He concluded his letter by praying for continued friendship between the two governments and that the Governor should consider the matter closed in the opinions of the Board of Management, its directors and Basorun.

The Governor did not agree to Johnson's explanation in the letter under reference. He wrote back to Johnson telling him that the Lagos government regarded Ebute-Metta as "Lagos Farms" and at no time had Egba did something to benefit or even protect the people South of Abeokuta, from whom they now which to collect tolls. To counter the Egba's action regarding the frontier issue, Governor Glover of Lagos went and recruited Hausa manumitted slaves, turned them into constables and placed them on the routes between Lagos and Otta, and on water up to Isheri. In preparation for an attack, he distributed arms to some people and this enraged the Egbas. The Egba war men led by Akodu the Seriki of Egba, and Solanke, the Jagunna of Igbein were combat ready for an attack and on the 13th of October 1867 the Egba warriors attacked the mission houses in Abeokuta and demanded for the expulsion of all European missionaries and foreign traders from Abeokuta.

Every house belonging to the missionaries was either destroyed or looted in the uprising. Libraries and the printing house of the local newspaper (Iwe Irohin) were not spared in the attack. The uprising was not a persecution of the Christians but a persecution of the Europeans because of the hostilities of the Lagos government to Africans in general and those of the missionaries like Townsend to the people of Abeokuta. The hostility of Townsend in particular to the people of Egba convinced the emigrant politicians that "all whitemen were the same" and it culminated in their decision to drive away the mother gorilla and retained her baby – the Christian community in their midst. The agitations of the natives came closer to victory in nearly all the cities and towns of the Yoruba country. But the Europeans who believed that European and Christian interests could be protected under European rule later redoubled their efforts and energies to see that such rules were extended from Lagos to the rest of the country. For upwards of about a dozen years after 1867, European missionaries were confined to the coast while the missionary work in the interior of Yoruba and the Niger was left entirely unto the hands of Africans led by Bishop Ajayi Crowther.

It would not go unattended the position of the Christian villages and communities during the Egba uprising. Life in the village missions was acutely distrupted while their churches were closed. Many converts, that left Abeokuta with the missionaries formed settlements in Lagos, Ebute-Metta and in some Egba farms of Agege and it's environ. The converts themselves knew that they were not the object of attack but the European missionaries. Now that they were sympatizers, they had to have their own share out of the gains of the uprising. When the cloudy dust of the uprising settled down, the African pastors and catechists were allowed to come back to their respective positions to continue with their jobs. The position of Bishop Crowther regarding the crisis was very straight and concise. He made it clear that he had no sympathy with the action or the idea of the E.U.B.M in a charge he delivered to his clergy in 1869 where he asked them whether the Africans are yet able to regenerate Africa without foreign aid?

He emphasized that if infact we have any regard for the elevation of Africa or any interest for the evangelization of her children, our wisdom would be to cry to those Christian nations, which have been so long laboring for our conversion, to re-double their Christian efforts. It was to the understanding of everyone that the uprising in Abeokuta was not to keep out European interests and influence from the country, but to emphasize that as long as the Africans continued to hold sway in the country, the policy of the 1865 committee was likely to succeed better than that of the annexation of enclaves; and that the missionaries should know that the policy of Henry Venn on the evangelization of Africa was infinitely wiser than that of Henry Townsend. At the end of this trouble time, Reverend Townsend himself realized and felt obliged to acclaim the wisdom in the policy of Henry Venn.

This was a remarkable period of training in self-government in Nigeria, which obviously laid down the foundation of subsequent governments of either the one of peaceful and progressive administration or the one with tyrannic in action or nature. Inch after inch and one step after the other, the colonial powers – the British and French were fast expanding in the land particularly in West African countries. The political process of the entire region was gradually being replaced one after the other thereby weakening the powers of the states to their own advantage. The African military set up they met when they first came was actually weak in terms of weaponry and commitment to military actions because of poorly developed sense of nationalism and total absence of racial solidarity, which combined to make the military effort much ineffective. One may agree with some of the past writers on African political system of the rock ages that the problem of why there were so many holes to fill in the body polity of Africa was for the absence of one important factor.

It has long being identified that one of the weaknesses of many African political systems was the absence of clearly defined rules of succession to the throne and because of this power struggle which will continue to be so unless the problem is attacked from its roots, its intensity would always destroy any program laid down for development of the people and the environment. It is obvious that where there are no clearly defined rules in the African context to the selection of our leaders, then the principles and policies being put in place would always find their ways to submerge into the premises of personal ambitions. Candidates for vacant stools or office positions in our public service sector, because of the support he is expecting from his lineage or friends may make him throw away the ideological position he might take to the advantage of his people. Because of this reason some of the African leaders of the past accepted foreign assistance to gain their ends and thereby plunged their people into perpetual darkness under the mercy of their foreign collaborators.

When the colonialists first came with their ideas of colonialism, they did not understand the political system and situations of the land. In the Tokolor Empire, Ahmad was fighting a number of pretenders and at the same time trying to control French advances. In Dahomey, the French supported the brother of the displaced King to occupy the throne. In Nupe, Lord Luggard dethroned the Fulani Etsu and replaced him with a candidate from a rival Fulani faction. It was often easy for the European power to secure the alliance of one group of people against the other so as to achieve their goals. Under this program, the British had the assistance of Ibadan against the Ijebu, the Itsekiri and Urhobo against Benin, of the Fante against Asante, while the French found allies everywhere in their journey from Senegal to Lake Chad. During this period too an issue of concern to everyone was the situation of how the European – led armies were made up of African soldiers.

Lord Luggard for example, conquered the Sokoto caliphate with the troops who were of Hausa origin by birth. At the time of partition, European powers became just another factor in the power struggle between hostile peoples of the same root, and also an instrument to be used by one African state or faction against the other. The divide and rule diplomatic method employed by the Europeans to conquer the powerful Kings and their Kingdoms in Africa of this time is still very much in use between the African people and states of today with slightly different in color and content. We still found some states or people in Africa looking upon a European alliance as an instrument of gaining ascendancy or finding equality with their neighboring rival states. Example is what is presently going on in some of the states in Central Africa.

The kind of diplomacy we are talking about was first used in Yorubaland where it was at its best by Governor Carter and close to its best in Sokoto caliphate by Lord Lugard; but this method met its worst and crudest in Benin and Asante because of the level of military power available at the disposal of the commanding officer at each station in those areas. For example, Carter and Luggard held only limited military means in Yoruba and Hausa lands, hence greater diplomacy was necessary to capture the people and their territories. Both Carter and Luggard were on the side of protectorate rather than building up a colony because it was essential for them to build a system whereby they would change little in the indigeneous system, but would succeed by establishing British paramountcy. Whereas the conquerors of Benin city and Asante from their side thought otherwise as if they were creating a colony whereby the institutions of the natives were to be completely destroyed so as to pave ways for direct British rule or at its worst through agents who may have held little traditional power or position.

In 1892, Governor Carter of Lagos used the system to crush the resistance of the Ijebus when he had noticed that there was a division between the Awujale and his chiefs. He quickly came in to confirm the Awujale in his position, as a direct hint to other Yoruba Obas that cooperation with him would not go without a reward. The same way he treated the Egba and Ibadan cases. He opened treaty discussions with them in which he showed his willingness to treat them with considerable respect, to negotiate and not to impose any of his terms on them. This diplomacy again worked and the Egbas secured its internal autonomy while after the second ammedment of the Ibadan treaty, their case was finally settled. The other Yoruba Obas followed this pattern and that was why none of them was either deposed or faced any harsh action from Carter in his Kingdom.

In Sokoto caliphate, Luggard's similar technic was commended. With his military strength, he conquered Nupe and Kontagora; he deposed the Etsu Nupe and installed a rival Fulani candidate and then wrote to the Amir al-Muminin at Sokoto telling him that he had taken such actions because of the oppressive rule of the two Emirs. He then requested that he should nominate another candidate to fill the vacant stool of Kontagora. All what these two governors were saying in effect was that they did not oppose the tradition of the people or hostile to their religion or faith. In the case of Benin City, the British used the mixture of force and persuasion and this later coursed a serious rift in the Oba's council, which in the end resulted in the burning of the capital and looting it of nearly 2500 of its famous artifats and famous bronze treasures. Oba Ovonramwen was as a result of this uprising deported and the British offered positions of importance in the city to chiefs who came out of their hidings and willing to cooperate with the Imperialist.

The principles of indirect rule established in Nigeria in the nineteenth century by the British diplomats ate too deep into the body and flesh of almost all Nigerians irrespective of their regions, communities, religion or culture. It created in them a Westernized class, which the missionaries among them contributed chiefly to the process because of the position they were to occupy as partners in business, religion and the administration of the country. Like all other places occupied by the British in the West coast of Africa, large numbers of Africans were needed to work for them in the colonial offices, in commercial fields and as well as in the churches administration. The partition, which gave the Brirish more larger territorial areas created much more problems for them in the areas of administration, personnel and finance as most of the newly acquired areas belonged to the interior part of the region.

In the meantime, those areas were to be managed by the Kings and the chiefs that were confirmed into their positions immediately after the take over of the territories by the British administrators under the new administrative name called the Native Authority (NA). To bring the total control of the British territory under its arms, the Colonial office in London began to bring in European administrators as fast as they could and in line with the growth of the finances available instead of them to accelerate the training of the educated Africans for administrative positions. In effect the larger part of the money coming from Britian was expended on their citizens working for them in their new land to take care of their emoluments, foods and wines and passages for them to go back home on holidays. Instead of the Africans to be elevated to higher positions in the administration their number were being reduced and replaced by the white boys either by custom or by enactment. In 1910 the Colonial office in London expressed its opinion that it was logical that they should be preferred over the Africans for the available senior positions in the colony.

Before 1914, separate entities called colonies in Nigeria were separately administered under different rules and regulations. But in 1914, the Colonial office mandated Luggard to join together all the various colonies that later made up the present Nigeria after his adopted system of indirect rule had been tested and found working satisfactorily and producing an effective economy. The indirect rule system that had now become Luggard's famous theory and guideline formular for the Southern states in the operatives of their administration was turned into a book after he had left Nigeria in 1919 – *The Dual Mandate* which later became an administrative handbook for the British officers everywhere in the country. In other colonial territories like in Tanganyika under the rule of Governor Cameron, in Ghana under Guggisberge and in the Gambia under Palmer all who were Luggard's admirers adopted his method to rule their territories.

The refurbished texture of the indirect rule system formed the basis of what is known today as local government administration, and which in its formative years was called by the name of native authority when the Obas, Emirs and notable chiefs in our communities were its instrument. By then the Obas or the Emirs by the authority in the instument would appoint all the officials that were directly responsible to him and he or whoever he chose among his senior officials would preside over the law courts. This was later changed to customary courts under the modern political system of recent years. His agents were the ones to levy taxes for the local treasury and part of the revenue collected would be sent to the central government while the remainder stayed home for local development and improvement on such projects as roads markets, schools, dispensaries and sanitation and for the payment of staff salaries.

Under this system, the king or the chief was responsible to a British officer usually the resident or district officer, who in turn was responsible to the central government. This white officers, as the case may be always remained at the background where they make changes and push them to the community as if the Kings or the chiefs made them. The general believe around this time was that if an agenda works perfectly well, it meant that the people loved and respected the king or the chief that had that authority as at that particular time and if such agenda was disliked and did not work well, it meant the opposite. This was the yardstick to measure the popularity or failures of any native government of the time.

The African natives tolerated the British rule for a period of time because as at that time they could not find any alternative not until around 1918 when the position of the British began to decline in the world that the Africans were asking for a faster pace towards self-government. At the beginning of their demand for self-government, some Europeans visibly doubted African capability and ability to evolve at all and some of them held more liberal views on the issue. Someone like Lord Luggard who lived and ruled for sometime in the heart of Africa felt that the Europeans were capable of transforming African society, but, not toward their own side but toward a distinctly African pattern. His views about the role of the British in the continent and his liberal views about the competency of the Africans on how to rule themselves gave him the reference title of "shapers of African society" by his English friends.

Right from day one when the British came out of their shells to blow open their colonial intentions in Africa, the people especially the educated group among them knew that empires were not created because of the general love of mankind and they accepted the fact that the British must expect some benefits from the deal. But what they hated most was the British efforts to hide their views under the slogan such as "paramountcy of African interests and white man's burden". Infact they did the little they could do by expanding educational opportunities into the interior, given them a voice in policy formulation, sharing of civil service positions, economic development which they thought could bring Africa into the industrial age of the whole world of the time and a wider national interests that would submerge the tribalistic tendencies of the society. The indirect rule system that Luggard started following his conquest of Sokoto was now gaining ground everywhere in the country. He confirmed the positions of those Emirs that cooperated with him, enthroned a new Amir al-Muminin at Sokoto, permited the Alkali courts and bureaucracy to continue functioning as before. The British took over from the caliphate and the rulers their former supervisory functions of the native governments in their areas; it confined the authority of Amir al-Muminin to strictly religious matters and the people that were supposed or appeared to build independent power around the Emirs were now being tuned to be working towards separate independent states of their own.

The effect of Luggard's indirect rule turned advantages into disadvantages to the people of the North generally. In the terms of the British relationship with the Emirs and their people, the British promised that it would not interfere with the Muslim religion meaning that Christianity would not be encouraged. This decision alone increased the isolation of the Northern Nigeria from the pronounced impact that Christianity was having on the people of the South. The shielding of the people kept them out of the stimulating influence of Christianity and slowed down their process of change. What the British could do in the area of education for them was to set up a few good schools for the aristocrats, which were then in competition with the existing Islamic schools. The northern products from the aristocratic school system were relatively small compared with the products from Islamic schools and as there was no place in the British Administration for the products of the Islamic schools, the few vacant positions reserved in the civil service, railways, postal services, electricity and commercial firms for Nigerians were being recruited from the south from those that graduated from the western education school system. It was a matter of regret for the British not to have seen the future implications of their protecting the northerners in this way. This mistake put an untold hardship on the people because it created a big problem for them on the day of eventual self-government. Throughout the days of trouble in the south with the British administrators regarding the way they were mismanaging the economy of the nation thereby stagnating the progress of the people, the northern aristocrats and their people were not much involved or affected as they were still being protected and enjoying that kind of immunity from the colonial administration.

The Luggard's indirect rule system could not perfectly work wonders in Iboland because the culture of the people was too heavy for that kind of mouse and cat game. There were only few chiefs that the British could control. If they were able to control the Ama – ala for example, the elders may not be able to control the village meeting, which was infact the grassroot institution of Ibo government and of which the elders were just only spokesmen. Interestingly the British and Ibo democracy were far from each other but both of them possessed a common quality among themselve - the supreme authority must come directly from the people. If a research is conducted on this theory, one may find out that the authority from the people is indeed more implanted in the Ibo culture than that of the British people because the practice in Iboland is an inheritance culture from generation to generation while that of British may be attributed to mixture of changes in governmental situations over a period of time and borrowed culture from elsewhere.

When the British began its journey in Iboland, they did not approach the Ibo people about the practice of the theories of "the dual mandate" because they thought the people of their new territory were one in culture and character. What they did was to create artificial chiefs whom they gave powers to in the courts while the lineage elders were left with small degree of powers. Whereas the best thing for them to do was to introduce the system of elected representatives who would have come from the village meeting to form a council for smooth administration. A jury system would also have been a better replacement for the Ama – ala in the courts rather than when the package of authority was given to one person, which may possibly not known or recognized in the society and particularly one that was imposed on them as against their tradition and culture.

When Luggard's theory was not working as expected among the Ibo society, the British was looking for a way of how they can now transfer the British political philosophy into the society. On studying them into an average level they discovered that one of the characteristics of an Ibo person was that he was the most troublesome person ever to live in West Africa. But later in the course of their relationship, the Ibos proved them wrong because during the period of the British observation that gave them such impression was the time when the Ibo society was undergoing rapid change that was emanated from the influence of the Yoruba educated class in their society. They used the co-operative strength of their clans to build schools, to educate their sons and daughters and knocked one mission against the other to get what they wanted for their own benefits.

The British administration in Iboland experienced series of failures, which called for so many re-organizations. As noted earlier Luggard's system did not work well with the Ibos for some obvious reasons and this prompted Luggard himself after he had taken over the administration of the amalgamated Nigeria in 1914 to send one of his Northern officers Mr. Palmer to the Eastern region to find out what was the chief problem of the Ibo society over the continued protests of officers who had been working in their midst for many years. The finding of Mr. Palmer was about the issue of the warrant chiefs that were given unrestrained authority and the control of their courts, which the people saw as miniature tyrants. The culminated anger in the people was visibly shown when the British attempted to impose direct taxation in 1929, which was followed by women's riot around the same time and as a result the main targets of attack were those chiefs and their properties.

Following the riot a lot of anthropology researches were conducted to discover Ibo traditional government and not until the 1940s that the British began to introduce their own local government system in the Eastern region of Nigeria. Donald Cameron the Governor of Nigeria from 1931 – 1935 who was considered a reformer of indirect rule system, during his tenure of office checked on the growing influence and independence of the Emirs in the North, elevated the Alafin in Yorubaland and was hailed for the emphasis he placed on the development of institutions rather than preserving them. He on his part introduced some selected western educated men and women into certain highly placed councils in Southern part of Nigeria.

The British race in Yorubaland was not so much different from what has been observed in other areas of the country because it was Luggard's belief that his system and diplomatic methods could be nationally adopted or slightly modified as the case may be in Yorubaland. One of the basic approved ingredients of his theory was the use of the traditional institutions to achieve the aims and objectives of his home government. The Yorubas had in the past ages been known to possess a centralized system of government, which would be headed by their Obas. These Obas would in turn extend their greatest respect to the supereme throne of Oduduwa and to his sons that established the major cities of Yorubaland particularly the Oni of Ife and the Alafin of Oyo the senior sons of Oduduwa.

By this traditional arrangement it could thus be too easy to see the Yoruba family of states as a looser arrangement of the caliphate style. Lord Luggard did not have much problem with the Yoruba Obas as he maintained them in their positions for the establishment of British rule through them. The only major problem that he had was when he attempted to return the condition of the eighteenth century by trying to make Oyo the chief power of Yorubaland. He quickly noticed that the refusal of the Yoruba Obas to accept this move was the main course of the disagreement that erupted into the Yoruba Wars of the nineteenth century that almost tore the family apart. In the 1890s, the British recognized Ibadan as one of the most powerful place in Yorubaland but during Luggard's administration, Ibadan was made subordinate to Oyo. It was during this time that the British officially placed Ibadan under Oyo and that Ibadan chiefs were being reduced to their lowest elb and carelessly called around the agents of the British rule. Their problem should be clearly understood as they were then helpless and no substantial action they could take to help the situation and as such they retired to their faith.

The educated Yorubas in the missionary and in the government being civilized and influential people that were also equal in status to the people ruling them were now becoming suspicious about the genuity of the British annexation of Nigeria territory. In Abeokuta for example, the educated Yorubas had taken over the control of almost everything there; in Ibadan they were now the advisors to the chiefs; in Ilesha one of them had become an Oba. But instead of Luggard to see reason with the type of the developments going on in this society, he deliberately ignored it and tried to go ahead with his program of indirect rule. As a result of this, he overthrew the native government of Abeokuta and gave it back to the chiefly government system of the past while he decided to elevate Oyo above all other places in the Yorubaland

It was thus not surprising that the educated class of Yorubaland became suspicious of Luggard and they were ready to lead opposition to his government and the British rule in the country. Part of his government's program to destabilize the cohesiveness of the Yorubaland was when he attempted to dangle into the Yoruba traditional methods of selecting their Obas and chiefs. He forgot that Yoruba people have their own traditional methods of selecting the Obas and chiefs of their choice. When the government wanted to come into the selection process and they failed, they resulted to doubtful methods such as threatening to take lands from un-cooperative family lineages and gave such land to those who were more readily accepted to their aims but yet this embarrassing situation did not make much impact on the decision of the people regarding the selection of candidates of their choice and according to their tradition. As the Yoruba people of this time were known to be dogged and articulate, so shall the Yoruba community be for many more centuries to come.

Chapter 23

Nigeria's Preparation for and at the gate of Independence:

The First World War created an atmosphere whereby the Germans had to surrender their colonies in West Africa, which thereby prompted the League of Nations in 1922 to grant mandate to the British and French to take over the administration of their former colonies in Africa. The British mandate, which consisted of two thin strips on the Eastern border of Nigeria was later known and called the Protectorate of Cameroon. The experience of European administrators in Nigeria is worth mentioning here for peoples judgment on the sixty years of the British stay in the country; managing their total affairs as if they were together the same blood brothers and sisters. It was correctly judged by someone like James Johnson to have asserted that, **"neither the colonizer nor the colonized had any real insight into the alien cultures they were faced with"**.

The situation faced by the two different people when they first started their race of cat and mouse could be likened to the relationship between two blind men or a deaf man and his friend who hears distinctly and both of them were co-habitating together in the same room. Certainly most of the discussions between the later two would always go into the thin air while the journey of the former two would end up in a ditch. Apart from the distance between the colonized and the friends that colonized them in terms of mileage between England and Nigeria and between the cities in Nigeria where they were living and the towns and villages in the interior, the huge cultural gulf between the two of them was anormous. Without mincing words, Britain and Nigeria were entirely two different worlds with nothing in common other than the history of slave trading. During the slave trade era, both of them were only trade partners and nothing else.

But when the era of colonialism came, it was necessary to establish a sort of camouflaged relationship between those that were to be colonized and those who were coming to colonise them. This kind of manufactured relationship was to enable both parties to move on safely on the dangerous pathway. The relationship was indeed manufactured in the sense that it suited only the British demands and it inevitably allowed them to achieve more out of the relationship more than the Nigerians. One of the first experiences encountered by European administration in Nigeria was like as if they were stepping back into the forgotten history of Europe and re-entering the medieval society of feudalism and patriarchy. This impression was what Abdul Jan Mohamed noted in his writing – ***Manichean Aesthetics*** as "an atmosphere of idealistic, paternalistic despotism". Based on this feeling, the administrators soon began to feel their king-like presence in the barbaric land they miraculously found themselves.

Certainly sure and not very long, they began to feel the disillusionment that followed their elevated expectations. Because of the language and finance problems that faced the visitors, many of them ended up their time in Nigeria disillutioned, isolated, and highly ambivalent in their opinions of both the natives and the Imperial project they agreed to undertake. Lack of effective communication posed a big threat to the well being of the forced marriage between the newly wedded couple. It represented a potent reflection of the shortcomings of the European administrative training. As Abdul Jan Mohamed explained the issue of lack of effective communication between the Africans and the Europeans; he used the case of one of the newly posted colonial officers to Nigeria from London to narrate the problem that such officer encountered when he first arrived Nigeria as a colonial employee of the Nigeria Political Service thus: "Joyce Carry virtually understood nothing about what the natives were saying.

But before leaving England, he had already passed all his Hausa language courses that never served him any useful purpose when he arrived at Lagos where a different language was being spoken by the natives there apart from the Hausa language, which he had a vague knowledge about". The colonial staffs in the cities where they were posted could not interact freely with the natives because they did not understand the native dialect of the people and vice versa the majority of the people including their Obas and chiefs could not communicate effectively with them because they too did not understand the English language at all. The language barrier that was a major factor in this apparent unwillingness reflected the truth of the situation in Achebe's ***"Things fall apart Book"***. In chapter 15 of this Book, Achebe narrated how the natives killed a white man who did not know enough of the language of the people to make him survive the encounter. According to Achebe, he said that "***the man said something, only they did not understand him"***.

Both parties in the deal suffered different fashions of the language problem. From the Nigerian side, they too suffered most because they could not communicate effectively in any form with their partners other than to go through some native halfbaked interpreters who may not be able to interpret the full text of the discussions between the two. This made them to retire to their faith in line with the dictates of God that were being preached to them every Sunday by the missionaries in the churches. The few natives that were employed as interpreters mostly in the interior sometime looked childish and stupid in the presence of their English masters because they could definitely judge their level of understanding of the English language right at the spot of the discussion. Conclusively the issue of language was perceived by both as one of the significant factor involved in the Manichean Opposition that placed the assumed superiority of the Europeans as an undeniable fact besides the inferiority of the natives.

This lack of effective communication also legitimized the argument that revolved around the people's opposition to the whole process of Imperial project in Nigeria. The colonial administrators themselves faced the inadequacies of the system itself, especially when the question of funding the project comes in. Undoubtedly the colonial project in Nigeria was nothing outside business venture and as such it was run the way and fashion all other businesses in the world would be run. In the diplomatic circle, Britain wanted to maintain its stand as peacemakers and civiliser in Africa, which was the case she presented to the whole world including the Africans themselves. But she could not finance the project the way a good business venture has to be financed because much fund was needed for the project and this was not forthcoming from England and because of this most of the development projects they started ended up in ragged fashions. This was confirmed in the independent opinion of Ranger in The Invention of Tradition in Colonial Africa P.215 when he stated that *"while life was been restructured in Britain itself…. Most of European activities in tropical Africa, whether official or unofficial, had remained tatty, squalid, rough and inefficient".* Therefore the only society that visibly gained from Nigeria's submission to an alien power was Britain.

Through various protests, lectures of firebrands and agitations of the educated Nigerians, immediately after the World War II, Britain first attempted to find a structure to meet African demands for political power. By 1951, the country was divided into three distinct administrative regions – Northern, Eastern and Western regions, each with its own House of Assembly. In the Northern region where the system of indirect rule fully started with the support of the Emirs, a separate House of Chief to reflect the strong tradition of tribal authority was established. A legislative council for the whole country was also put in place. The complex structure of the country was now rearing up its head out of the bottom of the water for everyone to see how beautiful or how ugly it looked like. In 1954 a new Constitution (the 3rd in eight years) was darfted and approved whereby the Federal Territory of Lagos was added to the Federation of Nigeria.

The struggle for the independence of African nations and freedom for the blacks all over the world have their own ways parallel to each other in content and nature. We cannot but mention about the activities of the freedom fighters of the past centuries for posterity purposes and to further encourage the Africans of this generation and beyond for any eventual similar type of situation that people faced during their own time and how they surmounted the pressure of the time. We should all take note that permanent condition does not exist anywhere, all it takes to deal with it is to remain focus and stand to the test of its time. The first to be remembered in this series was Marcus Garvey who stirred the black world as no one before or since until the rise of Kwame Nkruma of Ghana and host of other African nationalists.

Garvey was a Jamaican born Negro and was one of the outstanding orator of his time and race, who organized the biggest mass protest movement in American history with the backing of his movement called **Universal Negro Improvement Association (UNIA),** which by 1923 had claimed six million members. Garvey was and ardent preacher of racial purity, glorified the color black, upheld a black Christ and black Madonna and called upon his people to "forget the white Gods". His slogan was *"Africa for the Africans", " the renaissance of the black race" and "Ethiopia awake".* He demanded for the freedom of Africa and prophesied that "her redemption is coming like a storm, it will be here". Some of his achievements included the recruitment of a black army for the liberation of Africa, the setting up of the Black Star Shipping line, sent a mission to Liberia to negotiate for the settlement of between 20,000 and 30,000 American colored families who would be helped to immigrate back to Africa. In 1925, with the help of some American colored leaders, the United State government jailed Garvey and later deported him out of the States. Depite the persecutions he faced, his ideas pervaded colored American and West African thinking for many years to come.

Garvey's philosophy echoed the feelings of millions of blaks and turned them into a militant proud soldiers demanding and forcing concessions, equality in American, freedom in Africa, dignity for the black race everywhere and a share in the world economy. His journal **Negro World** was widely and eagerly read throughout West Africa and in Lagos. While his U.N.I.A met openly and discussed freely about Garveyism, the colonial powers were much worried about the doctrine of Garveyism now spreading like bush fire in West Africa. In Lagos for example the mission churches closed their hall doors and unitedly refused to allow any U.N.I.A. meetings in their premises. In Dahomey anyone caught with a copy of Negro World would serve a life imprisonment.

Marcus Garvey

The next name to come on board in the remembrance catalogue of freedom fighters among the world black community was a university professor and a prodigious writer named Dubois. Garvey's philosophy undoubtedly inspired DuBois and with the fall of Garvey, DuBois attempted to step into his shoes and approached the problems of the blacks the same ways that Garvey approached them. He believed that the Negro

Jacob Oluwatayo Adeuyan

who was suffering under the caste system in America, the West Indies and those under the colonialism in Africa must come together under one big umbrella for effective course to pursue. His own philosophy was that the struggles of the blacks for equality were all part of one movement, and that the blacks either in America, Africa or elsewhere could inspire and encourage each other, and that a gain for one was likely to bring a gain for the other. To drive his point home better he became the leading spirit of five pan-African congresses between 1919 and 1945.

Past Activists on Africa's Course

The first pan-African congress that was held in London in 1900 under the inspirational activities of a Trinidad lawyer discussed extensively about the inhumanities practiced by the Europeans in Africa during the partition. Another congress did not come up not until 1919 when DuBois with the help of Blaise Diagne organized it to take place in Paris and after being motivated by the ideas following the First World War. The congress was to be attended by delegates from the United States and other places but it was mainly the Africans living in Paris that attended because those that were to come from the United States were not granted travel permits to travel out of the States. The congress drew up a charter of Human Rights for the People of African Descent. The third congress was held in three sessions in 1921 at London, Brussels and Paris where Diagne presided; the fourth congress took place in London and in Lisbon in 1922 while the fifth one was held in New York. DuBois played a great role in organizing these congresses and as well as helped a lot to keep the pan-African unity of the black world together.

The hub of the black agitations all over the world around this time was through the students organizations based in London. The first of such organization started in 1917 with 25 members in 1921 and increased to 120 in 1924. In 1925, Oladipo Solanke, a Nigerian organized the First West African Students Union (W.A.S.U.), a center where social and political activities pertaining to the black movement were carried out. Solanke known for his zeal and interests in the advancement of African freedom traveled to the major cities of British West Africa to collect funds for his organization.

Blaise Diagne

This money was to enable W.A.S.U. to pursue its projects in Africa and build up strategic support for the African chiefs who saw reason with their ideological persuasions.

Highly placed personalities like the Alake of Abeokuta, the Emir of Kano and Nana Ofori Atta of Ghana became supporting patrons of the union. In those days, African students were skeptical of traveling to America for education but after the home coming of Dr. Nnamdi Azikwe and Kwame Nkrumah from the United States other African young men began to travel to America and in 1941, an African students organization with its own magazine was established and closely linked up with W.A.S.U to foster unity among the students and to move forward the wheels of their agitation cart. The protest of the blacks was now becoming more and more pronounced and widespread than ever before in history. Therefore no black organization throughout the world of this time that did not organized one or more protests to take their grievances to the people for judgment.

In New York, more than 20,000 black Americans demonstrated in support of Ethiopia against the Italian actions there. Similar demonstrations were also organized in South Africa, countries in West Africa, London and the West Indies in support of Ethiopia. W.A.S.U on their side organized an Ethiopian Defence Committee, which was one of the most successful pan-African committee ever to be organized by Africans and which went into action in London soliciting support for Ethiopia. Those that were connected with this international uprising were three Ghanaians that included J. B. Danquah, five West Indies, one Somalia and Jomo Kenyata of Kenya. This committee gave Emperor Haile Salassie a befitting reception when he arrived at London to begin his exile immediately after Ethiopia was taken over by the Italian forces.

In Nigeria the invasion of Ethiopia by the Italian forces re-opened the old wounds and brought forward the most national attention and response Nigeria had ever witnessed. Mass meetings were organized, which attracted large audience of over 2000 people at each meeting demanding for the withdrawal of the Italians forces from the Abyssinia. Money donated for this course continued to pour in for the Ethiopian Defence Fund; young Nigerians offered themselves to go to Ethiopia to fight the Italian forces; Italian firms operating in the country were victimized and boycotted while the emotion was so deep in the hearts of the Black people all over the world. The deal under which England sold Ethiopia to Italy was considered shoddy and provided enough evidence to convince many that the white world would always be each brother's keepers no matter what. Italian invasion of Ethiopia marked a strong follow-up of political movements in West Africa.

In 1919, the National Congress of British West Africa was established and in the following year it held its first conference in Accra. The moving spirit behind the congress was Casely Hayford of Ghana in consultation with Nana Ofori Atta and R.A. Salvage of Nigeria. The first meeting of the congress that was held in Accra-Ghana was attended by six members from Nigeria, three from Sierra Leone, one from Gambian and forty from the host country. Part of the resolutions passed at this meeting included the introduction of the franchise, equal opportunities for whites and blacks in the civil service, opportunity for higher education, and a clearer separation of the judiciary from the colonial administration. Furthermore, the congress decided to take their grievances to colonial office in London but they forgot that the colonial governors in the West African region did not like to see the future growth of the group, because they were collectively annoyed over the outcome of the Accra meeting and the intended deputation they

Casely Hayford

were to send to London. Governor Clifford of Nigeria was particularly very scornful and resentful about the congress more than the rest of his colleagues. He even at a time laughed at the idea that Nigeria would ever be a nation and because of the governor's resentments, the deputation of the congress sent to London could not achieve anything tangible. The congress was not totally disappointed but instead it continued to wax stronger, holding its meetings regularly in Freetown (1923), in Bathurst (1925) and in Lagos (1930).

British diplomacy being what it is known for from its day one creation came through the back door to effect some changes in line with the resolutions of the Accra conference. They claimed that the changes effected were purely theirs and not through any pressure from any organization. By 1925 limited franchise was extended to Lagos, Calabar, Accra, Cape Coast and Freetown; Achimota College was set up in Ghana in 1927 for higher education and the West African Court of Appeal reduced the influence and the control of the governors over judiciary matters. Unfortunately the Africans elected to the Legislative Council were powerless while the graduating students from Achimota College were denied gainful employment in the government civil service. But the spirit of the congress lingered around for sometime at least up to the death time of Hayford in 1930 when the congress passed away with him. Before Hayford died in 1930, he expressed his disillusionment with the elite leadership in this form:

> *The African God is weary of your wranglings,*
> *Weary of your vain disputations, weary of you*
> *Everlasting quarrels, which are a drag upon*
> *Progress and which keep from you, as a people,*

Jacob Oluwatayo Adeuyan

The good that is intended for you.

The relevance of nationalism was now walking its ways unto the hearts of the people of West Africa thereby increasing the heartbeats of almost everyone from all class of people. These people were beginning to see many administrative blunders of the colonial government from Lagos in Nigeria to Freetown in Sierra Leone; across the jungles of Ghana down to the rivers in Barthust; moving its Imperial wheels up the hills and mountains in the Cameroonian regions and hoping to end its race in the Orange Vaal in South Africa. From Nigeria emerged such opposition leader in person of Herbert Macaulay, the grandson of Bishop Ajayi Crowther and son of the founder of the first secondary school in Nigeria (C.M.S. Grammar School founded in 1859) by Thomas Babington Macaulay. T.B.Macaulay was himself one of the many distinguished people of Yoruba descent born in Sierra Leone of the "re-captive" parents. T.B.Macaulay was the eldest of the three sons of Ojo Oriare, a re-captive from Ore Aganju in Ikirun district and from Oyo, his mother was a granddaughter of the founder of the Ile – Ogo. His father "Ojo" was popularly known and fondly called "Daddy Ojo" at Kissi in the Sierra Leone colony. T.B. Macaulay like other children of the re-captives was a Christian of Church Missionary Society. In 1854, he was ordained and then married Abigail Crowther, the second daughter of Bishop Ajayi Crowther. Untill he founded the Grammar school in Lagos he ran the C.M.S. mission stations at Igbehin and at Owu, both in Abeokuta. He was noted for his contributions to the translation of the Bible into Yoruba language. He died on 17th January 1878 during the smallpox epidemic that claimed many lives.

His son Herbert Macaulay first came to the public limelight when he exposed the European corruption in the way they were handling the finances of the construction of the Railway lines in 1908. Thereafter he was the defender of the Royal lineage of Lagos, which the British normally treated with impunity unless they had some unpopular policy to enforce on the people that the institution would be dignified. In 1919 the government's action went over-board when it arbitrarily took over some lands in Lagos. Macaulay acting on behalf of the Chiefs carried the case to the Privy Council in London. He won the case and the government was asked to pay the some of twenty two thousand, five hundred pounds sterling compensation for the land. In 1920 in a retaliatory mood the colonial government deposed the King of Lagos and appointed another person to the throne. Macaulay again stood to defend the Royal house and for two times in ten years that the case dragged before it was settled, Macaulay had been jailed.

Interestingly he won the case by a Privy Council decision in favor of his client – the Oba of Lagos. The Oba was restored back to his throne in 1931. Albert Macaulay was all along known to be a bitter critic of his other educated leaders for one reason or the other and people attributed this kind of hatred to the support most of his colleagues were given to the colonial administration, which Macaulay himself did not like. His hatred for them got to a stage when he would lash them out in the press with loose anger; his statements against them now set a division among the Lagos politicians and created jealousy and bitterness between the elites and the populace. There was always one scuffle or another among the Lagos politicians and may be this was what Hayford had in mind when he spoke of "wranglings", "everlasting quarrels" and "vain disputations" in his last day's comments.

Macaulay was not known to be an ardent supporter to the ideals of the National Congress, as he did nothing spectacular to assist the work of the movement in Nigeria. Despite the role he played among the elites and the fact that he was very much the Victorian gentleman of his time, he, like no other politician of his age was very much in tune with the grass root people of the Lagos colony. With his close contact with the common people, he superseded his contemporaries in politics because his opponents saw themselves as being too big and high to stoop low to the levels of the common people in any form. This plus his repeated victories in the Privy Council over the colonial governors, earned him the high reputation the people accorded him and from henceforth Macaulay was regarded as the leader of Nigerian politics and father of Nigeria nationalism.

When the Nigerian Constitution was amended in 1922 to permit three elected representatives (one from Calabar and two from Lagos) to sit on the Legislative Council, and when the Municipal government of Lagos was set up, Macaulay's Nigerian National Democratic Party swept all the seats in the three elections of 1923, 1928 and 1933. As a result of these victories and others which included the restoration of the Oba of Lagos in 1931, the relationship between Macaulay and the colonial administration in Nigeria began to grow and improved tremendously. Because of this turn around relationship, people assumed that he and his party may have been tricked to dance to the tune of the conservatism music of the British politics because it was very glaring to people that Macaulay and the members of his family now attended government functions and social parties organized by colonial administrators.

The governors now hold conferences with his Democratic Party on regular basis at government House at Marina and elsewhere in the colony. The rebels of the 1920s had now become conservatives and darlings of the 1930s. The end of desire for change and reform swiftly came in because Macaulay and his chief supporters were the only members of the Lagos elite who did not support the **"Hands off Abyssinia"** campaign of 1935. His party **"The Democratic Party"** was the only African group that was recognized by the colonial power and from whom the government seeks political advice; whom the Europeans mixed freely with on the streets of Lagos and who received invitations to Government House balls.

It now became apparent that all administrative abuses of colonialism were to be ignored at least for the moment because of the temporary friendship between the government and the elites. This was the clever way the colonial governors always **"buy off"** their critics in West African colonies of the time. When the people noticed that their future life had been mortgaged by their own people they lost interest and confidence in such a party of Albert Macaulay and his co-partners in the running of the affairs of the country. In retaliation in 1933, out of the 3000 eligible voters in Lagos election, it was recorded that only 770 people went to the polls to vote meaning that the people had now used the power vested in them by the Constitution to say NO to the style of government they did not like.

Political situation in the 1930s was becoming too unbearable for the youths of Nigeria, Ghana and Sierra Leone and as such there was a wave of reaction against the older politicians in those three principal colonial states of West Africa. The new brand of Youth Leagues flatly opposed the conservatism of the old parties and the way the leaders were romancing with the colonial administrators was too irritating and disappointing to everyone. Prior to this era, the top elites in the society believed that it was themselves alone who could stage meaningful political protests, which would be recognized by the colonial administrators. Furthermore these top elites of the time never thought that the people in the rural areas of their countries too have grieveances to put across to the government and this obnoxious thinking made them to believe that all protests were to be confined only to Lagos, Accra or Freetown.

It was becoming very clear to the people that the older politicians only go to government to service their own interests and to improve their own personal positions or at best to serve the interests of the small group of elites at the top. For this reason and more to it, the Youth Leagues attempted to study the problems of their countries into details and from broader perspectives. In 1932, Eyo Ita in Calabar organized the Nigerian Youth League to support reforms in the educational system of the time. In line with his principles and philosophy, Eyo Ita established an industrial school called West African Peoples Institute with the primary aim of preparing the youths to be self-supporting rather than for them to be roaming the streets looking for white collar jobs under the government.

In 1934 in Lagos the Nigerian Youth Movement (N.Y.M.) was established on similar program to the one of Calabar. It sought to encourage national feelings, demanded for self-determination and Africanization of the civil service and industrial sector of the time. The organization opposed the setting up of Yaba College because it felt that technical colleges of lower standard that would support the needed industries like the ones in England would be an ideal institution of this time. N.Y.M. in Lagos also put up a strong fight on behalf of the then few transporters against whom the colonial government discriminated because of their competition with the railways. The movement later spread its tentacles to other parts of the country to make it truly Nigeria rather than to confine it only to Lagos.

In 1937 when Dr. Nnamdi Azikwe returned to Nigeria from the United States and established his West African Pilot, he supported the activities of the N.Y.M now being metamorphosed into a political party and which later derailed the Democratic Party in the elections to the Legislative Council in 1938. It may not be too far from the fact that the Nigerian Youth Movement was the first organization to possess a Nigerian image because of its concern for national interests in the areas of education, transportation and economic development. The youths in other areas of West Africa rose to the pressing challenges of their countries and they succeeded in forming themselves into formidable groups that later took over the mantle of modern and indigenous governments of their countries from the colonialists.

In 1938 J.B. Danquah organized the Gold Coast Youth Conference. In the same year, the strongest and the most purposeful of all the youth movements established in West African colonies was organized by Isaac Wallace-Johnson of Sierra Leone. The ensuing struggle continued and expanding from city to city and from generation to generation until the turn of the silent revolution came to the minds of people like Israel Oludotun Ransome-Kuti and others in the struggle for African freedom and independence.

Ransom-Kuti was born on 30th April 1891 some months before the death of Bishop Crowther to an Egba family in Abeokuta. He was an eminent Nigerian churchman, educationist, administrator and the founding president of the Nigerian Union of Teachers (NUT), which was known in history as the first largest professional group. His father was Reverend Canon J.J.Ransom-Kuti who was also a well-known churchman for his outstanding administrative competence and his talent for singing. His passion for singing earned him the nickname of the *"Singing Minister"*. Israel Kuti was educated as Suren village school, went to Lagos Grammar School and later returned to Abeokuta Grammar School as the first student when it was opened in 1908. In 1913 Ransom-Kuti matriculated at Fourah Bay College, Freetown with a B.A. degree and on his return to Nigeria, he took up an appointment as a teacher in his former Grammar School from 1916 until 1918 when he left for Ijebu-Ode where he was the principal of Ijeu-Ode Grammar School for thirteen years.

Kuti left Ijebu-Ode in 1932 and returned to his Alma-mata at Abeokuta where he headed the school and had twenty-two years of meritorious service there. During this period he visited Britian in 1939 and again between 1943 and 1945. He was appointed to serve as a member of the Elliott Commission that reviewed higher education system in West Africa. His achievements at Ijebu-Ode included the founding of the First Boys Scout Troupe, the town's spokesman pleading their course with the British colonial residents in the province and founder of the Association of Headmasters of Ijebu schools. Remarkably, while Kuti was forming his organization at Ijebu-Ode in 1926, Reverend J.O.Lucas, also a renowned clergyman had already formed similar organization in Lagos in May 1925, which he called Lagos Union of Teachers.

These two organizations later became the base from which the idea of a national organization that could bring together all the teachers from all parts of Nigeria under one big umbrella. Hence the birth of Nigeria Union of Teachers (N.U.T.) came to life and Israel Oludotun Ransome-Kuti was elected its first National President. After many times of re-election as its President, Kuti finally retired in 1954 at the age of 63 years. Kuti was known to be a strong, forceful and charismatic personality, who guided his union in its campaign for improved working conditions for the teachers and also against colonial education policy in Nigeria and elsewhere in the British territory in West Africa. With his super administrative skill and that of his colleagues in the N.U.T. executives, notably people like A.A.Ikoku, E.E.Esua and the Reverend (later Bishop) S.I.Kale, the N.U.T.

succeeded in winning recognition for the organization from the colonial administration and also secured benefits for its members that totaled 20,000 by October 1948.

Through the efforts of the organization's leadership, the Union rapidly grew and by the 1960s, it had become the largest professional organization in Africa with the membership that exceeded a quarter of all the teachers in the continent. The success of the Union today in Nigeria and the continent largely depended on the good foresight and dedication to duty of their founding father – Reverend Israel Oludotun Ransom-Kuti. He was a man with reputable family set-up. His children included professor Olikoye Ransom-Kuti one of the best Health ministers that Nigeria would ever produced and also a world class medical teacher known everywhere in the globe; Fela Anikulapo Kuti also a world acclaimed musician of the immediate past century; Dr. Beko Kuti a medical practitioner and a world class peoples defender. Their mother Mrs. Ransom-Kuti during her lifetime was recognized as the first Nigeria woman ever to drive an automobile and also a great woman leader of her youthful age that played spectacular roles during the Egba conflict with the colonial authorities.

The role-call of the African fighters for its independence desire may not be limited only to the few ones mentioned but extended to all that played one role or the other in any form or capacity, which space in this book may not be able to accommodate. The continent would forever remember their names and the individual roles they played in various forms of honor. Coming back to Nigeria situation, the rival claims of Nigeria's various regions become most evident after the World War II when Britian attempted to find a structure that would meet the African demands for political power. In this regard the country was visibly divided into three regions viz. North, West and East for more administrative convinience and ethnic grouping. This administrative decision was not enough to solve the complexity of the problems of the political and economic situations of the country, which had been ragging since the 1950s.

In 1957 the country had its first Federal Prime Minister and in the same year the Western and Eastern regions were granted internal self-governments, to be followed by the Northern region in 1959. In the following year full independence rights was granted to Nigeria in October 1 1960 by her colonial master – Britian. Nigeria was under the rule of the British for six decades (1900 – 1960). During this time, Nigeria's economy and the welfare of its people were completely being managed by the British government and people. The unsolved tension between the amalgamated communities of the country that have diversed cultures and different ecological situations now becomes the country's concern. The vaguely managed problems of the country in the past also becomes the concern of everyone from the state houses to the citizens living in the cities, towns, villages, creeks, on the hills and mountains and those living under the bridges in Lagos, Enugu or Kaduna.

Chapter 24

Independent Nigeria and the Civil War

The British domination of Nigeria by its Imperial Agents lasted for six decades from 1900 – 1960 amid chaos, pains, suffering and degradation. At different times during this period, there were uprisings against the intruders in almost all the regions of the country especially in the interior where colonial rule was not yet fully established or where forced labor was imposed on the natives which sometime resulted into crisis. The dangerous pathway that Nigeria threaded in the course of her growth into manhood could not be over-looked or simplified in all of its entire priod. The idea of amalgamation of Nigeria into one unit by Fredrick Luggard was for the economic gains of his masters in London who never considered the complications that would follow their actions. Fredrick Luggard, who assumed the position of High Commissioner of the Protectorate of Northern Nigeria in 1900, is often regarded as the model British colonial administrator.

He was clever enough to have devised a means of appealing to the minds of the rulers in the North whom he had previously defeated and now reassembled together and used to govern the Protectorate. As a result of this lion and anthelope relationship and a well-monitored pact that Luggard was said to have signed with the Emirs, the North remained largely sheltered from Western influence, especially in the areas of education and economic development. While nationalist movements were gathering momentum in the early twentieth century in Lagos and some other places in the South, the rulers in the North and their British advisors would not allow such movement to be born in the North not until in the mid 1940s.

The unification of both Northern and Southern Protectorates that was started in 1912 by Luggard after his return to Nigeria from Hong Kong did not come through not until 1914 on the eve of the World War I. The British side of the war enjoyed the heavy hands of Nigeria's patriots used as laborers and soldiers of high repute at the war front and only God knows the numbers of innocent Nigerians that were either killed or missing in the War. It was on record that the Nigeria Regiment of the Royal West Africa Frontier Force (RWAFF), composed of men from the North and South, gallantly fought against the German colonial forces in Cameroon and in the East Africa where the Africans were set in combat against each other in a War that hardly benefited them in any form and which was prompted by their colonial masters in an attempt to protect their colonial interests in Africa and elsewhere.

When Sir Luggard became the governor-general of Nigeria with his ostensible unification tactics, the individual administration of the three separated regions – North, East and West was yet under the direct supervision of the British governors who were mandated to maintain the policy of indirect rule in their regions. The success of this system depended on fairly centralized hierarchical political units, which functioned well in the North, with variable success in the West and poorly in the East. The pressure from the educated Nigerians for self-government was increasing on daily basis particularly after the World War II. As a result of this, succession of short-lived constitutions were put in place.

The constitution of 1954 that established a federal system of government equally extended the functions of the regional governments. The constitutional conference of May and June 1957 in London granted self-government for the Western and Eastern regions and the North to follow in 1959. Finally in response to the demands of Nigerian nationalists for independence and after the trial period of between 1957 and 1959 under the self-government system plus successive constitutions legislated by the British Government, Nigeria moved up the ladder toward independence in October 1960 as a federation of three distinct regions (Northern, Western and Eastern) under a constitution that provided for a parliamentary form of government – the replica of the British system in England.

Under the parliamentary system of government, the three regions of the federation retained substantial degree of self-government to themselves

The Journey of the First Black Bishop

and it enabled them to see clearly what the regional problems were and how best the wheels of the regional vehicles could move forward faster. Indeed a lot of changes and developments were recorded in the Western region where Chief Obafemi Awolowo was at the head of the government and in the Eastern region where Dr. Nnamdi Azikwe was the head of the government before he was called upon to become the Governor-General of the federation at independence. The competetion between the regions was very healthy and brought about the good governance of the people. The impact of the self-government was not much seen in the North because it only prepared them for the independence rather than for them to count on its blessings and difficulties as it did to the other two brothers.

The Federal Government was given exclusive powers to defend the territorial borders of the country, managed the foreign relationship between Nigeria and the nations of the world, be in-charge of commercial negotiations between the country and the foreign traders, partners and investors and also formulate policies that would make Nigeria proud and develop. In 1963, Nigeria slightly altered its relationship with the United Kingdom and proclaimed herself a Federal Republic and subsequently promulgated a new constitution. In that year a fourth region (the Midwest) was added to the family of the federation.

Past Nigeria Leaders

The Federal Government was headed by an educated notherner Sir Abubakar Tafawa Balewa with Dr. Nnamdi Azikwe as the Governor-

General while Chief Obafemi Awolowo became the leader of opposition in the Federal Parliament. Political parties maneuvered for position of power in anticipation to rule the country at independence. The three major political parties that emerged for 1959 general elections were the Northern Peoples Congress (N.P.C.) with Sir Ahmadu Bello- the Sardauna of Sokoto as its leader and Sir Abubakar Tafawa Balewa as the party's flag bearer for the election; the National Council of Nigeria and Cameroon (N.C.N.C.) with Dr. Nnamdi Azikwe as its leader, flag bearer and who later became the first Nigerian Governor-General by the fussion of NPC and NCNC to form the first Federal Government; and the Action Group led by its leader- Chief Obafemi Awolowo who emerged as the leader of opposition with the strong backing of his party stewalts like Chief Anthony Enahoro (the fugitive man), J. S. Tarka (UMBC) from the Middle Belt and others in the parliament.

Names such as that of Mallam Aminu Kano, Chief T.O.S. Benson, Shetima Alli Mungonu, Zana Bukar Dipcharima, Sir Odeleye Fadahunsi, Bode Thomas, Denis Osadebey, A. C. Nwapa, Michael Okpara, Chief S. L. Akintola, Sir Adesoji Aderemi (the Oni of Ife and the first native Governor of Western region) and host of others that contributed immensely to the structural design of Nigeria's growth will forever remain unscratched from our memories.

The British influence on the government and people of Northern region of Nigeria caused a lot of problems on the stability of the nation immediately after their exit in 1960. The internal disorders, which began to surface in 1962 and, which were caused mainly by regional sentiment over the domination of the Federal Government by Northern elements culminated in series of discontentments as was even seen by the reactions of the people from the minority groups in the North especially from the Tiv community, where late Hon. J. S. Tarka was the leader of the community and its minority party – United Middle Belt Congress (UMBC), an affliat of the Action Group of Chief Obafemi Awolowo from the West.

So also the followers of Mallam Aminu Kano the leader of Northern Elements People Union (N.E.P.U), which affliated itself with the National Council of Nigeria and Cameroon (N.C.N.C.) of Dr. Nnamdi Azikwe became a big thorn in the political body of the Northern Peoples Congress (N.P.C.), the senior party at the Federal level. One thing to note here is the home bases of these political organizations, which could hardly change the interests of their supporters because of the ethnic loyalty and affinity that bounded them together.

Predominant in the North, the religious unity among the Moslems made people to pitch their tents in the N.P.C. political field without reservation for ideological understanding and convictions. In the East and the West where Christianity was predominantly the religion of the people, tribal sentiments divided them into two different camps. The Yorubas followed Chief Obafemi Awolowo and his Action Group party purely on tribal sentiments while the Ibos never taught it twice to follow Zik and Okpara in their bid for political positions. The new Midwest state that was recently added to the family followed the same political patterns of its big brothers by recognizing the Osadebeys and the Akpatas in their political play field.

These wranglings were sufficient enough to distabilize the new nation as the tribal politics was already eating deeply into our bones and marrows. To find a way to kill this dangerous animal taunting us around, some military boys came through the doors of Coup d'etat on the 15th January 1966 to chase out the elected government of the people. The coup left its death marks on the Federal Prime Minister, Sir Abubakar Tafawa Balewa, the Premier of the Northern region, Sir Ahmadu , the Premier of the Western region, Chief Samuel Ladoke Akintola and Chief Samuel Okotie Eboh, the Federal Finance Minister. Some of the military and security guards of these notable figures were also killed for their failure to surrender their bosses to the Coup plotters on demand.

By January 17, 1966 General Johnson Aguiyi Ironse one of the nations finest and most disciplined soldier by world standard suppressed the revolt and took over the administration of the country as the Head of state and Commander-in-Chief of the Nigerian Army. He suspended the constitution, dissolved the Parliament, established a unitary system of government by decree 34 and appointed military governors to replace the popularly elected civilian premiers in the regions. Not very long and precisely on the 29th of July 1966, that mutinous elements in the army, majority of whom were the Northern officers, staged a countercoup at Ibadan while the Head of state General Ironsi was on a state visit to the Western region. He was killed along with his host Brigadier Adekunle Fajuyi the then governor of the region and Ironsi was replaced by Lt. Col Yakubu Gowon as the new Head of the military government.

The July Coup was seen and admitted by people as a revenge for the Northern leaders that were killed during the January 15 Coup because the Coup did not claim a soul from the Eastern region. In the revenge design, thousands of Easterners living in the Northern region of the country were massacred and more than a million persons of Ibo origin returned to their home region in Iboland. The counter-action of the Northerners was one of the hiding reasons why the country was plunged into the civil war that lasted for close to three years. Yakubu Gowon's military government divided the country into 12 states; 6 states were created out of the old Northern region; 3 from the old Eastern region while the Midwest, Western region and Lagos areas became separate states.

While the other two former regions North and West accepted the re-alignment, Eastern region leaders rejected it and on the 30th May 1967, the independent Republic of Biafra was born with Lt. Col. Odumegwu Ojukwu as its head of state. For Lt. Col. Gowon to move the wheels of the country forward, he had to repeal the Decree 34 of General Ironsi so as to allow him to revert the country back to Federal system of government and further to allow him within the legal frame work to established the 12 states he created on the 27th of May, 1967. The new states were the followings: Bendel, East Central, Kwara, Lagos, Benue-Plateau, North-Eeastern, North-Western, South-Eastern, North-Central, Kano and Rivers.

On 6 July, the Federal government declared war on the Republic of Biafra. During the prosecution of this war, many lives totaling over a million persons were perished through guns, diseases and starvation. By the time the war was ended on 12th January 1970, the landmass of Biafra had been reduced to about one-tenth of its original 78,000 Sq-Km about 30,000 Sq-miles area. Some European nations who never wished Nigeria a happy stay together as one indivisible entity supported the breakaway Eastern region with money, ammunition and diplomatic strategies. The rail line that connected Lagos with Enugu was disconnected while most of the Federal government offices in the East were taken over by the Biafran authority. Many Ibos from all over the country returned to their home state in Iboland to support their new republic.

The Nigeria civil war actually set back the hands of national devlopment and hindered the growth of the nation's economy. The military men especially the governors of the states now see themselves as perfect beings and God sent administrators who have come to rescue the nation from the mess heaped on the citizens by the politicians. They now began to employ different delay tactics as to when the country would deem it fit to return to civilian rule. By October 1970, General Gowon set 1976 as the target date for his Nigeria's return to civilian rule, and in 1974 he announced an indefinite postponement in plans for the transfer of power. His regime's recalcitrance in this and other areas, which included the power-drunk attitudes of some of his state governors and the high level of curruption in the government circle, which he was unable to put top to or checked led to his overthrow on 29th July 1975.

He was succeeded by Brigadier Muritala Ramat Muhammad, and Brigadier Olusegun Obasanjo as his number two man in the Supreme Military Council. His regime relieved in flushing out the inefficient and corrupt civil servants from the government service, which added more problems to the existing loaded ones in our sack. It was his government that kicked out most of our fine civil servants from the service and ever since then, our civil service sector has remained very unpopular, uncommitted and undedicated to the jobs they are employed and being paid for. The civil service became a place where job certainty is never guaranteed because any civil servant can be booted out of job without any recourse to his/her future and that of his/her family.

As such the purpose of his government to exterminate corruption was defeated by his actions and the level of corruption in the country instead of coming down went up astronomically. It became whatever you can grab; grab it before you are booted out. There may be good intention in the philosophy of Muritala/Obasanjo to change the attitude of the civil servants but the approach and the intent of its receivers made it so difficult to plant such idea into the hearts of the workers whom part of them were being used by the people at the top of government to defraud the nation on a large scale looting of our treasury. Instead of this philosophy to start lowering the flag of corruption, it continued to increase its level of knowledge, and graduating it from one class to the other. It must be remembered to its credit that the regime was the architect of the new national capital of Abuja.

On 13th February 1976, General Muritala Ramat Mohammed was assassinated in the course of an abortive insurgency led by Dimka and Lt. General Olusegun Obasanjo who was his Chief of Army Staff took over the reign of power and promised that he would definitely carry on with the program of his immediate past boss. In 1976, Obasanjo's government promulgated a decree to establish more states and the states of Nigeria were increased from twelve to nineteen. Along the line, political activities were permitted to come back again in late 1978. A new constitution was ratified and put in place on 1st of October 1979, which was the day that Alhaji Shehu Shagari took office as civilian president after thirteen years of military intervention in the political system of the country.

Alhaji Shagari's party – the National Party of Nigeria (N.P.N.) had to romance with the Nigerian Peoples Party led by the former president Dr. Nnamdi Azikwe to form the government which the marriage between the two of them did not last long enough when it collapsed in 1981 leaving Shagari alone in the middle of the sea with his minority members in the government. N.P.N stage-managed that government until the end of its four-year term amid chaos and big time corruption. In August 1983, president Shagari won a re-election bid into the office the second time but in late December of that year, three months after his second victory at the polls, the army toupled his government in yet another military coup led by Major General Muhammadu Buhari. The slate of the nation was wiped clean again as the second Republic of 1979 – 83 was thrown into the garbage can by our good old friend – the military men.

To be kindness, each profession has its expertise skills and knowledge. The soldiers for example are technically trained to handle weapons in use to defend the territorial boundaries of a nation and to protect the lives and properties of the inhabitants of such territories against external aggressions. Group of people in that territory called the politicians are specifically mandated by the people to arrange for how to rule them, formulate policies for them, determine the remuneration for the services of the security men, buy the adequate equipment and machineries with which they are supposed to use to protect them and not to sit in the fortresses to rule them and determine their future without asking for their opinions.

This was one of the courses why Buhari's government provoked growing public dissatisfaction because of its increasingly authoritarian and military character, and on the 27th of August 1985, his government was sent packing by his Army Chief Major General Ibrahim Babangida. As soon as he assumed office, he designated himself with the title of "President". There is always the fact in the sayings and thinkings of the African elderly people especially when they intend to marry psychology with events. One of such interesting areas is the saying that goes thus: "It is only in the city of the blinds that one eyed man becomes the king". The regime brought about a lot of new innovations and management skills into the college of corruption in th civil service unit; it conducted unsuccessful elections; it banned the Second Republic officials from participating in the politics of their land for ten years as punitive offence; it pledged a return to civilian rule by 1982, which never fulfilled; it inaugurated a "homegrown" Structural Adjustment Program (S.A.P), which would involve cuts in public spending, decreased state control over the economy, stimulation of exports, devaluation of Nigerian currency, and re-scheduling of our foreign debts. But funny enough his government's budgetary excesses undermined his SAP policy.

Babangida's military government was credited with lots of policies to be remembered and noted in the history book of the nation. It was the regime that forced two political parties – the National Republican Convention (N.R.C.) and the Social Democratic Party (S.D.P) on the country, a replica of American style of party politics. On 20th May 1992, his government banned all political, religious and ethnic organizations other than his two approved political parties and conducted legislative elections on the 4th of July 1992 from which S.D.P. won 47 of the 91 Senate seats and 301 of the 593 seats in the House of Representatives. Its counterpart N.R.C. won 37 and 267 respectively.

His regime also conducted one of the first successful censuses since independence the result which was announced in March 1992 and gave Nigeria a population of 88.5 million people, some 20 million fewer than the estimated figure. His government kept changing colors on the transition date and continued postponing the inauguration of the National Assembly that was to coincide with the establishment of the Third Republic. While the country was preparing for December 1992 Presidential elections and to the amazement of the Nigerian people, General Babangida dribbled everyone into his net again when on 17th November 1992, he announced a third delay in the transfer of power from 2nd January until 27th August 1993.

The dribbling style of his government steered up political violence and charges of electoral fraud and malpractices disrupted the first round of Presidential primaries. The second round too was flawed and because of the ineffectiveness of the electoral machinery, his government suspended the primary results in October and banned 23 of the presidential aspirants from future participation in the political competition of the nation. As a result of what followed the distruption, there were students and labor unrest and many were detained. Ethnic and religious fightings compounded the problem but instead of the government to see reason with the groaning of the people, it kept on promising the people of a possible date in 1993.

In March 1993, another round of presidential nominations took place and Chief M.K.O. Abiola of the S.D.P. and Alhaji Bashir Tofa of the N.C.R. both Moslems and close friends to Babangida won the tickets of their respective political parties as their flag bearers. The election that was slated for 12th of June 1993 was conducted amid a flurry of legal efforts to halt it and at the end of it all Chief M.K.O. Abiola of the SDP gallantly defeated Tofa according to unofficial results given Abiola 58.4% and Tofa 41.6%. On 16th of June 1993, the National Electoral Commission (N.E.C) on its judgment either right or wrong set aside the results of the presidential elections ever to be conducted in the country after independence. Based of this decision, our self-styled president, General Babangida annulled the election a week later using excuses of irregularities, poor turn-out and legal complications to justify his action. Abiola's tribal people from Yorubaland stood very strongly and solidly behind his demand to be certified as president-elect and when this demand was not forth coming from the government side; civil unrest erupted in Lagos and some other Yoruba cities.

When President Babangida could no longer handle the unwanted situations surrounding the nation and his presidency was in a terrible mess, amid hot and tensive climate, he resigned on the 26th of August 1993. As clever as he would always be, he handpicked a transitional council to be headed by a U.A.C. former chieftain, Chief Earnest Shonekan who incidentally came from the same Egba clan as Abiola himself. By mid-Novermber of the same year, Chief Shonekan was thrown out of the seat by yet another army general – General Sanni Abacha.

General Abacha in the usual military system of governance banned all political parties and any activities associated with them; he abolished all states and local governments plus the national legislature. He replaced some civilian government officials with military commanders; He ordered the strikers to go back to work and the following week, he named an 11 member of his Provisional Ruling Council, which was composed of mainly the generals and the police officials. Days later he created a 32 member Federal Executive Council to oversee the ministerial duties of the ministries under his government. He shopped around the country to put this group together from the pro-democracy and human rights activists and from the group of those who were his mentors when he was in the lower ranks in the army.

The moment of turn around to suit every ugly situation in the country than in the past was now strikingly and forcefully knocking at our doors. On June 11 1994 Abiola proclaimed himself the president of the nation, and because of possible arrest for his action, he went into hiding. Later that month he was arrested, an action that was to portend much of what was to come for Nigeria in the immediate near future. Nigerians in their usual manner protested against Abiola's arrest, but Abacha's repressive military junta quelled the demonstrators violently.

On July 6, Abiola was charged to court on three counts of treason, which he pleaded not guilty to those charges. The following day, Nigerian workers went on strike to support Abiola's mandate and within that month millions of workers had reportedly walked out on the streets of major cities and towns of the nation. They vehemently refused to talk it over with the government. While Abiola remained in jail, his wife Kudirat Abiola was assassinated in resemblance manner to the style Dele Giwa was assassinated by bomp-parcel delivery during the regime of President Babangida.

In August, General Abacha banned several newspapers, fired his army and navy commanders and declared that his government had absolute powers to do and undo things, which may in all ways contrary to the wills of the people. He vowed that he would not walk in cheaply into the demands of the pro-democracy demonstrators. By late September, General Abacha in his attempt to rejuvenate the machinery of the government, he removed all civilians from his Ruling Council. Three months later, he suspended habeas corpus and now throwing his opponents into prison-houses throughout the land. He rejected a court order for the release of Abiola from prison on medical grounds.

In March 1995, General Abacha ordered the arrest of his former Commander-in-Chief and Nigeria Head of government - General Olusegun Obasanjo on suspicion of treason. Later in the month, he dissolved the Labor Unions and put their leaders behind the bars. On 25th April, he canceled the January 1, 1996 deadline already earmarked for the return of the civilian rule and warned not to hear or discussed the issue any longer. The convictions of fourty suspected persons in secret trials brought the attention of international communities to the way he was governing the country and called for serious condemnation and demands of leniency from the critics of his government. On October 1, he relented and committed the death sentences of his convicted opponents and declared that he would relinquish power in 1998 to an elected government. Like his military predecessors in office, he too was fond of deceiving the people as to the manner and time he wished to hand over the power to an elected government. Saro-Wiwa's case and extermination was the tallest tower building of Abacha's regime. It was the most horrible and barbaric event one would expect to witness happening in this modern age.

Ken Saro-Wiwa was an intellectual of his age and the leader of the Movement for the Survival of Ogoni people in the river-rine area of the Delta where the nation's oil wealth has been sitting. He was arrested, charged and convicted to death with eight others on trumped-up charges steming from his opposition to a proposed drilling agreement in Nigeria's main oil producing region. The horrible executions of these Nigerians in early November called for a torent of criticism from the international community, which resulted in the suspension of Nigeria from the Commonwealth and placing an embargo on Nigeria by the European Union on arms aid to it.

In April 1998, four of Nigeria's five major political parties ganged up together to nominate Abacha as their presidential candidate at a rally in Abuja, a rally which gulfed up millions of Naira on entertainment sprey that may not be accounted for uptil today. It became apparent to everyone that the primary aim of General Abacha in doing all he flagrantly did was to succeed himself in office. The most difficult job that would have been left for him to do was to pull off the khaki uniform of the Nigeria army on him and simply replaced it with the big native robe called "Babanriga".

But unfortunately the man died on the 8th of June 1998 of sudden heart attack and the batton rolled into the waiting hands of another army general – General Abdoulsalami Abubakar. He took office amid lots of confusions, political unrest and bleaking pathway to progress. On the 7th of July, the sudden death of M.K.O. Abiola in the government custody was announced and people strongly believed that his blood was used to appease the gods of his fatherland. Under the administration of General Abubakar, elections for presidency and the national legislature were held on 27th February 1999 and General Olusegun Obasanjo who was recently released from Abacha's jail term and nominated as the flag bearer of the Peoples Democratic Party (P.D.P.) won the presidential ticket with 62% of the votes casted.

His counterpart in the race Chief Olu Falae of Advance for Democracy (A.D.) and one time Secretary to the Federal Military Government and Minister of Finance under Babangida's regime scored 38% while the 3rd party (A.P.P.) did not field any candidate. General Obasanjo's government was inaugurated on June 4 1999 and part of his proposed agenda included restoration of law and order, which had been grounded in the country, fighting curruption, and unification of Nigeria's ethnically and religiously diverse peoples.

Chapter 25

If African Continent is to be totally Free and Independent, What is to be done?

I must confess to my readers that during the script writing of this chapter, I wrestled a lot with my inner abilities before I could come up with the little contributions I am able to offer for the future of our mother continent – Africa. My living period in other parts of the world especially in America exposed me greatly to how life looks like in other places besides my continent of origin – the great Africa. On February 12, 1779 Samuel Adams one of the founding fathers of great America was discussing a point related to the "education of the head and the heart" with his friend James Warren in a letter he wrote to him. The title of the letter was that – *"If virtue and knowledge are diffused among the people, they will never be enslaved. This will be their great security"*. True to life this was the chief course of our problems in Africa and we seriously need to address the issue vigorously and aggressively. Without educated citizens, said James Madison (the 4th American President), "popular government is but a Prologue to a farce or a tragedy; or perhaps both". The fact remains that because in Africa we do not have enough educated citizens, yet our problems keep on mounting to the heights of our mountains such as Kilimanjaro Mountain in Tanzania. Popular government that is government by consent of civilized society will not in the views of our founding fathers, enough; but informed consent from informed society was what the African community would need to make them strong enough to enjoy their freedom and independence.

Our political institutions like all other political institutions of other places of the world were designed to take into account human depravity and self-interest. But, as dynamics, flexible and self-oriented as they were, our freedom fighters took all these assertions into consideration when they were at the war front fighting for the independence of the nations of Africa. Their hope was to raise-up men and women who would improve not just the material conditions of our people but the people themselves and that the people should be enlightened and virtuous enough to govern themselves. Other conditions attached to it was, that they should be able to select responsible and enlightened politically talented people among ourselves to govern us. In the days of our founding fathers, schools and homes were the two institutions where we could learn about our civic responsibilities. There we could be taught to temper our selfishness, respect the nation's laws and our elders so that we may become better human beings to our community and society. The big question ever being asked from generation to generation is "what is the chief end of a man"? As this question is being asked in America, so also it is being asked in Asia, Africa, Europe, Australia and elsewhere in the universe.

John Adams (the second American President) and his wife Abigael tried to answer this question when John once told Abigael to "let our Anxiety be, to mould the minds and manners of our children". Their eldest son, John Quincy Adams, grew up to become the sixth president of America. George Washington (the first President of America) wrote many letters to his stepson and adopted grandson, telling them to cultivate the habits and virtues that would make them not only successful individuals but useful members of their community; so also Thomas Jefferson (the third American President) exhorted his children to be good and honest – to let their "internal monitors" (or conscience) be their guide.

Our founding father's reasons for promoting the general diffusion of knowledge, was first to create within the society a "natural aristocracy" of genius and virtue. By this, they did not meant aristocracy of wealth, caste or privilege because genius and virtue are not limited to any particular class or tribe, but scattered randomly throughout the polity. Their intention therefore was to see that all children, no matter what their background, were to be given an opportunity to rise to their potential. By separating the "wheat from the chaff" as to the motives of leaders like Bishop Crowther, Johnsons, Obefemi Awolowo and others, they hoped to elevate worthy persons to guard the sacred rights of liberty. Secondly they were not content to rely simply on the elite – no matter how natural – to safeguard their nations from tyranny. They knew quite well the tendency of the nation to devolve into oligarchies or tyrannies.

Ultimately, the people would have to rely on themselves to feud off tyranny as it happened in Nigeria during the regimes of the military junta. Number three reason was the quality of education that the founders left behind. During their time, we all remembered that technology was just at its infancy in almost everywhere in the globe and because of this we may not be qualified enough to apportion blame to them for our inability to catch up with some other areas of the world. But the generations that followed that of the founding fathers enjoyed the better part of the educational system of their time because in addition to planting virtues in their hearts, and cultivating "natural aristocracy" among them, they harvest the patriots that later became the firebrand fighters in the continent.

These fighters were taught and encouraged to love their country so that they would become useful citizens in the future. Our founders believed that what is needed as at the time was a civic education, the one that would shape both minds and hearts to prepare the Africans for the requirements of self-government. They had it in mind that the civic education of the time was fundamental to the future prosperity of Africa and that the children would learn to revere their laws and to become acquainted with their heroes and ideals of their collective past. This was the reason for them to place much emphasis on the home education of their children before it could be built upon in the schools. Abraham Lincoln's defence on civic education to the Americans goes thus: let reverence for the laws….. be taught in schools, in seminaries, and in colleges; - let it be written in Primmers, Spelling books, and in Almanacs…. And in short let it become the political religion of the nation, and let the old and the young, the rich and the poor, the grave and the gay, of all sexes and tongues, and colors and conditions, sacrifice increasingly upon its alters. I honestly think the man was right in his judgment.

Whereever we may find ourselves on the surface of the earth, all we needed do is to take advantage of that environment and to study the varied scenes carefully so that we might arrive at a better judgment and understanding of ourselves, and the human nature in that environment. We should endeavor to let our ambitions be engaged to become eminent, and above all things, we should support a virtuos character and always remember that: "an Honest Man is the Noblest work of God". As John

Locke puts it: "virtue is harder to be got than knowledge; and if lost in a young man, is seldom recovered". We seldomly forget the fact that the proper end of any education is moral education and the chief of all education is the education of character.

Successes and difficulties are two inseparable twin brothers in life and no matter how clever a man is he must experience both either severally or jointly in his life ambition journey. Following Crowther's consecration in 1864, Henry Venn wrote to Mann in April 1865 appealing to all missionaries in the Niger Episcopal jurisdiction to place themselves under the Bishop's jurisdiction and authority and enjoined them to cooperate and work with him diligently and as brothers. He also assured them that, Bishop Crowther had been destined for great works by God. No matter how good or bad the physical structure of a man is, the hiding super structure in him would always dictate and control his outward appearance and behaviors. The consecration of Crowther bothered Townsend and this anger was shown in his letter to Venn when he gave an opinion that bordered on religious secession and claimed therein that he "could not see any necessary connection between the Episcopal office in a foreign country and the Crown of England". Initially, Venn knew that Townsend did not approve of Crowther's consecration when he forged ahead to make him a Bishop and Townsend's cumulative and suspected reactions of the recent times plus his political judgment on what ensued between him (Townsend) and Governor Glover of Lagos, Venn began to censure the language of his letter and became suspicious of his ambitions. Unfortunately Townsend built up his tower of hatred to such a height that he himself could not live to enjoy before his ambition crashed on him.

The Delta was a particular difficult area to work in the days of our founding fathers. The practice of the destruction of twin children in one locality or the banishment of the mother in another area were very rampat during the time Bishop Crowther stuck his neck and that of the members of his family to save that of others. He ruthlessly condemned the practice and the misery that the people always inflicted on their victims. He mounted serious crusade against the evil practice during his meetings, visitations, prayers and social interactions with the people. It is too hard to believe today that when Crowther was performing his first ordination service at Onitsha, there was still human sacrifice going on within the locality. It is also still a misery how Bishop Crowther succeeded in bringing the light of the Gospel to supersede the darkness of idolatory in Bonny where people worshipped alligators as deities. Around this time, it was said that the reptiles became menace in the streets and every corner of the town and it was forbidden for anyone to kill them. But when Bishop Crowther ordered them to be killed and sprinkle their bloods in the people's drinking water to prove that they were not better than ordinary edible meat that this practice was abolished.

On Easter Day of 1867, the Head Chief of Bonny announced the worship of the giant reptiles and with gradual pains an end was put to the worshiping of the animal. We have to re-visit here once again some of the persecutions that Bishop Ajayi Crowther went through in his attempt to lay the foundation of the church, the mission and the modern trading activities that generations after him built upon to make us proud as a nation today. An example of such was when mission station was to be built at Ghebe in Lokoja area. Bishop Crowther saw the influence and the development that the station would bring to the people of the locality if it were to be built there. He noted in his journal that the people of Ghebe were willing to hear the good news but he was very sad and upset on one occasion to learn that Ghebe had been plundered after being destroyed with fire. Such an important town of its time as in ruinous heaps and swept away from the face of the earth. No one group was spared from the persecution trials.

While the flock suffered theirs, so also the shepherd did not go unscathed. The Bishop and his son Dandeson once fell victim to the treasurous attitude of his one time friend – Chief Aboko when the chief ordered his men to sweep clean Crowther's boat of all cargo; his personal luggage and apparel were removed and he and his men spent the night outside while striped naked. Bishop Crowther and his men were imprisoned under the directive of his good old friend Aboko just because the English merchant failed to recognize him as the superintendent of the board of trade in that part of River Niger. Bishop Crowther was only to be released on the payment of a ransome of two hundred slaves to Aboko but after detailed negotiation through Abega, the chief asked for the payment of one thousand bags of cowries – the equivalent of one thousand pounds sterling of the time. In the end the negotiation failed because the demand would amount to re-approving or reviving slave trade. To get them out of the trouble, military force had to be used to release Bishop Crowther and his men from the trap of chief Aboko. The church at Lokoja on hearing this incident wrote to commend the spirit and character of endurance that Bishop Crowther used to quell the barbaric situation and confessed that they learned a great lesson from him.

Bishop Crowther faced a lot of difficulties which included covering a large area of the country on foot thereby qualified him to earn the title of "the man trecked a lot" when transportation was very irregular and in some instances not even available. The irregular movement of people and trade through waters was the order of the day as there were virtually no motor- ways or motor vehicles for use. His last days in the episcopate bore unpleasant events. This was the time the fruits of his commercial labor and his foresight for his people were beginning to bring out its blossom flowers and this time too was when the struggle between the European companies, the African coastal tribes and the Sierra Leonian merchants was rearing up its ugly head above the waters. Inevitably the African ministers in this Delta region took side with their Brass and Bonny neighbors while the European missionaries supported their own business people.

Bishop Crowther as he was known during his days was a very good educational strategist. His main weapon in his evangelical ministry was the estalishment of schools because he regarded education as a means to build an informed society especially where the texts used to educate people came from the Holy Scriptures. He believed that all "virtues" could be inculcated while all vices could be condemned. According to him, it is only when people are educated that all the superstitious of idolatrous worhip would be exposed and dropped. He therefore pioneered the self-supporting local school system by introducing fees; contributed immensely to Macaulay's (his son-in-law) efforts to start the Lagos Grammar School and showed his very best interest in the development of the Freetown Grammar School and the Fourah Bay College his Alma Marta.

Crowther being a carpenter and educationist, he encouraged his people to bequest technical education in the field of carpentary and joinery, mechanics of steam engines, mansory, and artisans in other related fields. Some of his time caterers, women tailors and domestic scientists owed their training to the efforts of his wife. He did not want Christianity to destroy national assimilation but hoped it would correct any degrading and superstitious defects attached to it. He also did not go against the Christians participation in politics but all he advocated for was that it should be played with caution, wisdom and meekness so that it would generate mutual understanding between them and the power holders. The hardships that his trusted people in the Church Missionary Society heaped on him in his last days caused his indisposition from which he did not actually recover thereafter. At last the one time strong man broke down. He was able to record his last attendance at the church of Christ in Lagos on Christmas morning in 1891 and on December 31 1891 at a quarter to one in the morning, our beloved Bishop, our son of hope, father to all the black communities in West Africa and beyond threw up the towel and answered to the call of his creator at the ripe age of 89 years.

God the creator of all things has been a familiar Being to the people of Africa before the coming of the white missionaries into the continent and it would therefore be a misunderstanding of facts and dead propaganda that the whites introduced God to the Africans. It is evident that they come to the continent for a purpose from the on-set and the question of using the Bible to evangelize the people was secondary intention. African people had already been solidly grounded in the knowledge of God, and the concept of Trinity was evidently present in their day-to-day worship. The traditional religious concept that was in existence many centuries back still do exist till today in the communities where such religion are been practiced.

An example of this fact can still be seen in some parts of Africa particularly in the East Africa from the region of Bukusu, an ethnic group in Western Kenya where the Supreme Being is being addressed in three dimensions: Wele Baba, Wele Mukhobe, and Wele Murunwa meaning God the Father, God the Herald, and God the Messenger. God the Father, Wele Baba was also adorned with a variety of attributes such as, Muumba, meaning The Creator. God the Herald, Wele Mukhobe, carries with it the concept of spokesmanship having the same attribute of "God the Son", which we refer to in today's modern churches. God the Messenger "Wele Murunwa", has the attributes of the Holy Ghost that was sent as a messenger to reveal the "mysteries" or the secrets of God to the people. An approach to individual religion may differ from the instinct of its believers to that of another but the bottom line is that the message they carry goes the same way and to the same source. In the African religion heritage the number three "Wele Murunwa" is a symbol in high esteem but yet they give equal power to the three personalities mentioned. An example is thus illustrated: The three can be equated to the three traditional firestones, which served important but equal roles in supporting and providing balance to the cooking pot - the famous ancient cooking method still in use in Africa and elsewhere in the world of today. None of the three persons of the Trinity is therefore subservient to the other.

Coming closer home in West Africa especially regarding to the culture and people of Yorubaland. The Yoruba version of the Bible we read today was interpreted from one language (English) unto it. The then laborious interpreters of the English language unto Yoruba dialect linked up with the custodians of the native religion achives before they could come up with what we see today. In this great task we give thanks and credit to people like Bishop Ajayi Crowther, Johnson James, Mojola Agbebi, Babington Macaulay and host of other reformists of their time that worked tirelessly to put Yoruba people and its language on top of today's evangelical movement almanac.

In an act of relationship, language plays a key role. Because of the inability of the Europeans not to understand the language of the Africans, they assumed that their ways of worshiping God significantly differs from theirs and as such African system of worshiping God must be crude and barbaric. Western missionaries failed to identify themselves with the ethnic ambitions and idiosyncracies, which they still do to this day. The continuing American presence in the running of projects in Africa prevents the full development of the African Christians because their presence destroys the superior physical qualities of African Christianity. It does not encourage their readiness to face difficulties as they themselves faced such difficulties when the building of America began. Their independence, courage and daring self-reliance were completely destroyed as their presence only increases the attitude of dependency and nothing more.

Another point is that the young Americans of today that goes to Africa to supervise their organization's projects in the continent or for any other reasons on their way back home still see Africans as primitive and static in development. Reason being that the so called self help projects are intentionally located in most of the remote areas of the continent for propanganda purposes and as soon as these young people from America steps unto those areas where developments have not significantly reached, they would form an opinion that the whole continent must in every aspect be like where they were. The early missionaries that went to Africa thaught that they could succeed to see that the continent was civilized only by introducing Christianity and formal education, but the colonists added capitalism, industrialization and work ethics. When these formulas came on board, all other subsidiary things followed. Rightly or wrongly we can then trace the string of our problems in Africa today to the time of these cancarous regimes because in their attempt to annex empires, the missionaries who were partners in business with the colonists collaborated with them to produce the Africans of their own image.

At the end of the partitioning, the colonial rulers as well as the missionaries began to condemn all things that were being done by the Africans. The Africans themselves started abandoning their African names, music, dance, art, marriages, systems of inheritance and the quality and cohesiveness in their traditions. All were excluded from schools, college curriculum and church programs. One of the major problems one would find in our primary and tertiary educational system of today is the re-inventing of the English language. In Yorubaland for example, the language of the people is almost abandoned both in the schools and at homes because the language that an average child in this community understands best now is English language. It has become a new culture that is fastly spreading across the community. Are we expecting these children to start learning the language of their mother tongue when they gain admission into Oxford University in England or when they become students at Havard University in Washington D.C. of Morgan State University in Baltimore – USA? To me this is yet another wave of self-introduction of perpetual slavery into the ranks of this new generation by their parents and leaders, as they would eventually become alien in their communities in the immediate near future. The final agenda of colonialism in Africa as it is now unraveling itself through foreign languages can be likened to an ice cream filled in a cone cup. We have licked the ice cream and about eating the cone cup to solidify its taste and texture.

The people of Congo today are facing the problems created by the early missionaries in collaboration with the European merchants. Simion Kimbangu and his wife Mivilu Marie were baptized in 1915. He hoped to become a teacher and an evangelist but he could not because he was not read enough to qualify him for his life ambition trade or profession. In 1918, in the year of the great worldwide influenza pandemic, Kimbangu began to have various callings asking him to be a healer and apostle. His case was not different from that of Jonah in the Bible. He fled his calling and ran to Kinshasa where he became miserable but the vision continued to hunt him around until he returned to his home town Ntamba, yet his hopes were once again frustrated. Finally he settled down in his home town to begin a ministry of faith healing in 1921 drawing crowds from everywhere in the region. His kick-off success alarmed the Belgian authorities, who feared that he might become focus for nationalist rebellion and for this purpose they attempted to arrest him in 1921, but he escaped with some of his followers only to submit himself to them three months later.

He was tried, and sentenced to 120 lashes of Cain and death. After protests by the people against this travesty of justice and that he had never been found of advocating any rebellion against the colonial powers but had constantly preached obedience to authority, his sentence was commuted and he spent the next thirty years as a model prisoner and yet he died in the prison in October 12, 1951. Kimbangu was known to be a leader who summed up in his own person the destiny of his people and their future. He would always pray for their weaknesses, their hardships, their poverty and sufferings, their powerlessness and apathy, and above all their captivity of evil and their need for deliverance. Through trumped-up charges, he was destroyed both ways – in his attempt to develop his people so that they would match-up with their contemporaries in the globe and to provide the service that others (the colonists) could not provide. The man and his ideas were intentionally and maliciously killed.

The Nineteenth century Xhosa Christianity, which was crushed between the Zulu and the British suffered major religious, social and political crisis in the beginning of this century. The crisis was prompted by the collapse of an effective traditional political power organized by the detractors of the system. Nxele who was a Dutchman grew up as a Christian who learnt its art on a Boer farm. In 1812, a year after the war between Xhosa and British broke out, he went through the ecstatic experience of a traditional Xhosa prophet and led his people to a war in which he saw a battle between the God of the whites and that of the blacks. According to him, he believed that the God of the blacks, "should be worshipped in dancing, the enjoyment of life and in love, so that the blacks would fill the earth, and not to sit and sing songs and pray with their faces to the ground and their backs facing the Almighty".

Nxele promised his people that the Xhosa ancestors would rise from the dead to help them in their battle, but unfortunately like the African leaders of his type, he was captured in the attack and imprisoned on the popular Robbin's Island of Mandela fame. In his escape bid he drowned. The improvers who were the Africans from his region and who had absorbed David Livinstone's ideals of "Christianity and Commerce" could not do much other than to mount protests upon protests that did not received the blessings of the British authority. Unfortunately the white settler community viewed economically successful black people as a threat and as such all they wanted black people for was cheap labor; much so, the colonial government of South Africa did all they could to prevent the Xhosa people from gaining economic and commercial quality as the white settlers of South Africa.

The swift economic and social changes that were brought into the continent by the Europeans in the twentieth century were as a result of the outcome and the participation of the Africans during the Second

World War. After the war, the educated Africans particularly from the West Africa noticed how their people were being used in a war that was neither concerned them nor benefited them passé. Strong pressure was built around the colonists demanding for rapid development and greater participation in the government of their countries. The Constitution of each country in the region was always short-lived as it was been drafted, discussed and approved by the imperial parliament of the mother nation ruling that country in West Africa.

Most importantly, these imperial powers always underestimated the urgency of demands of the people and as such all they would do was to screen the areas where the hardest, fastest agitations and militant political organizations came from to demand for imperial withdrawal. Preference would therefore be given to such region and push aside that of the conservative areas till later time and this was why places like Ghana became independent state before others on the West Coast of Africa. Sooner or later but within fifteen years after the war ended, almost all West African states had become independent. In Ghana for example, the centralizers won the battle and the country became independent with a unitary form of government. In Nigeria, though the regional feelings were strong among its natives but at the end of the day, the federal structure was preserved for the sake of national unity and feelings. In French West Africa, the federation there was gradually being weakened, thorn down to allow the various territories to merge as separate states.

In all of the West African states, Ghana was best favoured for independence because of her strong export commodities like Gold, cocoa and other mineral resources. Also considered along this line was her financial reserves, her standard of living; population of educated people in her territory, their longer period of political agitation and possibly the homogeneity of its people. Ivory Coast and Nigeria were next to being considered for this prestigious freedom obligation. In the case of Ivory Coast with its small population and limited number of trained personnel, she was obliged because of her rapidly growing and flourishing economy. Nigeria, having the heavy population behind it with its diversed economy, strengthened by the discovery of large oil reserves and adequate number of educated people being produced by her five universities as at the time, possibly had and approved for bright economic future of all. We should not forget that Nigeria has serious cultural and ecological problems that might curtail her chances of enjoying to the fullest the expected benefits to be accrued from all the resources at her disposal.

Other areas such as Sierra Leone, Senegal and Guinea were considered to follow later because of their inability to stand on their own without recalling the imperialists back for financial assistance in the nearer future. Sierra Leone as at this time was on her way to developing its diamond and Iron ore deposits, which gave her a good chance and promise that it would soon become prosperous. However, as for Dahomey, that had over-supply of personnel and under-supply of mineral potentialities as at this time; Gambia with its small territorial area and population; Mali, Upper Volta and Niger, which were denied an access to the sea by mother nature, their economic future was not promising. As earlier said, no imperial power that was ready to carry the burden of any of its territories that would be granted independence after they must have left and for this reason all of these states were asked to wait till the time they would be economically matured enough to carry their civic responsibilities without any recourse to any nation.

The reforms that started in West Africa at the beginning of the 20th century would have given the whole continent a broad view of what level the continental problems and aspirations would have reached say in the 21st century at least if the European system of divide and rule was not put in place in all of their territories across the continent. The London deputation of the National Congress in 1920 revealed the strength of unity among the people of West Africa of this time. The delegates that attended the London meeting represented the cross section and physical image of their respective territories with one accord and interests.

The members of the delegates who were carefully drawn from West African territory were as follows: Dr. H.C. Bankole-Bright (Sierra Leone), T. Hutton Mills (President of the Congress), Chief Oluwa (Nigeria), J. Casely Hayford (Ghana), H. Van Hein (Ghana), J. Egerton Shygle (Nigeria), H.M. Jones (Gambia), Hubert Macaulay (Nigeria and Chief Oluwa's Secretary) T.M Oluwa (Nigeria and son of the chief), F.W Dove (Sierra Leone), and E.F. Small (Gambia).

They all had one thing in common and this was how their suffering people in the hands of the imperialists would be free and become independent.

The powerful decolonizing drive of the National Liberation Movements in the colonies particularly those of the Black Africa was admitted to be as significant as the National Movements of Europe in the Nineteenth century. The agitations of the movements were loud enough to cause big headaches to the imperialists; otherwise Africa would have been repartitioned into federated units of their choices, which would have been afflicted with chronic weaknesses and to be governed by terror with the help of outsized police forces under the economic domination of the foreign countries. They will continue to use their mere tiny embassies as strings to pull in the wealth of the people as it was being practiced in some parts of Africa in the immediate past century.

The case of Guatemala would have been our lot where a foreign business firm, the United Fruit Company (US), overthrew the government there and replaced it with another that was amenable to the company's aims. This company must have definitely been taking instructions and orders from its big brothers in the U.S. If the Black Africa is to be protected from such situations and calamities, this is the time for us to drop those nasty ideals that had never worked from the time of Adam till the end of the world. We must stop fooling ourselves with minor patchworks and bring about the ultimate break with all those fake structures that were designed by our detractors for their own benefits and which have no good intentions and historical future for our people. Such of those structures are the Commonwealth and Eurafrica where the wealth that is meant for Africa as partners in these organizations normally goes to the big brothers in England and France. We can no longer tolerate to run with the hare and hunting with the hounds at the sametime.

These structured organizations have their intended dangerous programs for the continent as a whole, and if care is not taken as quickly as possible, something much more terrible than the era of slavery would befall the continent and its people. By the time we move off from all these bogus and meaningless organizations and face the reality of life at home rather than squatting around the bridges and road ways of Europe and America for possible dirty jobs, the economic situation of Africa with the natural potentials endowed it would in lesser time improved and stabilized. If we take West African economy alone for example, the region has an economic potential for greater than that of England and France combined. But the irony of it is that each time we have economic problems or we are unable to feed our people out of our personal greed in governance, it is they that would come out first to impose economic sanctions on us or making noice about food supply to African famine areas. The potentials we have are not fully tapped and where patchwork developments are seen, they are either mismanaged of developed to the disadvantage of the bonefide owners. Is it not time for us to come together to find a way to develop those great potentials nature has endowed us?

There is no doubt about the fact that African people have been staying too long in the house of poverty whereby their thinking has been oriented towards heavenly riches. It is very logic to conclude that someone who is impoverished in his own home would certainly carry such standard with him to wherever he goes to either you call it heaven or hell. Those who are responsible for our degenerated conditions are the so-called political football players among us. Those ones in the corridors of power are the ones who have not proved themselves up to solving our problems, who indeed have not given serious thoughts to them possibly because of their in-built greed and non-challant attitude towards the degrading conditions of their people, and who are terrified of taking the action which they conceive as economic weaning. All these put together rope them into servitude and in the end they would come back to blame the poor people for no just course. On the other hand, if we take the fertility of the landmass of Africa into play here, we would see that the continent is superfluously blessed with everything that are required for agricultural development, but yet the people are dying in millions every year because of hunger.

The farmland in Africa is virtually empty now while the cities are over-populated by people looking for every odd job for survival. Our rivers and lakes are rendered useless and underutilized, yet we import seafoods from Europe and elsewhere on daily basis. The Iron and Steel industry that would have lent its hands unto our agricultural machinery are yet to take-off the ground after fourty years of its birth. The Agro-allied industries that are supposed to take care of the fatal infectious diseases affecting the food products have been closed down either for political reasons or otherwise. Drinking water becomes an essential commodity in almost everywhere in the Black African region of the continent while the energy supply even to homes and not to mention industries is absolutely nothing to write home about, yet we have our own self-governments and our own people running those governments. Is there anything that is wrong with us physiologically?

To bring this book to its close, we should all examine the numerous speeches and promises of our past and present leaders concerning the type of vision they intend to sell to their people on assumption of the prestigious seats of presidency or whatever in their countries. I will beg for the indulgence of my readers to allow me to use my country Nigeria to drive home the concluding part of this text by making reference to the vision of some of my past leaders either in Khaki uniform or in Agbada (Babanriga) outfit. When the junior officers of the Nigerian army under the leadership of Major Chukwuma Kaduna Nzeogwu toppled the Abubakar Tafawa Balewa led Federal Government in January 15 1966, they told the nation that their objective and vision in coming to power was to end curruption, indicipline, political violence, disunity and maladministration of the then young government. He also promised that his regime would be brief and that as disciplined and patriotic officers of the army, he and his co-conspirators intended to handpick "civilians of proven honesty and efficiency" to govern the country.

When it was not possible for him to achieve these objectives through military arrangement, the military government of General Ironsi came to bridge the gap between the security ranks of the nation. On assuming power, he too promised us of a good and stable government devoid of all things related to disunity. Like Major Nzeogwu the pioneer coup plotter in Nigeria, all other coup plotters too argued that their mission in coming to seize power from their own brothers was to either restore the economy, clean the Aegean stable of corruption and abuse of power, or democratize the nation and then retreat to barracks; but yet for the larger part of our self-governance from 1960 todate, the army dictatorship regimes took the lion share and all of their regimes from the time of Major Nzeogwu to the present time of General Olusegun Obasanjo, currruption is still a major feature of Nigerian public and private life.

General Gowon came after Ironsi; Muritala Mohammad after Gowon; General Obasanjo completed the regime of Muritala and handed over the government to Alhaji Shehu Shagari who was there for a very brief period before his government was cheaply taken away from him by General Ibrahim Babangida the man popularly known and called by the people as military Maradona in Nigerian political field. Then came the ever-witnessed stellular government in Nigeria – Shonekan's regime followed by the most tyrannic government of General Sanni Abacha and finally ended up the army race in government with that of General Abubakar. Yet none of these fine and combatant soldiers was able to nip in the bud any of their visions.

We should then agree that we had problems with the Armed Forces that promised us heaven and earth that they would resolve our issues and differences the way we would like it. But the problem with the Armed Forces itself as analyzed by the editorial of the Post Express at one time echoes the concern regarding the invidious nature of factionalism in the institution and thus expressed its views:

[It was not only civil society that had suffered in the hands of our military. The military institution itself (even before the death of Abacha) reached the death of loss of esteem…. Even more devastating is the effect of prolonged political involvement on the institutional integrity of the military itself. Esprit de corps that the indivisible bond of respect for each other and for the professional hierarchy that binds modern warriors (serving and retired) to each other and to the profession had long vanished. Political factions emerged in the barracks with their own adherents and detractors alike. Mutual suspicion among factions, crude materialism and corruption among the officer's corps and rank and file alike have become the bane of our military.]

It became apparent to everyone of us that every segment of our national economy had been infected and rendered comatose by corruption, shady deals and gross fraudulent practices. The ceaseless use of state power and apparatus for private accumulation of capital that was in vogue during the military era in Nigeria refused to vanish but instead, it has taking a wider and sophisticated dimension that our country has been accredited for this dangerous practice and way of life the world over. We must not forget that none of the military regimes that governed the country who never had its own sorrowful and bitter anger over this unblessed disease. General Abubakar during his own regime and in his own contribution to this topic urged that the military should revert to its constitutional role, divest itself of involvement in politics and subordinate itself to civil authority. Likewise General Babangida in an address to his senior military officers at one time said:

[We should ask ourselves whether or not it will be in our own corporate and even personal interest to continue to intervene in the political process of this great country at the level at which we have done so during the past twenty years….. How can we… put in place structures, institutions, processes, and values that will make military intervention in the governance of the country irrelevant passé?]

During this second time of General Obasanjo's coming back into the government as civilian president and to which his people refers to as an intervention from God could as well be accepted as combination of idealism with charisma and truly African humility plus candor that seem to destine him to bring his people back from the edge. Being an engineer by profession, a devout Christian, and someone with a proven track record in governance, his people believed that he is up to the task of getting the theatre room ready for the surgical operations that our body politics needed. His government has so far taken a hard line on corruption and working to create a stable political and economic environment for the nation. His purge of politically aligned senior officers in the Armed Forces was initially presumed to be a joke but later heralded as a clear signal that military incursion will no longer be tolerated in the country. His promise to his people in his agenda included restoration of law and order, fighting corruption and unifying Nigeria's ethnically and religiously diverse peoples. He stated categorically that he will leave no stone unturned to ensure sustenance of demoracy because it is good for us, it is good for Africa, and it is good for the world.

It is a living fact that economics can never completely displace politics in West Africa because of the close ties and affinity between both of them. The current generation of Africa wants to see a continent that is politically and economically stable so that in either Abuja, Accra, Addis Ababa, Tripoli, Dare-Salaam, Maputo, Luanda, Conakry, Kigali, Bangui, Lusaka and all other capital cities of the states in the continent, they can pursue their primary global interests in the economic growth and the development of their people. The nations in the continent must pursue the ideology of doing business together and sharing of ideas especially those whose economies are rightly connected by the global system of trade so that they would have a natural incentive to promote good relations and stability.

Through this we shall be able to create powerful industries that would give primacy to industrialization, development and mechanization of agriculture. So also our technical institutes would be able to lay much emphasis on such learnings as nuclear physics and chemistry, electronics, aeronautics and all other applied science subjects. Lastly the people should work out an effective form of full representation for the female sector of their nations in all of its governmental and developmental areas of life especially those in the religious fields. If our children are to grow up to be among the "industrious and rational" rather than the "quarrelsome and contentious", they must be raised and thought with an appreciation of the importance of hard work. Work itself is ever known to be the best way to learn about its own virtues and rewards; another better way is from understanding what to do and when to do it. Therefore if thou love life, do not squander Time; for that is the ingredient life is made of. Do not live useless and die contemptible.

Chief Olu. Adeuyan is blessed with passion for knowledge search in all the key geographical locations of the world. He received his B. Sc (Hons) Applied Geology from Kiev Geological College in 1971; LLB (Hons) - JD Law Degree from University of Wolverhampton - UK in 1995 and his MBA Information Technology as Major from Morgan State University, Baltimore Maryland, in the year 2000 class. He has worked with many reputable engineering companies across the globe. He was one of the first group of Nigerian scientists deployed from the Geological Survey of Nigeria in 1971 to work with the Russian scientists that investigated and form the mineral exploration base for the nation's Iron and Steel Complex at Aja-okuta mill. Working for the Federal Government of Nigeria under this national scheme for many years and attained the position of Deputy Chief Geologist, he opted out to form his own company known and called Geotek (Nig) Services Ltd, a Consulting firm on Geological and Engineering business as its President.

In 1991, he moved to the United Kingdom for fear of political persecution from the hands of the then military junta ruling his country-Nigeria. In London where he sojourned, he worked for some Engineering, Law, and low ebb firms to make two ends meet and to pay for his education while in the Law School. in 1995, after graduating from the Law School, he moved to the United States to join his family that were already in the States. Here in the States, he continued to pursue his passion for knowledge. He enrolled at the School of Business studies, Morgan State

University and in the year 2000, he graduated with good grade. He went back to his basic engineering profession to work for some Engineering firms as Soil Advisor and Consultant. He is now retired to become a writer and business consultant. He has authored six books on different topics ranging from religious to business and from politics to personalties. He is widely travelled across the globe and happily married with children and grandchildren.